International Politics since World War II:
A SHORT HISTORY

International Politics since World War II: A SHORT HISTORY

CHARLES L. ROBERTSON, *Smith College*

John Wiley & Sons, Inc. NEW YORK LONDON SYDNEY

Preface

This book is a survey of international affairs since the end of World War II, primarily intended for students but, hopefully, one that may be of interest to others who have lived through these extraordinary times.

Like many other teachers I have found it hard to realize that twenty years have passed since World War II, and that to many of my students what I consider to be current events—the Marshall Plan, the Korean War, the Suez War—are nothing but vague historical events, comparable to, but often less well-known than, much earlier events. And I find that friends who have been adults (more or less) throughout the period have often forgotten much that has passed, or how much certain things have changed.

This book, then, is a summary and synthesis, drawn in large part from numerous secondary sources, but also from the plethora of memoirs and document collections on the period. It attempts to do a difficult thing: to both indicate the broad sweep of historical change and recall at the same time the numerous specific events that made up these changes. The result will certainly not satisfy most people: I have had to select and summarize, and many will object to what I have selected and to how I have summarized. I have tried to be fair and "objective." But objectivity does not preclude a point of view—one that I would like to make clear.

International politics differs from domestic politics chiefly because power to make authoritative decisions is decentralized among a number of distinct geographical units. A host of consequences flow from this, chief among which is the large measure of uncertainty and indeterminacy governing the conduct of foreign policies of states in the international system. Policy-makers act on the basis of assumptions, not the truth. Therefore when describing major events I have spent much time surveying the different assumptions on which policy-makers acted, and I am frequently unable to make any judgment about the validity of these assumptions. A second consequence is that whatever patterns do emerge come from the separate actions of numerous units. Generally, none of these units singly can create the political pattern of the world (although a number may cooperate to try to create one). The result is that the pattern of world politics will often be quite different from what the policy-makers of any single state worked for or foresaw, and they cannot often be blamed for this.

In the second place, I find it useful in teaching to spend time on how the nineteenth-century balance-of-power system worked, on the nature of conflict and the ways found to deal with it and to foster cooperation (developing therefore a view of units coexisting side by side in a constant position of both cooperation and conflict over their interests), and of how the desire for security impelled leaders, whatever their ideology, toward balance-of-power policies, even though these were in practice often modified by other goals or by ideological considerations. Upon this system were imposed the twentieth century changes in technology, mass communications, mass ideology. These have—in ways frequently almost incalculable to policy-makers—changed the system greatly. Yet states have tried to retain their political independence and legal sovereignty.

I find that these two points serve as a basis for understanding the workings of international politics, and I have therefore tried to summarize them in somewhat more detail in the first two chapters. The main body of the text then proceeds in a roughly chronological fashion, using these ideas.

The years since the war seem to me to fall fairly logically into the divisions I have made for reasons indicated in the text. The first two years after the war differed sharply from those that followed after, and 1955 marks a second great break, when the development of thermonuclear bombs and the means for delivering them produced a new set of assumptions for policy-makers. Within these broad spans of time, too, I found several quite natural divisions, which constitute the various chapters. In a number of cases, however, events did *not* fit within these divisions: I have no apology to my readers for this.

But I do apologize to many who will find little mention of their countries or of their interests. It is not that I consider them unimportant: to the people living in those countries, events I have passed over in silence often have supreme importance. But I have tried to select on the basis of what has most affected the entire international political system—the whole world—and I have tried to do so honestly.

My thanks must go to many people who have helped me: to Mrs.

Marge Erikson and Miss Ciba Vaughan who have typed and retyped so much for me, to Mr. Peter Rowe, who after reading the manuscript convinced me that the book could be useful, and to my students in Geneva who left me alone while I finished it.

Charles L. Robertson

GENEVA, SWITZERLAND
FEBRUARY 1966

Contents

Part I   *Background*

CHAPTER I   THE BREAKDOWN OF THE BALANCE OF POWER   3

Introduction — The Balance of Power and New
Developments — Conclusion: technological, political, and
social changes and trends.

CHAPTER II   WORLD WAR II AND THE MAP OF THE POST-WAR
WORLD   18

Introduction — Military Operations — Diplomacy in World
War II — The Yalta Conference — After Yalta — Potsdam —
New Organizations for a New International Politics —
Conclusion.

Part II   *1945–1955: The Atomic Age*

CHAPTER III   1945–1947: THE ATTEMPT TO REBUILD THE OLD
WORLD   47

Introduction — The Peace Treaties — Germany Splits —
Communization of East Europe — Winter of 1947 —
Europe and the Non-Western World, 1945–1947 — Iran
and Turkey — China — Korea and Japan — Disarmament
Negotiations — Conclusion.

CHAPTER IV   1947–1950: THE COLD WAR, BIPOLARIZATION, AND
CONTAINMENT   85

Introduction — American Initiatives — The Moscow
Conference — The Marshall Plan — NATO and the Berlin
Blockade — Point Four — The OAS — The Communist
Bloc: the Czech Coup and the Yugoslav Defection —
Developments in Western Europe — War in the Middle
East — Independence in Asia; Communist China — The
United Nations in a Divided World — The Atomic
Bomb, Military Strategy and the Balance of Power —
Conclusion.

CHAPTER V   1950–1955: HOT WAR AND COLD WAR   133

Introduction – Korea and Its Impact – A New War –
International Consequences of the Korean War –
American Reactions to Frustration: Initial Effects of the
1952 Political Campaign – The Death of Stalin and Soviet
Foreign Policy – Geneva, 1954: The Far Eastern
Settlement – More Stirrings in the Non-Western World:
Iran, Egypt, Africa – Latin America Enters the World
Stage – Europe, 1950–1955 – Developments in the United
Nations – Conclusion.

Part III   The Hydrogen Age

CHAPTER VI   1955 AND 1956: COEXISTENCE AND CONFLICT—A NEW
WORLD BALANCE   201

Introduction – "Deeds, Not Words" – Geneva in July –
New Soviet Initiatives – The Bandung Conference – The
Soviet Twentieth Party Congress – The Stalemate Shaken:
Suez and Hungary – Conclusion.

CHAPTER VII   1957–1964 (I): THE NEW STATES AND COMPETITIVE
COEXISTENCE   240

Introduction – The New States and Their Search for an
International Role – The Congo – White Africa –
Southeast Asia: Neutralism and Guerrilla Conflict –
Difficulties Among the New States – The Tragi-Comedy
of the Middle East – War in Vietnam – Regionalism in
Africa – Conclusion.

CHAPTER VIII 1957–1964 (II): THE OLD BLOCS AND COMPETITIVE
COEXISTENCE   284

Introduction – Europe, European Union, and the Atlantic
Alliance – Disarmament: 1957–1964 – Communist Foreign
Policies After 1956 – The Chinese-Russian Break –
Conclusion.

CHAPTER IX   CUBA, THE UNITED STATES AND LATIN AMERICA, AND
THE GREAT CONFRONTATION OF 1962   330

Castro and Cuba – The Missile Crisis – Conclusion.

CONCLUSION   346

BIBLIOGRAPHY   353

INDEX   365

International Politics since World War II:

A SHORT HISTORY

Part One

BACKGROUND

CHAPTER ONE

The Breakdown of the Balance of Power

With the advent of mass communications, everyone today is subjected to a flood of information on world affairs—sometimes detailed, sometimes oversimplified and distorted, frequently heavily biased. Most of us receive a hazy day-to-day impression of what is going on in the world around us. Too often, however, it comes in the form of suddenly finding out that there is a new crisis in some far-off spot: names of new places, names of new people compete for our attention. Sometimes the crisis drags on and we see its importance. Sometimes it disappears, along with the people involved. Which crises are "important"? Can we ever decide? Is it possible to see the forest and not merely the trees, to determine how events fit in to broader patterns of change? Is there, in fact, any pattern at all, or merely chaos and absurdity?

The "facts" rarely speak for themselves; interpretation is all-important. The account of international affairs in this book reflects a conviction that there are indeed discernible patterns and valid ways of making these patterns clear, that they result in large part from the interplay of current revolutionary developments in technology and ideology with persisting elements of the centuries-old balance of power system, and yet that the patterns are in part influenced by the very large measure of indeterminacy always present in human affairs.

In few other spheres of human endeavor does indeterminacy play a larger part than in the conduct of foreign policy. Those who formulate and carry out foreign policy for the states that make up the international community must constantly make assumptions about how their strategies will serve their various ends of security, economic welfare, or ideological expansion. In so doing they must constantly make assumptions about the aims and strategies of other states, and although policy-makers may try to equip themselves with as much intelligence and analysis as possible, they will always act on the basis of much speculation and hypothesis.

3

Thus, for the period immediately after World War II American policy-makers assumed that the Soviet Union would be too busy with internal reconstruction to set out upon a deliberate path of expansion. By 1947 this assumption had been revised, and a largely ideological explanation for Soviet hostility had replaced it. In 1950 the Korean War led to the assumption that the Soviets were now prepared to use force to expand. Yet all of these views were essentially unprovable, and to this day there remains much argument over their validity. Time may give the historian perspective to make judgments, yet the writing of history is a constant dialogue over just such matters. In the meantime, the policy-makers of states must act on the basis of these views whether they are correct or not. Furthermore, in the post-war period, there were people in every country ready to dispute these particular assumptions about the Soviet Union and to make far different ones, whereas a close reading of Soviet discussions of military strategy reveals some startling assumptions about the possible hostile moves the United States might make and which the Russians must be ready to counter. The North Atlantic Treaty of 1949, with its subsequent rearmament of Europe, was based on the view that the Soviet Union might at any time overrun Western Europe. Billions of dollars were spent in strengthening the alliance, and yet many people in Western Europe felt no such military intentions existed on the part of the Soviet Union. The statesman might argue that he could take no chance and *must* be prepared for the worst. Yet he could be answered that the very act of such preparation would in turn stimulate the Russians to strengthen their own military capacities in ways they had not previously wanted, setting off the vicious circle of an unwanted arms race. At the moment of major policy decisions accurate judgments can rarely be made about such matters, although policy-makers are always called on to justify their actions—to themselves, if not to others.

A narrative of international relations, though limited to telling *what* has happened, must tell something of *why* it happened; for what men think they must do is a part of what they do, and their views of the world around them and their responses to these views are necessary parts of the story. At all times this view is subject to dispute, and in this lies the inevitable indeterminacy of international affairs.

Yet the past always sets the stage and the limits within which current actions can take place. The international events of the last two decades can be understood only if seen in the context of radical change in the balance-of-power system which had bequeathed to the contemporary world the sovereign, independent nation-state and the methods of maintaining some kind of order in a political system lacking any central political authority.

The Balance of Power

The balance-of-power system arose out of the ruins of the preceding system, feudalism. Three hundred years of intermittent but often savage warfare had ended with the Peace of Westphalia in 1648. The new system meant that kings and princes had successfully repudiated the superior authority of Pope and Emperor and substituted the idea and reality of the sovereign independent state which commanded the loyalty of all inhabitants within its territorial limits. States might differ in size, power, and geographical location, but on the basis of the idea of absolute sovereignty and the concomitant rejection of the authority of anyone outside the territorial borders of the state, each state also claimed equality with all other states.

For the first century and a half of its existence the system rested upon dynastic legitimacy; sovereignty—though sometimes disputed—was represented by a hereditary monarchy. The French Revolution decisively challenged the dynastic principle, which was eventually supplanted by ideas of nationalism and liberalism. The ensuing half-century was a struggle between those who believed that the state should be composed of any group of people who felt that they constituted a separate nation, reflecting the principle of self-determination and those who clung to the idea that the state could properly and legitimately be ruled only by members of one ruling family. Almost everywhere the struggle ended in the triumph of liberalism and nationalism. The new middle classes came to share political power in the state. Petty principalities in Italy and Germany united into national states, and multi-national dynastic states like Austria-Hungary and Turkey experienced the increasing pressure that ultimately led to their breakup in World War I. Yet the struggle remained within the confines of the balance-of-power system.

There really was a "system" in the sense that the states of Europe, though lacking any superior authority or law, regularized their inevitable contacts with one another. They developed systematic methods of coexistence, of decreasing the frequency of their conflicts, and of controlling conflicts when they did occur.

When Thomas Hobbes, the seventeenth century English political philosopher, analyzed what would happen to any political system that had no absolute, central political authority, he argued that inevitably the units composing it would have to constantly strive to increase their power, fearful of the *potential* power of other members. Since each would calculate in this fashion, each would therefore be correct in his calculations. The result was bound to be a war of all against all unless an all-powerful sovereign could be installed to reassure individuals that they need not fear others. Machiavelli, writing a manual for Princes in 1513, argued that common, every-day morality could never apply to the actions of sovereigns. It was moral for them to do anything and everything necessary to strengthen the state against all its *potential* opponents.

Yet the balance-of-power system never fully assumed the characteristics attributed to it by Hobbes. Each state, of course, had to fend for itself, and the tendency toward arms races and the constant maneuvering for security inevitably made stability precarious. But the search for security or power rarely led to Hobbes' "war of all against all." The idea of preserving the balance of power as a means of security was sufficiently accepted to allow the creation of a crude international system in the sense that common rules of behavior were developed and observed. When one power threatened to become too strong, other states allied against it and, if necessary, fought against it. But if one of the allied states in turn emerged too strong, alliances shifted and it found itself facing a new alignment. When one state gained territory (and resources and population, the bases of power), there was general agreement that other states should obtain territory in compensation to maintain the balance. There was little regard for the wishes of individuals when one piece of territory was traded for another. When Europe discovered the rest of the world, the principle of compensation was further extended; much of the pattern of imperialism can be explained as the result of occupation of territory by one country in order to keep other countries from acquiring strength by occupying it, and of the other countries receiving compensation in the form of other territories. With the exception of the Napoleonic period, wars remained generally limited, the independence of most of the major states of Europe was maintained, and despite injustices, a general order was preserved.

Several factors helped maintain this decentralized system. Until the full impact of the industrial revolution was felt, the technology of destruction that had ended the supremacy of the armored knight and fortified castle of feudal times had remained static. The weapons used in the Napoleonic wars were scarcely different from the ones used two centuries earlier. It still required a massive effort to kill many people. Moreover, the states of the European system had a common cultural foundation. Their ruling classes intermarried and, perhaps most important, their diplomats came to think of themselves as an international class defending the *vital* interests of their countries but also willing, as European diplomats, to compromise and accommodate to maintain the peace.

In one way, liberalism helped buttress the balance-of-power system. The new bourgeoisie, as it rose to political power and vastly increased the productivity of state economies, instituted a relatively free and multilateral trading system based on greater specialization and exchange. Gold served as the currency of the new trading system, London as its financial center, and men, money, and goods flowed far more freely across national frontiers than in the days of the dynastic period when the prevalent trading pattern, known as mercantilism, had dictated close state control of the economy in order to develop a "favorable balance of trade." The strict controls of the mercantile period were designed to ensure an inflow of gold the new monarchs needed to pay for their new mercenary armies and centralized administrations; it had served its purpose. Proponents of the new liberalism not only argued that mercantilists had confused gold with wealth, but they also claimed that the increased links created by international trade would ensure perpetual peace. To a limited extent they were right; the international bourgeoisie, eager to ensure the security of investments and trade, developed a vested interest in peace. Members of the new class frequently pressed governments to forego strategic interests, confident that their counterparts in other countries would also renounce attempts to achieve military or political predominance. International law—previously concerned with defining boundaries, diplomatic immunities, and matters of citizenship—now reflected the common interests of the commercial classes in new rules to facilitate trade and communication.

Yet the whole international system had a more precarious base than most people realized and, later in the nineteenth century, the full impact of political liberalism and nationalism and their economic counterpart, industrialization, undermined it more. Increased reliance on trade and specialized economies made states more vulnerable to economic blockade. Now belligerents might be more tempted to carry war home to the mass of the population. The industrial revolution sparked the rapid development of weapons and communications technology that revolutionized warfare. A preview of modern war came in the American Civil War of the 1860s; North and South used magazine-loading rifles, crude machine guns, torpedoes, land mines and submarine mines, the field telegraph, wire entanglements, hand grenades, armored trains, and balloon observation of artillery fire. On February 17, 1864, a man-propelled Confederate submarine sank the U.S.S. Housatonic.

Then years later the Franco-Prussian War showed that the mobility provided by new railroads could have a decisive effect on hostilities. By World War I the modern submarine and torpedo were developed sufficiently to have as revolutionary an effect on naval warfare as the increased firepower provided by semiautomatic rifles, carbines, machine guns and rapid-fire artillery had on land warfare.

While the technology of destruction developed at such a rapid pace, the changed social structure of the new industrialized states presaged an equally important revolution in the conduct of foreign policy. Increased suffrage meant popular demands on government and a restricted freedom for negotiation by diplomats. In 1898 popular pressures brought about an American war with Spain that traditional diplomacy could easily have avoided.

Diplomacy failed to prevent the outbreak of World War I in 1914 and the carnage of the next four years revealed how much the old balance-of-power system had been undermined. Blockade *did* bring the war home to the mass of the people, and the new weapons produced the stalemate of trench warfare, the awesome casualties of the Western front, and unrestricted submarine warfare. All of these led to increased public pressure for a victory in which the vanquished would truly pay for the fantastic hardship that total war had brought. It was impossible to settle for a negotiated peace without victory.

The war had numerous consequences for the international political system. The stable basis for trade was gone; governments had learned that they could finance the war by inflation, and with fiscal policies conducted independently of the balance of payments, they resorted increasingly to tariffs, quotas, bilateral trade agreements, and exchange controls to channel the flow of trade. All of these made trade a more political matter; the war itself had showed that trade could be a weapon. War debts and reparations payments added to the burden on world trade and led to even more bitter quarrels. People held on to supplies of gold as a hedge against inflation, and by doing so limited its availability as an international currency. The war led to an increase of manufacturing outside of Europe and to liquidation of European investments abroad, further unbalancing trade and making the

United States and Japan powerful competitors with Europe. On the other hand, Europe was forced to limit its imports; its economic decline *vis-à-vis* the rest of the world had already begun.

The war brought revolution and the Communists to power in Russia. Except for its fruitless efforts to sponsor world revolution, the new Communist government withdrew from the world scene. A host of weak successor states emerged in Eastern Europe: Poland, Czechoslovakia, Austria, Hungary, and Yugoslavia joined Rumania and Bulgaria, and to the North, Finland, Latvia, Estonia, and Lithuania became independent. The French, deprived by the Communist revolution of their ally in the East turned to the weak new states on the other side of a Germany whose power they still feared. But England, distrusting France's attempts to keep Germany weak, dissociated itself from its wartime continental ally. The United States, refusing to join the League of Nations, participated on the international scene only to bring about a temporary stabilization of the Far East, to press for disarmament, and to attempt to buttress the German economy with short-term loans in the late 1920s.

The network of international short-term loans contributed materially to the spread of the depression from one country to another in the 1930s. As internal financial collapse took place in one country, it would call back its loans from another, thus causing internal financial collapse there. People who learned another hard lesson about the interdependence of the modern world tended to stress economic self-sufficiency and nationalism even more.

The depth of the changes in the international economy as well as in the distribution of power among European states and between Europe and new powers was hard to appreciate. But the war had emphasized how the balance of power could degenerate into arms races; it gave rise to demands for modifications of the whole international system. And so, at Versailles, the League of Nations came into being with three conscious attempts at major change.

The first involved an attempt to institutionalize the balance of power in a system of "collective security," under which every country would have the legal obligation to come to the aid of any country attacked by another. The uncertainty of the balance of power would be replaced by the certainty that overwhelming power would be brought against an aggressor.

The League of Nations incorporated a second major change in the international system though the creation of the Permanent Mandates Commission. The victors in World War I had wanted, in traditional fashion, to annex overseas territories taken from the vanquished, but they were forced to bow to the view that simple annexation was no longer possible. Instead, the victors were to act as trustees for the international community which would carry out a limited measure of supervision through the Mandates Commission. Mandatory powers were committed to goals of welfare and of development of the peoples within the mandate.

The mandate system was limited, incorporating within it only the territories lost by the Central Powers and Turkey. Only one mandate, Iraq, became an independent state during the life of the mandate system. Yet the attempt revealed a consciousness that people outside Europe could no longer simply be traded as pawns in the European balance of power; colonialism, with all its attendant evils, had brought stability and literacy to colonial areas and had begun to create the demand for independence and sovereignty modeled on the European pattern.

Finally, the League set up not only a Council in which the great powers would assemble as they frequently had in the past but also an Assembly. Here all countries, large or small, would have equal representation and could discuss world affairs. It was an unprecedented step, and no one was quite sure what the Assembly could do.

The 1930s gave the answer. Institutional modification of the international system was insufficient to cope with the challenge posed by states that repudiated the entire system—Nazi Germany, Fascist Italy, and Communist Russia—and a state like Japan that tried in the mid-twentieth century to do the kind of empire building Europe had done in the nineteenth. This challenge came at the same time that a worldwide depression cast doubt on Western society's ability to deal with its own problems and at the same moment that the bombing plane was developed. The challengers found an international system whose members had neither the will nor wit to respond. European states were still pervaded by memories of the horrors of the World War. The United States, disenchanted, had legislated itself into neutrality so that France and Britain could not look to it for help, and its Secretary of State preached a futile doctrine of free trade as the cure for all the world's ills. Collective security, as some statesmen had foreseen, proved a hollow promise. Countries were unwilling to take action against a distant state that seemed to threaten no vital interest of theirs. The aggressor of today might be the needed ally of tomorrow; it might be better to allow him to have his way.

The governments of Britain and France tried to offer the dictators limited gains, but they only grew more demanding. The Soviet Union, seeing the threat in Nazi expansionism, tried to return to membership in the international system and sought a rapprochement with the Western powers. But the effort to build a new coalition was doomed. The French, willing to use any means to avoid mass attacks against trenches, had adopted a strictly defensive strategy behind the massive defenses of the Maginot Line and could offer no real aid to the Soviet Union if the Nazis attacked. Moreover, both France and Britain failed to make a really serious effort to work out cooperation with Russia. Their leaders doubted the effectiveness of the Soviet Union as an ally, especially after the widespread purges of the late 1930s had liquidated the vast majority of the top rank of the Russian officer corps. They distrusted the Communist *volte face* and were afraid, too, of what Communist Russia might gain in Eastern Europe in a war. On the other hand, the Nazis could point out to Stalin that while the Western powers could not help him in a war Germany could offer the Soviet Union a buffer zone in Eastern Europe. Stalin decided to cooperate with the Nazis and on August 23, 1939, signed a nonaggression pact with Adolf Hitler, giving him the green light to go to war.

By the end of 1939, the Western powers that had dominated the world for the past three centuries were demoralized and unhappy and faced a situation in which they could only lose; neither alternative was attractive. On the one hand, German-Italian-Japanese victory seemed probable if the three could cooperate with Russia. Their defeat appeared assured only if Russia split off and joined the war against them, but this, the alternative to defeat by the Fascists, promised a much larger expansion of Soviet influence.

A series of lightning wars brought Nazi victory over Poland, Norway, Denmark, the Lowlands, France, and the Balkans. But the courage of a handful of British pilots, German strategic mistakes, and the unsuccessful German submarine attempt to cut British overseas communications were factors in the Germans' failure to win the Battle of Britain. Hitler mistakenly turned against the Soviet Union, leaving England as a strategic base from which attack could be brought both against his lines of communication and eventually against Fortress Europe. Meanwhile in the Pacific, the Japanese, faced with stiffening American resistance to expansion of empire, calculated that an internally divided United States would sue for peace after a series of quick defeats. They struck at Pearl Harbor and the Philippines, crippled a large part of the American Pacific fleet and moved rapidly through Southeast Asia. Within a few months they threatened Australia and New Zealand. On the mainland they moved through Burma toward India, at the same time cutting off land communications to China.

Early in 1942 the Axis was triumphant everywhere and the Western world was at its lowest point. German forces, moving through North Africa toward the Middle East, threatened to join the Japanese in India. Although they had suffered reverses in Russia, their spring campaign looked as though it would be successful.

By the end of 1942 the picture had changed. In the Pacific the Japanese fleet suffered a decisive setback in the Battle of Midway on June 4, 1942, and America had a breathing spell during which it could begin to draw upon its enormous latent industrial capacity and gradually to force the Japanese back from their extended conquests. On October 23, 1942, Field Marshal Montgomery turned back the German forces in North Africa at the decisive battle of El Alamein and began to chase them to ultimate defeat in Tunisia. Within a few months German forces surrendered at Stalingrad, marking the turning point in the German campaign in Russia. But it took two and a half more years before the Axis powers were finally defeated and World War II ended.

World War II caused many changes. It gave birth to two super-powers, the United States and Russia. Between the two was a broken Europe, its economy wrecked, society demoralized, and political structure grossly weakened. In attempting to displace the European powers in the Far East, the Japanese had encouraged nationalism among the Asians. When the Europeans were able to move back into areas evacuated by Japan, they found that this nationalist feeling persisted and that they could not regain their lost position. Moreover, the presence of Allied troops in other parts of the world brought many primitive peoples into contact with modern technology, medicine and communications for the first time. Again the result was to be the creation of new demands and social unrest in parts of the world previously dominated by Europe. The precise extent and implications of these major political changes took time to be appreciated and understood. However the enormity of the holocaust through which the world had gone gave rise to new demands for a general improvement of world politics.

Conclusion

This is still a world of nation-states claiming sovereignty and independence. But the foregoing sketch has indicated that the transformation and demise of the balance-of-power system based on the independent state was effected by fundamental changes. Changes in the technology of destruction, in the internal character of the states composing the system, and in membership in the system have meant that no state is now truly sovereign, no state is truly independent. These changes have only speeded up since World War II; they underlie all world events of our time.

The speedup is most noticeable in the field of weapons technology and communications. The rickety 90-mile-an-hour bomber of World War I with its load of several hundred pounds and range of a few hundred miles became, by the end of World War II, the B-29 that devastated Japanese cities, flying at 300 miles per hour with a range of 4000 miles and dropping a load of 10 tons of TNT. By the mid-1950s the American B-52 could travel to any point in the world at 600 miles per hour; by 1963 it had been almost superseded by intercontinental rockets that could travel at 18 thousand miles per hour up to 9000 miles. The latest of these were solid fueled and took only minutes to fire; they were protected against attack by being placed in deep underground concrete silos or by being fired from submarines cruising below surface.

More impressive were the developments in weapons that these carriers could deliver. During the terrifying blitz on London, the Nazis dropped 12,000 tons of bombs, killing 30,000 people and injuring more than 120,000. In World War II the Allies bombarded Germany with a total of 2 million tons of TNT. Then, in August 1945, the United States dropped a single 5-ton bomb over Hiroshima that released the explosive power of 20,000 tons of TNT that killed 78,000 people and injured 45,000 more. By the mid-1950s the atomic (fission) bomb had led to development of the hydrogen (fusion) bomb; its explosive power could be measured in millions of tons of TNT equivalent (the term used was "megatons"). In October 1961, the Russians exploded a 50-megaton hydrogen bomb. The new term, megaton, made people forget that this single weapon had an explosive power twenty-five times that of all bombs dropped on Germany during World War II. Moreover, such weapons have heat and radiation effects in addition to their blast effects. A 10-megaton weapon exploded thirty miles above the surface of the earth would sear an area of 5000 square miles, producing massive fire storms. Efforts to calculate the effect of attacks with these weapons have led to widely varying estimates. American Defense Department experts and Atomic Energy Commission scientists estimated that, in a small-scale attack by the Soviet Union on the United States,

Eastern cities such as Boston, Washington, New York, and Philadelphia would suffer immediate casualties of from 65 to 92 per cent; more would soon follow. An all-out attack on either the United States or the Soviet Union would cripple the economy and society of the countries involved for an indeterminable period.

Other weapons showed comparable development. During World War II the vulnerable, thin-skinned submarine was increased in range and firepower and equipped with the "snorkel," a device that enabled it to stay underwater while renewing its batteries and air thereby decreasing its vulnerability. By 1960, atomic-powered submarines could cruise underwater for weeks without refueling. The American Polaris submarines carried loads of solid-fueled missiles equipped with nuclear warheads. Automatic guidance devices, proximity fuses, radar—all these signified a revolution in the field of electronic devices adapted to warfare.

In contrast to the balance-of-power period, modern weapons allow states to be destroyed with little physical effort; they have also made it possible for the most squeamish to go about the task. When belligerents could kill men, women, and children, combatant and noncombatant alike, from a long distance, another restraint of the balance-of-power period disappeared. People could kill casually without having to see the bloodshed they caused, and actions of war condemned by the pre-World War I code, which reflected in law and morality the political fact of limited war, are now accepted as normal procedure. The United States finally went to war in 1917 because the Germans barbarously initiated unlimited submarine warfare; in World War II the first order sent to American submarines was to execute unlimited warfare. The American nuclear strategy of the mid-1950s spelled out by Secretary of State John Foster Dulles (a devout Protestant) was "massive retaliation"; as a strategy it committed the United States not to meet an armed attack directly, but rather to strike back at the enemy's homeland with the most destructive weapons. Few people found it morally repugnant.

Finally, the prevalence of the new weapons has led to a continuous debate about their implications—do they make total war more likely or have they reintroduced a period of limited war; can nations now withstand total war; has disarmament taken on a new urgency or will the presence of these new weapons for the first time guarantee peace; have small states been outmoded or, in a reversal of the trends of the past century, have they been given a new freedom and a new lease on life under the umbrella of a nuclear stalemate that prevents the major powers from resorting to use of their fearsome weapons.

But if the revolution in weapons development is striking, the effects of accompanying political and social revolutions are equally great. World War I destroyed the last dynastic states within Europe—Austria-Hungary, Ottoman Turkey and Czarist Russia—and enshrined the nation state. It also weakened Europe's hold on the rest of the world: if nationalism and national self-determination were proper for Europe, then why not for the peoples of Africa, the Middle East and Asia? Emancipation of peoples from European and American domination has proceeded at an ever-quickening pace: in 1945 the United Nations had a membership of fifty-one and in the fall of 1964 had 112 member states. Each of these new states claims the attributes of sovereignty and independence, derived from the reality of the balance-of-power system, at the very time that these concepts seem to have lost all meaning. Equally important, while the European-centered balance-of-power system rested on relative cultural unity, the new world system is composed of culturally divergent states, whose leaders find diplomatic communication far more difficult.

Moreover, since matters outside its borders greatly affect affairs within the state, mass pressures on national political leaders have also increased. Whether the flow of influence is primarily upward, as in essentially democratic states, or whether the process is one of attempted manipulation from the top, as in totalitarian states, mass opinion must be taken into account in various ways. Policy makers defer not only to political pressures within their states, but to a shadowy, hard-to-determine world opinion.

While the current revolution has increased the number and variety of states in the international system, and the scope of mass pressures on policy-makers, it has also caused the "revolution of rising expectations," an insistent demand by the leaders of the impoverished peoples of the world that something must be done to help relieve their poverty. Modern communications have tended to make the whole world one political community in which the juxtaposition of extremes of wealth and poverty inspires conflict and upheaval. Mindful of this, leaders of wealthier states have answered this plea, sometimes in a spirit of cooperation and sometimes in a competitive spirit designed to win the allegiance of the poorer peoples. Economic development for many of the economically undeveloped states involves profound cultural change and shock, and therefore internal conflict and, frequently, resentment against the very states that have tried to help. Conflict is endemic in a situation that is further complicated by the population explosion.

Modern medicine and transport have brought a drastic decline in death rates so that population continues to increase at a progressively faster rate. A world population of 500 million in 1600 took two hundred years to double; from 1800 to 1900, it had doubled again. The two billion of 1900 became three billion by 1960; thirty years will add another billion. If the current rate of increase were to continue for only 150 years, the world's population would reach 150 billion, compared to three billion in 1961. Fortunately, it seems highly unlikely.

In the meantime, the population increase becomes of importance to international relations. This growing population has not been distributed evenly. Europe, the United States, and Japan have been able to cope with the problem since production has grown at a faster pace than population. But in the rest of the world the reverse is frequently true. In many areas the standard of living is actually declining, while in others the economy barely holds its own. In such areas—the Caribbean is the most obvious to Americans—social and political unrest will increase unless population growth can be controlled. Many liberal-minded men think harsh measures are necessary, yet impossible to take without using totalitarian methods. The Communist position on this issue has had to change. In China, poverty was viewed as the result of maldistribution of wealth under capitalism, and the "population problem" as a capitalist bogey designed to keep the peoples of Asia and Africa small and weak; however, experience has taught the Chinese Communist leaders the urgent necessity of population control.

All these developments taken together combine to weaken national frontiers at the very time when the creation of many new states has added frontiers. Cheap and easy communication across national boundaries means that subversion—the attempt by outsiders to transfer loyalties of one part of the population from the current regime to a proposed new one—and its companion, propaganda, are commonly used techniques of modern foreign policies. The idea of the divine right of kings spread across Europe to supplant feudalism with the dynastic state; later liberalism undermined the dynastic concept and encouraged loyalty to the nation-state. Now the nation-state finds itself challenged by the class concept of communism; Fidelism can spread through Latin America; Nasserism finds its adherents throughout the Middle East. Competing claims for loyalty greatly increase the number of actors in international politics. Groups, organized interests, and classes within states are as much a part of international politics as the national leaders who presumably act for them. In some areas—Western Europe, the Arab Middle East, parts of Africa—deliberate efforts to transfer loyalties from the nation-state to larger units have tried to link together interest groups in many nations. These attempts at regional integration have only been successful in Western Europe, and even there, only to a limited extent. The nation-state retains a strong hold on its citizens, one that is reinforced by contemporary state regulation of the economy, by welfare measures, and by the ability of a society and government to generate "nationalized" versions of the truth.

It is hard for observers—and for policy-makers—to assess the impact of changes in technology, changes in the internal character of states, of population growth, of the increased number of states in today's world. Against this background of transformation and uncertainty only one thing emerges clearly: all of these developments have worked to unsettle the nation-state balance of power system, and the world is in a state of flux not seen since the feudal world dissolved in the upheavals of 1350–1650.

CHAPTER TWO

World War II and the Map
of the Post-War World

What kind of world would emerge from the war? In 1941, it appeared that either the Axis powers would dominate Eurasia or that the Soviet Union and the United States would emerge as superpowers, with Europe weakened, and with uncertainty the only certainty in the regions formerly controlled by Europe in Africa, the Middle East, and South and Southeast Asia. With the Axis turned back in 1942, the second alternative was assured.

Yet much remained in doubt: What would Russia and the United States do with their new-found power, how weak would Europe be, to what extent could European powers reestablish their overseas hegemony, could China finally find the strength and unity to supplant Japan as the dominant power in the Far East, and finally, could a new world organization be created to succeed where League and the balance-of-power system had failed to ensure world peace?

Statesmen and military leaders constantly face uncertainty; they choose a course of action with little assurance of where it may lead, however much they may be able to convince themselves of the opposite. During the war their strategies and diplomacy were crucial in defining the actual political map and the spheres of influence in the new postwar world.

Military Operations

To a limited extent military strategies were based on political expectations of the aims and power of other states. British statesmen seemed most conscious of the future political effect of military operations, though they possessed the least military power; the Russians groped their way to what military power could do for them; American statesmen were more uncertain and divided. Some distrusted the British attitude or were simply anti-British in an old American tradition; some

18

were naive; some were sure the American public and Congress would not tolerate an energetic overseas foreign policy in postwar years. But the main concern of military men was to achieve victory over the immediate enemy with the least cost in manpower.

After careful review, the Allies had decided on the war aim of "unconditional surrender." The phrase meant simply that the victors would set surrender terms without negotiating. Although Nazi propaganda chiefs tried to use it to convince their people that the Allies meant to destroy them completely, the rationale for policy was simple. In the years after World War I Adolf Hitler had convinced many people that his demands were justified because the Versailles Treaty had imposed far harsher terms than those proffered by Woodrow Wilson when the German Army first surrendered. "Unconditional surrender" would keep any new German revanchist from using the same tactic; it committed the Allies to nothing until the time for decisions arrived and it had, in addition, a good ring to it as a rallying cry. The unconditional surrender policy did little to prolong a war in which Hitler was determined either to win or drag Germany to utter defeat. In the Pacific, however, it brought a delay of several days while Americans debated accepting the Japanese condition that the Emperor remain in power: former American Secretary of State Cordell Hull—whose ideas were ultimately rejected—argued that the Emperor was the key to the system that had launched the Japanese upon military expansionism which would be repeated if he were not removed.

In support of the aim of unconditional surrender, overall Western strategy called first for an attack on Germany, the most dangerous and pressing enemy, and later a full-scale attack against Japan. With limited military resources assigned to the Pacific, General Douglas MacArthur devised an immensely successful strategy of island-hopping that bypassed many Japanese-held islands. The success of this strategy and the pressures to use most war materials against Germany and Italy meant that the Allies devoted relatively little logistic support to reopening routes to China and to operations within China proper. Consequently, when Japan surrendered, the Nationalist government in China could not easily take over the areas occupied by Japan, nor could it rely on masses of foreign troops in China for help. Strategy had dictated an uncertain future for Chiang's government.

The Allies' overall strategy of switching forces from the European theater to the Pacific after the German defeat relied on Russian intervention against Japan as soon as the Russians had time to mass forces in the Far East. Military planners assumed that the Japanese would make a fanatic last-ditch fight causing hundreds of thousands, perhaps millions, of casualties; that eighteen months after the defeat of Germany would be needed to subdue the Japanese, and that the Japanese still maintained an enormous untapped army based in and supplied from Manchuria. The Russians were to knock out this supposedly formidable force. The success of the super-secret atomic bomb project in late 1945 threw doubt on these assumptions but the machinery for carrying out military plans, once set into operation, was hard to stop, and uncertainty about the situation made planners hold to the original project.*

At the next lower strategic level—how the war against Germany ought to be prosecuted—the main concern was the direction of the Anglo-American effort. Russian troops had borne the brunt of the battle against the Nazis, and Stalin, who never let the Allies forget it, demanded an immediate cross-Channel invasion of France to relieve pressure on the Russian front. Winston Churchill, always eager to follow an indirect strategy and with an eye on the political future, argued for an alternative attack through the Balkans. Some historians have since contended that such an attack would have forestalled Russian military advance through, and subsequent political domination of, the Balkans. Others have argued that an Allied attack in the Balkans would have faced terrain as difficult as the rugged land that slowed their attack in Italy, and could have resulted in the Russians sweeping across the north European plain and dominating all of Germany. But the determining factors for choice of a direct cross-Channel attack were distance and supply, and recognition that such an attack would bring the Allies ashore close to the main German industrial complex where overall production was still increasing despite strengthened Allied air attacks. The Allies chose to attack the Normandy coast of France and named General Eisenhower to command the invasion force.

As a consequence of these decisions and of enemy action, by the end of the war Russia occupied most of Eastern Europe; the Allies were ensconced in Southern and Western Europe and the Mediterranean area; and Britain, France, and Holland were in a position to reoccupy Southeast Asia with the help of the United States. The United States emerged in undisputed domination of the Pacific and Japan, and

---

* As important a military man as Admiral William D. Leahy—President Roosevelt's liaison with the Joint Chiefs of Staff—had told the President the proposed atomic bomb would never go off—years of experience with explosives convinced him of this.

occupied the southern half of Korea; the Russians occupied Manchuria and northern Korea.

Diplomacy in World War II

While armies fought, political leaders tackled a two-fold job: they tried to clarify the lines of demarcation of their own advancing armies, and they tried to make sure the areas occupied by other coalition members were not falling too firmly into their grasp.

At Washington, in March 1943, representatives of Britain and the United States decided that they had to accept reincorporation of Latvia, Lithuania, and Estonia into the Soviet Union, as well as the portion of Poland east of the Curzon Line, and of Bessarabia. The Curzon Line had been the boundary between Poland and Russia suggested by a commission at the end of World War I, but Polish victories in subsequent hostilities had pushed the line well to the east. Now Stalin wanted this and other areas that Russia had previously lost; since the Red Army was about to overrun them, there seemed little point in arguing. Moreover, the Western Allies accepted the idea of compensating Poland with some German territory, and the possibility of dismembering Germany.

Churchill agreed that the United States should obtain the Pacific islands that Japan had controlled under League of Nations auspices and that had been fortified in violation of League commitments. Thus the United States extended its zone of influence far out into the Pacific so that it would never again suffer another Pearl Harbor. In May the British leader accepted American demands for the abolition of extraterritorial rights in China secured during the nineteenth century. The United States was mildly interested in making China a Pacific great power and though Churchill had doubts about the future success of Chiang's government, he was willing to go along; in his view this was essentially the American sphere of influence. Appointment of Lord Louis Mountbatten to the newly created post of Supreme Allied Commander in Southeast Asia symbolized Churchill's position that Southeast Asia was still a European sphere.

On July 25, 1943, Marshal Pietro Badoglio deposed Benito Mussolini, dictator of Italy since 1922. In September he surrendered to the Allies and on October 13 declared war on Germany. German forces continued to control the northern half of Italy. But in the part held by the Allies, a pattern of occupation controls developed that would later be applied to all occupied territories. The Western powers whose forces were in actual control of the area gave the Russians membership in a powerless supervisory organ while, despite all Russian protests, they actually ran matters themselves. In their turn the Russians followed suit in Eastern Europe where the Allies also complained repeatedly and ineffectively about actions taken without consulting them. Military occupation came to mean—by and large—political domination (though the Russians used their position of domination to much harsher effect than did the United States or Britain).

Stalin felt it was not worthwhile to occupy Finland, far to the north, and in September 1943 signed an armistice with the Finns. Finland would be spared Russian occupation at the price of ceding a large slice of territory to the Soviet Union.

Czechoslovakia was a different matter. It had a government-in-exile in the Allied camp, it was further to the west, and it had enjoyed relatively good relations with the Soviet Union in prewar years. Czech leaders felt their country had been abandoned by the Western powers to Hitler in 1938, and the course of military operations indicated that it would probably be occupied by the Russians. Consequently President Beneš decided that Czechoslovakia, while retaining good relations with Western powers, must follow a foreign policy of close ties to the Soviet Union. In this way, Beneš hoped, the country could serve as a bridge between Russia and the West. Late in 1943 he flew to Moscow where he signed a treaty of alliance with Stalin and received his assurance that Russia would favor reconstruction of the Czech state with its pre-Munich frontiers.

Yugoslavia and Greece posed complications, since they were part of the Balkan area—the Russian sphere—yet were also Mediterranean countries, thus falling into the zone of predominant British influence. Churchill tried to stave off trouble. Reorganization of Greek and Yugoslav governments-in-exile lessened the probability of Communist revolt; then the British suggested to the Soviet Union in May and June 1944 a delimitation of their respective zones. Rumania and Bulgaria would be Russian controlled, and Greece and Jugoslavia would be British controlled. The Russians accepted tentatively, but asked pointedly whether the Americans had been consulted.

When the British approached Secretary of State Hull, he objected strongly. The Secretary held a view, widely shared among his American colleagues, that Churchill was too eager to advocate military operations that would serve Britain's postwar interests. Hull also held the traditional liberal view that power politics, balance-of-power policies, and spheres of influence were bad. But President Roosevelt waited for the Secretary's absence to tell Churchill that he accepted the idea. The British began to work actively against Communist-led guerrillas in Greece. In Yugoslavia they found that Partisan leader Josip Broz-Tito led the strongest resistance movement, and they chose to work with him. But Marshal Tito was both nationalist and Communist, and his acceptance of British aid never brought him under British influence.

Although the relentless advance of Allied armies roughly outlined the areas that the great powers would continue to dominate in the postwar years, military strategy left in doubt the fate of certain areas that would be jointly or only partly occupied—Iran, Germany, Austria, Korea, and China. At a series of conferences the Allies tried to settle their future.

At *Moscow*, in October 1943, the foreign ministers and chiefs of staff of Britain, the United States and the Soviet Union met to set up the European Advisory Council, whose job was to work out conditions for occupation of Germany and to delimit occupation zones. They promised independence for Austria after the war, agreed to punishment of war criminals, and published a declaration in favor of creation of an international organization to ensure world peace.

Once more, Secretary Hull displayed an attitude toward foreign policy shared by many of his colleagues. For him, the Russian commitment to participate in a postwar international organization overshadowed all the other accomplishments of the Conference. He thought that creation of an organization that could guarantee international peace and security would remove all the incentive states had had in the past to occupy strategic areas and to maneuver for advantage merely to keep other states from becoming too powerful. As he saw it, Winston Churchill insisted on pursuing precisely these old objectives, and for this reason Hull distrusted the English statesman. Military operations should have no relation to future political boundaries, Hull believed; postwar settlements should be made around a conference table where military power would play no part. Now that the Soviet Union was committed to a new security organization, the Secretary of State saw his main task as obtaining Senate approval for American membership and avoiding the fiasco of 1919, when the Senate repudiated membership in the League of Nations. But events were bound to confute the Secretary's point of view, and American policy faltered and remained unsure.

At *Cairo*, November 1943, Roosevelt and Churchill met with Chiang Kai-shek, Generalissimo of the Chinese Republic. They worked out future operations against Japan, and agreed to strip Japan of all islands in the Pacific seized or occupied since the beginning of World War I. All Chinese territories Japan had taken would be returned—Manchuria, Formosa and the Pescadores. In due course Korea—long an object of struggle between China and Japan and under Japanese control since 1895—would become free and independent. Afterwards the American president and the Chinese leader told the press that the conference had recognized the right of the oppressed and ill-treated peoples of Asia to form their own governments. Winston Churchill, intent upon retaining control of the British Empire, remained silent.

From Cairo, Churchill and Roosevelt flew to meet with Stalin at *Teheran*, the capital of Iran. In this—the first meeting of the Big Three—discussions ranged widely over military policy, the issue of a warm-water port for Russia, ideas about the future United Nations Organization, and possible dismemberment of Germany, to guard against any postwar resurgence. To Iran, which they occupied jointly, they promised sovereignty and territorial integrity after the war.

The British and Americans continued their conversations in Cairo after the Teheran meeting. The Americans wanted a big military push in Burma to reopen land communications to China. Churchill argued instead for military operations in Greece to protect the Mediterranean sphere from undue Russian influence. He finally won the day by pointing out that the Russian commitment to enter the war against Japan had reduced the necessity of hazardous Allied mainland operations in China. But an increasing number of American officers distrusted the British stress on military operations which would be of political value to Britain.

These conferences gave some indication of the differences among coalition members. They became open, however, only in subsequent months as the issue of control of Poland came to the fore and political developments in Italy and France further muddied relations between Britain and the United States.

Britain had entered the war against the Nazis on the basis of its commitments to Poland, had sheltered a Polish government-in-exile, and had armed Polish refugees. As Russian armies approached Poland, Churchill was far less willing to countenance outright Russian domination there than he had been in Eastern European countries that were formerly Nazi satellites. But the Russians obviously held the upper hand. Their first move had been to break off relations with the Polish government-in-exile in London and to give diplomatic recognition to the Polish Committee of National Liberation, a genuine Polish resistance group dominated by Communists.* Churchill, to remedy affairs, tried to persuade the London Poles to accept Russian requests for boundary changes. They refused, and tried instead to negotiate directly with Russia. Stalin suggested they drop certain objectionable members of their government and accept most of the Polish Committee of National Liberation as colleagues. This led to an impasse, accompanied by brutal tragedy. The Red Army stood at the gates of Warsaw; within the town the underground Polish Home Army rose to attack Nazi defenders of the city. Instead of coming to their aid the Russians stood by, on the excuse of German resistance, while German troops wreaked a terrible vengeance on the Polish group. In the process the one armed force within Poland that would have favored the London Poles over the Communists was wiped out. Military force and the disposition of troops determined the political future of Poland, despite Churchill's diplomacy.

In the meantime, within the emerging Western sphere of influence, Americans and Britons clashed over events in both Italy and France.

In Italy the Americans charged Britain with supporting reactionary and unpopular figures, King Victor Emmanuel and Field Marshal Badoglio. Russian recognition of Badoglio and Italian Communist support for his government made the American position temporarily untenable. But when King Victor Emmanuel abdicated in favor of his son Umberto and a new government replaced that of Badoglio, the United States began to regain influence.

Meanwhile in France, General Charles de Gaulle had become another subject of contention among the Allies. Churchill disliked the single-minded and arrogant Free French leader but worked with him and was willing to recognize his Committee of National Liberation as a provisional French Government. Secretary Hull and Admiral Leahy (Roosevelt's liaison with the Joint Chiefs of Staff, and an influential adviser) hated the Frenchman. Leahy had been the American Ambassador to the Vichy French government during the early years of the war when the policy was to bolster this regime in resisting the demands of its Nazi conquerors. On the basis of this experience, Leahy insisted that de Gaulle would face bitter resistance in France.

But de Gaulle received a hero's welcome. On May 15, 1944 he transformed his Committee into the Provisional Government of the Re-

* The pretext was a Polish demand for an international Red Cross investigation into the massacre of Polish officers in Katyn forest. The Russians had charged Nazis with the crime, but the German government had insisted Russians had done it.

public of France, and received Russian recognition when he took several Communists into it. Confronted with such broad support, the Americans finally bowed and extended him *de facto* recognition on July 11.

Luckily, there were fewer troubles in other Western-liberated countries: Norway, the Netherlands, and Belgium.

In August 1944 Churchill flew to meet Tito of Yugoslavia for the first time. Britain had given him much support, but the meeting was not cordial, and the next month Tito secretly flew to Moscow to arrange for withdrawal of Russian troops. These were hardly necessary to bring Tito firmly into the Russian orbit, for—despite Churchill's attempts to persuade the Russians that Yugoslavia should be within the English sphere of influence—Tito was himself a Communist and had a solid base of domestic support.

The British statesman had by now arrived at his own view of what was happening. Russian power was spreading over Eastern Europe while everywhere else the Western powers seemed to be at loggerheads. Two tasks appeared necessary: a British-American concert must be established and Russia must be confronted with its existence to force an agreement limiting Russian expansion. Churchill and Roosevelt tackled the first at *Quebec* and at *Hyde Park, New York* in mid-September and in October Churchill flew to *Moscow* to undertake the second.

The Americans were as willing as the British to restore Italy to the family of nations; they agreed easily to a broad relaxation of armistice terms, exchange of diplomatic agents, and economic assistance for Italy. About Poland, however, there was little to say. That the Russians were in a commanding position, Roosevelt, concerned with voters of Polish background in the forthcoming American election, could not acknowledge. Although Churchill and Roosevelt concerted plans for operations in the Pacific, they got into a bad muddle on future economic relations between Britain and the United States and on the question of Germany.

Important divisions within the United States government compounded the difficult situation. Secretary of the Treasury Henry Morgenthau, long active in foreign affairs, had prepared a harsh plan for Germany that would strip the country of industry and turn it into a primarily agricultural land. At Quebec he appealed for British support, arguing that the plan would eliminate one of Britain's chief competitors and suggesting that the United States extend a large-scale loan to Britain for postwar reconstruction. He also proposed to continue lend-lease aid after the defeat of Germany and until the end came for Japan.

Roosevelt knew that his State and War Department advisers favored demilitarization and denazification measures for Germany, stringent controls over its government, and German reparations payments to the conquered countries it had systematically looted. Without consulting his advisers, therefore, he initialled the Morgenthau plan, and Churchill followed suit. It was with some amazement that President Roosevelt found bitter opposition on the part of Secretary of State Hull and Secretary of War Stimson when he returned to the United States. In the face of this he had second thoughts and withdrew approval of the plan. Instead of making a decision, he temporarily suspended all planning for Germany, with the unfortunate result that the European Advisory Commission was without direction and could make little progress on the task of coordinating Allied policy for Germany. Nothing concrete was done until the Potsdam Conference in July 1945. A further consequence was that the Morgenthau plan's influence was still felt in the first stages of the German occupation, though it was no longer a part of official policy. Nothing more was heard of the loan to Britain which Hull opposed because it had been suggested without any plan to extract concessions from the British.

With the first task only partly completed, Churchill flew to Moscow, where he met with Stalin and the American Ambassador, Averell Harriman. In return for renewed assurances of British preeminent influence in Greece he accepted Russian predominance in Rumania, Bulgaria, and Hungary. On the thornier issue of Yugoslavia, he obtained the best he could in a bad situation—an agreement to share influence on an equal basis. But Poland remained an intractable problem. Churchill brought the head of the Polish exile government in London to Moscow, but no agreement could be reached on the eastern boundaries of the country and Stalin insisted on just such an agreement before allowing the London Poles to take part in the new government of the Committee of National Liberation firmly established under Russian sponsorship in Lublin. Yet discussions of other matters went so smoothly that when Churchill flew back to London, he told the House of Commons:

I am very glad to inform the House that our relations with Soviet Russia were never more close, intimate, and cordial than they are at the present time. Never before have we been able to reach so high a degree of frank, friendly discussions of the most delicate and often potentially vexatious topics.

In the meantime General de Gaulle was adroitly using his limited diplomatic resources to rebuild France and its position in the world. His vision was clear; he had to assure governmental authority and stability in France against the chaos that might result if disparate political groups fought for power—a situation where the superior organization and arms of Communist resistance groups might well gain the upper hand for them. To avoid chaos he must inspire respect for his purpose and authority among the French people and create a feeling that the extraordinary problems left in the wake of defeat, occupation, and liberation—and their accompanying tremendous physical destruction—were being energetically tackled. In the second place, he must vigorously defend French interests abroad. During the surprise German offensive in the winter of 1944–45, General Eisenhower planned a withdrawal from Strasbourg and the surrounding area. De Gaulle, whose armored forces occupied Strasbourg, refused point-blank, even when the Americans threatened to stop his supplies. He knew that the Germans would take a terrible vengeance on the Alsatian populace which had so deliriously welcomed its liberators, and the effect on political morale in France would be disastrous. The incident confirmed de Gaulle's view that only a Frenchman could defend French interests and that the American allies were only too willing to ignore them. France, for example, had an empire which had provided de Gaulle a base on which to rebuild his army when France was occupied. Like Churchill, de Gaulle knew that the Americans were ready to speed the liquidation of all empires. France had vital economic and strategic interests in the European peace settlement, and particularly in the future of Germany; it therefore had to regain enough power to make sure that its interests could not be ignored by the United States, England and the Soviet Union, who had only grudgingly accepted any French role. Their annoyance at de Gaulle's demands for material to reequip his troops and his insistence that French troops be in the forefront of battle might have been even greater had they realized that de Gaulle intended to use these troops for political purposes—to buttress the French position in time of peace.

The French leader followed two approaches. He tried to persuade Churchill that a weakened Britain might also find its interests ignored by the United States and Russia, and that England therefore ought to make common cause with a France whose new unity and spirit was demonstrated to Churchill during his visit to Paris in November 1944. If the two acted together, he argued, they could form the nucleus of a third force between the two giants, and they would probably receive support from many other countries with doubts about a Soviet-American hegemony. But he also approached Stalin, arguing that, as continental powers, France and the Soviet Union had a common interest in preventing German resurgence, and that they could not count on the United States, which had its own preoccupations. Nor could they fully rely on England. Not only did England have an insular tradition, but as the center of the Commonwealth, she frequently had to defer to the interests and desires of Commonwealth members. In December 1944, in Moscow, he signed a twenty-year treaty of alliance with the Soviet Union on the strength of this argument.

The Allies kept one another informed of de Gaulle's maneuvers. Yet by playing upon their divergent interests and fears, he obtained not only the Russian alliance, but also *de jure* recognition of his regime as the French Government, and—at British urging—membership on the Advisory Commission charged with settling the future of Germany. Finally, at the Dumbarton Oaks Conference of 1944 that took the first steps to create the new United Nations Organization, France obtained permanent membership in the new Security Council.

The Yalta Conference

Despite the success of de Gaulle's diplomatic efforts he was not invited to the most important wartime meeting—the conference at Yalta, in the Crimea, February 4 to 11, 1945. It came after the successful repulse of the German winter offensive in the West—the Battle of the Bulge in the Ardennes Mountains of Belgium—and after renewal of the Russian offensive in Poland. Victory was in sight, bringing with it a host of problems needing resolution.

For the American participants, political problems in Europe were not as important as strategy toward Japan and the settlement of certain questions of international organization. Roosevelt still thought that public opinion would prevent the United States from keeping any troops in Europe for more than two years after the end of the war with Germany. It would therefore be up to the Europeans to settle their own affairs. But Roosevelt and his advisers also arrived at Yalta with increased distrust and suspicion of the British, who had recently been found shooting at guerrillas in Greece, opposing a proposed government change in Italy, and embroiled in Belgian affairs. In each of these cases Churchill's government, against considerable opposition at home, appeared to be backing a conservative and even reactionary regime against popular demands.

For the British, Allied policy toward Europe was paramount. And for Stalin it seemed that economic reconstruction of the Soviet Union (and therefore reparations from Germany) was as important as establishing friendly governments in the countries that lay between Germany and Russia. Although Communist parties were active in the Western areas of influence and in many cases were actually consolidating local positions of power, they did not seem to receive any particular support from the Russians at this point; Stalin appeared to be avoiding interference in the Western zone of influence. In turn, at Yalta he tried to block any Western interference in the Russian zone of Eastern Europe.

At the time of the Yalta conference, military men still estimated that it would take eighteen months after the defeat of Germany to subdue Japan. Roosevelt obtained Stalin's secret commitment to enter the war against Japan within two or three months after victory in Europe. Earlier in the war, Roosevelt, Churchill, and Chiang Kai-shek had declared that Japan would be forced to disgorge all fruits of past aggression. The price Russia demanded for its intervention was largely in keeping with these terms. The Allies agreed that Outer Mongolia— the Mongolian Peoples Republic—would remain independent, a condition no Chinese government could accept with enthusiasm. Russia regained the southern part of Sakhalin Island and islands adjacent to it, as well as the Kurile Islands. The port of Dairen on the tip of the Liaotung Peninsula was to be internationalized and Port Arthur to be leased to Russia as a naval base; a joint Soviet-Chinese company would operate the railroad across Manchuria to Dairen. "The pre-eminent interests of the Soviet Union shall be safeguarded," the agreement stated. "China shall retain full sovereignty in Manchuria."

This agreement, obtained as a *quid pro quo* for Russian intervention against Japan, also had to remain secret until the intervention took place. Roosevelt, in the light of what appeared to be military necessity, made a bargain in which he undertook to obtain Chinese consent. Sakhalin and its adjacent islands had previously been Russian and taken over by Japan. The railroad and port rights had also been Russian, extracted from a weak China in the nineteenth century, and then transferred to Japan. In the face of a China that was internally divided and whose military effort had been woefully weak, and of a Russia which would be militarily strong and would make a major contribution in the area, the bargain did not appear a bad one. Roosevelt felt that he had secured Russian support for China. When the Chinese Ambassador to the Soviet Union negotiated specific agreements to implement the terms of Yalta, he received assurances that the Russians would not support the Chinese Communists, and Chiang Kai-shek subsequently told the American Ambassador that he was "generally satisfied with the treaty."

Yalta also brought agreement on zones of occupation in Germany, and on the establishment of an Allied Control Council for Germany based in Berlin—which would still be a special zone under joint three-power occupation. Nothing more clearly illustrates the discrepancy between contemporary views and subsequent events than the fact that the main argument concerning the German zones was between the British and the Americans. They could not agree who would occupy the southwest zones as against the northwest. American military personnel feared for their communications through France, which they expected would be torn by revolution if de Gaulle tried to take over. Once this fear was assuaged, it became difficult to define their communication rights across the British zone to the north. No one, on the other hand, gave much thought to the question of access to Berlin; few thought that any problems would arise in that area.

Again the Allies discussed possible dismemberment of Germany, but no decision was made. Upon British insistence, the Americans and then the Russians agreed to give France a zone of occupation and a seat on the Allied Control Council. The Allied leaders exchanged views on the issue of reparations—German repayment for war damage that it had inflicted. The Russians demanded a large sum to be drawn from existing German capital goods and from production over the next ten years, amounting to $20 billion. But ever since the incident of the Morgenthau Plan the British and Americans had had second thoughts about the German economy and its role in the European economy, and they demanded further study of possible solutions; neither country wanted to subsidize starving Germans who would be working for the Russians. All agreed, however, that reparations would be apportioned both on the basis of suffering endured at the hands of the Nazis and the contributions made to Allied victory. The whole discussion of reparations was carried out against an extraordinary background of systematic Nazi pillage and exploitation of the areas they occupied, under a long-term plan of turning all the rest of Europe—inhabited by "inferior peoples"—into a semi-starved contributory area for the Third Reich.

Yalta really failed to settle policy for Germany—much was left for future decision. Discussions over East Europe were markedly different because they involved an area in which Russian military power was already well established. Stalin forced acceptance of the Curzon Line as the eastern boundary of Poland. He argued for the Oder-Neisse line as a western boundary, thus giving the Poles a substantial territorial compensation at the expense of Germany. The Western powers were put in the embarrassing position of opposing Polish claims; at Yalta they succeeded simply in persuading Stalin to agree to Polish occupation of the area, with the final boundaries to be fixed at the peace conference. Ever since then, the Poles have known that Russia supports their right to the western territories, and that the Western governments, in their bid for German support, have refused to accept this right.*

Concerning the make-up of governments within the Russian sphere the Western Allies could muster little strength. They could, and did, bring diplomatic pressure to bear on Stalin. They made him promise publicly in the Declaration on Liberated Europe that the end of the war would see "the earliest possible establishment through free elections of governments responsive to the will of the people," and accept the same conditions for Poland. Much later, when the myth of the "Yalta betrayal" gained wide currency in the United States and gave rise to a call for the repudiation of the Yalta agreements, the critics who finally got around to reading the agreements dropped their demands. It was Russian failure to live up to the agreements as the West understood them that was really objectionable. To claim that no agreement that depended on trusting Stalin should have been made was only to argue that the Western powers should have asked for nothing in Eastern Europe; the area was already within the Russian grasp. In the Far East, Russia relinquished its Yalta-based rights in Manchuria to the Chinese Communist government in 1954.

A number of other lesser political problems were briefly discussed, but time was short, and the Allies agreed to periodic meetings of their foreign ministers to deal with major policy issues. Agreements were also reached on certain matters of international organization, including a conference at San Francisco on April 25, 1945 to create a world security organization. The Yalta Conference ended on a note of satisfaction that the wartime Allies would be able to resolve their differences in peacetime.

On his way home President Roosevelt stopped at Suez to confer with Emperor Haile Selassie of Ethiopia, King Farouk of Egypt, and

---

* When de Gaulle was in Moscow, he accepted the Oder-Neisse line, but refused recognition to the Moscow-sponsored Communist-dominated Lublin government."

King Ibn Saud of Saudi Arabia. He asked Ibn Saud to admit more Jews to Palestine, but also promised to take no step in Palestine without consulting both Jews and Arabs. The conversations foreshadowed a more active American intervention than before in Middle Eastern affairs.

On April 25, American and Russian troops met at the Elbe River. May 8, 1945, marked the end of the war in Europe.

After Yalta

Toward the end of May 1945, Winston Churchill had a series of conversations with Joseph P. Davies, former American ambassador to the Soviet Union. Davies had been sent by the new President, Harry S. Truman, to talk about relations with Russia. Davies shared the suspicions of American military men and Cordell Hull about Churchill—that he wanted to include the Americans in an anti-Russian bloc to implement what Davies called the policy of "preserving England's position in Europe."

At the time of the talks Churchill had watched the Soviets continue to consolidate their control of East Europe. The presence of Western troops in Austria had blocked them there, but Yugoslavia, despite Stalin's agreement with Churchill, had moved into the Soviet camp and its troops had almost come to blows with Anglo-American troops when Tito tried to occupy the Trieste area between Italy and Yugoslavia. British and French troops had, in fact, fought each other in the course of de Gaulle's efforts to reinstall France in Syria, and the United States had begun to divert lend-lease shipments and troops for use in the Far East. Churchill felt that division among Western powers existed in the face of a strong possibility that the Soviet Union intended to dominate Europe—and told Davies his forebodings as he reviewed events. Davies' response could hardly have cheered him. the American asked him if he was now willing to admit that he had been wrong not to support Hitler. "For," Davies said in reporting the conversation, "as I understood him, he was now expressing the doctrine which Hitler and Goebbels had been proclaiming and reiterating for the past four years in an effort to break up Allied unity and 'divide and conquer.' Exactly the same conditions which he described and the same deductions were drawn from them as he now appeared to assert." *

* Quoted in Herbert Feis, *Churchill, Roosevelt, Stalin* (Princeton: Princeton University Press, 1957), pp. 650–652.

Nothing was done to resolve these differences in attitude before the Big Three met again in Potsdam, Germany after the defeat of the Third Reich. But the Big Three were no longer Roosevelt, Churchill, and Stalin.

Potsdam

Franklin D. Roosevelt, for twelve years President of the United States, died on April 12, 1945. His successor, Harry S. Truman, was a former Senator from Missouri known for little but his efficient conduct of an investigating committee during the war and his uncertain connections with the unsavory Pendergast political machine in Kansas City. Roosevelt had virtually taken control of foreign policy, and Truman had been Vice-President for only a short time before he succeeded to the presidency. Consequently he relied heavily at first on Roosevelt's advisers. Chief among these was James F. Byrnes, whom he made his Secretary of State. Byrnes, a former Senator, Supreme Court Justice, and Director of the Office of War Mobilization and Reconversion, had been a presidential troubleshooter; he had held no foreign policy positions. He had thought he would be chosen Vice-President in 1944, when he was passed over for Truman, and it seemed that he had been cheated out of the presidency. With the death of Roosevelt, the new Secretary of State was next in line for the presidency after Truman, and Truman thought he should choose someone prominent in American politics: Byrnes filled the bill.

The new Secretary of State had distinct views about his functions. He proceeded to liquidate many of the war-born foreign policy agencies in the field of propaganda, espionage, and economic warfare, considering these to be out of place in peacetime. His role would be to make peace, to devote himself to the task of negotiating peace treaties for former enemy states. As far as he was concerned the most important accomplishment of the Potsdam Conference was the creation of the Council of Foreign Ministers to draft the peace treaties. A few meetings, he thought, would be sufficient.

A comparable change took place in Britain, where a July general election, delayed during the war, turned out Winston Churchill's Conservative party and replaced it with a Labour government, headed by Clement Attlee. Churchill, it seemed, had been fine as a wartime leader. But the people looked to Labour in peace.

Thus, when the Allies assembled at Potsdam, Germany from July 17 to August 2, 1945, Churchill and Anthony Eden attended only for the first week and were then replaced by Atlee and his new

Foreign Secretary, a tough, former trade union leader named Ernest Bevin. Of the wartime leaders, only Stalin and Molotov were left. Germany had gone down in defeat; only subjugation of Japan remained, and the first experimental atomic bomb was exploded at Alamagordo, New Mexico on July 16, the day before the Conference opened.

The issue of Japan was therefore easy to resolve; the conferees issued a declaration calling on Japan to surrender or else be subjected to merciless bombing.

The issue of Germany was harder to deal with, but imperative, since the Yalta agreements had left much to be settled. Boundaries, reparations, and the economic treatment of Germany were all interrelated problems. The Russians had demanded large reparations at the same time that they insisted on the Oder-Neisse line as Germany's eastern boundary. But the Western Allies were afraid the new boundaries would deprive Germany of coal and grain areas necessary to its overall economy, and that if they accepted Russian demands for reparations from current production, they would find themselves feeding an impoverished Germany at one end while Russia funneled out their aid at the other. Under those circumstances Germany would become an intolerable burden on all Europe.

After bitter hassling, with Byrnes trying to act as an arbiter between Britain and the Soviet Union, the three agreed that Germany should retain enough resources so the German people could subsist without external assistance. Against Russian insistence that at Yalta the West had agreed to $20 billion, they concluded that the amount and character of industrial equipment *un*necessary for German peacetime economy (and therefore available for reparations) should be set by the Allied Control Council under policies fixed by an Allied Commission on Reparations. Meanwhile, in order to ease the difficult economics of the situation, Germany and its zones of occupation would be treated as a single economic unit.

The part played by military occupation again became evident. The Western Allies had to accept Russian annexation of the northern part of East Prussia and the ancient city of Koenigsberg. The Russians in turn were barred from a role in administering the great Ruhr coal-and-steel area under a tripartite scheme that they had advanced earlier. And the most the Western powers could do about the Oder-Neisse line was suggest that the frontier be left for final delimitation at the time of the peace treaty. Nominally, therefore, the area behind it was only under Polish occupation. In fact the Poles had already begun to treat it as a part of Poland and were expelling its German inhabitants.

The most bitter exchanges took place over Russian activities in Eastern Europe. Stalin demanded Western recognition of the new governments of Rumania, Bulgaria, Hungary, and Finland. British and Americans both demurred on the ground that the Yalta agreements on free elections had been violated. Stalin replied that Britain was promoting monarcho-fascism in Greece. To Western demands for improvement in the procedures of the Allied Control Commissions in Eastern Europe, Stalin pointed out that Russia was denied any influence in Italy. Nevertheless, he agreed to modification of procedures and promised Russian evacuation of Persia. The promises meant little perhaps, but Russia had been blocked from the Ruhr as well as Italy, and her demands at Potsdam for a trusteeship over Libya and modification of the convention governing the Turkish Black Sea straits—both moves that would have brought Russia into the Mediterranean—were also denied by the West. The demarcation lines appeared to have been drawn more clearly in Europe.

Once the weary participants had issued their communique and gone home, the one substantial area of agreement—Germany—proved to have been none at all. De Gaulle was not invited to Potsdam, and considered that the agreements reached there in no way bound France. Far more interested than the British or Americans in keeping Germany weak, he refused to treat his zone as a part of the rest of Germany, and blocked all moves in the Allied Control Commission during the next few months. By the time he relented, it was too late to know whether the Russians had ever really intended to carry out the Potsdam agreements. Soon the accord on democratization of Germany proved that the word could be interpreted in a variety of ways by the different occupying powers.

Events in the Far East then moved far more rapidly than had been anticipated and caught participants off guard. At Hiroshima and Nagasaki the first two atomic bombs were dropped upon an exhausted Japan. The Japanese government appealed to the Soviet Union for mediation, and received instead a declaration of war and the invasion of Manchuria. Although a war party in Japan tried to avert the action and tried to bring about a last-ditch stand that would throw the Allies back into the sea, Japan sued for peace, asking only that the Emperor remain as head of state.

New Organizations for a New International Politics

World War II had prevented the hegemony of a small group of powers, but at too high a cost. The attempt to patch over the old balance-of-power system with the institutions of the League of Nations had obviously failed to cope with underlying changes in the international environment. The war gave statesmen a second opportunity to rebuild, and they created a set of new institutions embodying a whole view of how international politics could be made to work under the new circumstances.

After preliminary conferences at Dumbarton Oaks in Washington, D.C. (September–October 1944), at Mexico City (February–March 1945), and finally at San Francisco (April 25–June 26, 1945), the long years of planning and thought culminated in creation of the United Nations. Its Charter drew heavily on experience of the League, but contained modifications that would, it was hoped, make the new organization more effective.

The Security Council (representing the concert of great powers) had its peace-keeping functions more clearly delineated and was given far more power to enforce peaceful settlement of disputes and to keep the peace through collective security measures. The five great powers, China, France, Great Britain, the Soviet Union, and the United States, were permanent members. Instead of the unanimous vote required in the old League of Nations Council, the new Council needed only a special majority of seven out of eleven for most of its recommendations for settling disputes. However, to keep the major powers from voting futile resolutions against each other which, if carried out, might result in war, collective security decisions—that is, those involving diplomatic, economic, or military pressures against a country threatening the peace—required unanimity among the five great powers. Since any one major power could veto this kind of resolution, it was hoped that this provision would make the powers seek solutions upon which all could agree. There was widespread opposition to the inclusion of the unanimity requirement. But few if any of the major powers would have accepted the Charter without it, and many commentators believed that if bad relations between the major powers kept them from reaching agreement on international political issues, the United Nations system would fail anyway. As it was constituted, the Security Council represented an attempt to give ultimate responsibility for keeping the peace to those who had the power to do so. But they would also have to consult with and secure the approval of at least some smaller powers.

The unanimity requirement extended to membership recommendations and Charter amendments. On questions of peaceful settlement a permanent member could veto a resolution unless it was itself a party to the dispute. The Soviet Union had demanded power to veto inclusion of items on the Council's agenda for discussion; only a

personal appeal by Truman to Stalin brought a relaxation of the
Soviet position. Delegates to the United Nations Conference at San
Francisco expressed hope that the permanent members would use
their veto power sparingly. All realized, however, that the United
Nations would at best only provide channels for political action and
some standards for conduct; it would not eliminate political power
nor discrepancies in power and their influence on political affairs.
The Charter still placed primary emphasis on states' own efforts to
resolve their differences, and only foresaw United Nations efforts
when traditional methods failed. It encouraged attempts by regional
organizations to bring about settlements. But it also envisaged a strong
role for the United Nations, for under the Charter the United Nations
was to be given what the League had never had. By special agreements
negotiated with member states, the Security Council would have armed
forces at its disposal to carry out its orders. Collective security would
have real teeth.

At San Francisco smaller powers successfully pressured the larger
ones to give broader powers of discussion to the General Assembly, in
which each state, large or small, was to have equal representation.
Unlike the Security Council, the General Assembly could not make
binding decisions, but like the Security Council, it would have broad
powers to initiate investigations, to discuss, and to make recommendations on virtually anything that might disturb the peace of the world.
And like the Security Council, the General Assembly also abandoned
the unanimity rule which had bound its League of Nations predecessor. When making recommendations on certain categories of important
matters a two-thirds vote was required; on others—mainly procedural
ones—a majority sufficed.

The system of collective security, under which all states agreed to
act against one declared to be an aggressor, was designed to guarantee
an existing *status quo* against any attempt to overthrow it by force.
But no political system—and certainly not the ever-shifting international one—can continually preserve an existing *status quo*. It must have
methods by which new political and social demands and new technological changes can bring about acceptable political change. Otherwise people will ultimately try to use force to bring desired revisions.
The United Nations Charter recognized this; the enhanced capacity of
the Security Council and the General Assembly to recommend peaceful settlement of the disputes, and therefore to provide change, was
viewed as the necessary corollary to collective security. But some
people viewed another Charter modification as potentially more im-

portant. This was the elevation of the old Mandates Commission to the status of a principal organ of the United Nations in the form of the new Trusteeship Council. Here, indeed, was an agency specifically charged with supervising major political change on the international scene, and whose functions, many hoped, would eventually include supervising the dismantling of the European empires created under the balance-of-power system.

The old Mandates Commission had had limited functions and powers. At the end of World War I, the victor nations had felt unable simply to take over the colonies of the defeated states, Germany and Turkey. They had therefore allowed a limited measure of international supervision through the Mandates Commission. Only one state, Iraq, had achieved independence during the existence of the mandate system. The new Trusteeship Council was given far wider powers of supervision and control, and most of the former mandates were placed under it. But at San Francisco, several non-European states expressed the hope that many colonies of victor states would also be placed under the Trusteeship Council, which would help them to achieve independence. Since, at the outset, this was only a hope, the Charter included in addition a declaration on non-self-governing territories, which bound member nations to follow certain principles in their colonial territories and to transmit information to the United Nations on progress toward self-government within them. All this indicated the deep feeling that a chief task of the United Nations was to guide the inevitable and desirable break-up of the old European empires. Only European leaders argued against haste and against the propriety of the task with which the United Nations was being burdened.

The Secretary-General of the League of Nations supervised the translating, printing, information, communications, and housing services required by the various League agencies. The role of the United Nations Secretary-General was potentially larger. Since the Charter charged him with annual reports on the work of the United Nations and with bringing to the Security Council any matter which in his opinion threatened the peace, he might become an important world political figure.

Least altered among League organs was the International Court of Justice—the judicial arm of the world organization through which rules of international law would be applied, interpreted, and eventually broadened.

Although the United Nations was created to encompass both order and change in the world of international politics, care was taken to see that, unlike the League, it would not be crippled by being tied to the peace settlement. Any inequities in the peace could be corrected later through United Nations action.

If the experiences of the interwar years seemed to dictate strengthened political machinery, they appeared to show that economic and social conflicts underlying international political conflicts must also be attacked through international action. The interwar depression had spread from one country to another as each tried to save its own economic skin at the expense of the others; depression had hastened the demise of weak democratic political institutions and brought fascism and militarism into power. These in turn had produced the war.

To avoid repeating this sequence of events new agencies were created. The Economic and Social Council would act as the General Assembly's agency to supervise various economic and social commissions and committees charged with promoting human rights, higher standards of living, full employment, economic development, cultural and educational cooperation. The International Bank for Reconstruction and Development would stimulate the flow of international capital that had buttressed the nineteenth century order but had been inhibited by the uncertainties of the twentieth. It would help in the task of reconstructing devastated areas, thereby avoiding some of the strains that earlier produced the depression and its sequence of events, and it would provide funds for the underdeveloped countries, thus helping to eliminate international conflict between "have" and "have not" nations.

The new International Monetary Fund would rectify the situation created by the abandonment of gold as an international currency. The fund was based on the idea that stabilization of exchange rates between currencies would create a climate of confidence and allow expansion of mutually beneficial trade and investment. By providing other methods than exchange devaluation of currencies for rectification of trade imbalances, it would prevent the competitive devaluation that had been so self-defeating in the 1930s. Finally, a third major economic organ, the International Trade Organization, would guarantee observance of trade rules which in time would diminish use of discriminatory tariffs, export subsidies, import quotas, and other restrictions. The lend-lease agreements negotiated during the war had committed the countries involved to this kind of program at the end of hostilities. But the Charter of the proposed ITO, signed at Havana in March 1948, unlike those of the Bank and Fund, was never ratified. Its place in rebuilding international trade was eventually taken by a simplified bargaining arrangement known as the General Agreement on Tariffs and Trade, a series of periodic multilateral meetings where major trading nations might conclude a series of bilateral agreements that would be extended to all members, and could agree on trade rules.

These and other organizations which facilitated communications (the International Civil Aeronautics Organization, the International Telecommunications Union) or helped curb the spread of disease (the World Health Organization) or had still other purposes (the United Nations Educational, Scientific and Cultural Organization and the International Labor Organization), were designed to cope with the impact of the new developments treated in Chapter I on the system of presumably sovereign and independent states. Taken together, the organizations formed a neat, well thought out, world system reconstructed on the nineteenth century system. The signing of the United Nations Charter at San Francisco on June 26, 1945 while the war was still in progress and its ratification by the United States Senate on July 28, 1945, by a vote of 89 to 2 were seen as a triumph of human reason. The problem of creating a viable, flexible political system under the basic condition of a lack of a central political authority had been solved. Presumably the United Nations would eventually come close to being such a central authority, and its organs of social and economic cooperation would bring about the underlying economic and social conditions which political theory teaches are necessary to the creation of an acceptable political community.

Among many statesmen and commentators, however, expectations were less sanguine. They knew that the United Nations system could not eliminate international politics but would only channel them. They were aware of critical weaknesses. The collective security provisions depended on continued great power agreement and could not be used against any one of the great powers. In the attempt to give responsibility to those countries that had the power to assume responsibility, the only acceptable solution was one which gave each major power a veto on whatever enforcement action it disliked. Furthermore as the pieces of the postwar international puzzle became identified, it soon became apparent that the economic dislocations caused by the war were far greater than the resources of the IBRD, the IMF, and the proposed ITO could cope with. The economic deterioration of Europe *vis-à-vis* the rest of the world, was far worse than was first realized. In 1943 the Allies had created the United Nations Relief and Rehabilitation Administration which soon began to disburse funds in the liberated areas of Europe. By the end of its lifetime in December 1946, it had distributed $4 billion worth of emergency supplies of which the United States supplied approximately $2 billion. Yet the conditions with which it was supposed to deal, though they would have been far worse without UNRRA, were no better at the end of that time.

Conclusion

From the point of view of international politics, the nineteenth century ended in 1914: World War I exhibited once more the inherent instabilities of the balance-of-power system and proved how much the economic, political, and social factors sustaining the system had changed. The dislocations produced by World War I seem to have led almost inexorably to the next act in the drama, World War II. The outbreak of this second, disastrous war meant that the Western powers' efforts to rebuild a more stable world through the League of Nations had failed. But the war also ended Nazi, Fascist, and Japanese attempts to build their own peculiar type of world system on the ruins of the nineteenth-century system.

What did it mean for the future? What sort of world political system could possibly emerge from this even more destructive holocaust?

Among the few certainties one stood out: Europe, which had dominated the world system in the past, would have a hard time doing so in the future. Germany and Italy lay shattered; de Gaulle appeared to have ambitions overreaching French capacities; it would be difficult for the Dutch to reinstall themselves in Southeast Asia. Only Britain appeared to have emerged capable of carrying out world wide responsibilities. But even for Britain, appearances were deceptive, and perceptive observers could note her worn-out and badly damaged industrial plant, and her radical shift from world creditor to world debtor. This new position would make any expenses incurred overseas in support of her far-flung responsibilities a terrible strain. On the other hand, Russia, though sustaining such enormous losses that most observers thought all her efforts would have to be turned to rebuilding, nevertheless occupied all of Eastern Europe, where even greater weaknesses existed. The United States, which had not suffered bombardment or occupation, emerged with a tremendously enlarged industrial capacity, new prestige, and greater resources for action.

The war also produced the shifting and shadowy outlines of a new political map of the world, in which—at least temporarily—the spheres of influence of the two new major powers were delimited, along with the more traditional English and French ones. The future of certain areas remained in doubt: China, it was hoped, would emerge as a reunited power to take Japan's place in the Far East. In Southeast Asia the nationalism that had been fanned by Japanese occupation was a force that opposed the efforts of weakened European powers to reassert their power under Anglo-American protection.

The war also left a legacy of doubt about the aims of the two new major powers and also of the three other powers which joined them in permanent membership on the Security Council. The United States had thrown all its energies into prosecuting the war. Would it now withdraw from the vast area that, willy-nilly, it had come to occupy as a result? Churchill had already given a gloomy answer to the same question when it was asked about the Soviet Union; yet other leaders were not so sure. Churchill, among others, was highly dubious about China's capacity to establish its own control throughout its territory; observers who knew something of the Far East wondered, in addition, what Chinese aims would be if the country were really consolidated under the Nationalist regime. Did not the Nationalists lay claim to large areas of northern India and Southeast Asia?

If these questions about individual countries' aims indicated an extraordinary uncertainty about the future and therefore about what policies to follow, there was also uncertainty about the new international institutions that had been created with such fanfare. Presumably these were meant to reshape the international system after the crisis that had convulsed it from 1914 to 1945. The sovereign state of the earlier system was still retained as the basic unit, and the new institutions even reflected a desire to break up empires and add to the number of sovereign states, each claiming to control its own affairs, its own borders, and its own armies. In the 1930s collective security principles had clashed with balance-of-power principles; on the basis of the former, England should have acted energetically against Italy when the Fascists invaded Abyssinia, and against Japan when the Japanese invaded Manchuria. On the basis of balance-of-power principles, however, England had still hoped to keep Italy from a firm alliance with Germany, which would have been the inevitable outcome of collective security action, and similar considerations played a part in lack of action against Japan. Only if collective security could really provide a firm guarantee could nations afford to ignore balance-of-power considerations. Did the new United Nations Charter provide the basis for such confidence? Did it rectify the weaknesses of the League? Many observers were already willing to answer that the existence of the veto—necessary, to be sure—proved that collective security could have only limited effectiveness. Russia's concern for

securing strategic frontiers, France's search for military alliances, and
the interest evinced by American military men in retaining islands
captured from the Japanese in the Pacific for security reasons, all
seem to show that no one was willing to trust collective security
measures completely. In addition, questions were raised about the possibility of collective security in the atomic age: What would be the
relationship of such security measures to national ownership of nuclear
weapons? Was not the Charter a preatomic document? Or did the
new weapons call for revised thinking about the necessity for disarmament at a time when disarmament was being played down, because, when reviewing the sequence of events leading up to World
War II, it seemed that the weakness of Western powers had invited
aggression by the Nazis and Fascists?

Would the other organizations and institutions such as the IMF,
the IBRD, the ITO that clustered around the United Nations serve
the functions assigned to them? They were based on a reading of
the past and a desire to avoid the disasters of the 1920s and 1930s. But
could the new organizations cope with the economic and social
legacies of World War II? And what would be the effect of defeat
of the major powers, Germany, Italy, and Japan? De Gaulle, the
British, and the Russians were determined that these countries would
never again be allowed to disturb the peace. But was this to be done
by keeping them divided and impotent, in the manner envisaged by
the French—or by the American Morgenthau Plan? Or was it to be
done by restoring the countries so that the kind of grievances that
led their peoples to select leaders like Hitler and the Japanese milita-
rists would not arise?

In the face of such uncertainties, conflicts and disagreements were
inevitable, and the thousands of individuals trying to devise policies and
carry out day-to-day operations faced extraordinarily difficult tasks.
Grappling with these uncertainties and overwhelmed by immediate
necessities, what kind of answers could they provide? What patterns
would emerge?

Part Two

1945–1955:

THE ATOMIC AGE

CHAPTER THREE 1945-1947

The Attempt to Rebuild the Old World

In the excitement and general chaos marking the end of World War II, many people realized that fundamental changes had taken place in the international system. But few foresaw the nature of the changes; only in 1947 did people come to finally accept that Europe could no longer stand alone, that European countries would find it impossible to reassert control over the rest of the world, and that the Soviet Union and the United States would emerge as the two chief contenders on the world scene in a system that could be characterized as "bipolar." Bipolarism emerged gradually, for from 1945 to 1947 leaders in both countries moved cautiously in testing their positions of power, and in the first year and a half policy makers devoted much political effort to creating a new world in the image of the old. In the widely prevailing view of this period, Britain appeared to be Russia's chief contender in Europe and the Near East, and the European problems seemed to be drawing up peace treaties and reconstructing shattered economies. Distrustful Americans were ready to withdraw from Europe once the peace was made, and then the United Nations was to become the chief arena of international politics.

The Peace Treaties

Under this prevailing point of view, the United States devoted much of its diplomatic and policy-making manpower to concluding the peace treaties. The Soviet Union followed suit, because peace treaties would remove any last excuse for Western intervention in areas that the Soviets were finding it easier to control. Since Western statesmen both perceived and opposed Soviet aims, and the Soviets used the technique of arguing that they should have influence in the Western-controlled areas in return for Western influence in East Europe, negotiating the treaties proved to be no easy matter.

The Council of Foreign Ministers had been charged with the job of preparing the peace settlements, and its first meetings took place in

September–October and in December 1945, when any earlier optimism should have been dispelled. The first meeting broke up, ostensibly because of procedural differences, but in reality because the Western Allies objected to Soviet activities in Eastern Europe. They demanded that the Soviets implement the terms of the Yalta Declaration on Liberated Areas, and refused recognition to Eastern European governments until these were broadened in composition and legitimated by elections. Soviet Foreign Minister Molotov apparently found these demands outrageous since he had been told by Western powers that they favored governments friendly to the Soviet Union in Eastern Europe. Now Molotov's tactic was to make harsh demands on Italy; he wanted the Italo-Yugoslav boundary to be shifted considerably westward. He repeated the Soviet request for the right to administer Tripolitania as a trustee under the United Nations, and asked for reparations of $600 million, of which a large part would go to Russia and Eastern European countries. As the arguments wore on, Molotov also asked for more control in the occupation of Japan. December brought a measure of compromise. The Russians agreed to modifications in the governments of Bulgaria and Rumania, and Britain and France recognized the Rumanian government on February 5, 1946, although they still objected to the Bulgarian situation. The Western powers also agreed to new arrangements for the Japanese occupation, though final control was still left to General MacArthur.

Subordinates of the foreign ministers then got to work on the text of the peace treaties. But the Council of Foreign Ministers met again on April 25, 1946, partly because the subordinates had made so little progress, partly because tempers had frayed and the conflicts patched over in December had come out in the open. The Russians had delayed their withdrawal from wartime occupation of Persia and Manchuria, guerrilla warfare between Communists and non-Communists had intensified in Greece, and the Russians had attacked Western efforts to reimpose rule in their own spheres, particularly in Indonesia and the Middle East. In Germany the issue of reparations had begun to complicate the occupation.

If these events were part of an emerging conflict, Stalin and Churchill helped intensify the conflict by defining its nature—as they saw it—in a very public fashion. In a speech delivered on February 9, Stalin reminded good Communists everywhere that World War II was not to be seen as an isolated and unique incident, but as a part of a pattern of developing conflict between capitalist-imperialist powers. He thus linked the Western Allies and Germany together in a conflict which would ultimately lead to the downfall of Western capitalism and the triumph of the Communist world. To this ideological interpretation of the world situation, Churchill, now leader of the Conservative opposition in Britain, responded in a speech given in Fulton, Missouri on March 5. "Nobody," he said, "knows what Soviet Russia and its Communist international organization intends to do in the immediate future, or what are the limits, if any, to their expansive and proselityzing tendencies . . . from Stettin in the Baltic to Trieste in the Adriatic an Iron Curtain has descended across the continent." He went on to say that in the face of the Soviet attempt to expand the Western democracies must stand together, that the strength of their union would prevent a war that the Soviet Union did not want either.

In the United States, however, opinion remained strongly divided over the meaning of the events to which Churchill had referred. Most people still hoped for a return to normalcy, and to many Americans brought up on older traditions, Churchill's speech was merely another attempt to get the United States to pull British chestnuts out of the fire.

Against this background, the April meeting of the foreign ministers produced so little result that Secretary of State Byrnes concluded that the Soviets had little desire to end their military occupation of Eastern Europe. But in June the stalemate broke, and sufficient agreement was secured to call a peace conference of the twenty-one United Nations members that had been at war with the Axis satellites. The proceedings of the conference (which lasted from July 29 to October 15, 1946) were dominated by Russian efforts to impose harsh terms upon Italy (these were opposed by the United States and Britain) and by Russian attempts to obtain her own terms for the Axis satellites that were now within the Russian sphere. Finally, delegates of the twenty-one nations approved the drafts that were to serve as recommendations for the Council of Foreign Ministers, which met in New York, November 4, 1946, to draw up the final treaties. Here, incredibly, the debate started all over again, and Western delegates registered their incredulity at what they thought was Russian obtuseness. Suddenly, on the threat of American withdrawal, Molotov agreed to most of the terms set at Paris. He had found that he could obtain nothing more from the Western powers. The treaties would also obviate Allied excuses for further intervention through the Control Commissions in Eastern Europe, where Communist consolidation now appeared far more promising than before. In spite of the peace treaties, the necessity to maintain Russian communication lines to occupation forces in Germany and Austria meant that Russian troops would remain in the Eastern European countries. Perhaps Molotov agreed also because the peace treaties would remove Western controls in Italy where the Communist party showed great strength. In any event, to American participants and observers the Soviet assent appeared to be a victory brought about by continued firmness in insisting on certain terms. At the same time, Soviet attempts to gain a foothold in the Mediterranean had been blocked.

Peace treaties with Italy, Rumania, Hungary, Bulgaria, and Finland were signed in Paris on February 10, 1947. Italy lost small border regions to France and some of the province of Venezia Giulia and a few islands in the Adriatic to Yugoslavia. Ethiopia immediately regained its independence. Other African colonies were given to the temporary trusteeship of Britain, with their disposition to be decided within a year. The port of Trieste, which Yugoslavia had claimed with Russian backing, was made into a free territory under the protection of the United Nations Security Council. Italy's armed forces were given a fixed limitation and she was to pay $360 million in reparations, of which Russia was to receive $100 million. The remaining Axis satellites and Finland had to pay substantial reparations, mostly to the Soviet Union, and submit to severe restrictions of their military establishments. Rumania lost Bessarabia, which had long been Russian before 1918, and northern Bukovina, inhabited largely by Ukrainians, both to the Soviet Union. She regained northern Transylvania, which Hungary had tried to acquire during the war. Bulgaria returned certain wartime territorial gains to Yugoslavia. In the north, the Russians took the Petsamo district from Finland, thus regaining a centuries-old common frontier with Norway. Finland had to grant the Soviet Union a 50-year lease of a naval base at Porkala and agreed to the reestablishment of the Russian-Finnish frontier as it had existed after the Finnish defeat in 1940. Finally, the Council of Foreign Ministers in New York called a meeting in Moscow for March 1947 to start work on the German and Austrian peace treaties. But events in those two countries since the Nazi defeat dimmed the prospects for any easy success.

Germany Splits

During the war the Allies had considered dismembering Germany; never again would the German people—addicted to militarism and metaphysics—be permitted to rise to disturb the peace. But common sense had prevailed at Potsdam, where the Big Three agreed to treat

Germany as an economic unit and to adopt common policies for the restoration of local self-government and democratic political parties. They reckoned without France, however, whose representatives proceeded to block all attempts to implement the Potsdam agreement through the creation of the rudiments of a central German administrative apparatus. By October 1945, the Allies suspended their efforts and began to establish local administrations very much on their own patterns. Necessity impelled them. They might believe in denazification and educational reform, but if production facilities and channels of distribution were to be reopened so that Germans would not starve, order and authority had to be reestablished. Moreover, the Western zones were swollen by millions of eastern Europeans of German descent (the "Volksdeutsch," expelled from their homes), of displaced persons unwilling to return to homes occupied by Soviet Russia and hostile national governments, of Germans expelled from the eastern area occupied by Poland. By the winter of 1945 Western zone authorities began to import food. Deliveries from the Russian-occupied breadbasket were not forthcoming, although the Russians continued to press the Westerners for reparations from their occupation zones. The occupiers had agreed on the level of industry necessary for Germany, beyond which equipment could be considered surplus and available for reparations, and the Soviets asked for delivery. But Western zone authorities answered that the agreed level depended on treating Germany as an economic unit, a policy which was prevented by the French at the level of the Allied Control Commission and also by the Russians, who found a good use themselves for whatever was produced within their zone.

Secretary Byrnes tried a new tack to break the impasse: Would the Russians accept a twenty-five year demilitarization treaty for Germany if the United States would be an active guarantor? Surely this would allay their justifiable fears. But Molotov temporized. What about reparations? Perhaps this really was the crux of the matter; perhaps, on the other hand, the Soviet Foreign Minister had no desire to see the United States pledge itself to such an active role in Europe. In any event discussions returned to the matter of reparations. To Western exasperation, the Russians argued that what they had taken so far need not be accounted for, since it constituted war booty and not reparations. Britain, whose worn economy was particularly burdened by occupation costs, shared fully in the American attitude that finally led American Commandant Lucius B. Clay to suspend all reparations payments on May 3, 1946.

Secretary Byrnes went one step further on July 11 when he offered to merge the American zone with any or all others; on July 30 the British accepted, and lengthy negotiations lead to creation of "Bizonia" on January 1, 1947. The Russians attacked the move as a flagrant violation of Potsdam. In the meantime, however, the whole picture changed as both Russians and Americans gave evidence that they had decided on a different policy than the one followed before. The Soviets announced their intention to help rebuild Germany while denouncing Western attempts to hold the Germans in subjection. Secretary Byrnes, in a speech in Stuttgart on September 6, took up the challenge and announced that the United States, which was in Germany to stay if necessary, would help to rebuild the German economy whose health was so necessary to the well-being of Europe. Germany, he declared, should be given primary responsibility for running its own affairs, and the United States favored early establishment of a provisional German Government for all of Germany.

The meaning was clear: The Russians, who had first thought only of stripping their zone, had decided to stay, to rebuild it under their domination, to appeal to all Germans. The Americans, at first concerned only with how soon they could get out, had arrived at the same decision. Peace treaty discussions were scheduled for 1947, but Germany was split. Still, the attempt by both sides to appeal to all Germans showed that the split was not yet considered irrevocable.

Communization of East Europe

The Western Allies had shown an early appreciation for Russia's desire to have friendly governments on its borders; at Yalta and later they tried to convince Stalin and his colleagues that broad-based, truly democratic governments might also be friendly. But as the months went by the Soviets clamped more and more rigid controls on the countries they had occupied. Eastern Europe had been notoriously unstable in the interwar period; the political spectrum had ranged from Communism to fascism, and violent nationalist hatreds had been expressed in many ways. Yet agrarian and small-holder parties with liberal or socialist leadership had also emerged. In the postwar period the Russians claimed to be eradicating fascist remnants from political life in the area; in fact, during the two years after the end of the war in Europe, they eliminated by various means all but Communist parties. The process varied from country to country, depending on the conditions the Soviet masters encountered.

For Yugoslavia and Albania there was little problem, since in both

countries the Communists had come to dominate the resistance movements, and in the process had destroyed their internal opponents. Both
emerged from the war firmly in the Russian camp on the basis of their
own efforts.

Rumania had fought first on the side of the Axis, then switched
to the Russians. When the Red Army came through, it left in its wake
friendly officials, usually Communists, and a tough cadre ready to
take to the streets. Non-Communist officials, shaken by Communist-led
riots in February 1945, appealed for public support, and the Russians,
fearful of the consequences, interfered directly. They forced King
Michael—recently decorated by Stalin—to install a government in
which Communists held the vital posts of Interior, Justice, and National Economy. Communist control of the first two posts meant that
police would arrest and jail non-Communists while giving free rein
to their own comrades; the latter meant the resources and power for
rewarding good behavior and punishing opposition.

Opponents of the new regime under Premier Groza appealed to
the West for help; in the impotent Allied Control Commission, at
Potsdam and at meetings of the Council of Foreign Ministers Americans and British protested, refusing to recognize the new regime. The
Soviets then broadened the government in January 1946, and Western
recognition followed. But in ensuing months—as the split between
Russia and the Western powers widened—the opposition parties operated only in a semilegal, semioppressed condition. They were subject
to continual harassment; their leaders were arrested, their funds seized,
newsprint denied them, and their meetings broken up. By 1948 they
were totally destroyed and King Michael was forced to abdicate.
Rumania had become a Communist state and a Russian satellite.

Most of Hungary's leaders had sided with the Nazis; as the Russians fought their way through, the country suffered bitterly. The
Communists began their political campaign in a popular front coalition, and obtained only one-sixth of the vote in the first, more-or-less
free, elections in 1945. But with Russian support they initiated the
same tactics used in Rumania. In February 1947, direct Russian intervention took place. Bela Kovaks, Secretary-General of the large Small
Farmers' Party was arrested and its leader, Ferenc Nagy, was forced
to resign a month later. Under Communist terror a new election took
place in August. Non-Communist newspapers were suppressed, the
Small Farmers' Party was dissolved. Though Communist "toughs"
voted more than once, the Communists secured only 22 per cent of the
vote. But the list of allied parties to which the Communists belonged

obtained 65 per cent, enough to ensure the formation of a government in which the Communist secured the key posts through which they could destroy first their opponents and then their allies. By the end of 1948 their domination was complete, and the next year Hungary adopted a Soviet-style constitution.

The process was considerably easier in Bulgaria. The country had a tradition of friendship with Russia ever since the Tsar had helped it secure its independence from Turkey, and although it had been at war with the Western allies, its leaders had resisted Nazi efforts to push it into war against the Soviet Union. On September 9, 1944, as Russian armies crossed the border, the Communist-dominated Fatherland Front—a coalition of resistance groups—staged a *coup d'état*, seized control of the police and organs of local government, and purged fascist sympathizers and potential opponents. Elections in November 1945 produced a Communist victory, which Western observers attributed to an atmosphere of terror and falsification of results. At a result of Western prodding, the Soviets instructed the Bulgarian Communists to broaden the base of the new government. But non-Communist leaders balked unless they were given genuine power, and so the Communists continued to consolidate power that was never threatened; they abolished the monarchy, and obtained 78 per cent of the vote in new elections in 1946. By 1948 they crushed all opposition parties and Bulgaria adopted a Soviet-style constitution.

Although Poland benefited from a greater degree of Western interest, the Russians had the advantage of their physical presence and Poland's wartime experiences. The first they could use brutally; the second gave the Communists genuine broad appeal. Nazi plans for depopulating Poland were even worse than the horrors they had actually perpetrated, and while Westerners had been able to do nothing to save Poland, the Russians shared with the Poles a common border. The Communists emphasized Western reluctance to acknowledge the Oder-Neisse border and adroitly used Byrnes' Stuttgart speech to claim that the Americans favored rebuilding Germany. The Warsaw uprising had helped destroy non-Communist leadership within Poland, and the Russians kept refugee leaders from returning except under terms imposed by the Communists. In February 1947 the Polish government adopted a provisional Soviet-style constitution, and by the end of 1948 all other parties had disappeared, leaving only the monolithic Communist party.

Western leaders expressed dismay at the process that unfolded in the Soviet sphere. But since it was gradual, their attention was frequently turned to other pressing problems. Only the occasional dramatic incident made headlines—the resignation of Hungary's Ferenc Nagy or the departure from Poland in October, 1947 of Mikolajczyk, the Peasant party leader and former premier of the Polish government-in-exile. Economic chaos and political weakness in Europe, demobilization of Allied armies, the disturbed situation in China, fighting in Southeast Asia, the American desire to throw off wartime controls and resume normalcy—all competed for attention. Many people could believe that the process of Communization in East Europe was a unique phenomenon and that the Soviets were being just a little overzealous in their standards for "friendly" governments; others could easily be persuaded that much of what was going on involved a domestic process in which "progressive" political movements were sweeping away old "feudal" structures and leaders. Besides, Finland and Czechoslovakia proved that outside of the troubled area just on their European border zone the Communists could get along with other parties.

Czechoslovakia had welcomed Russian military successes, and the government formed in March 1945 was a coalition of Communists, Social Democrats, National Socialists, and leaders of the People's Party (Catholic). The Communists held the posts of Interior (with its crucial control of the police) as well as important positions in the Army, Agriculture (responsible for land distribution), and in Information and Education. They held controlling positions in the border areas from which over two million Germans were expelled. But their behavior and that of the Russians was circumspect. Cession of Sub-Carpathian Ruthenia—the eastern tip of the country—to the Soviet Union had caused little ill-feeling, and the Soviets withdrew their troops in December at the same time that a smaller American force withdrew in the west. When genuine elections were held in May 1946, the Communists received 38 per cent of the vote, although they received something of a setback in more heavily Catholic Slovakia, where people objected to Czech centralization.

Communist Clement Gottwald became Premier in the new government, and Dr. Eduard Beneš, the prewar democratic leader, retained his wartime exile position as President. Despite the events taking place in neighboring countries, the coalition worked, and, under considerable pressure, the Communists observed the constitution. As 1947 drew to a close many people still hoped that Czechoslovakia might serve as a bridge across the widening gap between Russia and the West.

Winter of 1947

If any one thing brought home the realization that the world was going to be very different from what it had been before, it was the bitter winter of 1947.

Before World War II Western Europe had exported industrial goods and bought foodstuffs and raw materials from Eastern Europe, the Far East, British Dominions, and Argentina. The United States, as a massive buyer of colonial products (such as tin and rubber from European colonies) supplied Europe with the dollars needed to purchase its exports. The depression and then World War II changed all this. Destruction in Europe was enormous. Not only were houses, industrial plants, roads and railroads demolished, herds and flocks were killed—and these would take even longer than factories to replace. Moreover, currencies were almost everywhere in disarray, and without a stable unit of exchange a modern complex economy cannot function. In 1945 productivity in Western Europe was perhaps one-third that of 1939. In 1938 western Germany produced 220 million tons of coal and 18 million tons of steel. In 1947—two years after the end of the war—production had painfully climbed back to 143 million tons of coal and only 5 million tons of steel.

Neutrals like Switzerland and Sweden kept their economies intact. Belgium, partly because wartime shipments to the United States of uranium and other metals from the Congo were credited to its account, emerged in fair economic shape and was able to carry through a harsh but effective currency reform in 1946 that restored confidence and encouraged investment. But for the rest, the war was a disaster and Britain—the great prewar creditor nation of the world—although spared the invasions that raged across the continent and through much of Southeast and East Asia, emerged with $15 billion of overseas debts. Everywhere, in the year and a half after the war, hunger and deprivation stalked the land, and all efforts to rebuild were hampered by the very fact of the shortages that rebuilding was designed to correct.

The United States, in contrast, found itself at the end of the war with a revitalized industry able to produce a gross national product of almost twice that of prewar years, and an agricultural plant able to produce an enormous surplus—even though American consumption of meat, for example, had risen from 125 pounds per capita prewar to 163 pounds per capita in 1945. But American citizens—through savings enforced during the war years—also had a large pent-up demand for American production waiting to be released. The question for the rest of the world was whether representatives of the American people, clamoring for normalcy, would use part of this productive capacity to help restore a stable world order, or would insist that it be used for domestic consumption.

The United Nations Relief and Rehabilitation Administration, established in 1943, helped to sustain Eastern Europe with $2 billion worth of food and clothing. In addition, in the months of transition from war to peace, the American army and navy distributed relief supplies in liberated and occupied areas to the extent of $750 million. Private and voluntary organizations contributed hundreds of millions more. All these showed that Americans were willing to help. But the abrupt termination of lend-lease shipments by President Truman on August 21, 1945, came as a shock. Lend-lease was interallied aid; Britain, for example, was credited with the port services or shipping that it supplied to other Allies, the United States with the munitions and food that it supplied. And the United States had provided the lion's share: $48.5 billion from March 1941 to V-J Day, August 14, 1945.

The British had expected that the United States would negotiate a tapering-off plan, and Secretary of the Treasury Morgenthau had talked of a large-scale reconstruction loan. Both would have helped cushion the period of transition, but neither was offered.* The American government did, however, offer long-term credits to help pay for lend-lease supplies already negotiated and contracted for, and the liberal terms it gave Britain in the first settlement of wartime lend-lease accounts showed that it was not going to burden the already disastrous postwar world economy with a debt structure like the one that followed World War I. The settlement also represented the view that funds expended against a common wartime enemy should be written off. In 1946 the United States reached settlements with France, India, Turkey, Australia, New Zealand and Belgium, and, in 1947, with South Africa. There was never any settlement with the Soviet Union, which had received $11 billion worth and supplied $2 million in reverse, but which had also suffered considerably more casualties and damage.

The United States, through these interim measures, as well as a large loan to Britain in 1946 (see below) had responded to a chal-

* President Truman later acknowledged that the sudden cancellation was a mistake, based on Congressional specifications that lend-lease was not to be used for reconstruction and on the unforeseen rapidity of the Japanese collapse.

lenging situation. If mass starvation and complete economic breakdown were to be averted, the rest of the world had to look primarily
to the United States—the only country with a large exportable surplus beyond what was needed to maintain a high standard of living.
Compared to 1939–41 food exports of $350 million, 1946 food ex-
ports rose to more than $2200 million.

Yet within the United States the predominant view was that although relief measures might be necesary, there would be a rapid
return to normalcy. It was summed up in the lend-lease clauses pledg-
ing free trading practices, in the sharp cut-off of lend-lease, in the
creation of the International Bank for Reconstruction and Development and the International Monetary Fund and in the rapid elimination
of rationing within the United States, where caloric consumption was
twice that of Europe. Despite severe drought in 1945 and 1946 in
Argentina, Australia, South Africa, French North Africa, India and
China, and despite warnings from UNRRA officials that the outlook
for 1946–47 gave cause for "profound alarm," the American government abandoned UNRRA.

General Eisenhower and former Mayor LaGuardia of New York,
Director-General of UNRRA, pleaded for it. The United States, La-
Guardia said, wanted to give aid only to those countries "chosen,
picked and acceptable to our government." But, he went on, "We are
not giving aid to governments. We are giving aid to the men, women,
and children throughout the world who suffered so much during the
war and who to this very day are still in need." In November 1946,
however, Secretary of State Byrnes and Assistant Secretary Acheson,
in opposing the continuation of UNRRA, foresaw the position Congress would surely take. International aid *was* going to countries whose
governments were unfriendly, and the United States should control
its own foreign aid through bilateral agreements. Since the major
problems had been solved, the problem was now one of foreign exchange, and this could be attacked through the IMF, the IBRD, and
through normal extension of purchase credits by the Export-Import
Bank. UNRRA, deprived of its major supporter, ceased to function
in December 1946.

American officials were aware of a bad situation. But the first post-
war effort to cope with it after the collapse of UNRRA took the
form of a bilateral loan to England. The conditions of this kind of
loan could be more stringent, and the loan was extended to a more
reliable and friendly government than some in Eastern Europe that
had received UNRRA money. Nevertheless, the debate over the $3.75

billion longterm, low interest loan negotiated at the end of 1945 revealed confused attitudes in the United States about the state of the world, and Congress took seven months to provide the money.

The loan was designed to set the stage in which the United Nations system already described would work: prewar Britain had been a net importer using interest on its overseas investments to finance the import surplus. But during the war it had sold its assets and piled up debts of $15 billion, held in blocked accounts in London, that is, the countries which now held British notes could cash them in only when the British government allowed them. To resume its position in world trade Britain would have to export more than it imported in order to pay the debts and rebuild investments overseas; yet its industry was worn by war and far less productive than that of its rival, the United States. Moreover, Britain was trying to meet heavy overseas commitments; there was the aid to Greece against Communist guerrillas as well as action in Palestine, the German occupation, and restoration of order in South and Southeast Asia (see below). Unless Britain's position were secured, the world trading system envisaged when the United Nations organs were established could not be attained, and war-time commitments to multilateral trade would never be realized.

The arguments against the proposed loan—mainly from the Republican side—were that the United States should have secured more in return, that British policy in Palestine was all wrong, and—an echo from prewar days—that the United States was supporting British imperialism. But the answer to this came from House Speaker Sam Rayburn:

I do not want Western Europe, England, and all the rest pushed further into and toward an ideology that I despise. I fear if we do not cooperate with this great natural ally of ours, that is what will happen. If we are not allied with the great British democracy, I fear somebody will be and God pity us when we have no ally across the Atlantic Ocean, and God pity them, too.

In the face of increasing tension with Russia, the loan passed the Senate 46 to 34 and the House 219 to 155.

But the various forms of piecemeal aid, the loan, and the resources of the IMF and IBRD were all insufficient. In Eastern Europe the situation varied from country to country. Hungary and Rumania suffered most; recovery was slow to begin and trade with the rest of Europe lagged. Not until 1946 did Poland and Rumania, the traditional suppliers of coal, grain, and oil to Western Europe, begin to resume exports.

Then throughout Western Europe the winter of 1947 brought a grim situation. German industrial revival slowed; the Western zones were cut off from foodstuffs of the east. In France the shaky political coalition of Communist, Socialist, and Christian Democrat, seeking an acceptable political framework, had made too little economic headway, and inflation and the black market flourished. In the unusually cold winter of 1947 between three and four million acres of wheat planted in the fall were lost. This meant importing two or three million tons of wheat at a hundred dollars a ton. But there were no dollars. Throughout Western Europe the situation was repeated. With few consumer goods to buy and with rampant inflation, the incentives to work and to invest were lacking. Hopelessness and frustration helped to weaken governmental authority, reducing the capacity of governments to take the necessary drastic actions. Imports were needed; they cost dollars; but there were no exports to earn dollars. This was the "dollar gap."

Britain's situation, detailed in a series of government White Papers of early 1947 and Cabinet Surveys was particularly crucial. The British did not face a sizable internal Communist party ready, like the ones in France or Italy, to take advantage of a desperate economic, social and political situation. But Britain's extensive overseas commitments were a debilitating economic drain. Britain, with its sterling debts to the Empire and British banking and financial institutions, stood at the center of an economic complex heavily dependent on these institutions and on British industrial capacity. Yet in January, the government revealed that instead of improving its position, each month saw Britain going further into debt as imports continued to exceed exports; the great dollar loan was being used up far faster than had been expected. In other words, Britain was living far beyond her means and would have to retrench. Worse, in January and February, the impossible happened: Britain—the country in which the industrial revolution started, the island built on coal that had fueled that revolution—ran out of coal. Industries came to a halt. Those depending on electricity found their power was shut off several hours a day; there was not enough coal to generate it. The worst blizzards in memory halted trains carrying coal and froze barges carrying the desperately needed fuel. Crops of winter wheat froze.

It would take months to recover from this new blow. Exports would be reduced by hundreds of millions of dollars. Suddenly, to the rest of the world that had not been watching economic indicators closely, came the revelation that Europe was close to total disaster; a few blizzards could cripple the continent that had been the center of the entire world. In February it became clear that Britain, facing a deficit of close to $2 billion for the year, was on the verge of bankruptcy. The British might have to give up maintaining order in the Middle East, withdraw from Asia and the occupation of Germany, forego contributions to relief, default on foreign debts, and—against the rules of the game instituted in the IMF, the IBRD, and the ITO—impose the most rigid trade restrictions.

By midwinter 1947 the full effect of the war was felt in Europe: not only had the international system *not* been rebuilt—it seemed about to collapse entirely.

Europe and the Non-Western World, 1945–1947

In the four centuries before World War II, Europe, in a series of erratic steps, had exerted its control over the rest of the world. At the end of the eighteenth century and the beginning of the nineteenth, much of the Americas was lost. But the end of the nineteenth century brought the last great surge of empire building: the European powers carved up Africa and began to divide China. Even as they seemed to be consolidating their hold, the export of European administrative and legal systems, the structural changes they wrought in colonial economies, and their exploitation of natural resources stimulated na-tionalist opposition to European control. The process was inexorable, and World War II greatly speeded it.

France had used the resources and manpower of its vast empire to counterbalance Germany's greater population and industry. In World War II, although conservative colonial administrators tended to side with Vichy, the empire nevertheless provided the base—along with England—from which the Free French could work. But every-where in the empire the weakness of France was seen and understood. Moreover, in Southeast Asia, the Japanese followed the process they used in the British and Dutch territories they overran. First they con-solidated their hold and developed a system of economic exploitation, and then put local nationalist leaders into power. Thus, when the Chinese occupied the north of Indochina and Anglo-French troops en-tered the south, they found a Japanese-installed government in Viet-nam, and independent kingdoms in Cambodia and Laos. In Burma the Japanese had created an "independent" regime in 1943, and in the former Dutch-controlled East Indies the Japanese Supreme Council for the Direction of the War announced the independence of the area in July 1945. On August 17 Indonesian leaders proclaimed the birth of the Republic of Indonesia.

In the Mediterranean the Axis powers had also appealed to nationalist leaders to resist the control of the Allies. But more important was the extent to which people could see that the Europeans could not maintain their status without American troops and materiel. All through the Mediterranean, the Middle East, South Asia, and Southeast Asia, emergent nationalist leaders made demands for a new postwar status.

The reactions of the various European powers showed considerable continuity with their specific prewar policies.

The French had ruled directly from France through colonial administrators, and had tried to remake the alien cultures they ruled so they reflected French culture. The policy, known as assimilation, included close tying of the economies of the overseas areas with that of France. Postwar French governments recognized the need for reform, and initiated a policy of overseas investment to raise standards of living among the natives, and, in the "French Union," established institutions in which colonial representation seemed significant. But they also tried to reimpose direct rule from Paris.

In North Africa, after exiling nationalist leaders who gained prominence during the war and after quelling Algerian riots in May 1945—riots that gave evidence of widespread Moslem disaffection—French authorities held onto power.

In the Middle East—in Syria and Lebanon, which France had held as mandates under the League of Nations—the Free French, partly because of British pressure, partly to compete for wartime support from the Arabs, had promised independence. But in May 1945, during negotiations for the terms of independence, de Gaulle landed a small contingent of French troops in Lebanon, and tried to insist that the Syrian and Lebanese armies remain under French command. Direct British intervention forced the French to withdraw their demands. The Syrian and Lebanese governments had declared war on the Axis, thus gaining admission to the San Francisco conference; in March 1945 they had helped to create the Arab League. They had been granted recognition as independent states by many other countries without mention of any special status for anyone, and thus they had effectively become independent.

De Gaulle, however, saw the British intervention as a deliberate effort to supplant French influence by British influence in an area where

French interests were as important as those of the British. He accused the British of abetting Arab armed action against the French: "It can never be forgotten," he told the British Ambassador. Churchill, on the other hand, saw the matter as a minor misunderstanding in which a mistaken French move had caused unwelcome unrest in the Arab world at a critical moment, and he tried to smooth matters over. Not until the end of 1946 were all French and British troops withdrawn, and the matter came up in the United Nations, where the Soviet Union used the situation to reply to charges about its own conduct in Eastern Europe.

In Indochina, British troops in the south facilitated the return of the French, but Nationalist Chinese troops in the north, more inclined to work with the local nationalists, did not leave until well into 1946, after the French had made numerous concessions to them. In March 1946 the French and the Democratic Republic of Vietnam—a heterogeneous grouping of Nationalists headed by Ho Chi Minh, founder of the Indochinese Communist party—signed an agreement making Vietnam a "free state" within an Indochinese Union, and a member of the French Union. French authorities proceeded to reestablish themselves in a dominant position in Laos and Cambodia. But implementation of the agreement with the Vietnamese failed, incidents between the Vietnamese and French troops advancing into the north as the Chinese withdrew multiplied, and serious fighting broke out in December 1946. Once more—after a lull of only a year and a half, France was at war. It began on a small scale, but it was to drag on for seven years.

Just as the English had been willing to help reestablish the French in Indochina, they were willing to help restore the Dutch in the vast and important East Indies. There, as in Indochina, an independent state had been proclaimed and a government established, with which, of necessity, the British worked in the first months of their occupation, since they lacked manpower and transport sufficient to govern. Dutch reoccupation was motivated by a reluctance to give up a possession that had been Dutch for three hundred years, and by their feeling that the varied peoples in the widespread archipelago in no way constituted a "nation." Moreover, there were 200,000 Japanese troops to repatriate and 200,000 Dutch nationals on the islands who had suffered through the wartime occupation. Underestimating the growth of nationalist sentiment, and returning to the islands in force and by force during 1946, they negotiated an agreement with the self-proclaimed Republic in November 1946. To the Dutch, the agreement meant only that the Republic would be one among several states in a loose federation in a union with Holland. But the Indonesian nationalist leaders—Sukarno, Sjharir, and Hatta—wanted more. Within a few months the agreement broke down.

The British, whose overseas interests were as vast and varied as those of the French, responded in a different manner, and demonstrated more flexibility in meeting new situations. There had been less centralized authority in the prewar empire than in the French empire and British administration worked through existing native institutions to a much greater extent. Moreover, the evolution of Dominion status within the empire for advanced overseas territories had provided a way of developing complete self-government while ties to Britain continued. Like the French, the British planned an important increase in overseas investments; they also planned a gradual shift from indirect rule through existing tribal or other native institutions to the development of more modern forms of government.

Africa south of the Sahara posed relatively little political problem since the area had not been subject to the influences of Axis invasion. Egypt, however, had proved indispensable to the Allied war effort and the Suez Canal remained a lifeline; Britain therefore resisted Egyptian demands for withdrawal of all British troops. A December 1946 agreement that the Egyptians maintain British bases while the troops withdrew failed to be implemented because, first, there was no accompanying agreement about the future of the Anglo-Egyptian Sudan which Egypt now claimed, and subsequently because the cold war with Russia developed and the Suez Canal base to which the British had withdrawn their troops gained new importance.

Britain held Transjordan under a League mandate. During the war the British promised Emir Abdullah independence for his little country at the end of hostilities. The British delegate to the United Nations therefore announced that Jordan would not be proposed as a trust territory. On March 22, 1946, Britain signed an alliance with the Emir in which the British undertook to defend his state against external aggression and to subsidize his army, the Arab Legion, in return for certain base rights within Jordan. Britain proceeded to recognize the independence of Jordan, and other states followed suit, despite Jordan's obvious dependence on British support.

Britain's other Middle East mandate, Palestine, posed far more problems for the Labour government in London. Since the turn of the century, as Ottoman control over the Middle East dissolved, the land had become an object of struggle between Zionism and emerging Arab nationalism. The British promise to the Jews in World War I that they could establish a "national home" in Palestine (in the famous Balfour Declaration) clashed with the British attempt to cultivate the Arabs and stimulate their revolt against Turkey, then an ally of Austria-Hungary and Germany. In the period between the wars Jewish immigration increased and the well-organized Jewish community bought land and established its own institutions of self-government. Nazi persecution of the Jews intensified Jewish immigration, and riots and incidents multiplied. The British (who held Palestine as a mandate after World War I) tried to restrict Jewish immigration and institute a local government in which Arabs would predominate.

World War II brought an end of Arab guerrilla warfare in the area, partly because immigration declined, partly because Allied divisions were present. But as the war wore on, illegal immigration increased under pressure of the monstrous Nazi extermination policy, and Jewish terrorism grew. The Jews now found increasing support from the American Jewish community through the American Zionist Organization, which in 1942 had asked for the creation of a Jewish state in Palestine, unlimited immigration, and the formation of a Jewish army. Then, at the end of the war, the camps teeming with displaced Jews from Eastern Europe and the survivors of Hitler's extermination centers intensified the problem. President Roosevelt had told King Ibn Saud of Saudi Arabia that although he thought more Jews should be admitted to Palestine, no step would be taken without consulting both Arabs and Jews. But President Truman addressed an appeal to British Prime Minister Clement Attlee in August 1945, asking for immediate admission of 100,000 Jewish refugees to Palestine. The British, appalled at what they thought was a failure to consider the effect on relations with the Arabs in the area, proposed the creation of an Anglo-American Committee of Inquiry to study the matter. Thus the British in Palestine, although still directly administering the area, shifted part of the burden of responsibility to the United States.

State Department and Foreign Office officials emphasized that Soviet influence in the area might increase if the Arabs were alienated, but the Committee of Inquiry nevertheless recommended the admission of the proposed number of Jewish refugees and the transformation of the mandate into a trust territory. However, a higher-level official committee from the two countries charged with working out implementation revived an older British policy of creating a federalized Arab-Jewish state with continued Jewish immigration dependent on Arab consent.

Jews in Europe and the United States were bitter, particularly as news spread of British internment of illegal Jewish immigrants. Immediately before the congressional elections of 1946, President Truman renewed his demand for admission of 100,000 immigrants.

The harsh winter of 1947 was crucial for the Labour government faced with what appeared to be irreconcilable demands. Getting out of Palestine would relieve the British of a costly burden which produced nothing but hatred. On April 2, 1947, they requested a special session of the United Nations General Assembly to consider the whole question. The session met from April 28 to May 15 and created the United Nations Special Committee on Palestine composed of eleven states to prepare and present a report to the regular fall session of the General Assembly. Although Arabs objected that the General Assembly had no jurisdiction in the matter, by mid-1947 Britain was ready to get rid of another outpost of the empire.

Further across the southern perimeter of the Eurasian continent, the British demonstrated their willingness to divest themselves of imperial responsibility in India, Ceylon, and Burma. For a half-century the British had gradually granted more and more self-government to India; in response, the nationalist movement grew faster and demanded more. At the outset of the war its leaders refused to join in the "world struggle against tyranny and aggression" when India was not free and when it was faced with "an arrogant imperialism which is indistinguishable from fascist authoritarianism." At about the same time, the Muslim demand for a separate Muslim state began to make itself felt. Neither Hindu nor Muslim was willing to accept British war-time proposals for a free India after the war; both demanded immediate independence and threatened to initiate a mass campaign of non-violent resistance. In the face of imminent Japanese invasion, the British responded by imprisoning the important leaders of the Congress movement—Nehru, Gandhi and others.

The situation did not augur an easy renewal of relations. But at the end of the war the British quickly made clear their determination to actually transfer power. The Muslim League also made it clear that it would press for a separate Pakistan. After the failure to reconcile Hindu and Muslim leaders, Prime Minister Attlee, on February 20, 1947, announced a British decision to transfer power into Indian hands by June 1948. It was hoped that agreement would be reached between both parties by then, and that the Labour government could transfer power to some form of central government that would rule the whole area, but power would be transferred then in any case. Lord Mountbatten was to be sent as the last Viceroy, charged with liquidating the British Raj. Said Winston Churchill, speaking for the Conservative opposition, "In handing over the Government of India to these so-called political classes we are handing over to men of straw of whom in a few years no trace will remain."

Lord Mountbatten arrived in India on March 22, 1947. After sounding out Hindu and Muslim leaders, he was determined to speed the transfer of power. The dominant nationalist organization, the Congress Party, strove to maintain unity, and argued for a secular state within which religious minorities would be free, but Muslim leaders balked. Islam has an inherent tendency to dictate the organization of society. When fears of Hindu domination were added to this, it was too much, and the fateful decision for partition resulted. Gandhi, to whom partition was repugnant, said, "The British Government is not responsible for partition. The Viceroy has no hand in it. In fact he is as opposed to division as Congress itself. But if both of us, Hindus and Muslims, cannot agree on anything else, then the Viceroy is left with little choice." On July 4 an Indian Independence Bill was introduced into the British Parliament. By the 18th it had passed and received the royal assent. It provided that "from the fifteenth day of August, nineteen hundred and forty-seven, two independent Dominions shall be set up in India, to be known respectively as India and Pakistan."

Britain and India both faced an enormous administrative task to accomplish within a terribly short time. The armed forces, civil service, and various forms of government property had to be divided. Even more difficult was the drawing of boundary lines and the problem posed by the 562 Indian states with semi-autonomous local rulers through whom the British had acted in the past. Varying enormously in size, they covered some 45 per cent of the land and contained 28 per cent of the population. Through persuasion and pressure, the newly created States Ministry induced the leaders of all but Hyderabad, Kashmir, and Junagadh to sign an Instrument of Accession, thereby guaranteeing unity within the two major states, India and Pakistan. But two of the three that failed to sign proved to be serious problems in the future. And to Indians the presence of a few small enclaves still ruled by France and Portugal after two or three hundred years also remained for some years cause for irritation.

On the night of August 14, when the Constituent Assembly met to hail independence, Nehru declared, "At the stroke of the midnight hour, when the world sleeps, India will awake to life and freedom."

Unfortunately, the moment was accompanied by an almost uncontrolled orgy of violence.

No boundary commission could have put all Muslims in one state and all Hindus in the other, nor would all the people have wanted it. But when the boundaries were announced on the day after independence, Hindu attacked Muslim in India, and Muslim attacked Hindu in Pakistan. Millions of refugees left their homes and streamed across borders, under attack all the way. Trains arrived filled with mutilated corpses, and in many areas not only did the constabulary prove ineffective, but in some cases joined in the fanaticism. Neighbor set upon neighbor, burning, looting, killing. The governments cooperated in trying to stem the rioting and in moving and resettling refugees in camps. By the middle of 1948 over 12,000,000 people had crossed the Indian-Pakistani borders. The memories of the dreadful months are still alive. So is the issue of who was responsible for what, and the property claims involved. Relations between the two countries could not help but be bad from the beginning.

These bad relations were also exacerbated by the Junagadh and Kashmir issues. The Muslim ruler of the former, a small state with a predominantly Hindu population, acceded to Pakistan, which accepted it. The population rioted, the ruler was forced to flee, and, on the invitation of a lesser official, the Indian government sent in troops. In February 1948, a plebiscite held at Indian insistence gave an almost unanimous vote for accession to India. In January 1949, the merger took place.

The Kashmir question involved a much larger, richer state. Strategically located near the borders of the Soviet Union and adjacent to Sinkiang province in China, it contained the headwaters of the important Indus river. Here the reverse situation existed; the Maharajah was Hindu, and the population predominantly Muslim. The Maharajah hoped to remain independent, but under pressure from Pakistan, and facing Muslim tribal invaders from the wild northwest frontier area, he appealed to India for military aid. In order to get it, he acceded to India. Indian troops were sent immediately, and pushed back the invaders, who by this time were receiving aid from the Pakistani government. Lord Mountbatten had assured the Maharajah that the accession was provisional, and that a plebiscite would be held. Nehru, too, echoed the view. India brought the matter as a case of Pakistani aggression to the United Nations Security Council in January 1948, and the Security Council has since maintained representatives in the area to supervise the cease-fire that occurred, but no plebiscite has ever been held. At first no one could agree on the necessary preliminary steps such as demilitarization. Subsequently India shifted its position, and rejected the idea of a plebiscite. Pakistan claimed that what was right for Janagadh was right for Kashmir. And there the issue rested, but for one thing: in 1957 Kashmir adopted a constitution and India came to regard Kashmir as integrated into India.

Hyderabad posed few problems, since it was completely surrounded by Indian territory. The Nizam, ruler of this, one of the largest, most autocratic and backward of the native states, was a Muslim; the majority of the populace was Hindu. The Nizam refused to accede to Indian pressures until, in June 1948, India clamped on a complete economic blockade and then three months later sent in troops. Under the circumstances the Nizam finally acceded and withdrew the request for aid he had sent to the United Nations Security Council.

Both Pakistan and India remained members of the British Commonwealth of Nations, the loose grouping of states previously part of the British empire, and still held together by currency arrangements, trading patterns, and similar systems of law and administration. But Indian leaders decided to make India a republic, and the question arose whether it could remain part of the Commonwealth while other dominions continued their nominal allegiance to the British Crown. A special Conference of Commonwealth Prime Ministers, meeting in London in April 1949, solved the issue by simply declaring that India could be a partner and accepting the king as the symbol of the free association of the Commonwealth's independent member nations and as such, the head of the Commonwealth.

Further to the east, in Burma and Malaya, matters had been complicated by Japanese occupation. The fighting there had often been severe, and had resulted in much devastation. The Burmese economy lay in ruins, and bitter opposition existed between rival political groups and between the dominant Burmese and other smaller ethnic groups. A White Paper of May 1945 defined British policy: the promotion in due course of self-government for Burma within the British Commonwealth. Until the Burmese people could draw up and adopt a new constitution, there would be a renewed period of British direct rule.

But events in 1946 revealed a determination on the part of leaders of Burmese nationalist factions to resist even this period of rule. Strikes and insurrections led to a change in British tactics. In January 1947 the Labour Government reached an agreement with Aung San, leader of the dominant Anti-Fascist People's Freedom League, for immediate election of a constitutional assembly that would bring Burmese independence. The British could not resist expressing the hope that Burma might decide to remain a member of the British Commonwealth. But the elections took place in April, and the new Assembly resolved to set up an independent republic outside the Commonwealth.

Malaya posed an entirely different problem from most of the other British controlled areas. Like the Dutch East Indies, it was an important dollar earner through its exports of rubber and tin, and its dollars, paid into the common pool of the sterling area, contributed enormously to British ability to continue to pay for American imports. In addition, there was no Malay nationalism. The area was an ethnic conglomeration—one third Chinese, one third Indian, and one third Malay. At the southern tip of Malaya lay the great strategic port of Singapore, the supposedly impregnable symbol of British imperial might before the war that was, in fact, easily conquered by the Japanese. The returning British, facing a chaotic situation in Malaya, saw the problem not as one of nationalist resistance but rather of creating some semblance of a nation. The first British attempt, in 1946, was to give a separate status to Singapore (whose population is 77 per cent Chinese), and to amalgamate the states of Malaya into a Union in which the local sultans would retain little power. Strong Malayan objections forced the British to withdraw the plan, and they proceeded— at a more leisurely pace than was possible in other areas—to create a more acceptable federation.

One other great imperial power, the United States, faced the problem of emerging nationalism. But the United States, unlike its allies, had entered the war already committed to the eventual independence of its chief Pacific colonial possession, the Philippines. The war left the islands with a shattered economy, enormous physical destruction, and a complete social breakdown. Of twenty-four Senators in the previous Philippine Congress, seven were dead, seven under arrest as collaborators. Of ninety-eight Representatives, seven were under arrest, twenty others had been in a Japanese-sponsored wartime assembly, eleven others had taken jobs under the Japanese, and many others had been killed or were missing. Yet many Filipinos had strongly resisted the Japanese. Independence came to this broken country on July 4, 1946.

The United States helped; there were large relief operations before the end of the war, and the new government received emergency loans, tax refunds, and more than half a billion dollars to satisfy war damage claims and to underwrite rehabilitation. Unfortunately, in the chaotic situation that prevailed and in the face of immense shortages, corruption in the use of the funds was enormous. Moreover, agrarian unrest was fanned and led by the Hukbalahaps—the anti-Japanese Peoples Liberation Army—a Communist-led organization. For years after independence the countryside suffered from warfare between undisciplined military forces and terrorists who lived off the land. Although greatly reduced in number, the "Huks" continued guerrilla warfare through the 1950s.

By 1947 "decolonization," the process of breaking up prewar empires, was well under way. Those empires had been created by the curiosity, ambition, idealism, or greed of Europeans, coupled with their technological superiority and greater political strength. But their delimitations had usually proceeded from balance-of-power maneuvering within Europe. Unlike the United States, which could expand across an almost empty continent, and at the expense of weak neighbors, European powers had expanded outside of their own continent. An increase in empire by one country was viewed as an increase in power; since none wanted any single power to become too strong, all joined in the race in order to maintain the balance, and often they agreed on rules to follow in dividing up the world.

But the European and American rulers of empires had introduced modern education, transportation, European systems of law, and western forms of trade and finance. Indigenous societies were disrupted, and a new group of leaders adopted the doctrine of their overlords—nationalism. In the postwar period their demands, the revealed weaknesses of their rulers, the prodding of the Soviet Union, China, and the United States, the increased voice given to the small, poorer countries in the United Nations General Assembly and the Trusteeship Council, and the fact that the war was fought in the name of democracy and self-determination, all had an effect in the drive for independence.

It met resistance. The colonial powers had investments to protect: large groups of settlers and descendants of settlers, many of whom had been born and raised in the colonies, felt that all modern developments were due to colonial endeavor. Foreign office and military personnel worried that hasty decolonization would create a power vacuum into which new imperialism might move. Political analysts wondered how an international system including many new powers with abundant reasons for quarreling would function. What would it be like without the sort of safety valve that they had provided for balance-of-power struggles within Europe?

In the early postwar period, no one predicted how far decolonization would go. Africa seemed untouched. But in the Middle East and in Asia, the struggle had begun in earnest.

Iran and Turkey

Iran and Turkey were the first non-Western countries where the Soviet Union showed an active interest during the postwar period; the first two years of the period brought Soviet retreat in both.

At the start of World War II Iran had close ties with Nazi Germany. When the Soviet Union came under Nazi attack, Iran appeared to be the most logical supply route from the south, and the Allies asked the Shah to expel German technicians who might sabotage shipments. The Shah refused; on August 25, 1941, the British invaded from the south and the Russians from the north. The Shah abdicated in favor of his son, and Iran was forced to cooperate with the Allies. Soon American services created an enormous supply base in the country, and the Allies signed a treaty with Iran reaffirming its independence and promising withdrawal of troops within six months after the end of the war.

Within Iran various extremist groups became active, and the Russians openly encouraged Communism. They supported separatist agitation of Armenian-, Kurdish-, and Turkish-speaking minorities, and intimidated Iranian officials, while pressing Iran for an oil concession in the north. The British, though obliged to cooperate with their Russian allies, continued traditional British policy towards Iran and helped stiffen Iranian resistance; the Americans, by and large, held themselves aloof, but provided economic assistance and technical aid to the Iranian government. Although Roosevelt was unwilling to actually enter into the political fray, he persuaded the Russians during the Teheran Conference to endorse a section of the final communique reiterating the Big Three's "desire for the maintenance of the independence, sovereignty and territorial integrity of Iran." It was the British, however, who actively opposed the Soviets.

Then, in the last months of 1945, when the war was over, the Soviet Union sponsored the creation of a separatist regime in the Soviet-occupied region of Azerbaijan, and another, less important, Kurdish one in Mahabad. The Soviet Army kept Iranian troops from entering and continued its occupation after the six-months deadline for withdrawal lapsed. It looked as though the pattern in other occupied areas was to be repeated. Faced with a *fait accompli*, the Iranians, who had embarrassed the Russians by bringing the matter to the newly created United Nations, turned to negotiate with their northern neighbor. Britain and the United States, who had completed their troop removal from Iran, appealed to the Soviet Union. The Russian price for withdrawal was an oil concession in the north, the admission of several Communists to the Iranian cabinet, and withdrawal of the Iranian complaint from the Security Council Agenda. Iran acquiesced and to the surprise of many, the Russians withdrew their troops. Perhaps Stalin was still hesitant to alienate foreign opinion which was not yet unalterably hostile to the Soviet Union; perhaps the main Soviet desire was for the oil concession. In any event, once the Soviet Union had withdrawn, the Iranian army reentered Azerbaijan and the rebel regime collapsed in December of 1946. The next year the Iranian parliament—the Majlis—refused to ratify the Iranian-Soviet oil agreement.

The Turkish case was quite different. Following the disastrous World War I alliance with Germany and Austria-Hungary, Turkey had switched between the wars to a policy of alliance with France and England. But as Nazi power advanced toward the Eastern Mediterranean the Turks found it necessary to be circumspect; Allied leaders understood, and despite Nazi blandishments (which became easier and easier to resist as the Nazi tide receded), Turkey remained neutral during most of the war. In the early period of the war the Soviets, then allied to Nazi Germany, were annoyed by Turkish alignment with France and Britain. Once the Nazis had invaded Russia, Russian leaders became annoyed at Turkey's neutrality. But beginning in the spring of 1944, the Turks gradually severed economic and political relations with Germany, and on February 23, 1945, in order to gain admittance to the United Nations Conference at San Francisco, they finally declared war on the Nazis.

Although the Turks took pains to dissociate official policy from Pan-Turanianism—an agitation for union of all Turkish-speaking peoples which the Nazis had encouraged in an effort to win Turkish support—they faced increasing hostility from a triumphant Russia. For the first time the Russians felt themselves in a position to push for a warm-water entrance to world trade. The way led through the Turkish-controlled straits between the Black Sea and the Mediterranean, and the Russians asked for revision of the international convention which controlled movement through the straits. They demanded a special position for Russia, with military bases in the Bosphorus and the Dardanelles. The move—coupled with the demand for a trusteeship over the former Italian territory of Libya—would have made them a Mediterranean power. In addition, they began to push for cession of Turkish border regions—Kars and Ardahan—and for revision of the Turkish border with Bulgaria in favor of the latter state, now, of course, Communist-dominated.

Through 1946 the propaganda and diplomatic barrage from Moscow increased in intensity and Turkey continued to maintain martial law. (The Russians made much of Turkish wartime relations with the Nazis.) In December 1946, the Turks took vigorous action against Communist groups in Turkey. Relations with Russia had never been more strained, and the Turks faced 1947 with justifiable apprehension. All through the nineteenth century the British had propped up the tottering Turkish Empire against Russian efforts to dismember it. Much of that empire had been lost when the Turks had sided with the Central Powers in World War I, and the Turks had turned again to England. But the winter of 1947 demonstrated the weakness of their supporter, and brought into question their whole policy. They might well be apprehensive about the future.

China

While America tried to make peace, while the lines between Communist-held areas in Europe and the West hardened, while the West faced mounting resistance from areas outside Europe that it had hitherto dominated, the enormous area known as China knew no peace. During the first two years of the post-World War II period the Nationalist government of Chiang Kai-shek attempted to extend its control to all parts of the country, and to reincorporate under the Nationalist regime all Japanese-occupied regions. During this time the United States continued to support the Chinese Nationalists, but, doubting their ability to seize control of the whole area, and faced with pressure within the United States to reduce expenditures, the United States tried to persuade Nationalist and Communist Chinese to enter a coalition.

Throughout the nineteenth century increasing chaos had unsettled the last Chinese dynasty. Revolution within was compounded by pressure from without as the Great Powers maneuvered for spheres of influence in the form of grants of extraterritoriality, exclusive concessions, and outright cession of Chinese territory. Russia, Japan, Germany, France, Great Britain, and the United States vied with one another for influence and control. Early in the 20th century the United States—drawn in after annexation of the Philippines led to American concern for order in the region—tried to establish the rules under which influence would be exercised: this was known as the Open Door policy in China. But the United States was prepared, if agreement could not be reached, to secure its own exclusive rights. However, not until Japan threatened to overrun all of China and more of the Far East besides, at a time when American security was also threatened in the Atlantic, was the United States ready to take decisive action to enforce the Open Door.

In 1911 the Manchu Empire, which, unlike the Japanese, had been unable to cope with the strains imposed by contact with modernism, had come to an end. Sun Yat-sen, leader of the Kuomintang (National People's Party), guided the revolt that established a new Republic and attempted the task of modernization. Before his death in 1925, he was unable to establish the Republic's control over the whole area of China. Leadership passed to Chiang Kai-shek, who continued the effort to consolidate internal control and to eliminate great power rights. His break with the friendly Soviet Union also involved a break with the Communist faction within the Kuomintang. The Communists moved into opposition and ultimately established their own territorial base in North China and their own army. Japan, fearing a strong united China, invaded Manchuria in 1931 and easily overcame resistance. In 1937 it attacked China proper. Although an uneasy truce was established for a time between Communists and Nationalists in an attempt to promote a common effort against the Japanese invader, each party conducted hostilities against the invader in a way that would put *it* into the situation of best advantage in case of victory. The Chinese welcomed United States entry into World War II, but (as we have noted in Chapter II) they were disappointed by the United States decision to downgrade China as a main theatre of war. The United States, perplexed by how to deal with a government that could not give orders to its subordinates, had chosen to give priority to its operations in Europe and to MacArthur's island-hopping strategy; all efforts to work with the Chinese seemed to pay off too little. Dismayed, too, at how much Chinese effort went to continue the sporadic civil war, American missions tried to unite all the Chinese against the common enemy. Japanese success in the great offensive of 1944 further weakened the Nationalist government. The United States tried to compensate for its military strategy by building up China diplomatically—by giving it permanent membership and a veto in the United Nations

Security Council, obtaining abolition of foreign rights in China, and securing Russian support for Chiang Kai-shek.

At end of the war the Nationalists had elements of both strength and weakness. They had a large army but it was disorganized, poorly trained, and paid only what its generals saw fit to disburse after pocketing what they wanted. (Some generals wanted little, but many wanted a great deal, and the government was virtually helpless.) Although the Japanese were defeated, the Nationalists who had to move into regions that had been occupied by the Japanese lacked the transport and administrative apparatus necessary for the takeover. The United States supplied the Nationalists with transport, but Russian troops in Manchuria hampered their movements and the Russians dismantled Japanese factories and removed machinery from the area. Although the looting supports the belief that Moscow was not very confident of a Communist victory, still Russian withdrawals sometimes facilitated the entry of Chinese Communist rather than Nationalist troops, and thus the Communists obtained a large stock of Japanese weapons.

More weakness was to be seen in the overall economic picture which was marked by inflation and shortages. Worn out by war, the Nationalists were unable to cope with the inevitable black marketing and speculation. Disaffection was obvious, and observers were quick to note how much better morale and political and military discipline were among the Communists in the north. Communist propaganda capitalized heavily on these differences. They claimed—with much success—that they, not the Nationalists, were the true heirs of Sun Yat-sen's revolution. As the Nationalists, dependent on the wealthy for support, failed to institute reforms and turned to more and more repression of opposition, the opposition grew—especially among the educated classes.

American observers impressed upon Chiang the need for reforms, but he found it impossible to carry them out. Changing the structure of the army to make it more efficient would undercut the power of local commanders, who would thus resist reform. Land and fiscal reforms would hit many of the people providing the chief support of the Nationalist government.

The Nationalists proceeded in two directions. Strongly encouraged by the United States, they negotiated with the Communists. At the same time they moved into the north. In retrospect it may seem strange that anyone could expect an acceptable coalition to emerge from the talks, but within the context of the times it was not so unrealistic. Relations with the Communists appeared difficult but not impossible; there were coalitions in many countries (and in those never occupied by Russian armies, such as France, the Communists who had entered into the coalition with the hope of capturing more power failed in the end). The Nationalists themselves had long carried on negotiations. Late in 1944, a dispatch from General Hurley, the American ambassador in China, noted that Chiang Kai-shek believed the Soviet Union did not consider the Chinese Communist party to be Communist. Hurley thought Russia was not supporting the Chinese Communists, did not want civil war in China, and wanted better relations with the Nationalist government.

Negotiations for a coalition government failed in 1945. Communist demands proved too much for the Kuomintang leaders, to whom an arrangement preserving their separate Communist military power was unacceptable. The Communists in turn felt sure that any arrangement that did not do this would give the Nationalists the opportunity to destroy the Communist party. They had no reason to think that the Nationalists would provide a genuine democratic choice—any more than did the Nationalists think that the Communists would play according to the rules of any democratic game. Since the United States continued to provide financial and military aid after the end of the war—including the moving of troops into the north—the Communists were able to charge that the Nationalists were using support from outside to improve their strategic position against the Communists. At one point (in August 1945), after the signing of the Sino-Soviet Agreement of August 14 in which the Soviet Union agreed to treat the Nationalists as the sole legal government of China, Mao Tse-tung actually met with Chiang Kai-shek in the Nationalist capital of Chungking, where they did agree on principles. But as the troops of both sides maneuvered for position in the north and in Manchuria, negotiations for implementation broke down.

The United States remained committed to the support of the Nationalists, but many American observers became convinced that the Nationalists might well fail. Therefore, on November 27, 1945, President Truman announced that he had dispatched General George C. Marshall as his representative to try to bring about unification and a cessation of hostilities. Marshall brought with him all the distinction of having been Chief of Staff of one of the two most powerful armies in the world, and an immense personal prestige. But his mission failed: during 1946 the Nationalists continued to move into the North and to clash with Communist troops. Their apparent success strengthened their determination to proceed by force; their troops were three times as numerous as those of the Communists, and they seized city after city. They cleared the rail lines leading from China proper, and with an all-out offensive reached the peak of their success at the beginning of 1947.

It may therefore seem paradoxical that General Marshall, leaving China in January of 1947, announced the termination of his efforts to bring about a peaceful settlement. He apportioned blame to both sides and cited their deep mutual hostility. The statement held out hope for a new democratic constitution and the assumption of leadership by liberal elements, but the tone was one of failure. The reasons were not only the continuation of fighting, but also the growing conviction of many Americans that the Nationalist position was weaker than it appeared to be. The Communists had avoided any major engagements, had maintained their better-disciplined armies intact, while the Nationalists were operating through extended lines of communication that passed through country they could not hold. Their forces in the urban rail centers could not gain control of the countryside.

Thus, at the outset of 1947, when Marshall returned to become the new American Secretary of State, the situation in China was still unsettled. Though the Nationalists seemed to be winning, the base of their victory was precarious.

Korea and Japan

In Korea and Japan, as in Europe, military occupation was the decisive factor in determining subsequent political alignments.

In Japan, General MacArthur, acting for the American government, resisted the efforts of all other wartime Allies to obtain a real voice in occupation policy.

Unlike Allied commanders in Germany, MacArthur still had an intact Japanese administrative apparatus to work through. It was greatly weakened by the American policy of purging the old, militarist leadership, since few new leaders existed who were dedicated to democratic ideals, but MacArthur proceeded with reforms that eliminated old leaders and created new political forms. Administration—particularly police administration—was decentralized, and on January 3, 1947, after one Japanese draft for a new constitution had been rejected, the Japanese adopted a second draft drawn up by the Americans. This constitution established popular sovereignty and Western-style civil liberties. If the Japanese could not be democratic by themselves, democracy would be imposed on them from above! In accordance with ideas about the relationship of social and political forms to aggressive foreign policy, the Americans began to dissolve the large Japanese business cartels, or *zaibatsu*, that had dominated Japanese economic life, and inserted a clause in the new constitution that renounced forever the use of armed force in the conduct of foreign policy. Communist leaders were allowed to resume active political life, and trade union activity was encouraged.

Yet, just as in Germany, reform began to falter almost as soon as it began, principally because of the change in world outlook that was shaped by the events of this period. Both Japan and Germany began to be seen as outposts on the edge of a menacing Soviet bloc, and as outposts whose cooperation might be needed. In both countries the attempt to purge old leadership had provoked resentment—more in Germany, where all democratic political parties disassociated themselves from "denazification" and the punishment of Nazi leadership. But in Japan, too, reform was often seen as revenge, as the imposition of an alien pattern by a victor, as a question not of right, but of might, and the change in foreign policy orientation tended to reinforce cynicism.

For Korea, the story was different. The Allies chose the 38th parallel as the arbitrary demarcation line between Russian occupation in the North and American occupation in the South. Korea had long been the subject of great power rivalry between China and Japan; Japan had decisively defeated and eliminated China in 1895, and then, in 1905, eliminated the new contender, Russia. Outright annexation of Korea followed in 1910, and only with World War II did Korea face the prospect of independence. But the occupying authorities made no progress in setting up joint administrative organs on the spot, so in December 1945 they turned the problem over to the Council of Foreign Ministers meeting in Moscow. The Council established a new joint commission to help form a provisional Korean democratic government. The commission failed to agree, however, on what groups within Korea could be considered democratic enough to be consulted in planning the provisional government. Each power feared the consequence of a hostile united Korea, and soon, as in Eastern Europe, the Russians, who had cultivated native Communist groups, installed a puppet regime in the North.

In the south the United States found that the strongest group was led by Syngman Rhee, a long-time Korean nationalist-in-exile. But Rhee was impatient with the failure to bring about Korean unification and annoyed by continued American occupation. The United States government found itself maintaining a costly operation while under pressure to economize and at a time when demobilization had placed a premium on manpower. In return it received Korean hostility. If the burden could be laid down, the charge that the Korean occupation represented American imperialism would be rebutted. Thus, in 1947, the Administration determined to call on the United Nations to handle the problem of Korea. The United Nations, unfortunately, would find it no easy problem.

Disarmament Negotiations

The power of the atomic bomb—demonstrated at Hiroshima and Nagasaki—was awesome. The political developments that indicated growing tension between Western powers and the Soviet Union, also evoked a terrible dismay: was it possible that not only had World War II failed to produce a new and better world of harmony, but that it might now be superseded by an infinitely worse World War III? The United Nations Charter did not stress disarmament the way the League Covenant had. Experience with Nazi Germany had suggested that unilateral disarmament might invite aggression, and that it was impossible to guarantee disarmament by all nations. The advent of "the ultimate weapon" changed this attitude. To many, disarmament now seemed more important than ever; it also seemed possible. Fascism, with its doctrine of the right of the strongest, was dead; the Soviet Union, which had suffered extensive damage in the war, would have to devote its resources to reconstruction. Thus Russia would undoubtedly welcome a system that would eliminate the reliance on military force, particularly when force now included atomic weapons. The very existence of the bomb might now force nations to abandon war as a means of foreign policy. The attitude of expectancy has been well summed up in the phrase of James Phinney Baxter: the atomic bomb had "blasted the web of history and, like the discovery of fire, severed the past from the present."

The first major step took place in November 1945 when the United States, the United Kingdom, and Canada, who had all participated in development of the weapon, issued a joint statement offering "to share, on a reciprocal basis with others of the United Nations, detailed information concerning the practical industrial application of atomic energy just as soon as effective enforceable safeguards against its use for destructive purposes can be devised." The offer to share the secret of the bomb led to a widening of the debate over the wisdom of the move. Many Americans asked whether the United States should not keep the secret. President Truman's advisers, however, did not expect the "secret" to be kept for long; other nations would learn to develop the weapon within several years. In the meantime, if the move were not taken, disarmament and security would be unattainable. Could any nation trust the United States completely? Time, therefore, was short; it had become imperative to establish a system of international control so that the United States could afford to "give up" the bomb. Questioning senators were reassured: the United States would continue to hold it as a "sacred trust" until sufficient controls had *first* been established.

In December, with the Anglo-American-Canadian declaration as the impetus, the Russians agreed to the establishment of an Atomic Energy Commission of the United Nations. It was created on January 26, 1946, and directed to report to the Security Council. On June 14 it received the American proposal, the Baruch Plan, named for the American on the Commission, Bernard Baruch. Five days later the Russians presented their own plan.

The Baruch Plan proposed an International Atomic Development Authority to which would be entrusted "managerial control or ownership of all atomic energy activities potentially dangerous to world security," the "power to control, inspect and license all other atomic activities," and which would itself be "the world's leader in the field of atomic knowledge and development." To this radical proposal to separate atomic matters from national sovereignty, the Russians answered with a suggestion for immediate prohibition of the use, production, and accumulation of atomic weapons and for the destruction of existing stockpiles within three months after the conventions had come into force. Each nation would enact domestic legislation to punish violators of the convention.

All through 1946, attempts to negotiate on these matters proved fruitless. The Russians insisted that there need be no prior provision for inspection and control, and the Americans insisted precisely on the need for a thoroughgoing system of control before any further action. The Baruch Plan, the Russians argued, since it obviated the all-important veto, was a capitalist plot to dominate the Soviet Union through an international monopoly in which capitalist powers would always have a majority voice, and where their agents could spy on all aspects of industrial and military activity. Besides (though they did not say so), the plan would have prevented their own national atomic research and development. On December 31, the Commission submitted to the Security Council its first report, which had been adopted by a vote of 10 to 0, the Soviet Union and Poland abstaining. The report recommended that the Security Council accept substantially the Baruch

Plan. The Security Council requested the Commission to undertake further study and make recommendations. In the following years it made no progress, and in 1949 the Soviet Union exploded its first atomic bomb.

Conclusion

The first year and a half of the postwar period witnessed the end of the war-born alliance. As European recovery faltered and the attempt to reestablish European rule in the rest of the world failed, the United States and Russia emerged as superpowers. But both moved cautiously. Within the United States, political pressure to throw off wartime controls, to demobilize, and to cut taxes all combined with the lingering isolationist impulse, distrust of Britain, and some feeling that Russia was being thrust into the role of the villain. The result was considerable confusion about what the United States ought to do beyond providing some relief. But while Europe and the United States attempted to consolidate their hold on the non-Russian part of the world, they parried the thrusts of Russia into the Mediterranean, Iran, West Germany, and Japan. The Russians proceeded to consolidate their hold on their own sphere and block Western intervention into it.

Those who supported an all-out effort to get along with Russia had strong arguments; the alternative was dreadful to contemplate and no one could choose it until it was certain that cooperation was impossible. In the light of history, Russians had good reason to fear the West; even more, the emergence of two superpowers surrounded by weak states appeared to create a situation in which hostile competition was far more likely to emerge than in the multipower situation of past centuries. Many people believed, therefore, that greater efforts were required to avert a conflict that neither power wanted, a conflict provoked not by Russian arms, but by the nature of the bipolar situation. Finally, many argued that Russia was bound to devote most of its efforts to internal reconstruction. The war had devastated the Soviet Union: its resources for reconstruction were limited, and it had expressed a desire for a large American loan. If America were willing to aid Russian reconstruction, would this not alleviate Soviet fears and provide some cementing ties? Were not the everyday clashes—of which many Americans and the American press were making so much —merely the kind of constant political maneuvering that normally takes place on the international scene, but whose importance the United States, emerging from its long period of isolation, tended to magnify?

Were not the Russians merely probing into areas that had always been their concern in the past, even before Russia became Communist?

Within Europe many people asked the same questions. But, even more, most people were more concerned with reconstruction efforts, or merely with recreating an acceptable private life after the shattering war years. In France, de Gaulle—who had aspired to great power status for France and had seen an opportunity to become an arbiter between the new giants—resigned in disgust when many of the old political forces that had governed the Third Republic reemerged. In 1946 France had adopted a constitution favored by only one-third of the voting public; it was governed by an uneasy coalition of Christian-Democrats, Socialists, and Communists; it had already begun to fight in Indochina. French leaders found that their capacity to influence the international situation was limited; neither the United States nor the Soviet Union appeared to pay much attention to them, and their foreign policy goal of keeping Germany divided and weak was blocked by growing Russian-American rivalry for the allegiance of the Germans.

In Britain the Labour government, facing an unprecedented economic crisis, had worked out a policy of austerity—keeping consumption down so that Britain could import only what was strictly needed, and export enough to pay for essential imports. At the same time, the British were trying to reequip worn-out industries and to rebuild investments overseas, and also maintain the posture of a great power. By mid-winter 1947 the effort had failed. Many Labour supporters had long thought that capitalism was the main cause of international conflict and that a Socialist government would be able to get along better with everyone. But Ernest Bevin, Labour's Foreign Secretary, was less sanguine than many staunch American capitalists about how well the West could get along with the Russians.

In Russia the war had been the occasion for relaxation of controls on art, literature, religious practice and on contacts with the West, apparently to enlist support of the Russian people against the German invader. Now that the war was over, the restraints were reimposed in even more rigid form. Although a large-scale demobilization took place, a large army still remained. Economic reconstruction concentrated on heavy industry rather than on consumer goods. Reprisals were taken against those whose participation in the war effort had been half-hearted, and prisoners of war were not released; instead they were kept on in Russia doing forced labor on heavy construction jobs.

Although the Western powers, particularly the United States, were painted in the darkest colors in the Soviet press, Soviet foreign policy was curiously halting. In Iran the Russians retreated. They abandoned some of their goals in other areas. In Eastern Europe consolidation proceeded spasmodically; in the Far East Stalin did not expect a Chinese Communist victory and was ready to work with the Nationalist government while awaiting the outcome. Soviet strength only became clear as the weakness in surrounding territories was felt. Stalin formally annexed only territories to which Russia had some historical claim. Nevertheless, the Soviet Union was not ready to renounce all claims to what it felt were war-born rights in areas outside of the Soviet Union. The winter of 1947 revealed the weakness of former world powers and the extent of world chaos. Stalin faced a situation that gave him unprecedented opportunity for widespread gains, whose achievement, however, depended on two factors: what he *really* wanted, and how Americans would view this situation and decide to act upon their view.

CHAPTER FOUR   1947–1950

The Cold War, Bipolarization,
and Containment

Every year is heralded at its outset as a turning point in world affairs—a year during which great decisions must be made, a year that will determine the course of history. Unlike most years, 1947 was actually one of these. In 1947 the Truman administration, in a series of radical new policies, crystallized a view of the world scene, and evolved a new role for the United States. Despite subsequent criticism, the overall policy, summed up in the term "containment," was followed by succeeding administrations.

Containment was based on the assumption that the Soviet Union was bent on a course of limitless expansion, and that this Soviet policy was inspired by the Communist world view of inevitable conflict between capitalist and "socialist" societies.* The containment policy, embodied in many American actions, assumed that the Soviet Union would therefore press outward by every possible means, and that its pressures must be met with positions of strength. In geopolitical terms, containment involved a United States commitment to defend the "rimlands" of the Eurasian continent against pressures from the "heartland." In the period 1947–1950, it came to have two aspects: enough military power should be developed to meet Soviet military thrusts or their threat, and the economic, social, and political health of the non-Soviet world would be strengthened to impede Soviet expansion through subversion and revolution by native Communist movements led by Moscow. Proponents of containment hoped that ultimately, the Soviet Union, finding expansion impossible, would relax its efforts as revolutionary dynamism and certainty of world victory faded. As the interpreters of Soviet ideology found that the capitalist world

---

* The term "socialist" must be used cautiously. In Communist parlance, only Communist-bloc countries are truly socialist. The Labour government, in England, which considered itself socialist, was therefore by definition not.

did not behave according to Marxist-Leninist categories, they would be forced to revise their ideology to conform to reality.

Thus, in 1947 the United States launched a program of economic and military aid to Greece and Turkey accompanied by the Truman Doctrine that "it must be the policy of the United States to support free peoples who are resisting attempted subjugation by armed minorities or by outside pressures." Later in the year the Marshall Plan began, a long-range commitment of large-scale economic aid to help rebuild the faltering economies of Europe. In 1948 the impetus of the previous year led to the formation of the North Atlantic Treaty Organization (NATO), and the commitment of American troops to the defense of Europe, along with large-scale programs of military aid. Then, in 1949 President Truman launched the program of technical aid to underdeveloped countries, known as the Point Four Program. The policy of containment, with its commitments, was underway.

The Soviet Union responded by hastening to consolidate Communist control in Eastern European countries, by abetting Communist attempts at take-overs in France and Italy, by bringing about a coup putting Czechoslovakia definitely into the Soviet orbit, and by a squeeze on the Allied outpost in Berlin. But tightened Soviet control led to the break by Tito's Yugoslavia and the subsequent constant threat of "Titoism" within the Soviet bloc, which foreshadowed some of the future complexities of "bipolarism."

The move to unify Europe gathered steam, under the impetus of the Marshall Plan and the growing awareness that a world dominated by several powers had been replaced by one where there were only two superpowers. In the Middle East the continued British withdrawal led to the Palestine War, the emergence of independent Israel, and new bitterness toward the West. In other parts of the world the march toward independence continued; in China, it took the form of a Chinese Communist victory over the Nationalists.

American Initiatives

In January 1947, General George C. Marshall, recently returned from his mission in China, became Secretary of State. His first policy task was to prepare for the forthcoming Council of Foreign Ministers meeting, to be held in Moscow in March, presumably to draft peace treaties for Germany and Austria. In the weeks before Marshall left for Moscow, the seriousness of the European situation became apparent. At the same time the new Republican-controlled Congress was in a mood to cut drastically the administration's budget demands. On Friday, February 21, 1947—some three weeks before the Moscow Conference—the British Government delivered to the State Department a note which, in effect, declared Britain's inability to continue the effort to stabilize the eastern Mediterranean area over which it had gained control during the last century. Greece would need a minimum of $240 to $280 million during 1947 to enable it to cope with the Communist guerrillas and keep its people from starving. It would also need substantial aid in subsequent years. Without this aid, Greece would simply collapse. The British stated flatly that they would be unable to meet Greek needs after March 31. Turkey's army, although kept in a state of readiness, desperately needed modernization. In late 1946 an American naval task force on a courtesy visit to the country had bolstered Turkish resistance to Soviet demands. But if the Russians continued to press them, the Turks could offer little military resistance. Britain could no longer provide the financial resources either to strengthen the Turkish economy or reequip its armies.

Within the administrative branch of the American government there was quick agreement that in some way it must step into the breach, that the loss of Greece and Turkey to the Communists would jeopardize not only the whole of the Middle East but also Europe. The United States would have to give long-range economic and military aid to Greece and Turkey, notwithstanding other troubled areas like Korea and China, and despite the limitations of American military and economic resources and the strong pressure for economy in government. In conversations with Senate and House leaders, the administration determined that strong public appeal was necessary and that unless the wording of the commitment to aid Greece and Turkey were stated within a broader context of aid to free peoples everywhere public support for this particular case would be hard to gain.

Thus, when President Truman made a dramatic appearance before a joint meeting of Congress on March 12 to request funds and announce the new policy, he spoke in terms of an ideological confrontation between the two systems. The debate that followed revealed considerable opposition. From Republican Senators Robert Taft and Everett Dirksen on the right to former Vice-President Henry Wallace on the left— and from many in between—came the attack. This was a proposal to pull more British chestnuts out of the fire. It was nonsense to invoke the slogans, "free people" and sustaining "democracy," neither Greece nor Turkey were democratic countries. The administration was asking for a blank check. The policy was a retrogression to the power politics

that had previously characteriezd Europe. It would divide the world
into two armed camps and lead to war, and it bypassed the United Nations. The United States would be intervening in the domestic affairs
of Greece, since the plan involved the presence of a large American
aid mission to carry out administrative and military reorganization.

It was not easy to answer the criticisms that the policy bypassed
the United Nations. The Greek problem had been before the United
Nations Security Council several times. Once the Soviet Union had
complained of continued presence of British troops, and when the
Russians had repeated the complaint, the British replied heatedly that
Communist guerrilla attempts to impede elections were responsible
for British presence. In December 1946, a Greek complaint that
Albania, Bulgaria, and Yugoslavia were harboring the guerrillas resulted in the creation of a Security Council Committee of Inquiry
which was actually *in* Greece at the time of the American debate.
The administration, however, felt there was no time to work through
the United Nations, that the UN Commission would be hamstrung by
the Soviet Union, and that the United Nations was not the proper
organ for the task that had to be performed. But it did accept modifications of the Congressional aid bill. Provisions were added that the
President could be empowered to withdraw American aid if and
when the United Nations could assume the necessary tasks and notified the United States to that effect, if the Greek and Turkish Governments asked for an end to the aid, or if the President found that
other intergovernmental agencies were accomplishing the purposes of
the Act.

Notwithstanding the President's note of urgency, it took until April
22 for the bill to aid Greece and Turkey to clear the Senate, by a
vote of 67 to 23. The House approved it on May 8, by a vote of 287
to 107. On May 22, the President signed the bill. But appropriations
had to follow authorization; the administration was asking not only
$400 million for Greece and Turkey, but also $350 million for general
aid to other countries, $725 million for reconstruction and occupa-
tion costs in Germany, Austria, Japan, and Korea, $78 million for
relief in Korea, and $73.5 million for the International Refugee Or-
ganization—a total of $1626.5 million. More time was taken for the
appropriations to be made, and Congress served notice upon the administration that the piecemeal approach was not satisfactory.

In June and July bilateral agreements were signed with Greece and
Turkey and the programs of technical, military, and economic aid
got under way. The economic aid programs remained independent for

only nine months; in 1948 they came within the purview of the new Economic Cooperation Administration of the Marshall Plan (see below). But the military program had economic effects also, since it provided for the modernization of roads and transportation, as well as military reequipment and training. It was a success. By the end of June 1949, Greece had been almost cleared of guerrillas. The program, however, was not completely effective until July, 1949, when Yugoslavia's Communist boss, Marshal Tito, successfully defied Stalin, and closed the Yugoslav border to Greek Communist guerrillas.

Success of the Turkish program was harder to measure, but observers reported that the effectiveness of the Turkish armed forces had increased, while the pressure on the Turkish budget of maintaining them was relieved.

The Moscow Conference

Part of the immediate opposition to the Truman Doctrine arose because it was announced at the very moment when Secretary Marshall was in Moscow for the Conference of the Council of Foreign Ministers. Opponents suggested that a declaration of ideological warfare at this point would surely wreck the conference. But the discussions that took place in Moscow support the view that the positions of both nations were, for the moment at least, irreconcilable.

The conference, which lasted from March 10, 1947 to April 24, was supposed to draft peace treaties for Germany and Austria; the United States also proposed a German disarmament treaty, designed to see if alleviation of Russian fears might lead to a relaxation of Russian pressures. But the gap could not be bridged. The United States and Britain wanted a higher level of industry in Germany than the French did. The former felt that European recovery depended on a German contribution. For political reasons the French wanted the level kept low, but they also wanted a higher share of German coal (and more would be left for export if German steel production were greatly restricted). More important, the Russians continued to insist on a high level of reparations from current production while the Western powers argued that that would mean they would be pumping in goods at one end while the Russians went on siphoning them off at the other. The Russians now urged the creation of a strong central authority, where the Communist-dominated East Zone Socialist Unity party would presumably have a leading role. The French, although they had had to abandon their earlier desire for dismemberment of Germany, wanted to begin the reconstruction of political units at the local level, with central units to come later. In between stood the British and Americans, who wanted economic unity and the central political organs this required, but wanted them to be based on a federalism that would leave much power to the states. The West, too, tried to argue about the boundary with Poland, while the Russians wanted it accepted as final. France wavered, since Foreign Minister Georges Bidault wanted the coal-rich Saar excluded from Germany (possibly to be incorporated into France) and also demanded international control of the Ruhr and the Rhineland. The Russians might support France's demands if France accepted the new Polish boundaries, and the French certainly cared little for German feelings in the matter. The Russians tried to bargain: they would work for unity if the British and Americans halted actions to merge their zones, and if they accepted Soviet claims about reparations and the Polish border. But no bargain could be concluded.

There was to be a subsequent meeting of the Foreign Ministers in November, where procedure would be discussed (should there be a central German government before a peace treaty, or a peace treaty before a central German government?) Here Western demands for economic unity countered Soviet demands for reparations and the ending of joint British and American administration of the West-zone. The Moscow meeting of March and April had really settled the issue of Germany: it would remain divided. Events of the months between the Moscow and London Conferences made sure that the London meeting was only an exercise in futile countercharges.

The Marshall Plan

While aid to Greece and Turkey and Truman's speech were being mapped out, further long-range studies of the European situation were begun in Washington. The work was hastened by the dismal comedy of the Moscow Conference and by the growing crisis in Hungary. On February 26, Kovaks, the secretary general of the Smallholders' party, was arrested by the Russians after the Hungarian Parliament had refused to bow to pressure to act against him; a general purge of the party followed, and Western protests were to no avail. Open intervention by Russia culminated on August 31 in rigged elections and the subsequent elimination of all further opposition to the Communists.

On May 8, 1947, Under-Secretary of State Dean Acheson, in a speech to a group of business and agricultural leaders, anticipated the thinking of the administration on the question of long-range aid. He noted the imbalance between what other countries needed from the

United States and what they could sell to it, and described United States interest in seeing the enormous gap filled. Then, on June 5, General Marshall delivered the Commencement Address at Harvard that initiated the European Recovery Program.

In his speech, Marshall again reviewed the situation. It was logical, he maintained, for the United States to help fill the gap between European requirements and what they could afford to pay—the alternative would be "economic, social, and political deterioration of a very grave character." He added that this policy was "directed not against any country or doctrine but against hunger, poverty, desperation, and chaos," and that European nations should cooperatively work out programs matched to their requirements.

The speech stressed cooperation among European nations. More than that, in deliberate contrast to Truman's speech announcing the program of aid to Greece and Turkey, it concentrated on economic factors. It declared that poverty and chaos—not Russia or Communism —were the enemies. In fact, the speech appeared to allow for Russian and Eastern European cooperation in development of the new venture.

This aspect was quite deliberate. On the one hand, it was designed to counter growing European and American criticism that the Truman Doctrine was "negative"—that it was only anti-something, that it was a declaration of ideological war. Though it was all very well to be anti-Communist, this would not strike at the roots of the problem, which was economic chaos in Europe. It was hoped the Marshall initiative would be looked on as "positive," as indeed it was. Moreover, Western European leaders still saw East Europe as a necessary supplier of grain, coal, and oil for their own countries; the economy of the West was not viable without the East. The Marshall Plan put the burden of choice on the Russians: participation in the Plan would entangle their economy with the West and make it more difficult for them to follow the belligerent path they appeared to be taking. It offered them the possibility of peaceful and mutually beneficial cooperation instead of mutual hostility. Despite the clashes we have so far noted, Stalin had continued to give indications that Russia wanted and needed peace and expanded trade. It was still possible to argue that Russia had expected a more or less free hand in the defensive zone it occupied, wanted to prevent a strong coalition forming against it, and expected that the capitalist United States—to avert a depression—would need trade with the Soviet Union. Also, the Soviet Union did not have the atomic bomb while the United States did. If these were the factors uppermost in the minds of some Soviet leaders, they might still be induced to sacrifice long-term Communist goals for short-term economic needs. In the past they had made internal compromises; egalitarianism and the withering of the state had been postponed indefinitely in the interest of building a strong industrial state. On the other hand, if the Russians fought Marshall's initiative, it would put the onus on them.

In Europe, the British and French Foreign Ministers, Bevin and Bidault, took the initiative and invited Foreign Minister Molotov to Paris for a conference at the end of June to consider the American offer. Here it became clear that the Russians would consider the offer only on one condition: that its cooperative aspect assume a very minor role. They proposed that each state take stock of its needs, which would then be reconciled or scaled down in terms of what the United States was prepared to offer. Each would then go ahead with its own plans. The French and British argued that the whole proposal depended on a *European* inventory of needs, resources, and possibilities of mutual aid. The result was a deadlock. Russia dropped out.

What about the rest of Eastern Europe? On July 4, the British and French invited twenty-two other countries to attend a conference in Paris on July 12; the invitation was also sent to the Soviet Embassy with an expression of hope that Soviet refusal was not final. But when the conference convened eight countries failed to attend: Finland, Poland, Czechoslovakia, Hungary, Yugoslavia, Rumania, Bulgaria, and Albania. Their presence had been forbidden by the Soviet Union.

Though it was hard to accept a division of Europe that they had been trying for two years to avoid, the European representatives gathered at Paris created the Committee of European Economic Co-operation and rapidly drew up a four-year projection of the European economy and its needs. Given the uncertainties of the situation, the projection had to be rough. For a four-year period, it forecast a balance of payments shortage of $29 billion—an enormous sum. In addition there were differences among the participating countries. France was still reluctant to see the German economy revive; others saw German reconstruction as imperative to their own rebuilding. There was American criticism, also. The report was too much of a shopping list and not enough of a survey of how intra-European trade could be increased; it failed to specify the fiscal and financial measures European countries could take, failed to propose specific reductions in their trade barriers. The report was revised and in September of 1947 presented to the United States. It now forecast a gap of $22 billion, 3 billion of which could be filled from the International Bank for Reconstruction and Development, leaving 19 billion to come from the United States.

In the meantime, different groups in the United States had also proceeded with surveys. They included the special Harriman Committee (appointed by the President), and a special committee of the House of Representatives, headed by Christian Herter (Republican, Massachusetts). Besides looking at the European situation, they surveyed the general world trade picture and prepared estimates of the impact of the possible program on the American economy. On the basis of these and the European suggestion, the administration prepared a program to present to Congress in January 1948.

Events in Europe hastened action by the administration. In June 1947, Italy was forced to stop all dollar expenditures except for coal, cereals, and petroleum products. France followed suit two months later. Economists expected that both would run out of foreign exchange by December 1947. Consequently, President Truman asked for, and received from Congress, interim aid of close to $600 million as well as extra aid for Germany. The request—which was for relief, not reconstruction—was buttressed by a review of the planning under way for the European Recovery Program, a plan which would presumably obviate the need for relief in the future.

In February 1948 came the coup in Czechoslovakia that installed a Communist government and decisively moved that sorely tried land into the Soviet bloc (see p. 103). In France, Communist-led strikes and riots gave evidence of the Party's determination that it should be taken back into the government. As a result, Congress' interest in the Marshall Plan was quickened. On April 2 (some two weeks before the Italian general elections in which it was suspected that the Communists would make a strong showing), Congress passed the Economic Cooperation Act.

There was much battling over the scale of the aid, the way it would be administered, the forms it would take, the countries that would be eligible for it. Congress agreed to authorize expenditures over a four-year period, but insisted on appropriating the money each year. The actual funds made available the first year (including loans) totaled $6220 million, the second year, $4060 million; and the third year, $2254 million.

From the American side, the European Recovery Program (ERP) was carried out by a new agency, the European Cooperation Administration (ECA) headed by industrialist Paul Hoffman. At the insistence of a distrustful Congress, it was separate from the Department of State. The enabling legislation had specified that the aim of the Act was to encourage unification of Europe. Hoffman spelled this out:

The long-range goal I put before the OEEC was the effective integration of the economy of Western Europe—the building of a single market of 270 million consumers, in which quantitative restrictions on the movement of goods, monetary barriers to the flow of payments and eventually all tariffs should be permanently swept away.

It did not happen.

But out of the Marshall Plan—once called the greatest creative act of statesmanship of modern times—grew the Organization for European Economic Cooperation and the European Payments Union, both made up of participating members. The former undertook studies, suggested legislation and treaties, and supervised the various forms of cooperation devised under the spur of the Marshall Plan. The latter helped the shaky European currencies to achieve stability and permitted multilateral clearing of payments, thus arresting the long-term trend toward bilateral clearing of payments and trade; the restoration of multilateral rather than bilateral trade in Europe was one of the great achievements of the postwar era. By helping to strengthen European economies, it subsequently helped them to participate fully in the wider-spread United Nations agencies—the International Monetary Fund and General Agreement on Tariffs and Trade. Until the success of the Marshall Plan, the inability of Europe to export and its desperate need for imports had kept the multilateral features of the two organizations in abeyance. Once Europe, revitalized by the Marshall Plan, had recovered and even begun to exceed prewar production levels, European countries could take full part, and at least some of the hopes for the world envisaged during World War II began to materialize. Europe was now free of many inhibiting trade restrictions that had been resorted to in the 1920s and 1930s during periods of inflation and depression.

The OEEC and the EPU were substantial steps in the right direction. Europeans took a further step when German production resumed after the currency reform of 1948 and it became clear that despite French objections German economic expansion would take place. As a consequence, the French proposed a revolutionary scheme, the European Coal and Steel Community—the so-called Schuman Plan.

Most people found it difficult to understand what the Schuman Plan called for, but they were ready to applaud any initiative toward

European unity; the time was ripe for the many groups to work for unification in some form. The Schuman Plan (which took eighteen months to negotiate) eventually removed substantially from national sovereignty the coal and steel industries of six continental European countries: France, Italy, Germany, Belgium, the Netherlands, and Luxembourg. It created a complete set of supranational institutions to effect the common market in coal and iron and steel. Ultimately, the success of the European Coal and Steel Community inspired another and more important venture—a European customs union that developed in the late 1950s.

The Marshall Plan did much more than give the impetus to integrate the economies of European countries: it gave Europeans some measure of confidence in their own future. Once this confidence was established, governments and industries began to plan and invest. The results were impressive. By 1950 total industrial production had increased by one-half over 1947, exceeding the 1938 level by a quarter. Agricultural production outstripped the prewar average. Marshall Plan officials predicted that if nothing intervened the overall goals of the program would be attained by 1952, and Europe would be self-supporting. Unfortunately the Korean war, with its necessity for an expensive rearmament, did intervene. Hard choices had to be made; American aid tended to shift to military help. But the ECA had laid a real foundation which was not to be shaken by the events of the 1950s.

NATO and the Berlin Blockade

The year 1947 gave rise to the Marshall Plan; 1948 gave birth to the North Atlantic Treaty Organization. Both were part of the new United States commitment to the support of Western Europe.

Failure of the Moscow and London foreign ministers' conferences stimulated Britain, France, and the Benelux countries to sign the Brussels Treaty, a fifty-year defensive alliance with permanent peacetime coordinating and planning committees. Foreign Minister Ernest Bevin presented it to Parliament in January 1948, and on March 17— hastened by the Czech coup—the six countries signed it. But from the beginning they knew that European military power, even if pooled, would be inadequate if the Russians decided to use the large peacetime army that they maintained. They hoped that if the Europeans took a joint initiative in the military as they had in the economic realm, the United States might respond in the same fashion. There had been diplomatic hints to that effect, and in March Bevin proposed American participation to Secretary of State Marshall. In April the Canadian government publicly endorsed the idea. But to the United States the idea meant a drastic reversal of a century and a half of foreign policy, summed up in the phrase "no entangling alliances."

The impetus of the Truman Doctrine and the Marshall Plan was still there, however. Moreover, events in Germany now added urgency to the pressure provided by the Czech coup. In response to the Western creation of common governmental organs for the Western zones of Germany, the Russians instituted a blockade of Berlin. Beginning with restricting military traffic in and out of the city in March, they began to harass and finally completely to stop all land communication on June 24. It seemed inevitable that the Western powers would be starved out of the city of two and one-half million, and would be compelled to agree to Soviet terms.

Instead, under the prodding and direction of the American commandant, General Lucius D. Clay, the Western powers organized an extraordinary airlift to the city. Clay told a worried administration that the action would not mean war:

We have lost Czechoslovakia. Norway is threatened. We retreat from Berlin. When Berlin falls, western Germany will be next. If we mean . . . to hold Europe against Communism, we must not budge. We can take humiliation and pressure short of war in Berlin without losing face. If we withdraw, our position in Europe is threatened.*

Occupation authorities had calculated that forty-five hundred tons of supplies per day would maintain Berlin at a subsistence level (without any private home heating). In anticipation of the blockade food stocks sufficient for thirty-six days and coal for forty-five had been built up. It took until December before the airlift, begun on June 25, could handle the necessary forty-five hundred tons. But after this the tonnage climbed steadily, and by the spring of 1949 an average of eight thousand tons per day were being flown into the city. On May 4 an announcement from the United Nations indicated that the Soviet Union had capitulated. Negotiations there had led to agreement that ground communications would resume, and on May 11 the first trucks and trains crossed the border for Berlin.

In the meantime, the Berlin crisis had had its effect within the United States. To make sure that a proposed security treaty would pass the Senate hurdle of the necessary two-thirds majority (which required Democratic and Republican support), Republican Senator Vandenberg had been prevailed upon to introduce a resolution in favor

* Lucius D. Clay, *Decision in Germany*, Doubleday (New York, 1950), p. 361.

of American participation in regional alliances "in accordance with the purposes, principles, and provisions of the Charter" of the United Nations. On June 11, 1948, the Vandenberg resolution passed the Senate by a vote of 64 to 6. With Senate support secure, conversations began in July in Washington, while American officers began to participate in the work of the Brussels Treaty committees in Europe. Although the first draft of the treaty was completed in November, negotiations continued into 1949. The question of membership was thorny: could an ex-enemy like Italy be asked to join? Its strategic location in the Mediterranean appeared to answer the question, but the Italian legislature, with its heavy Communist representation, balked. After months of debate the Christian Democratic government obtained support for the pact. Portugal, Iceland, Norway, and Denmark also joined. Sweden and Switzerland maintained their traditional neutrality. Spain was still outside the pale. On April 4, 1949, eleven countries signed the North Atlantic Pact and on October 22, 1951, Greece and Turkey were admitted to membership.

The main purpose of the pact was clear—to keep the United States in Western Europe to help counterbalance Soviet power. Many United States Senators made explicit their objections before the pact was ratified, for it committed the United States to action in circumstances that would negate Congress' power to declare war. In fact, the pact made the obligation to act in case of an attack on one of the signatories contingent on the constitutional processes of each country. But the deterrent power of the pact rested on convincing the Soviet Union that an attack on one would really be an attack on all, and that the United States would not wait while Congress leisurely declared war. Thus the United States would have to keep troops in Europe in the line of Soviet fire. An attack upon Western Europe would then inevitably involve the United States. Senate critics therefore concentrated their attack on this commitment and also challenged the constitutional authority of the President, in his capacity as Commander in Chief, to move troops abroad. But they were beaten back, and the Senate received an education on reconciling the Constitution with the necessities of foreign policy once isolation was no longer possible. It approved the pact by a vote of 82 to 13. Republican Senator Taft, voting in the opposition, still claimed that there was no Russian military threat to the United States.

In subsequent months the Congress also approved the first military aid to the countries of Western Europe to strengthen their own armed forces, with an initial appropriation of $1.3 billion in aid. Finally, the pact led to the creation of an elaborate North Atlantic Treaty Organization, with a Supreme Headquarters, Allied Powers in Europe (SHAPE) outside of Paris, a series of joint regional commands, and periodic meetings at the ministerial level for coordination of foreign and military policies and for determining and apportioning the financial burdens.

Point Four

The last chapter in the wholesale reversal of American attitudes toward its role in world politics came in January 1949. President Truman, in his inaugural address, proposed several policies, the fourth of which set off a whole series of programs in subsequent years.

We must embark on a bold new program for making the benefits of our scientific advances and industrial progress available for the improvement and growth of underdeveloped areas. . . . For the first time in history, humanity possesses the knowledge and the skill to relieve the suffering of these people. The United States is preeminent among nations in the development of industrial and scientific techniques. The material resources which we can afford to use for the assistance of other peoples are limited. But our imponderable resources in technical knowledge are constantly growing and are inexhaustible.

Here was an acknowledgement that the nineteenth-century era of empire was over, a recognition of the desire for independence for new states and of the social revolutions within them as people began to ask, not merely for independence, but for something more than subsistence and subservience. Britain and France—especially France—had initiated large-scale postwar development programs in their overseas dependencies. The United Nations, in strengthening the powers of the General Assembly to discuss almost any matter and in the enhanced status of the Economic and Social Council, had recognized these developments. The increased international interest in Trust Territories and non-self-governing areas had been written into the Charter. One month before President Truman's inaugural address the General Assembly had in fact passed a resolution providing for a long-range program of technical assistance to under developed areas, but it would have been ineffective without the support of the United States.

President Truman's speech began a debate that still continues. In the subsequent battle for legislative support, the program—like the Marshall Plan before it—took anti-Communist overtones; unless technical aid was provided the new countries would lapse into chaos and the Communists would take over. But despite this ideological slant, and despite the various forms of opposition to Point Four aid, the various programs came to represent a new phase in international politics. The wealthier nations of what was coming to be an international community found it necessary to help the poorer members. The flow of private capital was insufficient for, with the exception of a few attractive investment opportunities in such resources as oil, private investors found more profitable fields in the wealthier countries.

In the early years of implementation, when large-scale funds were still flowing to Europe under the Marshall Plan and in military aid, there was little direct capital aid as a result of the Point Four speech. Moreover, not until September 1950 was Congress willing to appropriate $34.5 million for technical aid. In that same year the United Nations began its own modest program of multilateral aid, with the United States paying up to 60 per cent of the total. In the years before the Korean War, the International Bank for Reconstruction and Development also began to find a few worthwhile projects in the underdeveloped countries, and to aid in their financing.

The Organization of American States

The United States directed its primary initiatives under the containment policy toward Europe, the region that appeared to be in the greatest danger; Point Four policies gave belated recognition to an emerging new world in other areas.* Both before and after these new departures in American policy, the Roosevelt and Truman administrations had continued to try to strengthen inter-American bonds through creation of a genuinely multilateral American security system in the Western Hemisphere.

The idea of the "Western Hemisphere" and the vision of a special relationship among the countries in it has long existed in American writing and political discourse, but ideal and reality were very different. The United States tended to dominate the pre-war relations—primarily economic—among the nations and frequently used its military power to ensure domination. Once the Panama Canal had been dug,

* When Henry A. Wallace, Secretary of Agriculture and Vice-President under Roosevelt, gave early wartime recognition to the need for such a postwar program, he was deluged with ridicule: Congresswoman Clare Booth Luce (wife of *Life* Magazine publisher Henry Luce and later Ambassadress to Italy) labeled his ideas "globaloney," and the phrase "milk for hottentots" helped to dispose of the whole issue—until a few years later when Wallace's estimate of the situation appeared to have been correct.

allowing for easy passage between the west and east coasts of the United States, the Caribbean took on the strategic status of an American lake; the approaches to the Canal must be under American protection.

When trade, investment, and travel take place between those that are rich and those that are less rich, although both may benefit, the poorer may only feel exploited. This happened in Latin America. Moreover, the gains from trade too often went to a small group that dominated politically, and part of their continued ability to dominate lay in the wealth amassed from trade with the Colossus of the North.

In the 1930s the United States had tried to change the Latin American image of the United States, in which the Monroe Doctrine was equated with domination and exploitation. The United States, which renounced the use of military intervention, did practice what it preached when Mexico nationalized American oil properties in the late 1930s. The attempt to create a Western Hemisphere community, however, was hampered by the difference between strong and weak, rich and poor, and the enormous internal economic and social differences between the Latin American countries and the United States as well. Although the former vary greatly, they have the common heritage of a Hispanic and Catholic colonial past, with its ethos radically different from the Anglo-Saxon society to the north. The contrast is not only between Protestant and Catholic, but also between capitalist and aristocrat, civilian and military control of government, a more-or-less fluid, egalitarian society devoted to technology, and a stratified society characterized by a vast gap between the few rich and the many poor, especially the peasants.

The depression in the 1930s had a strong impact on Latin American countries since many of them depended on the export of a single raw material or commodity whose price was likely to vary radically on the world market. In spite of the spread of liberal ideas in the nineteenth century, the typical form of Latin American government remained a military dictatorship. Only in Argentina, Chile, Uruguay, and Brazil did a growing middle and professional class appear to create conditions for the growth of somewhat liberal political parties and a free press. The Mexican revolution that began in 1910, and lasted for decades, was a genuine social revolution, which brought the masses into political participation for the first time. It also inspired other groups throughout Latin America. But the depression brought an alliance between radicalism and mass movements with military power all through the area, and a growth of fascism and more or less fascist dictatorships: Italy, Spain, and Germany exemplified how mass politics could be harnessed to dictatorship rather than democracy, and their influence was strong. In response, left wing radicalism also grew. Only Chile, Uruguay, and Colombia maintained liberal forms of government. The Good Neighbor policy of the Colossus of the North had little effect on these developments, although the lowering of American tariffs through the Reciprocal Trade Agreements Act and United States creation of the Export-Import Bank, which helped finance American exports to the area, were of some aid in easing relations.

World War II helped even more by creating a rich market for the export of Latin American commodities. Under pressure from the United States and its allies and—after 1942—in response to the fairly certain defeat of the fascist powers, the left tended to gain power. Only in Argentina, whose exports of beef and wheat had long made it competitive with the United States, did a fascist form of government emerge with Peron's seizure of power in 1945.

With the war's end and the emergence of plans for a postwar United Nations world, the governments of Latin America and the United States shared interest in the creation of a stronger regional grouping. If the United States really intended to participate in a world organization, the votes of the Latin American states would mean something to it. If all the nations in the area voted as a bloc, the smaller states would thus have a louder voice in international politics. At a meeting in Mexico City in February and March 1945, the American states signed the Act of Chapultepec, which promised the creation of an inter-American security system. Thus armed, they proceeded to strengthen the regional provisions of the United Nations Charter at the San Francisco conference where they also joined with smaller states from other areas to broaden the authority of the General Assembly. But difficulties had arisen. The Mexico City conference had been limited to those "cooperating in the war effort," in order to exclude Argentina, which had given and continued to give aid and comfort to the Axis powers. The United States felt that Argentina had to participate in any regional system—otherwise Argentina might exert a strong counterpull for many Latin American states, and might head its own bloc. Still, the United States could hardly support Peron. In subsequent months severe diplomatic pressure was put on Peron by publishing documents proving his complicity with the Axis, and denunciation of him by the American Ambassador, Spruille Braden, who also encouraged opposition to Peron.

But the intervention failed; Peron survived the attempt to overthrow his military regime and, with the aid of the trade unions, he consolidated his power in October 1945. The United States was compelled to accept the situation and in return Peron made some conciliatory gestures. By August 1947, after several postponements, it became possible to convene the Inter-American Conference for the Maintenance of Continental Peace and Security at Rio de Janeiro. Here, after several unsuccessful Argentine attempts to weaken its terms, the American states drafted a security treaty binding themselves to settle their disputes by peaceful means, declaring that an attack on one of them by an outsider would be treated as an attack on all of them and, finally, setting up an inter-American security system in which a meeting of foreign ministers, by a two-thirds vote, could enforce sanctions against any American state committing aggression against another. The next year, at Bogota, Colombia, the same states drew up and signed the Charter of the Organization of the American States (OAS), which created a permanent multilateral political organization for the region. It set up a permanent Council at the Ambassadorial level (in Washington), created organs that would meet periodically (the Inter-American Conference and the Meeting of Consultation of Ministers of Foreign Affairs), made the already-existing Pan-American Union a permanent Secretariat for the OAS, and defined the relations of the OAS to various regional specialized and technical agencies. It spelled out the rights and obligations of American states and defined the machinery for the settlement of disputes. Thus, unlike NATO, where political and economic cooperation were aimed at creating military strength against an external enemy, the OAS was far more concerned with establishing a regional collective security system designed to settle quarrels among its members and prevent them from exploding into war.

The Rio Pact (passed pursuant to the Act of Chapultepec of 1945) and the Bogota Charter also represented in part attempts to reconcile the overwhelming economic and military power and influence of the United States with the desires of Latin states to be politically independent and legally sovereign. Nothing more than partial success could be hoped for in the endeavor.

While political and security relations were made multilateral, the United States also continued war-born bilateral military cooperation with Latin American states. Throughout the 1940s it continued to provide military training to their armed forces and military equipment on a modest scale. The action was presumably taken to strengthen the security of the Americas. But military aid appeared to ignore the fact that a well-equipped and trained military group has internal political significance far beyond its numbers in almost any Latin state, and in the years after World War II the military continued to play an active political role.

The Communist Bloc

Communization of Eastern Europe began well before President Truman's speech to Congress on March 12 calling for aid to Greece and Turkey. It was completed in the ensuing months, during which Russia also forbade the Eastern European countries to take part in the Marshall Plan. Czechoslovakia, whose coalition government still maintained a precarious balance of power, at first accepted the invitation to come to Paris, only to be informed by Stalin that such an act would be deemed unfriendly to the Soviet Union and a breach of the Pact of Friendship and Mutual Aid between the two as well.

From July to February 1948, the Communists maintained a constant political crisis in the hapless country. They discovered Fascist conspiracies, packed the leadership of trade unions and the police, and interfered with the activities of other parties and branches of the government that were not yet under Communist control. On February 12 non-Communist members of the government instructed the Communist Minister of the Interior to reinstate eight non-Communist Prague police chiefs whom he had planned to replace with Communists. When he refused, they resigned in protest, thus precipitating a governmental crisis. Russian interest in the affair was made clear with the arrival in Prague of former Soviet Ambassador Valerian Zorin, now a Deputy Foreign Minister. The parties that had brought the crisis to a head hoped to force an election—one the Communists would lose. Unfortunately, President Beneš, aware of the power of the Soviet Union, hesitated; so did leaders of the Social Democrats, one of the major parties. Detachments of Communist-led factory workers paraded through the streets of Prague while gangs of toughs occupied the ministries whose heads had resigned and the headquarters of the parties to which they belonged. Communist "action committees" sprang up all over the country; the police arrested prominent anti-Communists and accused them of conspiracy against the state; a Communist-armed workers' militia revealed itself; finally, the pro-Communist Minister of Defense made sure that the army remained neutral. The only other possible source of opposition—the Western Allies—were unwilling to act. They were caught by surprise, unable to fully foresee the outcome, and hesitant about what they could do. They knew they had little armed strength at hand, while the Red Army could easily intervene. Communist control of the press and radio ensured that the Communist party leaders' demands would be met: they insisted on the formation of a new government without the participation of the other parties and without any elections. President Beneš gave in on February 23. All the key posts in the new government were held by the Communists; a few representatives of the other parties chosen by the Communists were admitted.

On March 10, Foreign Minister Jan Masaryk, who with President Beneš had carefully worked out the policy of cooperation with the Soviet Union in order to keep Czechoslovakia a democratic bridge between East and West, was found dead in the courtyard of the Foreign Ministry. The death of Masaryk, son of the first great President-Liberator of Czechoslovakia, brought home the tragedy of Czechoslovakia as nothing else could have.

At the same time that Czechoslovakia was drawn into the Soviet camp, Finland, to the north, came under pressure. Like Czechoslovakia, Finland had been dominated by the Red Army in the course of military operations of World War II. Unlike Czechoslovakia (a "liberated" state), Finland had fought against Russia on the side of Germany. On September 19, 1944, it signed an armistice confirming the 1940 borders (whose establishment after the Winter War of 1940 had involved cession of certain Finnish territories to Russia). A Russian-dominated Allied Control Commission was established, with nominal British participation. Reparations were fixed at $300 million, and Finland ceded several military bases to Russia.

The peace treaty between Finland, Russia and Britain was signed at the Peace Conference at Paris on February 10, 1947, and the Russian Control Commission departed, leaving behind a coalition government in which the Communists played an important part. In this case the coalition government lasted and Finland implemented the terms of the peace treaty. In late 1947 and early 1948 Stalin pressed for a defensive alliance that would allow Soviet troops to move into Finland, if, in Soviet judgment, they might be needed to forestall a German or other attack that also threatened Russia. Under pressure, the Finnish government sent a delegation to Moscow. It agreed to a treaty of mutual friendship and assistance, some of whose terms were ambiguous, but which clearly prohibited Finland from entering into any alliance or coalition aimed at the other signatory. Russia subsequently decided that the Marshall Plan fell within the scope of this clause, and thus Finland did not participate. In this, as in other matters, the Finns moved carefully to avoid any provocation of the Russians; the

Communist party continued to operate within the framework of Finnish democracy.

The year 1947 also saw the birth of the Communist Information Bureau (or Cominform), with headquarters in Belgrade. The organization was part of a Soviet effort to tighten its control over the Communist parties of Europe; apparently the Red Army, the presence of Soviet secret police, and the constant journeying to and from Moscow of leading functionaries of the Communist parties, were insufficient. In 1947 there had been dissension among the party leaders on the question of participation in the Marshall Plan; Yugoslavia's Tito had resisted Soviet efforts to bring his regime under closer control.

Consequently, in late September 1947, a group of leaders of the European Communist parties were brought to a meeting in Poland, where they were required to report on their activities. Then the reports were criticized, and they were told how to act correctly. Then all agreed to the creation of the Cominform, which published a newspaper titled *For a Lasting Peace, For a People's Democracy*. Printed in Yugoslavia, it was actually subject to a stringent censorship from Moscow. While articles written by Communist leaders from all over the world were published, the censorship ensured that the Soviet-dictated line would be transmitted to all, and the Cominform served as another device to consolidate the bloc. In fact, it was a reincarnation in different form of the Communist International (or Comintern), an organization which until its dissolution in 1943 had also acted to coordinate the policies of every Communist Party under Soviet direction. Stalin had dissolved it to assure the Western allies of his good will, but also— probably—because he foresaw a different world situation in which the Communist movement would have a different place. The new Cominform was not merely an assembly of revolutionary and conspiratorial parties to be molded to Stalin's will; it was an organization many of whose participants were now the absolute rulers of their countries.

In the months after rejection of the Marshall Plan, the Communist countries began to adopt long-range development plans based on the Soviet model, and also oriented their trade more toward the Soviet Union. This was particularly true of countries like Czechoslovakia and Poland, and to a lesser extent, Hungary, all of whom had been trading more with the West in the years 1946 and 1947. In 1948 the Soviet Union sponsored the Council for Mutual Economic Aid (Comecon), presumably to coordinate the economic development of the Eastern European countries. But in fact it also had another purpose:

to help organize the boycott by Cominform countries of Communist Yugoslavia, which, in 1948, was forced to break with the Soviet Union. The consequences of this break were to be momentous in the years ahead.

The schism in the Communist bloc was a direct consequence of increased subjection of the parties to Moscow. All through 1948 and 1949 purges of "nationalist deviationists" took place in Eastern Europe; the break between Yugoslavia and the Soviet Union essentially represented the unwillingness of Marshal Tito to accept the degree of subjection demanded by Moscow, and the subsequent attempt by Moscow to purge him. In the complex Communist world the position of the single dominant Communist party is based on the claim that it, through its possession of Marxist-Leninist knowledge, is the only bearer of the Truth. Since it alone knows the Truth, competing parties, which could only reflect untruth, are unnecessary. But since Marxism-Leninism can unfortunately lead to many interpretations of what is going on and what should be done, the totalitarian leader must claim that only *he* is ideologically pure, that only *his* Marxist-Leninist interpretation is correct. Thus the claim of ideological purity is essential to buttress the claim to a monopoly of political power. Once this monopoly was challenged by Tito in 1948, he and the Soviet leaders were bound to engage in a round of denunciations of the purity of the others' Marxist-Leninism, and Tito, one of the most vehement and faithful of Communists in the past, became an "imperialist agent" in the eyes of the Kremlin. But the ideological charges simply veiled a struggle for power. Only later would the competing centers of Communist power, each claiming ideological correctness, become an important source of strain for the Soviet bloc.

The move against Tito came when Stalin was preparing to bring into line all the Communist governments of Eastern Europe. In the process of consolidating power and hastening economic recovery they had all come to terms with varying local conditions. Some moved slowly in collectivizing farms, conscious that they could not yet cope with a recalcitrant peasantry. Others, on their own initiative, were beginning a hasty industrialization. Now that the Cold War had intensified, however, Stalin was ready to solidify his control over the bloc. Tito—the most ardent of Communists—appeared also to have the strongest base of independent power. He had emerged as the strongest leader in the Balkans, and he had envisaged a Balkan federation. He had disputed Soviet criticisms of his economic policies and resisted infiltration of his administrative apparatus by Soviet agents who were being sent throughout the bloc to foster its consolidation.

The break came when letters sent to all Cominform members detailed a series of charges by Moscow against the behavior of the Yugoslav comrades and a demand that the Cominform investigate them. Yugoslav replies denied the validity of the charges—which involved such matters as mistreatment of and spying on Russian soldiers—and told the Russians they had been misinformed. Moreover, the Yugoslavs, justly fearing arrest, were unwilling to send a delegation of their top officials to discuss the matter. Such argument and arrogance could not be tolerated. At a June 1948 meeting of the Cominform in Bucharest, Yugoslavia was read out of the Communist bloc, and an appeal was launched to good Communists within Yugoslavia to take whatever action might be necessary to rectify the situation.

Stalin may have expected Tito to give way; he probably expected him to be overthrown from within. Neither happened. Arguing strenuously that he wanted to maintain good relations with the Communist party of the Soviet Union, Tito secured the support of his own party and people. A nationalist wave of support swept through Yugoslavia, particularly as other Communist bloc countries under Soviet direction brought pressures to bear on Tito in the months that followed. They initiated an economic boycott, carried out a worldwide campaign of anti-Tito propaganda, abrogated various treaties of assistance, and concentrated troops on Yugoslav borders. Late in 1949 the Soviet Union expelled the Yugoslav ambassador and the *chargé d'affaires.* Purges of other leaders suspected by Stalin of recalcitrance now proceeded apace, and the accusation of "Titoism" became common. But the Yugoslav regime remained firm. Tito at first hoped for reconciliation, and found it difficult to reorient his own world view. Once a steadfast member of the Communist bloc, he had now become an outcast, yet one who remained the firmest of Marxist-Leninist-Stalinists. Under the circumstances, however, he began to look to the West. At first he met only suspicion. Many observers felt that the break was a fraud, and that aid to Tito would only be a help to one Communist government among others. But in 1949, the Truman administration decided that aid to the Tito regime, which represented a real schism within the Soviet bloc, was worthwhile. In 1949, the Export-Import Bank extended loans to Yugoslavia totalling $55 million. Tito also received financial assistance from the International Bank and International Monetary Fund. Although Congress lodged certain objections, the United States extended more aid in subsequent years, both for capital investment, relief in time of drought, and, beginning in 1951, direct military aid.

One immediate consequence of the Yugoslav break was the collapse of the Communist guerrilla movement in Greece. A secondary consequence was the attraction that the continued existence of Tito's Yugoslavia exerted for Soviet-bloc members who wanted Communism without Russian domination and dictation. Tito seemed to prove that such a thing was possible and, therefore was always a threat to the idea of a monolithic bloc.

Developments in West Europe

The achievement of some measure of European cooperation, of economic recovery, and of the creation of NATO has already been recounted, since American initiatives to "contain" Russia within Eurasian rimlands concentrated first on Europe. But this was only one stage in a more complex development.

The growing split in Europe and the hardening of the Soviet sphere changed the position of Communist parties in Western European countries and affected their politics accordingly. There was no Communist problem in England, where, under the relatively stable two-party system now headed by the Labour government, the American initiative was looked on as fundamentally sound (if at times erratic). In Catholic, continental France and Italy, however, large Communist parties existed, and shared in governmental power. They had gained prestige and respectability during the war when the Nazi attack on the Soviet Union enabled them to combine Communism with patriotism and resistance to the Fascist and Nazi oppressors. They still hoped to triumph, for in France Communist boss Maurice Thorez headed the Ministry of Defense. But on May 4, 1947, some two months after the proclamation of the Truman Doctrine, the Communists were ousted from the governing coalition of MRP (Catholic), Socialist, and Communist. The Communist party had supported the revolt of the Vietminh movement against the French in far-off French Indochina; it seemed intolerable to have them in charge of the Ministry of Defense. Several months later, in November 1947, the Communist party staged a series of strikes through the Communist-controlled labor unions. Domestic conditions provided plausible excuses, but the strikes were designed to put Communists back into the Government. The police, however, reorganized by a Socialist Minister of the Interior, Jules Moch, maintained order and the strikes were broken. The labor unions split, and never again in the life of the Fourth Republic were there Communist ministers. In subsequent years, however, the Communist party was always able to obtain between a fifth and a quarter of votes in French elections; to have an equivalent part of the French Assembly permanently opposed to the government meant that right and center opponents of any subsequent French government could always count on Communist votes to help bring it down; but to reconstruct a new one was a different matter. Thus the position of the Communist party was a decisive factor in the continued weakness of governments in the Fourth Republic, and in its final demise.

In Italy, too, Communists had shared power with Socialists and Christian Democrats. June 1946 brought the end of the monarchy; December 22, 1947, brought the adoption of a new constitution. But in May 1947, as in France, the Communists were pushed into opposition, and as in France, November witnessed a wide series of Communist-led strikes and riots.

Although the strikes failed to topple the government and to force it to accept Communist participation, elections in April 1948 (the first under the new constitution) gave the Party one more chance: as the largest outside the Soviet Union, its leaders felt there was a real opportunity to win sufficient electoral support to make sure that no government could be formed without Communist ministers. The Catholic Church brought all its influence to bear in opposition; Italians in the United States barraged families in the "old country" with letters; the United States announced open support for various Italian demands for revision in the peace treaties. And the Christian Democrats won a decisive victory, gaining 307 seats to the Communists 182, with 80 seats going to other parties.

In Western Germany the Communist party always remained a negligible factor, and as political life renewed under the occupation, two parties came to dominate the political scene: the Christian Democrats and the Socialists. In the first general elections in 1949, these two parties polled 60 per cent of the vote and gained 67 per cent of the seats in the new German Parliament; in 1953, 74 per cent of the vote and 83 per cent of the seats; in 1957 and 1961, 82 per cent of the votes and 88 per cent of the seats. From the beginning the Christian Democratic party, under the leadership of Konrad Adenauer, dominated the government established in 1949, and the foreign policy of West Germany was Adenauer's foreign policy. He wanted to rebuild Germany economically, to tie it to some form of Western European unity, to receive American military protection, and to reunify Germany under conditions of free elections. In all but the last he was to have gratifying success.

The Berlin blockade had been a Soviet effort to stem the formation of a West German state; it only hastened the actions of the occupying powers. In September, 1948 a German parliamentary council met to draft a new constitution, and the military governors of the occupying powers met to draft a new occupation statute defining the limits within which the new constitution or "Basic Law" would operate. On May 5, 1949, the Basic Law was promulgated, and West Germany came into being, though still under certain limitations, chiefly concerning continued disarmament. Faced with this and the failure of the blockade, the Russians persuaded the Western powers to meet with them in Paris in return for lifting the blockade. But the May-June Foreign Ministers meeting did little more than rehearse familiar charges, and West Germany became a reality.

Within Western Europe, the American initiative of 1947 was greeted with mixed feelings. Still suffering from the ravages of the war, the people and many of their leaders were unwilling to accept that the world was in fact divided, even that another war threatened. It was easy to accept the view that *both* sides were responsible, and the Truman Doctrine, seen as a declaration of ideological warfare, was received with distaste. It was easy, many felt, for a prosperous United States, spared the destruction of the war and now armed with atomic weapons, to put forth this point of view. But to most Europeans, it was too much to take. The Marshall Plan, however, which first suggested breaching rather than widening the gap, was received with enthusiasm, though after Russian refusal the Communist parties of Western Europe did their effective best to bring it into disrepute.

In England there was somewhat less dissension, primarily because a Labour party was in power. Many of its supporters had long felt that it would be able to get along with the Soviets better than any Conservative government. But Foreign Minister Ernest Bevin came to accept very much the views of Churchill and the Americans on the Russian threat, and carried some of Labour's support with him; Conservative supporters by and large needed little convincing. In France, however, where de Gaulle's early efforts had been to patch up the pre-1914 alliance with Russia, where the chief preoccupation of foreign policy was to keep Germany divided and weak, where leadership in foreign policy was divided, opinion also remained divided. The Hungarian coup in early 1947 and the Czech coup of 1948 did shock the

French, but many could still rationalize them as responses to American aggressiveness. Ways must be found, it was argued, to reassure and get along with the Russians. In Italy there was much the same feeling among non-Communists, so that Italy was slow to join the North Atlantic Treaty Organization, which the Parliament did not ratify for several months.

Italy continued to be preoccupied with the fate of Trieste and its former colonies. The peace treaty had made Trieste a free territory whose governor was to be chosen by the United Nations Security Council in consultation with Italy and Yugoslavia. But months of irritated wrangling, proposals, and counterproposals produced no agreement on a governor, Yugoslavia charged that the West was attempting to turn Trieste into an imperialist base; the Western powers countered by proposing its return to Italy (only a few people failed to notice that this was done in March 1948, immediately before the first Italian elections). As a result, Trieste continued to be governed in two zones by the British and the Yugoslavs. With the break between Marshal Tito and the Soviet Union, the Western powers softened their support for Italian claims to the territory. There the matter rested until the mid-1950s.

The former Italian colonies of Libya, Eritrea, and Somaliland also remained a matter of dispute throughout this period. These last remnants of Italian ambitions to rival the empires of England and France, of Mussolini's tragi comic attempt to rebuild the Roman Empire, were placed under temporary British administration after the war. By the 1947 peace treaty they were to be subject to Four-Power decision; if the Four could not agree within a year, the matter would be referred to the United Nations General Assembly. Of course, they could not agree, and the General Assembly placed Libya under United Nations administration to await independence in 1952; it united Eritrea with Ethiopia on a federated basis; in 1950 Somaliland was made a United Nations trust territory with Italy as the trustee. But Somaliland was given a ten-year deadline, during which time it should be prepared for independence. Another indication of the prevailing view that Western control of non-Western areas should be continued *only* with a view to their development toward "self-government" and that the international community had an interest in their welfare, Italy's administration was supervised by an Advisory Council composed of Colombia, Egypt, and the Philippines.

The reluctance to accept the division of the world into two blocs—a widely evident view among groups not in power, but shared by those

in power—gave impetus to the move for European unity. The movement for some kind of unification had a long history and took various
forms. The combination of individual weakness, Russian pressures,
American inducements, and the desire to be more than merely part of
the American bloc brought it to fruition.

American initiatives, largely inspired by the idea of containment,
led to the creation of the Organization for European Economic Co-
operation and the European Payments Union—both fruit of the
Marshall Plan. The Americans supported Labour Foreign Minister
Bevin's view of the Russian military threat, and out of the Brussels
Treaty Organization and Western European Union they formed
NATO. But there were purely European moves that reflected different
aims.

Earliest of these was the Benelux Customs Union of Belgium, the
Netherlands, and Luxemburg. Their governments-in-exile in England
negotiated and signed the convention establishing the Union in September, 1944. Liberation of the countries raised enormous difficulties in
implementation, largely because Belgium emerged in better economic
shape than the Netherlands or Luxemburg. A series of negotiations
finally led on January 1, 1948 to the institution of a common tariff.
Continued differences, however, in internal taxation policies, economic
controls, and levels of economic activity necessitated further arduous
negotiations during the next few years. Eventually, in the late 1950s,
the creation of a broader economic unit in Europe largely superseded
Benelux.

On the political front, Winston Churchill's call for a "kind of
United States of Europe," delivered at Zurich University on September
19, 1946, helped to inspire the work of a host of new organizations
devoted to the idea. Their own activities, Cold War developments,
and popular response led to the signing, on May 5, 1949, of the Statute
of the Council of Europe. It received sufficient ratifications to come
into force in August.

The Council of Europe and the accompanying Committee of Ministers were essentially cooperative rather than supranational organs,
reflecting the reluctance of all the governments concerned to surrender
any of their powers. They all feared the consequences: the English
distrusted the instability of continental countries, the French were
fearful of a Europe which contained Germany but neither England nor
the Scandinavian countries, and the Germans were afraid a united
Europe would be meant to keep them subjugated. Socialist parties
all over, traditionally anticlerical, distrusted the fact that the European

movement was being supported by Christian Democratic, that is, Catholic parties. Yet some Socialist leaders, notably Paul-Henri Spaak of Belgium, were in the forefront of the movement.

The Council, composed eventually of some 180 delegates, was weighted roughly in terms of population: France, Britain and Italy held 18 seats, as did West Germany when it was admitted in 1951; countries like Belgium, Greece, Sweden, and the Netherlands had 6; Luxemburg 3, Norway, Ireland, and Denmark 4, and Turkey 8. Delegates were elected by their parliaments, and roughly represented the apportionment of parties within them except for the Communist parties, which were excluded by virtue of the Statute. Article I stated that all members must accept the rule of law and fundamental human rights and freedoms. Delegates sat neither by country nor party, but alphabetically, thus stressing their independence and responsibility only to the European idea. In contrast, the Council of Ministers was made up of the foreign ministers of the participating states; there was no question whom they represented.

The Council's basic purpose was to suggest ways of effecting European integration. Since it could only recommend, while governments disposed, a split rapidly developed between the Council and the Committee of Ministers: the Council charged that the Committee kept it from doing any useful work. Within the Council itself another split occurred between "federalists" and "functionalists"—those who wanted to develop a set of viable political institutions first, and those who wanted to build "from the bottom" and thus create forms of economic cooperation, common institutions with limited functions, all of which would eventually serve as the foundations for political organs.

Further developments hinged on Franco-German relations. The earliest French view had been of a postwar world in which Germany would be kept permanently weak and divided and in which the wartime coalition would be maintained and strengthened for that purpose. It was in pursuit of this aim that de Gaulle had signed his military alliance with the Soviet Union in 1944. But the world developed in a different way. Germany became a prize, and one that the United States and several European countries felt had to be rebuilt. As a result, the French were forced to revise their tactics. They were forced to accept the creation of West Germany, but they obtained the safeguard of an International Ruhr Authority, consisting of the United States, the United Kingdom, France, and the Benelux countries. Created in December 1948, it would allocate German coal through a system of consumption and export quotas, so that German industry would, at least, be under international controls during its reconstruction. The French went even further. In 1946 they had unilaterally included the coal-rich Saar region of Germany in a customs union with France. (The Saar, adjacent to the French border, was within the French zone of occupation of Germany.) Within the Saar they sponsored pro-French political movements, and on March 3, 1950, the Prime Minister of the Saar and the French Foreign Minister signed an agreement which virtually meant its economic annexation by France. It seemed none too soon to the French: in 1949 German steel production had exceeded that of France.

Yet German reconstruction proceeded so fast that to accommodate it French Foreign Minister Schuman had to do even more. He devised a scheme—the Schuman Plan—that would allow for German reconstruction and yet guarantee that it would pose no threat to France. The German and French coal and iron and steel industries would be pooled under the control of a high authority. Removed from the sovereignty of existing governments, the steel industry would no longer provide the foundation for military aggression of one against the other. The story of the negotiation and establishment of the European Coal and Steel Community comes later. As a French adaptation to the new unforeseen pattern of world politics, it was a stroke of genius. But on June 13, 1950, before the actual negotiations got under way, it produced an event that would have long-lasting repercussions: the British Labour Party stated it could not participate: "European peoples do not want a supranational authority to impose agreements." The European movement was now split. On the security level it comprised an Atlantic Community; on the political level it included Western Europe as a whole. But on the economic level, although cooperation among all the Western countries was guaranteed through the OEEC and EPU, the little Europe of the Six began to emerge.

The matter of *what* countries would constitute *what* Europe was complicated by the Scandinavian situation. There were, in the postwar years, discussions of some form of Scandinavian federation. But their outcome was bound to be limited. Finland, which in 1948 got rid of its Communist Minister of the Interior, had to tread warily to avoid provoking the Soviet Union. Norway and Denmark, however, were interested in Atlantic security, whereas Sweden, geographically in between and with a history of successful neutrality, preferred to follow traditional policy, especially since if Sweden remained neutral the Soviet Union would have no pretext to come to Finland's "aid." The Swedish government calculated that seventy divisions would be needed to overcome its army and air force and, since Sweden was not on the main Soviet route toward the West, it might be able to avoid hostilities if war broke out. Moreover, Sweden was one of the first of the small powers to calculate that the United States might well come to its aid even if it did *not* join an American-sponsored alliance. The United States tried persuasion, for American military men were unhappy about the fact that Swedish neutrality would release Soviet armed forces for use elsewhere. But the Swedes were adamant, and there was little opposition to the government's course. To maintain neutrality, Swedish armed forces were kept as well-equipped and trained as possible; by 1950 the Swedish air force was the fourth largest in the world, and Sweden was well on its way to equipping itself with air-raid shelters and underground production and storage facilities. Although weapons developments in the atomic age might render these obsolete and make it possible for the Soviet Union to simply deliver an ultimatum with which Sweden would have to comply, the government took its chances.

Finland was forbidden by the Soviet Union from taking part in the Marshall Plan. Sweden, however, became a party to it, and a member of the Council of Europe. But the Swedish government always maintained reservations about involvement in activities the Soviet Union would consider hostile. Norway and Denmark were fully involved, Swedish diplomatic efforts to keep them neutral having failed. But they were not privy to the new, smaller grouping of the Six.

Monetary stability is necessary to the successful functioning of a modern economy. The International Monetary Fund was designed to help stabilize international rates of exchange so that the international economy could function as it had failed to do during the 1930s. But it could not cope with the pent-up purchasing power and lack of goods in postwar countries. Inflation, with its concomitant effects— speculation, discouragement of investment, and encouragement of barter and black-marketing—plagued Western Europe during the postwar years. Belgium, with a relatively strong economic position, was able to stabilize its currency through a drastic monetary reform in 1946. Not for another two years were France and Italy, with Marshall Plan help, able to devalue and stabilize their currencies. The most dramatic reform took place in West Germany in June 1948 when occupation authorities replaced the old currency with a new one. Confidence in it so revived trade that within weeks goods began to reappear in store windows, and within a year and a half industrial production doubled. The reform was a major step in West German recovery in the face of Soviet pressures.

Devaluation of the English pound on September 18, 1949, made the biggest headlines. Nothing could better have symbolized the political and economic change in the world since the beginning of the twentieth century. In the nineteenth century, the pound sterling, solidly based on gold, was *the* international standard of value, and Britain the heart of the world trading system. Now Britain's exports could no longer finance her imports; foreigners would—if they could—trade pounds for dollars, and in the winter of 1947 Britain was on the verge of bankruptcy. American interim aid and the Marshall Plan helped tide it over, while American assumption of British responsibilities in the Middle East lessened overseas expenditures. But the British economy, despite the austerity program of the Labour government, was still in trouble. To reduce imports and increase the exports which could pay for them, the value of the pound was changed from $4.03 to $2.80.

It was no simple matter; the basic situation was complicated by the British decision that it must repay in full its wartime debts to Commonwealth countries, as well as a host of internal factors. The final pressure for devaluation came as people began to speculate that the British *would* devaluate the pound. Once such speculation occurred, people deferred purchases of British goods, since devaluation would mean they would get them cheaper. At the same time they tried to divest themselves of holdings of pounds sterling, which might be worth less in the immediate future. But Britain had to continue importing, and pay for its imports with holdings of foreign currencies, while suddenly earning less. The government could have either tried to convince people it would not devalue, thereby encouraging them to resume purchases and to hold British pounds, or it could devalue. It chose the latter course, and thus dramatized the end of an era in world politics.

War in the Middle East

During the period, 1947–1950, European reconstruction began in earnest, colored by an anti-Soviet tinge and made possible by American support. In the Middle East, however, the central fact of political life had nothing to do with either Communism, the Russians, or the rebuilding of a previous existing structure. Rather it was the creation of a new state, Israel. All the Arab states were involved; to their leaders, whether by conviction or reluctant expedience, Israel became the focus of political life, and the exacerbated national resentments against the West were directed against its existence.

The United Nations Special Committee on Palestine (see p. 66), reporting to the regular session of the Second General Assembly in September 1947, delivered a majority and a minority report. The majority recommended a partition of Palestine into an Arab and a Jewish state linked in a United Nations-supervised economic union with Jerusalem as a separate entity. The minority, composed of India, Iran, and Yugoslavia, warned that the Arab states would not accept an independent Jewish state, and proposed instead a single federated state, into which immigration would be limited. By a vote of 33 to 13, with 10 abstentions, the Assembly adopted the partition plan. It recommended that a United Nations Commission assume administrative authority from the British to effect partition, that the Security Council meet any threat to the peace represented by attempts to alter the partition plan by force, that the Economic and Social Council assume responsibility for bringing about the economic union, and that the Trusteeship Council be assigned the administration of Jerusalem.

But the plans were never carried out. Britain, fearful of further encouraging the anti-Western bias of Arab nationalism, failed to turn over administration of Palestine before surrendering the mandate. In the meantime terrorism—by both Arab and Jew—increased, and Palestine became a battleground. On May 14, with the withdrawal of the last British garrisons, the state of Israel was proclaimed; it was immediately recognized by President Truman. Just as promptly, Egyptian columns began to enter from the south, Transjordanian and Iraqi armies from the east, and Lebanese and Syrian forces began to move in the north. But because the more cautious American State Department shared British apprehensions about Arab hostility—fears prompted partly by the growing American interest in oil—the Security Council faltered. It decided that it lacked the constitutional authority to enforce a political settlement recommended by the Assembly. At one point the United States even tried to get the United Nations to abandon partition—which the United States had supported—and work out a trusteeship arrangement.

Consequently, when the Arab invasion of Palestine took place, the United Nations resorted to *ad hoc* measures and established a United Nations mediator whose task was to bring about a cease-fire and political settlement. The thankless task was delegated to Count Folke Bernadotte, President of the Swedish Red Cross. The first truce went into effect on June 11, 1948. Both sides received some respite, but the Jews took more advantage of it to consolidate their governmental and military administrative apparatus. Fighting broke out again within four weeks; neither side had been willing to make the necessary concessions—the Jews because Palestine had been invaded and they felt themselves gathering strength, the Arabs because they would now lose face if exaggerated early reports of their victories were revealed to be false. The renewed fighting, which lasted ten days, resulted in a series of Israeli victories that left their armies in control of much more territory than had been allotted to them under the partition plan. A second truce gave rise to a series of secret meetings between Arab technicians and Jewish leaders. They reached armistice agreements marking out lines based roughly on the location of each side's troops at the time of the truce, with demilitarized zones on either side and a Mixed Armistice Commission of representatives of both sides and of the United Nations to supervise the carrying out of the armistice provisions.

Both sides were forced by outside pressures to accede to the armistice. On the part of the Jews, facing Arab leaders who had made grandiose statements about driving the Jews into the sea, there was a strong sentiment for renewal of the war to convince the Arabs there was a need for real peace. But Israel was warned of possible sanctions; in September 1948, shortly after he had recommended an alteration of the demarcation lines in favor of the Arabs, Count Bernadotte was assassinated by men presumed to be Jewish extremists. After the shock, more moderate voices prevailed. An American, Ralph Bunche, took over the task of mediator. In 1949, when the armistice agreements were completed, Israel was admitted to the United Nations.

The short war left a bitter legacy. Six hundred thousand Arab refugees crowded camps around the borders of Israel, and in future years hundreds of thousands of Jews whose homes had been in Arab states left to enter Israel. The Arab states, claiming a right of repatriation for these refugees did nothing to relieve their misery, since such action might give weight to the argument that they would and could be resettled in Arab lands. Henceforth they and other Arabs were continually taught that it was their duty to help destroy Israel; no peace was possible, and the burden of refugee relief was assumed by the United Nations.

The war also revealed the weakness of the Arab states and the divisions among Arab leaders, and did much to discredit them at home and abroad. None would commit his armies wholly to the fight: each was afraid the others would then take advantage of him. Only the British-trained and equipped Arab Legion, which belonged to King Abdullah of Transjordan, really fought well.

Moreover King Abdullah then proceeded to alienate other League members by unilateral annexation of the Arab remnants of Palestine at a time other League members were promoting a new all-Palestine Arab government. Thus he doubled the population of his kingdom, which he renamed the Hashemite Kingdom of Jordan. Heavily dependent on British aid, Abdullah nevertheless emerged as a new leader in the Arab world, devoted to the creation of a unified Fertile Crescent through union with Iraq and Syria. But Abdullah was the only Arab leader who dared consider the idea of peace with Israel and the only one who remained friendly to Britain. Consequently he was assassinated in a mosque in Jerusalem in 1951, and rule passed first to his son, Talal, then to the young Hussein. Both vied with other Arab leaders in proclamations of fidelity to the idea of destruction of Israel.

Although Arab reactions to the Palestine War stimulated ideas of real Arab unity, it also discredited the Arab League, which had been formed in 1945. It increased Arab distrust of the West, particularly the United States. Without the West, Arabs argued, Israel could never have come into being: it represented the new—but last outpost of—imperialism. In subsequent years the Soviet Union—which had supported partition—by simply switching to an anti-Israeli position became the natural friend of any Arab who saw the necessity of destroying Israel.

Finally, the war did much to help weaken leaders of Arab governments whose bungling and corruption had helped bring about the loss of Palestine. In Egypt it strengthened the determination of groups of officers already set to cleanse the Egyptian body politic. In Syria it produced the *coup d'état* of March 1949 by Army Colonel Husni Zaim, who in turn was deposed and executed in August by Colonel Sami Hinnawi. Hinnawi lasted only until the end of the year, when Lieutenant Colonel Adib el-Shishakli assumed the power that he was to hold until deposed in 1954. The political turbulence marked definite shifts in foreign policy. Zaim favored the Fertile Crescent grouping of Jordan, Iraq, and Syria. This was favored by the British, still strong in Jordan and Iraq, but opposed by the United States, whose oil investments in Saudi Arabia prompted it to side with King Saud, an Arab who feared the strength of a Fertile Crescent grouping. Hinnawi was pro-Egypt, but el-Shishakli switched back to a pro-Fertile Crescent policy. The el-Shishakli regime became violently anti-American as continued American support went to Israel. Disarray of the Arab lands was complete.

Independence in Asia

The weaknesses of postwar Europe that impelled new American commitments in 1947 also forced European states to hasten their surrender of control in Asia. In the 1947–50 period Ceylon, Burma, India, Pakistan, and Indonesia all became independent, while the French attempt to hold onto Indochina required a greater and greater military effort.

The small island of Ceylon off the southern tip of India offered many problems, not the least of which was the status of a large part of the working population—Tamils from south India—who moved fairly freely back and forth. Other groups in Ceylon discriminated against them (they had only a limited suffrage compared to full suffrage for the Buddhist majority and Moslem, British, and Dutch minorities), and relations with India were bad as a result of the discrimination. Self-government in all but matters of external affairs and defense came first, then the Act of Parliament granting independence, and in February of 1948, with the signing of a defense treaty with Britain, Ceylon became a full-fledged Dominion within the British Commonwealth of Nations. In October the capital city of Colombo was host to a conference convened to discuss economic and political problems of Southeast Asia. From this conference came the important mutual-aid program known as the Colombo Plan, to which both the British and Americans subsequently contributed.

In Burma (see pp. 69–70), British attempts to move by easy stages toward independence were rejected by nationalists. But internal chaos verging on civil war made Aung San, leader of the catch-all anti-Fascist People's Freedom League, negotiate on terms that might include a military alliance with Britain. To do so, he was forced to expel one of the many Communist factions from the AFPFL, and as a result he and six of his colleagues were assassinated. U Nu, who took over the responsibilities of prime minister, negotiated complete independence for Burma, though Britain retained access to certain bases. In January 1948, Burma became a new state.

But internal chaos followed when minority groups revolted and the small potential governing elite splintered into irreconcilable factions. Former anti-Japanese guerrilla fighters contributed to the fratricidal warfare. Patiently, combining force and inducement through a broad welfare program, U Nu helped pacify his country. By 1951 he felt he could risk general elections. But in the meantime a sobering sense of reality concerning the state of the Burmese economy had replaced the early optimism of independence.

The story of Indian independence and its aftermath has already been told (Chapter 3, pp. 66–69). Further to the east the 1947–50 period saw the struggle for independence continue in French Indochina and in Indonesia. In French Indochina the nationalist movement had come under the leadership of a Communist, Ho Chi Minh; the Indonesian nationalist leadership was non-Communist. Therefore, in Indochina, the French made no attempt to come to terms with Ho. Instead they tried to create an opposition government under the Emperor Bao Dai, a playboy who had collaborated with the Japanese, and who preferred the Riviera to his own country. They found some unrepresentative Vietnamese who were willing to support him; the mass of the people, insofar as they were politically aware, did not. Within France left-wing parties pressed for more negotiations with the Vietminh, but they were overruled by right and center groups. As Communist victories mounted in China, and as French policy in Indochina continued, the Communists gradually established a firm hold over the resistance. The French Government could now represent its effort as a part of the overall Western policy of containment.

In Indonesia, Dutch belief that their colony was too primitive for self-government was reinforced by anger at reports of atrocities committed against Dutch civilians and resentment against a revolt by an "ungrateful" people. These attitudes clashed with the facts of power, however: the Dutch Government lacked the resources completely to subdue the islands, and, in 1946 it agreed to a federal union of Holland and the Republic of Indonesia. Presumably the Republic would be only one of several states in the islands that had been the Dutch East Indies, but the Indonesians wanted more—a treaty between two sovereign powers, with the Republic having jurisdiction over all the islands. The federal union, they were sure, would merely perpetuate Dutch rule.

In March 1947, at Linggadjati, the two parties signed an agreement defining the terms of federal union. Both made some concessions and both expressed considerable optimism. But all through 1947 and 1948 the two parties tried merely to improve their relative power positions in order to change the consequences of the agreement. The Dutch moved in more troops and blockaded the Indonesian nationalists, while the Indonesians tried to build wider political support both at home and abroad. In mid-1947, Dutch troops went into action to carry out what were described officially as "police measures of a strictly limited character," but were actually designed to narrow the area in which the Republic had real jurisdiction. During a cease-fire they tightened their hold on newly gained areas and created new states within them, and then, in December 1948, struck again. This time the attack was based on an estimate that all organized resistance could be crushed and the Republic would crumble.

Two factors determined the subsequent Dutch failure. First, within Indonesia, support had grown for the Republic, and political groups that had favored federation on the basis of the diversity of the islands now switched to the Republican cause. Thus passive and active resistance proved to be a severe financial and military drain on the Dutch.

But in the second place, the outside world manifested too much opposition to the Dutch venture. The first cease-fire had resulted from a combined Indian-Australian appeal to the Security Council. Here the whole matter became too public for Dutch taste. The United Nations rejected their claim that the whole problem was merely one of domestic jurisdiction—a claim supported only by England, France, and Belgium, also colonial powers—and the United Nations-sponsored cease-fire was buttressed by a United Nations Consular Commission, while a Committee of Good Offices sought to bring the parties to terms. When the truce it arranged aboard the USS *Renville* broke down with the second Dutch attack, events moved apace. The Committee of Good Offices was reestablished as the United Nations Commission on Indonesia, with a broader mandate to make recommendations for "the establishment of a federal, independent and sovereign United States of Indonesia." In the meantime in New Delhi Prime Minister Nehru of India had sponsored a conference of Asian and Middle Eastern states to recommend Indonesian independence, and had threatened to bring the matter before the United Nations General Assembly. These pressures, combined with the continued cost of the military action, brought a change of government in the Netherlands, one more prone to a change in policy. The last straw was American withdrawal of Marshall Plan aid destined for use in Indonesia.

The Dutch bowed to circumstances and agreed at a Round Table Conference in The Hague, August 23 to November 2, 1949, to a transfer of authority from the Netherlands to the Republic of the United States of Indonesia, the two to be joined in a union under the Dutch Crown, in emulation of the British Commonwealth of Nations. The outlook for the future was not particularly bright: the United States of Indonesia was beset with difficulties from the beginning. The provisions it had accepted for special treatment of Dutch economic interests in Indonesia were likely to cause intense irritation, and the fate of Western New Guinea (West Irian, as the Indonesians called it) was unsettled. The Indonesians claimed it as a "natural" part of the Republic; the Dutch argued that it had no ethnic, cultural, or national relationship. But at least independence had been achieved.

Western attitudes toward the Indonesian affair differed from those toward Indochina for two reasons. Geography played a part—Indochina was directly on the Eurasian rimland, while Indonesia was not. Second, Indonesian leadership remained non-Communist. In fact, there, as in Europe and other parts of Asia, the Russian reaction to America's world-wide initiatives had resulted in direct Communist action against popular nationalist leadership. From mid-September to mid-November 1949, bitter fighting occurred between Communist-led units and troops loyal to the Republican leaders, Sukarno and Mohammad Hatta. In the end, loyal army forces suppressed the insurrection.*

In China, the 1947–50 period revealed that early Nationalist successes in their campaigns to retake the north were based only on an illusion of strength. July 4, 1947 marked the end of an era of attempts to negotiate, to establish temporary truces, and to reach accommodations: the Nationalist government proclaimed the Communists outlaws. In the meantime, however, the military initiative passed from the government to the Communists, who began a series of successful military offenses early in the year. Bad morale among Nationalist troops, supply failures, the hostility of the local populace in the north whom Nationalist garrisons had treated like conquered people, all contributed to the debacle. Continued economic deterioration and government weakness in dealing with it led to increased inflation, speculation, corruption, and the alienation of most groups that might have supported the government. Intellectuals whose attempts to form rival parties to the Kuomintang had been frustrated turned to support the Communists. American military missions, surveying the situation, were unanimous in their insistence that military aid could accomplish little without drastic administrative and economic reforms; but the Nationalist government appeared unable to carry them out.

The Nationalist government entered the civil war with a three-to-one ratio in its favor of troops, territory, and population, and an even greater preponderance of industrial potential. It received American economic and military aid and diplomatic support. But continued

---

* The Communist Party of India had attempted such a direct action campaign at roughly the same time, but was also crushed by vigorous government action. Significantly, these attempts at Communist armed uprisings took place soon after similar attempts in West Europe: the resort to direct action appeared to have been well-coordinated; it was also a total failure, not to be repeated.

knowledge that such support could have at best a limited effect led the United States to try to use the aid as a lever for prying reforms from the Kuomintang. The effort failed. Larger measures, such as a massive military intervention, were never contemplated in the face of Congressional unwillingness to spend more, in the light of heavy commitments to Europe, and in view of the very real possibilities that such an intervention might fail, might further alienate the Kuomintang from the people, and could well provoke large-scale Soviet intervention. Russia never did much to help the Communists beyond maneuvering in Manchuria, and its actions there and Stalin's private utterances to high-ranking Communists reveal that under the circumstances Soviet leaders did not expect much from the Chinese Communists. But the United States had to face the problem that this attitude might change; the possibility that it would seemed very real.

In 1948, reorganized Communist troops cleared Manchuria of Nationalists, depriving them of much of their materiel and destroying some of their best troops. In the early months of 1949 the Nationalist retreat became a rout, the capital was moved from one city to another as each in turn fell to the Communist "People's Liberation Army." In 1949, Chiang retired from the government. Elements in the Kuomintang felt that without him it might still be possible to negotiate with the advancing Communists. The effort failed; the will to fight was gone, and in the autumn of 1949, having resumed the presidency, Chiang ferried as much as he could of his army to Formosa, ninety miles from the mainland. In the face of the extraordinary collapse before the Communist onslaught, most people expected that within a year the 600,000-man demoralized and poorly equipped army on Formosa would also suffer defeat.

But there was a pause. In October the new Communist regime proclaimed itself the People's Republic of China and established its capital at Peking, imperial capital of the Manchu Dynasty. In this way it established its link with the old China broken by the Kuomintang, who had tried to turn Nanking into a new capital. Mao Tse-tung outlined the position of the new regime: it would be essentially Stalinist. Agriculture would be collectivized, heavy industry developed, and counter-revolutionaries ruthlessly suppressed. For an indefinite period the regime would be a multiclass dictatorship, led by the Chinese Communist party and composed of a coalition of representatives of workers, peasants, the national bourgeoisie, and petty bourgeoisie. Minor democratic parties would be allowed to exist within the framework of the united front. But on the international scene there would be no doubt of the Chinese stance: China would belong to the Socialist camp led by the Soviet Union. Late in 1949 the regime began its preparations to complete the liberation of Formosa, now called Taiwan, and began also to aid Ho Chi Minh in Indochina. In December Mao Tse-tung and his Premier and Foreign Minister Chou En-lai went to Moscow to negotiate the formal ties that would bind them to the Soviet Union.

They went to Moscow in different circumstances than most other Communist leaders. Although Russian participation had helped defeat Japan, the Chinese Communists had obtained power by their own efforts, not through the Soviet Red Army. But they desperately needed aid, and the Soviet Union was already established in Manchuria by the terms of the Yalta agreements. The result was compromise on both sides. The Soviet Union extended credits of $300 million; it would turn back the port of Dairen to China immediately and return its share of the Manchurian railways and Port Arthur by 1952; it signed the Sino-Soviet Treaty of Friendship, Alliance, and Mutual Assistance, and agreed to provide military and economic advisers. But the loan was strictly a loan, and repayment would have to start in 1954. Moreover, the Chinese accepted a series of joint stock companies in the fields of civil aviation, mineral and petroleum extraction, and shipbuilding and repair, similar to those through which the Soviet Union dominated the economies of the Eastern European countries.

The Chinese Communists were thus partially dependent on Russia; if they were to make any progress in reconstructing and modernizing China's society and economy, they would need massive amounts of capital that would not be forthcoming from Western powers and would be hard to generate internally. But their victory in China brought a dramatic change to all of Asia: now the Communist bloc bordered troubled areas like Indochina and Burma, and extended to the undefined frontier area between China and India. The victory put the future of Formosa in doubt and brought fear to Japan. Only time would tell whether Communist China would act strictly in concord with the Russians, and whether the new Chinese rulers would be able to consolidate their position: both issues posed puzzling problems for the policy-makers of other states.

The United Nations in a Divided World

In the years before 1950 the United Nations system never operated as its planners had originally hoped. The peace treaties that were to have delineated the world map, to be preserved by the United Nations security system, had not changed the situation. The agreements that would have placed military contingents at the disposal of the Security Council for purposes of collective security were not forthcoming, and the necessary unanimity of the great powers on the Security Council had vanished in the Cold War. Economic dislocations were so much greater than had at first been realized that the escape clauses in the International Monetary Fund were the ones most resorted to. Negotiations for the International Trade Organization, the third of the great international economic organizations, dragged on; but the same factors that restricted the use of the I.M.F. and made the International Bank for Reconstruction and Development inadequate, delayed signature of the I.T.O. treaty. It, too, became riddled with escape clauses, and in the end it was never ratified.

Moreover, the protracted disarmament negotiations had bogged down; indeed, they had turned into an effort to achieve stabilization through rearmament. The Baruch Plan seemed out of the question; the Soviet Union had conducted a propaganda campaign to ban the bomb and then shifted policy to support international control through the Security Council after all weapons had been destroyed. Overwhelming General Assembly support for the Baruch Plan brought no further modification in the Soviet position, and it became doubtful that, given the current international situation, the American Congress would have accepted the international ownership and management set forth in the Baruch Plan. The great powers had come to act outside the channels of international diplomacy provided by the United Nations: the programs of American aid to Europe and the creation of NATO to provide for Western security against the Soviet Union, indicated how little the powers relied on the United Nations.

Still, the United Nations organization had played an important role in a number of the developments so far detailed—though not the role envisioned for it by many of its supporters, nor one always popular with its member nations. In the Palestine situation, on the Greek borders, in Indonesia, in the secret negotiations that ended the Berlin blockade, the United Nations had provided mediation, fact-finding, and face-saving formulas for ending the wars. In the fields of technical cooperation and of supervision of the trust territories, work immensely useful to UN members and the trust territories had begun. As the breach between the great powers enhanced the inherent weakness of the Security Council system, the energetic Norwegian Secretary-General, Trygve Lie, used all the resources of his office to try to ease conflicts between the powers. Rather than remain a quiet international civil servant, heading a staff that provided secretarial and translating services for international conferences, he had seized upon the diplomatic potentials of his office. When the Communist Chinese came into power, he took the initiative in drafting a memorandum suggesting that a country that refused to recognize the new regime could nevertheless vote for its membership in international bodies. This was part of an overall effort on Lie's part to break the diplomatic stalemate that had developed in the five years since the end of the war, and had brought the world to the brink of another war. In the course of this effort he visited world capitals, urged a new course of action on world leaders, and sketched a "Twenty-Year Program for Achieving Peace through the United Nations." But 1950 brought his endeavor to nought.

In one area the United States had given the United Nations General Assembly a task with which it could not cope. American authorities decided to cast off the burden of occupying South Korea in 1947 and the General Assembly created a United Nations Temporary Commission to oversee elections to be held throughout Korea. But the Soviet bloc refused to cooperate, the Commission was denied access to North Korea, and eventually, under American prodding, the Commission supervised elections in South Korea alone. Other states were reluctant to accept them as valid. It seemed that in still another area of the world the warborn borders were being reinforced rather than eliminated. Nevertheless, by a vote of 4 to 2 the Commission declared that the elections in the south met standards set by the General Assembly, and on December 12, 1948, the Assembly held that the new regime was the lawful government of South Korea. It then appointed a new United Nations Commission on Korea to report on the transition to independence and also to try to unite Korea. The efforts at unification were again in vain. The Soviet Union, however, announced withdrawal of its occupation forces in the north (leaving behind it a Soviet equipped and Soviet-trained North Korean army and joint Soviet-Korean companies to control main centers of the economy), and the United States then felt constrained to withdraw its own unpopular and relatively weak occupation forces in the south. In speaking of unification, both sides took a threatening tone, and during 1948 and 1949 the United Nations Commission kept an uneasy watch on border forays.

The Atomic Bomb, Military Strategy, and the Balance of Power

In the early years of containment, American military policy was based primarily on the atomic bomb. Although the NATO commitment of the Truman administration called for an increase in the number of American troops in Europe, the pressures to keep the military budget low and traditional American views of warfare forced the administration to rely primarily on the Air Force and its capacity to deliver an atomic strike against Russia to deter the Soviets from military expansion. The bomb was to compensate for the Russian superiority in manpower and materiel: Russian armed forces were variously estimated at between three and five and a half million well-equipped men. (Geographical considerations meant that dependence on massive retaliation involved building or expanding air bases around the Russian perimeter, a policy that gave the Soviet Union handy and most useful ammunition for the charge of American imperialism.)

This overall policy rested on one basic assumption: that the Russians would need a long time to make an atomic bomb. But, on September 23, 1949, both the White House and Downing Street issued announcements confirming rumors that an atomic explosion had been detected in Siberia. The estimates concerning the time required for the Russian development had been wrong. One reaction was the opinion, widespread and persistent, that the barbaric and unfree Russian Communists could not have done the job themselves, but must have stolen "the secret." More responsible opinion, however, was concerned with another question: How long would it take the Russians to turn one atomic explosion into the actual manufacture of bombs and to have the means of delivering them? And what were the implications for Western strategy of containment and of reliance on American atomic bombs? Would the United States really attack the Soviet Union in response to a Russian drive on some perimeter region if this involved the possibility of direct Russian retaliation on the United States? Would not Russian possession of the bomb mean that war would no longer be limited to a retaliatory attack upon Russia? Could the "in-between" countries of Europe afford such a war?

One answer came in the growth of "neutralism" in smaller countries—the view that it was better to try to remain outside the military blocs sponsored by both major powers. In the United States, newspaper columnist Walter Lippmann devoted an article to the "Breakup of the Two Power World." The new Russian weapon would make smaller countries realize that the atomic bomb no longer promised protection as it had during the period of the American monopoly; instead it promised destruction. The desire to rely less on American protection was bound to be strengthened. Smaller countries would try to escape the conflict between the two superpowers, and let them fight things out for themselves. Neutralists in other countries echoed Lippmann's words, adding only that the new course might enable them to act as mediators between the United States and the Soviet Union, as some had hoped to be able to do five years earlier.

The year 1950 would have to bring some reevaluation of the course so far followed.

Conclusion

Two opposing trends dominated the years 1947–50: development of a bipolar world, and continued breakup of old European empires. The first trend seemed the crucial one; in the United States as well as the Soviet Union bipolarism came to be accepted as the correct world view. For the Soviet leaders there was the "Socialist camp" and the "imperialist camp." To Americans there was the Soviet bloc and the "free world." People in other countries held more varied views. Yet for the moment, as the superpowers faced each other, other voices were barely heard.

The United States, after a faltering start, had decisively entered the world arena on the basis of this world view and had reversed a century and a half of policy to take the lead in building a military coalition against Russia and assuming large-scale commitments for economic reconstruction and development outside the Soviet bloc. Its intervention had helped to save a bankrupt Europe, now beginning to show signs of vitality. Yet every step had provoked discussion: What would successful containment lead to? Was it to be an end in itself; if so, how long must it last and at what expense? Was it supposed to lead to the freeing of people under Communist domination? If so, what would be the response to a situation like Yugoslavia's? The commitments of containment had brought major constitutional changes to the American government, and each of these had occasioned further argument. The discussions had even led people to wonder if the American form of government was suited to the needs of consistent, unsentimental foreign policy. Had de Tocqueville been right in the nineteenth century? "Foreign politics," he wrote, "demand scarcely any of those qualities which a democracy possesses; and they require, on the contrary, the perfect use of almost all those faculties in which it is deficient . . . a democracy is unable to regulate the details of an important undertaking, to persevere in a design, and to work out its execution in the presence of serious obstacles. It cannot combine its measures with secrecy and it will not await their consequences with patience." He was frequently cited in the years under review. The English writer J. B. Priestley wrote that being in the company of the

United States was "like being locked in a house with a whimsical, drunken giant." *

There was no question that European governments wanted and welcomed American commitments. But the recipients of aid had lost what had been a high status, and as older, more experienced, but impoverished relatives, they could hardly be expected to welcome charity without resentment or criticism. Americans who expected gratitude were sadly misled. Other Americans, more sophisticated and understanding, nevertheless failed to realize how hard it was for Europeans to accept the break with Eastern Europe. Many Europeans rejected the idea that so long as Communist governments existed, the breach would persist, and looked instead to an eventual reestablishment of useful relations with Soviet-bloc countries.

Yet developments within the Soviet sphere—the hardening of the bloc and the Czech coup—hardly augured well for this view. Yugoslavia had escaped Soviet domination, but people had yet to understand what this might mean for bipolarism. Some, failing to see different situations within the Communist countries, hoped that it might serve as a spur to others. Unfortunately, one effect of the Yugoslav break with Russia was to hasten Russia's extension of control over the other members. China appeared to have joined the bloc; yet its leaders had fought their own way to power with little Soviet help, and from the outset some analysts hoped that China might follow the way of Tito. A widely held view in the United States, however, was that Tito was still a Communist and a dictator, and therefore his defection was no victory for the free world. In this view, too, the Chinese Communist success signified Russian enslavement of the Chinese people whom the United States had long befriended and fought for. How bipolar was the world? The disagreements persisted. Official United States view had hardened into bipolarism; yet the Truman administration acted to help Marshal Tito defy Stalin.

In the five years after the end of the war Russia had tried to intervene in areas outside its control: Iran, Turkey, Libya, Greece, the Ruhr in Germany, Japan, Berlin, and less directly, through Communist parties, in Italy, France, India, Indonesia, and elsewhere. These attempts had met with failure and provoked the hardened Western position. Stalin had therefore sought some settlement. But so long as each major power persisted in proclaiming as its ideal the ultimate destruc-

---

* "You Worry the World," *Magazine of the Year*, October 1947, cited in Harold and Margaret Sprout, *Foundations of National Power*, 2nd Revised Edition, Van Nostrand (New York, 1951), p. 415.

tion of the other's form of government and society, any settlement was difficult to reach.

Implications of the second major trend, decolonization, were just as hard to discern. In the official Communist view, the new states had not left the "imperialist camp," since they were led by "bourgeois nationalists." American leaders did not give too much thought to areas outside the main spheres of conflict with the Soviet Union; they accepted the liberal view that empires and colonies must come to an end and therefore supported independence for Indonesia, Burma, India, and others. They tended to see colonial conflicts in terms of the benefit that might redound to the Communists if colonial countries tried to suppress nationalist revolts.

But American policy-makers had had to begin to face a major dilemma: with great difficulty they had conceived an alliance with a Europe they were helping to regenerate. At the same time they were supporting colonial revolts against European countries. They could hardly expect cheers from their allies. The French, fighting in Indochina, tried to convince their American allies that this, too, was part of the overall battle to contain the Communist bloc on the Eurasian rimlands; the Americans, although seeing merit in the French argument, tried to persuade them to make greater concessions to non-Communist nationalism in Indochina.

The Soviet Union, having abandoned many of its efforts to expand directly into areas outside the bloc, and having failed in its main attempts to use large-scale Communist party subversion, turned primarily to propaganda. Its chief target, naturally, was the United States, which was painted as a war-mongering imperialist state, brandishing its atomic weapons and bent on resurrecting a vengeful Nazi Germany. Its propaganda was often successful. It spoke to a world in revolutionary upheaval, and it was easy for Russia to support revolution with little thought to the consequences, while the Western countries, trying to maintain order or bring about orderly change, were in an inherently conservative position. In France Communist propaganda did much to discredit the Marshall Plan among the mass of the population by asserting that the benefits of the Plan went only to the rich. Since the Plan did, in fact, channel its funds into capital reequipment and renovation, its immediate effects were not apparent to the farmer, worker, or consumer, and the Communist arguments appeared valid.

Development of bipolarity hampered the United Nations even more than did the basic, inherent weaknesses in the United Nations system. The main political developments of these years took place outside the

United Nations framework, where the Security Council, in particular, found its work paralyzed by the bipolar confrontation.

By 1950 the world was in a precarious state. Polls showed that, only five years after World War II, most people expected another war soon. This time it might well be an atomic war, for Russia, too, now had the Bomb.

CHAPTER FIVE   1950–1955

Hot War and Cold War

If the years before 1950 were marked by deepening conflict between the Soviet bloc and the Western powers, the years that followed were dominatd by the eruption of the conflict into war in Korea. Although fighting remained confined to that unhappy land, the war had ramifications and consequences throughout the world, hastening rearmament, bringing new alliances, imposing strains on the economies of countries only just beginning to recover from World War II, and speeding the development of new weapons. Explosion of the first hydrogen bombs during these years foreshadowed a new era in international politics, one whose outlines could hardly be forecast. The war and the bomb, however, combined with the inability of European powers to maintain their hold on their empires, gave new impetus to another development that had accompanied the Cold War: the attempt of more and more countries to avoid aligning themselves with one side or the other, despite pressures and inducements from the United States and Britain to join new alliances prompted by the Korean War. To new non-Western nationalism was joined new neutralism.

If war dominated the early years of the period, a groping toward a series of political settlements dominated the latter part of it. The war had led to a hardening of positions and greater hostility; it had brought Communist China into a direct conflict with the United States that might otherwise not have occurred. But the cost and exhaustion of an indecisive war led to explorations of possible settlement. The death of Stalin in 1953 prompted Western statesmen to explore the intentions of his successors. To an uneasy peace in Korea was added an even more uneasy peace in Southeast Asia. In Europe, on the other hand, ways were finally devised for rearming Germany, and the Soviet response was creation of the Warsaw Pact alliance. Finally, in the mid-1950s, a new trend in world politics began to become apparent: Europe—apparently shattered by World War II—

showed amazing signs of new life following the disruptions of the Korean War. Americans and Russians had become accustomed to seeing the world in bipolar terms, and the development of hydrogen weapons by the two superpowers appeared to confirm this view. But in Europe as in non-Western areas, the view began to look quite different.

Korea and Its Impact

Victory of the Chinese Communists in China led to a broad reassessment of overall American foreign policy. Europe came first; the Marshall Plan's scope and NATO commitments indicated this. Military commitment in Asia would therefore remain limited, and the containment effort would primarily be directed at helping Asian peoples develop healthy and popular governments and economies. The lesson of China—summed up in the State Department's *China White Paper*, published in 1949—was that internal conditions had led to Communist success. The lesson would have to be applied elsewhere. In line with this thinking, most people in the administration were prepared to abandon the remnant of the Chinese Nationalist regime on Formosa, and try to reach some *modus vivendi* with the victorious Communists, who were proving prickly. Some students of Far Eastern affairs already spoke of possible "Titoism" on the part of Chinese comrades: like the Yugoslav leader, the Chinese had come to power largely on the basis of their own efforts, and might be expected to operate somewhat independently of Russia. Conditions were different within the country, and some of its fundamental long-range national interests might prevail over the ties of Communist ideology in the minds of Chinese leaders, particularly since Tito's case proved that Stalin would tolerate no show of independence on the part of other Communist bloc leaders.

There were many differences of opinion within the administration. But the view prevailed that the heavy weight of American responsibilities in Europe dictated a course of limited commitment in the Far East. Given the nature and limitations of American power, this was the only answer that could be consistent with the containment policy, the only answer possible since its inception. Secretary Marshall once recalled:

I remember, when I was Secretary of State I was being pressed constantly, particularly when in Moscow, by radio message after radio message to give the Russians hell. . . . When I got back, I was getting the same appeal in relation to the Far East and China. At that time, my facilities for giving them hell—and I am a soldier and know something about the ability to give hell—

was 1⅓ divisions over the entire United States. That is quite a proposition when you deal with somebody with over 260 and you have 1⅓rd.*

Twice, in 1947 and again in 1948, President Truman had vetoed tax cuts passed by a Republican Congress. In 1949 a Democratic Congress had refused him a $4 billion increase. Without the money, little force to sustain commitments was possible. The new Secretary of State, Dean Acheson, made clear that the United States would fight to defend Japan and the Philippines. But he argued that the other rimland countries would first have to be able to defend themselves and that the United Nations would then have to be called in to aid them. Lurking in the background was the case of Indochina, where the French attempt to suppress an insurrection was hopelessly bogged down. French use of unpopular local elements had allowed the Communists to capture the Nationalist movement. The administration obviously wanted to avoid such a course. In the meantime, since other countries were ready to recognize the new Chinese regime, the United States was reluctant to isolate itself by pursuing a different policy.†

Nevertheless, among the rimland countries of the Far East, Korea presented a special case. It had a United Nations-legitimated government over an area that bordered directly on a Communist state. While the Truman administration had largely turned the problem over to the United Nations, and—to the dismay of Korean President Syngman Rhee—had withdrawn all forces but a 500-man training mission, it also signed a military assistance agreement with Korea in January 1950, and persuaded a reluctant Congress to approve substantial economic aid.

Border incidents between the two halves of the country occurred with increasing frequency in the first half of 1950, and, although both sides professed a desire for reunification by negotiation, the North laid down impossible conditions. Both obviously felt that if negotiation was impossible force would be necessary. Intelligence reports revealed that the military forces in the North were being strengthened. (North Korean forces were about the same size as the army in the Republic of Korea in the South, but, with Soviet-provided materiel, were better equipped.) John Foster Dulles, a Republican leader in foreign affairs entrusted by the Truman administration with negotiat-

---

* John C. Sparrow, *History of Personnel Demobilization in the United States Army* (Washington, 1951), p. 380.

† The People's Republic of China received recognition by the USSR in October 1949, by Burma and India in December, by Great Britain in January 1950, and by the Netherlands in March.

ing a peace treaty with Japan, visited Korea, and in a speech to the National Assembly, promised that the United States would stand by the country.

Then, on June 25, war broke out. North Korean troops crossed the 38th parallel at several places and made numerous amphibious landings. At the same time the North Korean radio claimed that South Korean troops, which they said had begun the hostilities by crossing into the north, had been repulsed.

In Western Europe, among the newly independent countries of Asia, and in the Communist bloc, there were people prepared to believe that not only had a belligerent South Korea started the fight, but had done so with American assistance. To most historians studying these events, sufficient evidence exists to prove the opposite. Far more important for developments at the time was the fact that the United Nations Commission on Korea was in South Korea and reported immediately that "the invasion . . . was an act of aggression initiated without warning and without provocation in execution of a carefully prepared plan." On the basis of this report from a neutral commission, national leaders throughout the world accepted the fact of North Korean aggression.

They therefore supported action taken by the United States, and gave it United Nations sanction in the form of Security Council resolutions. The first, on June 25, by a vote of 9 to 0 with Yugoslavia abstaining, found that an armed attack by North Korea had taken place in violation of the United Nations Charter. It called for immediate withdrawal of troops, a cease-fire, and asked United Nations members to help execute the resolution and refrain from giving assistance to North Korean authorities. The Soviet Union, which was then boycotting the Security Council because of continued Chinese Nationalist presence when, it argued, the Communist should have taken their seat, was not there to veto the resolution.

On June 27, President Truman announced that he had ordered American air and sea forces to give air cover and support to troops of the Republic of Korea. Later that same day, the Security Council, by a vote of 8 to 1, recommended that United Nations members furnish such assistance as was necessary to repel the attack and restore peace in the area. Yugoslavia opposed sanctions, calling for mediation. India, at first abstaining, voted in favor after receiving instructions from home. The Egyptian government, still opposed to previous United Nations action in Palestine, refused to support the United Nations resolution.

Three days later President Truman authorized General MacArthur in Japan to use American ground forces in Korea, to institute a naval blockade of the entire Korean coast, and to bomb targets in North Korea. On July 7 the Security Council recommended that all military units be placed under a unified command, that the United Nations flag be used, and that the United States name a Supreme Commander. On July 8, Truman appointed MacArthur to the post.

Meanwhile, and through July and August, North Korean forces continued to drive south. American occupation troops from Japan, peace-time enlistees, ill-trained and ill-equipped for fighting an unforeseen kind of war, were hurried into the breach. In short order the North Korean attack pushed them, along with the small British units rushed from Hong-Kong, into an eighty by sixty mile pocket on the southeast tip of the Korean peninsula. But there they were able to gather strength while more American personnel moved into the Far East. On September 15 General MacArthur effected a successful amphibious landing 150 miles to the north, at Inchon on the west coast of the peninsula, while simultaneously launching an attack from the southeast perimeter. Within a matter of days, the whole situation had changed radically; enormous numbers of North Korean prisoners were taken, and the rest rushed pell-mell back toward the north. The war had entered a new phase.

The entire action so far was highly improvised, and hardly an example of what had been expected under the United Nations Charter. Absence of the Soviet Union from the Security Council, the presence of the United Nations Commission on Korea and the presence of American troops in Japan were the factors that made possible United Nations action under a recommendation—not a binding decision—from the United Nations Security Council. The Soviet Union was always to argue that the action was illegal since the Soviet Union had not concurred in the votes, and since the affair was a civil war rather than an international matter in which the United Nations could interfere. The American-named commander in the field had extraordinary leeway. The only link between him and the United Nations was a periodic meeting, held at the State Department in Washington, of representatives of the sixteen nations that had contributed troops. Here they were informed of United States actions and could give their thoughts on matters at hand.

In all, forty-five countries contributed troops, or supplies or transport. But the United States contributed the lion's share: nine-tenths of the non-Korean troops in action were American.

The American decision to face the attack in Korea was itself no simple one. The basic decision to restrict military commitments in the Far East to areas more easily defended had already been taken. Once the Korean attack came, there were military advisers who felt all the more strongly that this policy should be continued; they argued that the Soviet Union was not directly involved, that this might well be a diversionary attack while the Soviets prepared to use their strength in a still-weak Europe or a weaker Middle East, and that the United States should be ready to face these eventualities. There were those, too, who feared that presidential use of troops in the area would incur the wrath of Congress, some of whose leaders were already upset that the presence of American troops in a potential front line European situation had virtually pre-empted Congressional power to declare war. On the other hand, even though there was no knowledge of the extent to which the Russians or Chinese were involved, American leaders assumed close Soviet bloc coordination. They also felt that if the United States did not back the Korean government against invasion, other governments would feel uncertain about United States backing in other areas. In this particular case the presence of the United Nations Commission on Korea and its report made it far more difficult for people to accept the Soviet position, and ensured general United Nations support of the American move.

Finally, and no less important, the domestic political situation exerted tremendous pressure on the administration. Its overseas commitments to stop the Communists were expensive; it therefore faced the charge of spending too much. On the other hand, the containment policy seemed negative to too many people, and the administration therefore faced the counter-charge of not doing enough, and of only reacting to Communist moves. Since the requirements of foreign policy had led to strengthening the military branch and the executive in general, the administration was also charged with too much centralization in government. But most important, many Americans, since the announcement of the Open Door Policy in China in 1899, had felt some sentimental attachment for China (though this did not extend to allowing many Chinese to immigrate into the United States). American opposition to Japanese incursions into China had finally brought the United States into World War II. Now China had been absorbed by a far more formidable enemy—the Communist bloc. Charges were made that treason was involved, and that the State Department was directly responsible for losing China. An obscure, ineffective, and somewhat disreputable Senator from Wisconsin, Joseph R. McCarthy, had vaulted into national prominence through demagogic and unprovable charges of heavy Communist infiltration into the Department of State. In an extemporaneous section of a speech delivered at Wheeling, West Virginia, he held aloft a paper saying, "I have here in my hand a list of 205—a list of names that were known to the Secretary of State as being members of the Communist Party and who nevertheless are still working and shaping policy in the State Department." The paper was in fact a letter written in 1946 by the then Secretary of State, James F. Byrnes, that said nothing about Communists, and the figure McCarthy had used was whittled down to 81, and then to 57. Eventually the charges came to nothing. He was to use successfully the misrepresentation of documents for similar purposes in the future.

It was true, however, that there had been limited Communist infiltration into the government. A long-drawn out dramatic case that skyrocketed into prominence the young California Congressman Richard Nixon, who had uncovered it, resulted in the conviction of Alger Hiss for perjury. Hiss had held a high rank in the State Department, had traveled to Yalta, and was, at the time of his trial, head of a private scholarly foundation, the Carnegie Endowment for International Peace. Now he was convicted for having lied in denying that he had passed secret government documents to a confessed former Communist, Whittaker Chambers. Other Communists, too, were discovered in the Treasury, Commerce, and Justice Departments; still others had served on legislative committee staffs. President Truman had set in motion a harsh loyalty program as early as 1947. The number and influence of Communists in government was never strong, and some—having joined out of the most patriotic motives—left the Party fairly soon. But denials by persons high in the government that *any* Communist infiltration had taken place seemed misplaced. Demagogues like McCarthy—and many who should have known better—charged that American policy was virtually directed by Communists; that those who were not actually Communists—such as General Marshall, Dean Acheson, President Truman—were dupes of the Communists, and by implication, guilty of treason.

The historian finds it ironic that members of an administration who had set the United States upon the unprecedented course of containment, and who had accepted its underlying assumptions about Soviet policy, should have found themselves charged with being "soft on Communism." Political discourse reached an extraordinarily low level and assumed an unreality that would have important consequences in the next few years.

It is hard to tell whether and how much the political atmosphere in America influenced the course of decisions on Korea. Europeans, looking at what they considered to be anti-Communist hysteria in a country where the Party was small, weak, and ineffectual (in their own countries it commanded a large and faithful following) were sure that it did. Those involved in the decisions are equally sure that they acted in what they felt were the best American interests, regardless of public denunciations. To those who argued that the administration had abandoned the Far East to the Communists, the Korean decision appeared to be a successful change in policy forced by militant public opinion. But to the Truman administration it was a continuation of previous policy in a set of new circumstances.

In one way, however, Korea did force an immediate change. President Truman ordered the American Seventh Fleet into the Formosa straits, primarily to protect the Chiang regime on Formosa from Communist China.

To Americans, the decision to link defense of South Korea with defense of the Nationalist remnant on an island that properly belonged to China seemed natural: Communist aggression was one and the same thing. To most people in the rest of the world the action was a mistake; the former was legitimate defense against aggression, the latter interference in a civil war in a country not directly involved in Korea. They argued, further, that the move would prevent any possible accommodation with the new Chinese regime, would force it into closer cooperation with Russia, and, as it could be represented as another example of Western imperialism, would discredit the West in the eyes of Asian nationalists. Certainly it can only have served to confirm Chinese Communists in the view that the United States was *the* enemy, the one power halting reunification of the country and preserving a regime that challenged Communist authority. In the face of the American action, the Chinese halted their build-up of troops in the area opposite Formosa and began to move them to the North, near Korea. For the moment the Chiang regime was safe, but the implications of the action were unclear.

The Korean War served to harden Western assumptions about Soviet foreign policy: leaders throughout Europe and in the United States now accepted the view that because early Soviet efforts to expand in Western Europe had been blocked by the American initiatives of 1947–48, Soviet policy had now entered a new, hard phase characterized by reliance on military force. The Korean venture was one example of new Soviet policy, warfare in Indochina another. In a third area, Malaya, the Communists—as in other areas of the world—had gone over to the offensive in 1948, in the form of riots and strikes. Their failure prompted a shift to guerrilla warfare. Communist guerrillas never numbered more than five thousand and Malaya had no common border with any Communist power that could have given them supplies. But the large Chinese minority in Malaya was sympathetic to the guerrillas, and by 1950 a British army of 35,000 men was tied down in the fight, while hundreds of thousands of constabulary assumed police duties.

The new view of Soviet policy—correct or incorrect—could only lead to a strengthening of Western efforts to counter the Soviet military threat. But the pace of the war in Korea did so much to mold this response and its consequences that we must turn first to the course of that war.

Within two weeks of MacArthur's successful Inchon landing in September, his United Nations troops had reached the 38th parallel, where the war had started. From Washington came a directive that the General's objective should be "destruction of the North Korean Armed Forces," and he was authorized to cross the 38th parallel if there were no indication that Soviet or Chinese forces planned to enter the campaign. In China, Chou En-lai warned that the Chinese People's Republic would not "supinely tolerate seeing their neighbors being savagely invaded by imperialists" and that "if US or UN forces crossed the 38th parallel, China would send troops to the Korean frontier to defend North Korea."

To the commander in the field pursuing retreating troops, a pause that would allow them to regroup would be foolish in the absence of other overriding reasons. In Korea MacArthur had received permission to advance, and did so. The administration then went to the United Nations General Assembly—the Security Council being deadlocked after Soviet return to it—and secured a somewhat ambiguous resolution reaffirming the Assembly's desire for a "unified, independent, democratic Korea," and recommending that steps be taken to "insure conditions of stability throughout Korea." United Nations forces were to remain in Korea only long enough to achieve these objectives. To transform the anticipated military success into political reality, the Assembly created the United Nations Commission for Unification and Rehabilitation of Korea. In the meantime MacArthur's forces continued to pursue the enemy. From India's ambassador in Peking came warning that the Chinese were, indeed, likely to intervene if the move into North Korea continued. So that the Chinese Communists might present their side of the issue directly, India suggested that they be represented in the Assembly. But this move failed.

On October 15 President Truman flew to Wake Island in the central Pacific to meet with MacArthur, his Far Eastern commander, and receive from him an on-the-spot report. MacArthur predicted an early victory and reunification, and told the President there was little danger of Chinese intervention—the Chinese had too few troops and materiel. When Truman told him that the administration was particularly concerned with strengthening the defenses of Western Europe and wanted to avoid a war with China at all cost, MacArthur replied that one division could surely be spared from Korea to be transferred to Europe by the end of January 1951.

A New War

In November, however, as MacArthur extended his lines, he began to run into substantial numbers of Chinese units and notified the United Nations to that effect. At first, contact was sporadic and estimates of the numbers of Chinese troops remained low. Then on November 24 MacArthur launched an offensive with the announced intention of bringing the war to an end and withdrawing the Eighth Army to Japan by Christmas. Two days later an enormous Chinese force—subsequently estimated at 850,000 men—counterattacked, splitting MacArthur's forces, and sending them in a headlong, though orderly, retreat.

MacArthur now insisted that the new war required greatly expanded measures—bombing of Chinese bases in Manchuria, blockade of the Chinese coast, the use of Chiang Kai-shek's forces on Formosa to attack the mainland. But the Truman administration, with full approval of the Joint Chiefs of Staff, preferred to keep the war limited. Full commitment in the Far East might leave the West vulnerable in other parts of the world and might lead to an all-out war for which it was ill-prepared, particularly since Russia by then had the atomic bomb. America's allies, far more vulnerable, were particularly concerned that the war not spread. When a press corps eager for news pushed President Truman into saying that, since any nation in a fight always had to consider what weapons might be used, the administration was considering the use of atomic bombs in Korea, Prime Minister Attlee immediately flew to Washington to argue against such a course, and the newspapers of the world were filled with scare headlines. While groups within the United States pushed for more strenuous action against China, allies and neutrals pleaded for restraint.

Charges and countercharges flew. A Communist Chinese delegation came to the United Nations to argue that the United States was the aggressor in Formosa, Korea, and Manchuria, whose air-space it consistently violated. Meanwhile American troops recovered and regrouped and began again to move northward from their positions in South Korea. Faced with possible alternatives, including the ones suggested by General MacArthur, administration leaders had decided to keep the war a limited one of pressure and attrition which would eventually force the Chinese into negotiations. In the meantime General MacArthur sought to build up public support for his position and build a backfire to force the administration to adopt his ideas. Unable to accept what was clearly insubordination, Truman removed him from his command in April, 1951. "MacArthur left me no choice—I could no longer tolerate his insubordination," he wrote. "And the Joint Chiefs of Staff unanimously recommended that he be relieved." * He appointed General Matthew B. Ridgway in MacArthur's place.

MacArthur's recall led to an extraordinary emotional public display in the United States. The General moved through city after city in a series of tremendous parades, and addressed a joint session of Congress that was televised to sixty million viewers.

Republican opposition, hot on the trail of a winning election issue and sensing the extent of public frustration with the administration's inability to "win the Cold War," fanned emotions. Some asserted that treason had caused the hobbling of MacArthur, just as it had been behind the loss of China, and Senators called for impeachment of President Truman. Secretary of State Dean Acheson, General Marshall and others who had formulated the containment policy, were subjected to an extraordinary campaign of vilification; *Time* magazine called Acheson the leader of a State Department group that was "the last to identify the real enemy as Soviet Russia."

The campaign only began to die down when a lengthy Congressional investigation revealed the bases of administration action, and when it became evident that Congressmen and Senators who talked belligerently were totally unwilling to take the responsibility of declaring war. Extending the hostilities would risk involving the whole of the American economy and American society in another war with all its controls and costs—but this time with the presence of atomic weapons.

While people in Europe and Asia looked on in bewilderment, hav-

* Harry S. Truman, *Memoirs* (Garden City, 1956), Vol. II, p. 561.

ing applauded the President's action, the war went on in Korea, where enormous casualties were inflicted upon Communist Chinese troops. The United States, although using military pressure to force the Chinese to negotiate, had also succeeded in having the United Nations General Assembly brand Communist China an aggressor in Korea. Many members were reluctant, arguing that this would make negotiations harder, and the Indian delegation opposed the action on the basis that the West had been given ample warning of what would happen if the military move were made into North Korea—the Communist sphere. It argued, furthermore, that the Communist Chinese were right in insisting that the United States had intervened in Chinese affairs by supporting the Nationalist remnant on Formosa. On the other hand, the United States effort to obtain the resolution was made easier by the Chinese refusal to meet with a cease-fire group of India, Iran, and Canada in December unless the United States withdrew from Formosa and Korea and unless they were given representation in the United Nations.

Military pressures succeeded in forcing the Communists to discuss an armistice, beginning in June 1951. But for the next two years the Communist Chinese, partly perhaps because of their century of humiliation by the West and partly because events seemed to have confirmed their ideological preconceptions, used every propaganda device possible to discredit the Western negotiators in the eyes of the Chinese and other Asian people. They portrayed the United Nations forces as defeated and begging for peace. They parlayed charges of germ warfare into a worldwide propaganda victory. They succeeded in having agents planted among prisoners of war in American-guarded camps where they organized riots and the capture, in one case, of the American camp commander. To secure his safe release, the second in command agreed to terms that implied the United States had been mistreating prisoners, and the Chinese lost no time in making good use of this. They also gave extensive publicity to the decisions of eleven American prisoners of war to remain in China, while the United States retaliated by publicizing the far larger number of Chinese who declined repatriation to Communist China.

Eventually, military pressure and the economic impact of the war, as well as Indian efforts at securing compromise, brought an armistice agreement in July 1953. Nominally, it was to be the prelude to negotiations for reunification. In fact, few believed it, and Syngman Rhee, President of South Korea, tried to disrupt the armistice negotiations and force the United States to continue the war. He was unsuccessful;

but the United States promised economic and military aid and a mutual security pact to protect South Korea against a future attack, and he had to be satisfied with this.

International Consequences of the Korean War

The savage battle on the Korean peninsula gave a new shape to international politics throughout the rest of the world: in Europe, where the movement for unity was warped by the new haste for rearmament; in New York, where the United Nations assumed a new posture; in China, where the new leadership altered its plans and came into abrupt and direct conflict with the United States; and in the United States, where the long period of Democratic rule came to an end.

In January 1950 the Truman administration had adopted a new policy paper on overall strategy that reflected State Department dissatisfaction with the adequacy of American response to Soviet pressures. It had rejected preventive war—advocated by some who felt that the United States should strike at the Soviet Union before it turned its new capacity to carry out an atomic explosion into nuclear weapons and added them to its overwhelming strength on the ground. It rejected a turn to a "Fortress America" isolationist policy, publicly advocated by some of the old-guard Republicans, notably former President Herbert Hoover. Instead, it argued for a rapid and large-scale build-up of both atomic striking capacity in the air and of ground and naval power to deter expansion on the ground by more conventional means, along with a strengthening of American allies. The State Department estimated that the cost would amount to $35 billion annually, at a time when the actual ceiling on military spending was around $13 billion. Curiously enough, a number of military men argued strongly that the American economy would be unable to stand the strain.

The Korean War resolved the issue. Within the United States, military expenditures rose rapidly, not only to prosecute the war, but to build up existing armed strength and mobilization potential in general. In the January 1950 policy paper, 1954 had been named as the danger year in terms of increases in Soviet armed strength. The date was now advanced to 1952 on the basis that the Korean War and Chinese intervention were evidence of a new hard, aggressive Soviet policy, inspired by Russian possession of the atomic bomb.

In September 1950, even before the Chinese attack, the North Atlantic Council had met in New York. Until this time, NATO represented little more than a paper agreement backed by America's atomic striking force. The United States, under the Mutual Defense Assistance Program, had appropriated over one billion, three hundred million dollars in military aid for NATO allies in December 1949, and bilateral agreements on administration of the aid had been signed in January. In July 1950, the second year's appropriation, for a similar sum, was passed. But in August the President asked for, and was granted, another $4 billion. Until this time, however, the governments concerned had only begun to transform appropriations into armed force. Now Secretary of State Acheson proposed concerted action along two lines. He argued that an integrated force with a centralized command should be built up, and he further argued that an effective force could never be built up unless West Germany contributed to it, to the extent of twelve divisions.

The subject of possible German rearmament had been bruited about for at least a year, and at least some English and French political leaders had spoken in favor of it. But French acceptance meant an even longer and harder step than the ones it had already taken since 1947 in turning to association with the United States and Britain and to a rapprochement with Germany. Nevertheless, in the light of the Korean War, European defenses were found wanting. On October 24, 1950, French Foreign Minister Schuman therefore presented the so-called Pleven Plan, which presumably would make German rearmament acceptable. In brief, it envisaged the creation of a European army with units contributed from national armies merged at the lowest level. For this army there would be a European defense budget and a European defense minister responsible to some European Assembly, perhaps that of the Council of Europe. All European countries except Germany would contribute the units from their existing armies; Germany would contribute only to the European army, and would still have no national force of its own. About the time that the French presented the Pleven Plan, Western negotiators also decided upon modifications in the German Occupation Statute. It would be impossible to obtain German participation in European defense unless Germany were also allowed some greater measure of sovereignty. Therefore, Germany would be allowed a Ministry of Foreign Affairs and a regular diplomatic establishment, and Allied controls and restrictions over industry and review of German legislation would be reduced.

The growing importance of Germany in the new structure of world politics became far more apparent in the ensuing weeks of negotiation, and one of the strongest cards in the German hand was that of internal opposition to rearmament. Part of the opposition was moral; part of it was simply of an "oh, not again!" sort; part of it, particularly from certain Social Democratic leaders, reflected a feeling that German rearmament posed real security dangers for Germany. It might provoke Russian retaliation before the defenses of Western Europe were restored. Even worse, Germans might become cannon fodder because of a strategy that provided for neither liberation of East Germany and its reunification with West Germany, nor real protection of West Germany itself. Given the relative ground strength of the Russians and the West, in the event of war West Germany would serve only as a battleground over which the West would retreat to defensive positions. Therefore, argued some Social Democrats, only if other Western powers planned a militant strategy that would carry them *forward* in the event of hostilities could Germany afford to contribute to armed strength.

The internal opposition enabled the Adenauer government to press the other Western powers for more concessions, particularly since many people found merit in the German arguments. The opposition gave force to the German government's requests: unless they were met, Germany would *not* participate in Western rearmament and in its own defense, now so urgently desired by the Truman administration and approved by the British and French.

And so, in the laborious negotiations that followed, Germany was given more than it had originally requested. But although negotiators performed the difficult task of transforming proposal into policy during the next two years, and signed the treaty setting up the European Defense Community in 1952, it now appeared that French reluctance to allow German rearmament might doom it even in this guise. Added to this reluctance was a conviction that the European army would be unworkable, the fact that the British—with responsibilities throughout the rest of the world—refused to join it, and the opposition of many French political leaders to do anything that would diminish the possibility of independent use of a *national* army. Some observers became convinced that French leaders had in fact devised the unwieldy plan merely to postpone the day when they would have to yield to American pleas for German rearmament. If this could be delayed for a matter of months, or better yet, years, who could tell what might happen? Since no French government anticipated a life of more than a few months, delay might mean that at least it would not fall over the German issue; some future government would face it. And in the meantime the French used the matter to obtain acceptance of the Schuman Plan for a Coal and Steel Community; without this, they would not consent to German rearmament in *any* form.

The EDC issue was not actually settled until 1954, after the death of Stalin and the peace settlements in Korea and Indochina. Under the impact of these, the French Assembly rejected EDC. But German rearmament took place in a different form (see p. 186).

The diversion of EDC slowed the process of German contribution to Western armed strength, but NATO planning began to produce results on other fronts. Besides establishing a unified command structure for NATO in the form of Supreme Headquarters, Allied Powers Europe (SHAPE), and appointing Eisenhower as Supreme Allied Commander, Europe (SACEUR), work was begun to create a network of supply, communication, and airfield facilities behind the lines in Germany. (Before the Korean War, the British and American supply lines in Germany, instead of running vertically to the front, had paralleled it, to Bremerhaven and Hamburg. In places they had been within a few miles of the Russian lines.) Equally important were the complicated diplomatic maneuvers of military planners trying to convince their governments that in the face of Russian military power NATO would need one hundred divisions for a holding operation instead of the twelve divisions they had possessed before the Korean War. Each government tried to tell others in NATO what share they should contribute to the buildup. Each argued that what was asked of it was too large and politically impossible.

Nevertheless, although the force levels of almost one hundred divisions agreed on at the Lisbon meeting of 1952 were never to be achieved, by 1953 the impetus of the Korean War had transformed the situation in Europe. Weak divisions had been turned into a larger number of heavily armed divisions with appropriate supporting forces —tanks, artillery, and tactical air forces. There were fifteen ready on the central front, Denmark and Norway could supply two more, and Italy from seven to nine. If time permitted, even more could be mobilized. Korea also led, in 1952, to NATO membership for Greece and Turkey—scarcely North Atlantic countries. The negotiations were arduous, since some northern and western members were dubious about extending NATO guarantees to the eastern Mediterranean, a region particularly difficult to defend. At any rate, the United States was already committed to the defense of Greece and Turkey. On the other hand, since Greece and Turkey would add another twenty divisions to NATO, and the possibility that in case of war the Soviets would have to divert substantial forces to the area, the two countries were desirable allies.

The Korean War and the urgency it gave to American efforts to build an alliance system affected two other countries: Spain and Japan.

Spain, racked in the 1930s by a civil war that brought Franco to power with the help of Nazis and Fascists, maintained neutrality throughout World War II. Franco resisted Hitler's efforts to bring him in on the Axis side, and Britain and the United States—despite strong domestic protests—helped him to sustain the precarious Spanish economy. To liberals who saw World War II as a crusade against fascism of all forms, Franco Spain remained a detestable anachronism; it was excluded from the San Francisco conference and France closed its Pyrenees frontier in February 1946. America published a White Book detailing Spanish assistance to the Axis, and soon demands were made in the United Nations for action against Franco.

Presumably the very fact that Franco espoused fascism made him a threat to the peace. But since the loudest demands for action came from the Soviet Union, other powers began to question the wisdom of an effort to overthrow the Spanish dictator: What would follow? Thus, they resisted attempts to impose economic sanctions, and the General Assembly recommended instead that states withdraw their heads of mission in Madrid, without severing diplomatic relations.

By 1948, in view of conspicuous lack of result, the French reopened their borders and a number of states returned their ministers and ambassadors. In the fall of 1950, after the start of the Korean War, the General Assembly revoked the recommendation passed in 1946, and Spain was allowed to join United Nations Specialized Agencies. Only a few European countries held out against the revocation; Arab and Latin American states spearheaded the battle for a change and were warmly thanked by the Franco regime for having stood by it during four years. The same year the American Congress, having previously refused to appropriate any money for loans to Spain, reversed itself and provided money in the Mutual Security Aid bill; President Truman declared himself not obligated to spend it.

In 1951, however, the Truman administration found itself in the position of seeking a formula by which Spain could be associated with NATO. American military planners stressed the desirability of bases in Spain, and though the Spanish army was ill-trained and poorly equipped, it was large; with the disparity in manpower under arms between the Soviet bloc and the NATO powers, the Spanish army of between two and four hundred thousand men began to look like an attractive force.

But European governments, faced with emphatic anti-Franco opinion at home, refused to countenance a move whose expediency they felt would lose them more support than any possible military gain would be worth—and many questioned any military gain. Thus negotiations through 1952 and 1953 continued on a bilateral basis. In September 1953, under the Eisenhower administration, the discussions brought agreement that gave to the United States the right to build and use military bases in Spain in return for large-scale American economic and military assistance. Although conclusion of the treaty—after the extended negotiations—brought little stir in Europe, it contributed to distrust of the United States by left-wing groups. They were well aware that much of the impetus had come from Americans—Senators and others—who felt that a Fascist anti-Communist was a sturdier and better one than a Socialist anti-Communist.

On the other side of the world, the Korean War led to the conclusion of a peace treaty with Japan, thus ending the occupied status of that country. Though a treaty had posed delicate and difficult problems, the United States was determined to have one. The administration wanted to bind Japan by another defense treaty by which Japan would allow American troops and bases to remain within its borders in exchange for a guarantee of American protection. Moreover, the United States was determined that the treaty would not give legal sanction to return Japanese lands to Russia or imply that Formosa (whose return to China had been promised in World War II) should go to Communist China. Under the circumstances, a number of countries that had fought the Japanese in World War II were bound to oppose the treaties—not just the Soviet Union, but also countries like India, Burma, and Yugoslavia. All of these refused to attend the final peace conference at San Francisco in September 1951, or to sign the treaty. The settlement imposed no reparations on the erstwhile enemy, but left individual agreements to be negotiated between Japan and its former victims.

At the same time that the United States secured the Japanese bases that proved so vital in the Korean War, it signed two other mutual defense treaties with Asian countries, one with the Philippines, the other with Australia and New Zealand, creating the so-called ANZUS grouping. An attempt to enlist Arab states in a Middle East Command failed in the face of Arab hostility.

Finally, the Korean War had considerable impact on the United

Nations organization. While some viewed action under United Nations auspices as a first proof that collective security could be made to work against an aggressor, others felt that Korea mainly indicated how weak and ineffectual any collective security attempt would be unless the first prerequisite, written into the Charter, could be effected: great power unanimity on whatever action was to be taken. In the Korean situation the Charter provisions for collective security had never really been implemented; it resembled far more an old-fashioned war, but one fought under the threat of nuclear weapons.

Events seem to bear out the second contention, though it, too, was not entirely accurate. The Korean action was improvised, since the agreements that would have provided the Security Council with national contingents for collective security action were never made. It could only be taken under United Nations auspices because the Soviet Union was absent from the Security Council at the time of the invasion.* It could only be done because of the proximity of American forces in Japan. And finally—of supreme importance—the presence of the neutral United Nations Commission on Korea provided definite and reliable information identifying the aggressor. Subsequently, under other circumstances, countries that wanted to avoid being drawn into conflicts between the great powers were to use the excuse that precise knowledge of who was culpable in a conflict could not be obtained. In the Korean War, although the Formosa issue clouded the matter and the subsequent march north of the 38th parallel went beyond the meaning of collective security, at least it was clear that North Korea had been the initial aggressor.

The fact that these particular circumstances—absence of the Soviet Union, presence of American troops, and presence of the United Nations Commission on Korea—had made possible the Korean action led to changes in the structure of the United Nations, in hopes that in future crises the organization would not have to rely on chance. Early paralysis of the Security Council had already made countries use the General Assembly more freely in matters of international peace

---

* This fact led some to conclude that the Soviet Union had actually wanted the United States to be drawn into Korea in the way it had, thereby leaving other areas open to aggression or putting a heavy financial and military burden on the United States. There are many reasons to doubt this interpretation and support another, that the Soviet Union made a mistake so far as the United Nations was concerned. Had it blocked the United Nations action it seems likely that the United States would have acted alone, and thus lost some of the moral prestige of United Nations support.

and security. Now the move was made more formal in the Acheson Plan, or the "Uniting for Peace" proposal. Adopted by the General Assembly in November 1950 with only the Soviet bloc opposed and Argentina and India abstaining, it provided that if the Security Council were deadlocked, the General Assembly could meet on twenty-four hour notice and recommend collective measures including the use of armed force against an aggressor. This would solve the problem that would have arisen at the time of Korea had the Soviet Union stayed in the Security Council. Moreover, to avoid the difficulties that would have occurred had American troops not been available, the plan recommended to members that they keep within their armed forces contingents ear-marked and organized for possible service as United Nations units. To eliminate the element of chance in the decisive presence of the United Nations Commission on Korea, the Assembly created a permanent Peace Observation Commission of fourteen member states that could observe and report on trouble spots anywhere in the world. Finally, the Assembly established a Collective Measures Committee to make recommendations to strengthen the peace machinery.

Of the four innovations, only the first became an important part of the United Nations machinery. The others were doomed, mainly because Korea had really demonstrated how many countries of the world would *not* support collective security measures in distant parts of the world where their immediate interests were only remotely involved. The burden of the Korean War was largely carried by the United States, and many Americans felt that conduct of the war was unduly hampered by restraints exercised by countries whose contributions were minimal. But in other contributing countries in many cases people took the opposite view: they found themselves committed to courses of action about which they were unhappy, precisely because the United States carried the largest share of the burden and could thus act without deferring to their opinions. Many United Nations observers concluded that the Korean experiment would probably not be repeated, that Korea had demonstrated the inadequacy of the concept of collective security almost as effectively as the Ethiopian experience had done in 1936. But the increased role of the General Assembly in diplomacy involving matters of security became an established fact.

Finally, Korea had a direct impact on the leaders of Communist China. They had not been involved in preparations for the North Korea invasion and had weakened their military strength in the north in preparation for the final takeover of the island of Formosa, whose return to China had ben promised during World War II. The sudden American interposition of the Seventh Fleet blocked this move. To the Chinese, it was seen only as a direct intervention in their civil war. Then, when American and other United Nations troops crossed the 38th parallel despite Chinese warnings that this was an area of direct interest to them and that the Chinese would act to protect their interests, their hostility was reinforced. The Chinese Communist world view had already set in a hard ideological mold; but events had merely served to confirm it: imperialist America, everywhere in direct conflict with legitimate Communist Chinese interests, was obviously the main enemy. The regime—drawn into an expensive and unforeseen military venture in Korea—hastened the pace of the internal development necessary to produce the power to cope with American enmity. Sooner rather than later it would exert all possible power on the world scene in opposition to the "western imperialists."

American Reactions to Frustration: Initial Effect of the 1952
Political Campaign

The United States was the leader in securing general acceptance of the assumptions upon which containment was based and of the policies involved in building the grand coalition against the Soviet Union. Yet the strains and frustrations of a policy whose success led only to its own continuation instead of to final victory also had political consequences within the United States, and these political consequences, in turn, had widespread repercussions on international politics in the next few years. There were other factors behind the political upheavals of 1950 to 1952; but the containment frustration pervaded them.

One has already been mentioned, the growth of McCarthyism. Though it could not have been successful unless there actually were some spies and subversives, it led to the kind of wholesale vilification of scapegoats that had not been seen for many years in America. If there was no victory, someone must be responsible: the Communists in the Federal government, Harry S. Truman, Dean Acheson, American allies, the United Nations. Men whose only claim to fame lay in their ability to concoct wild charges vaulted into political prominence.

The acclaim given to General MacArthur, who, it was believed, could have "won" the Korean War was another result. Once given a serious hearing by those who would have to take the responsibility of action, he faded away. But more irresponsible men continued to echo his memorable if somewhat meaningless phrase: "There is no substitute for victory."

More complex but equally serious was the strong move to amend the Constitution to curb the foreign policy power of the executive. At a time when many were calling for *stronger* foreign policy action, the suggestion seemed odd; the origin of the so-called "Bricker Amendment" lay in the conviction that executive action was what had strengthened the Soviet Union and weakened the United States. In a sense, like the constitutional amendment limiting any president to two terms in office, it was retaliation against a dead president, Franklin D. Roosevelt. Happily, the "Bricker Amendment" failed—but the margin was surprisingly slim.

Herbert Hoover, Robert A. Taft, and others espoused a "fortress America" concept, and condemned the Truman administration for assuming its commitments in Europe. A more serious school of foreign policy thinkers declared that the moribund policy of containment must give place to a dynamic one of "liberation" or "rollback" of Communist power. The most prominent exponent of the idea was John Foster Dulles, Republican foreign policy spokesman who would have been Secretary of State had the Republican candidate, Thomas Dewey, won in 1948, and who did become Secretary of State under President Eisenhower in 1953. Dulles—who espoused the "Bricker Amendment" only until he became Secretary of State, at which point he reversed his stand—spelled out his views in a May 1952 issue of *Life* magazine. Here he wrote that, in contrast to the "static, passive" policy of containment, which promised at heavy cost only that the United States could "live with" peril, not live *without* it, the nation must develop a "dynamic" policy using "ideas as weapons . . . conform[ing] to moral principles." Such a policy could lead, in two, five, or ten years, to the freeing of substantial parts of the captive world. This would be accomplished through "freedom programs" whose precise content, however, defied definition. He declared that the United States did not want "a series of bloody uprisings and reprisals," but pointed to Tito's defection from the bloc as the form of change to which policy should be directed. In January 1953, testifying before a Senate Committee, he said, "Those who do not believe that [liberation] can be accomplished by moral pressures, by the weight of propaganda, just do not know what they are talking about. . . ."

At the same time that the whole basic containment policy was under fire for being insufficient, the administration faced widespread charges of irresponsible spending. Opponents of the Truman administration promised that a change would bring a reduction in the federal budget of twenty-five, forty, or fifty per cent. Since the only area in which such a cut could occur was in defense spending, with perhaps a smaller cut in the field of foreign aid (which was now primarily military), it was rather hard to reconcile the two arguments.

Nevertheless, in the 1952 presidential campaign, foreign policy frustrations played a large part. Charges were made of Communism in government, the weakness of containment, too much spending, and one other—corruption in high places. The sweeping Republican victory rested on these and on the personality of the Republican candidate, General Eisenhower, who had returned from his position as Supreme Allied Commander in Europe to wrest the nomination from Senator Taft of Ohio, leader of the Republican old guard.

There were several immediate consequences for American foreign policy and world politics.

Although Americans were accustomed to campaign oratory that has little relevance to what the victorious party will do once in office, the effect of such oratory was now international. In Eastern Europe, talk of "liberation" rather than "containment" raised high hopes among many people. There might be little chance to revolt against totalitarian power (regardless of Dulles' views, the Yugoslav case was unique, and hardly a model for what might happen in other Soviet satellites). But the thought that outside aid might be forthcoming added an element of hope. The extent to which American politicians had believed their own campaign oratory was revealed in early 1953 when a "Captive Peoples" resolution came before Congress. It repudiated past secret agreements made by the United States that permitted enslavement of other peoples. But as debate began, it became clear that in fact the agreements under attack—the Yalta and Potsdam Declarations—were the only documents signed by the Soviet Union that constituted clear engagements *not* to do what it had done in Eastern Europe. Eisenhower therefore worked to prevent passage of the resolution. He was supported by the Democrats in Congress, while his own Republican supporters, who had blamed the Democratic administration for allowing the Russian takeover, finally and reluctantly shelved the resolution.

But the debate had convinced people further that liberation was not an empty phrase. Then the administration took another step that served to bolster this conviction: on February 2, 1953, in a message delivered to Congress in person, President Eisenhower told the world that he had rescinded Truman's order forbidding Chiang Kai-shek to attack the mainland from Formosa. In popular parlance, the President had "unleashed" Chiang. In fact, the original Truman order interposing the Seventh Fleet between Formosa and the mainland had been designed to prevent the capture of Formosa by the Chinese Communists, while minimizing the extent to which the Administration could be charged with interfering directly in the Chinese civil war. Moreover it was subsequently revealed that Chiang's forces had been engaged in hit-and-run raids ever since Chinese intervention in the Korean War. And despite grandiose campaign utterances, the Nationalist Chinese forces had insufficient strength to do anything more. The order therefore appeared to be designed primarily for domestic consumption, but it, too, had its effects abroad. Allied statesmen, who could see no hope of liberation without the force of arms, were beset by the real worry that the United States might now be willing to risk war. Since Dulles, however, continued to disclaim any intention to use force, they expressed puzzlement at exactly what American policy was to be. More European leaders began to ask themselves whether some form of neutralism might not disengage them from a struggle in which the United States now appeared to be becoming more irrational.

Then, on June 16 and 17, 1953, workers in Berlin and other towns throughout East Germany revolted. The East German regime, unable to handle the situation, maintained power only because the Russian army quelled the revolt. The immediate causes were economic hardship, purges, and increased work norms, as well as ferment in Communist leadership brought by the death of Stalin three months earlier. From the point of view of international politics, several things were made clear: the East European regimes had failed dismally to create mass support, and the Soviet Union would probably have to be wary of depending on their armies. More than this, however, the United States, faced with a revolt within the Soviet sphere, did nothing despite appeals for help, and it and the other occupation powers disclaimed any part in the uprising. The talk of liberation had apparently meant nothing. Not until 1956, when a revolt in Hungary assumed even more widespread proportions, was this certain. But again the American administration did nothing. Liberation had not replaced containment, though it had raised high the hopes of many in the captive nations.

A second outcome of the political campaign put further strains on alliance policies and further clouded the international picture. In an effort to reconcile campaign pledges to cut expenditures drastically and also to pursue a more vigorous anti-Communist foreign policy, the new administration in Washington chose a new formula for military strategy: "massive retaliation." First described by Dulles in his

Life magazine article, the doctrine became official when the administration took office, and in January 1954, Secretary Dulles spelled it out in an address to the Council on Foreign Relations. In essence, the doctrine would abandon the attempt to contain the kind of Soviet probe on the periphery of the Communist bloc that had occurred in Korea. Instead of meeting limited force with limited force, the United States, Dulles declared, would "retaliate, instantly, and by means of our own choosing. We can now," he declared, "shape our military establishment to fit what is *our* policy, instead of having to try to be ready to meet the enemy's many choices." In line with this policy came the "New Look" in the American military establishment. It involved a reduction in overall manpower, as well as in American manpower overseas, and placed more emphasis on nuclear air power.

The key in the attempt to shift military strategy was development of the hydrogen bomb. The potential power of the H-bomb was a thousand times greater than that of the first atomic bombs that devastated whole cities in Japan. The first American hydrogen explosions took place in November 1952, at Eniwetok atoll in the Pacific, a month after Britain tested its first atomic bomb. In August 1953 Stalin's successor, Malenkov, announced that the United States no longer had a monopoly of hydrogen bomb production.

Many Westerners first reacted with the feeling that the Soviet premier must be exaggerating or lying. Dulles commented that Malenkov's statement could only be accepted "with some skepticism." Within hours, however, the Atomic Energy Commission of the United States received confirming evidence. Moreover, it revealed later that the Soviet Union had proceeded with somewhat more advanced techniques than had the United States—thus refuting claims that the Communists had "stolen" the secret of the bomb.

The new era had not yet really begun. The United States still had a far larger stockpile of nuclear materials and claimed to possess means of delivery that the Soviet Union lacked. But the Russians had not failed to see the importance of the latter point, and while speeding nuclear development, also pushed forward rapidly with construction of long-range bomber striking forces and a rocket force. The 1954 May Day parade, which featured a fly-over by the new four-jet Tupolev intercontinental bombers, gave dramatic evidence that their progress had been surprisingly rapid. In the West, the developments caused an extraordinary moment of confusion.

Upon reports that the Soviets had exploded their bomb, the director of the American Office of Defense Mobilization declared that "Soviet

Russia is capable of delivering the most destructive weapon ever devised by man on chosen targets in the United States." But the Secretary of Defense said it would be "three years before they have a reasonable number of bombs and airplanes that could deliver them." On the other hand, the recently resigned chairman of the Atomic Energy Commission argued that within one or two years the Russians could destroy the United States.

One thing clear amid the babel of different views was the awesome power of the new weapon. When coupled with the emphasis on the American "new look" and "massive retaliation," it gave statesmen a new source of confusion and doubt. Would the United States actually use massive retaliation against a local attack in the future if the Russians had the capacity to strike back directly at the United States? Would other countries depend on an alliance with the United States that counted on deterrence rather than upon local defense? If deterrence failed and the Soviets attacked, the result might be a holocaust. Given the reduction of American ground forces and hints of possible further withdrawals, would the United States, unable to defend on the ground, rely on a deterrence it would then find either impossible or suicidal to use? Adlai Stevenson, the defeated Democratic candidate in the 1952 presidential campaign asked, "Will we turn brush fires and local hostilities into major conflicts? Are we, indeed, inviting Moscow and Peiping to nibble us to death?"

These questions arose not only in the United States, but in Europe and Japan—where they contributed to growing neutralist sentiment. As a result, administration spokesmen qualified their position: massive retaliation would not be used under all circumstances; American units would be kept in Europe. But the planned troop reductions continued and the confusion persisted. In an attempt to offset the reduction, the administration argued that other countries should provide more of the manpower requirements of the "free world"—a suggestion most of them found politicially unpalatable.

In the end the new administration continued to follow the basic policy lines laid down by the previous administration, but with the shift in military emphasis dictated by budgetary considerations. To compensate for the lack of available means for implementing the more "dynamic" aspects of proposed policy, Administration spokesmen, including Secretary Dulles, continued to indulge in the blustering rhetoric of the campaign. Thus the realities of foreign policy were obscured for the American people, and fear continued to be aroused in other countries that the United States would do something rash.

Dulles' tendency to see the whole Cold War—and the position of any country in relation to it—in terms of a gigantic struggle between good and evil, between which there was no possible compromise (when in fact compromise was being made every day), made this brilliant but limited man the most mistrusted American statesman in a long time. In some cases, as in French Indochina in 1954 (see p. 164), it appeared that he and those around him had been carried away by their own words. In other cases, as at the time of the Geneva Conference of 1955, it appeared that the other side of this blindness had come to the fore (see pp. 203–205).

The Death of Stalin and Soviet Foreign Policy

Since the late 1920s Stalin had been the virtually unchallenged dictator of a Soviet Russia that had grown enormously in industrial strength and world power. In later years the almost oriental potentate ruled in an atmosphere of mystery, terror and seclusion, the object of sycophantic adulation that was fostered by an enormous propaganda machine. At times supple in policy, he could also be enormously rigid; although the Soviet state had grown, his mistakes had been great, and only the devices of historical rewriting and repetitious propaganda kept them from becoming evident. The Nazi-Soviet pact had almost cost the Soviet Union its independence; the obtuse insistence on the imminent failure of American capitalism after the war had led to a bold policy that had brought the American reorientation to containment with its concomitant commitments abroad—a policy that had effectively blocked further Soviet expansion in spite of an enormous and costly Soviet rearmament effort. The prolonged Korean War stimulated a further stiffening of the Western effort and meant the decisive defeat of Stalin's efforts to keep West Germany from rebuilding and rearming within the Western European orbit. The attempt to penetrate Western Europe, Turkey and North Africa had failed, and Yugoslavia had slipped out of Soviet grasp.

Under Stalin, himself, however, the Soviets had retrenched in later years, while continuing to push their nuclear arms project in an effort to match the United States. The Nineteenth Party Congress reflected changes in policy; whether it was because the old dictator was losing his grasp or whether he himself had sensed the discrepancies in his own policies, the greater flexibility that came to characterize his successors' foreign policies began even before they took over. To Western leaders the changes meant that the Soviets acknowledged their failures and recognized that the new dangers inherent in the possession of the hydrogen bomb necessitated an accommodation of sorts with the newly strengthened West. Thus, as the war in Korea dragged to its negotiated conclusion, the Russians, in late 1952, came forth with new offers for a German peace treaty designed to be particularly attractive to the West Germans. They were never explored by the West.

At the Nineteenth Party Congress a more flexible attitude toward the nationalist leaders of new countries appeared. Heretofore they had been stigmatized as bourgeois nationalist lackeys of imperialism. Now they began, in Soviet parlance, to become a part of a worldwide progressive movement with which Communists could cooperate. To some Westerners this new attitude appeared to pose more dangers; others saw it as a sign of mellowing and the need for retrenchment. Finally, structural changes in the moribund Party apparatus gave evidence of Stalin's intention of bringing new blood into the Party. Then, with the death of Stalin in 1953 and the uncertainty that this brought to his empire, the changes came more rapidly.

Within the Soviet Union the ensuing struggle for power was not resolved until Khrushchev emerged victorious in 1957. In July 1953, when Beria, the head of the dread secret police, attempted to seize power, he failed and was executed. In 1955 Malenkov fell by the wayside. In 1956 came Khrushchev's supreme gamble: a long, secret, bitter denunciation of Stalin and his rule to the Party Congress. His position was shaky, but adroit and wily, he defeated the old adherents of Stalin—Molotov and Kaganovich—who had allied themselves to Malenkov and others. Khrushchev then dumped the World War II hero, Marshal Zhukov, whose popularity had led Stalin to down grade him, but who had returned to support Khrushchev. As an ally, he had become too powerful. Finally, in early 1958, Khrushchev demoted Bulganin, who had been his partner in the new diplomacy that began in 1955.

In the meantime, as the new leaders sought to consolidate their power by dismissing or discrediting the older generation of Stalinists who could be made scapegoats for the hardships of earlier times, they put their own claims to legitimacy to a severe test. In East Germany the test came in June 1953, accompanied by rioting in Czechoslovakia. It was successfully weathered, although it revealed weaknesses in the Soviet structure of power as well as weaknesses in Western ability to capitalize on them.

The new Soviet leaders made many concessions outside their own sphere. They pressured the Chinese Communists to accept the neutral nations' plans for exchange of prisoners of war in Korea. As a consequence, the Korean armistice was signed on July 27, 1953. It was supposed to be followed by a general peace conference within three months, and President Syngman Rhee of South Korea, who had unsuccessfully tried to sabotage the peace discussions in order to keep the United States in the war, declared that if unification did not result from the conference, he would not feel bound by the armistice. There was no conference, however. Attempts to bring it about finally failed in mid-1954 over the issues of its composition and agenda, but the real reasons lay in the basic conflict itself and in continued American and Chinese opposition over Formosa and a seat for the Chinese in the United Nations. Rhee had to content himself with continued American military support for the independence of South Korea, a new military security treaty, and large-scale economic aid.

Russian fence-mending took place elsewhere, too. At the United Nations, Secretary General Trygve Lie had long been opposed by the Soviets for his support of the Korean effort. He had previously come under American attack for his support of Communist Chinese membership, and was now under fire for his personnel policies. In November 1952 he resigned; Russian intransigence made choice of a successor difficult. But in March the Soviets agreed to the appointment of the Swedish diplomat, Dag Hammarskjold.

Other conciliatory moves included resumption of diplomatic relations with Yugoslavia, Greece, and Israel, renunciation of postwar claims to certain parts of Turkey and abandonment of Russian demands for joint Soviet-Turkish control of sea and air bases around the Turkish Black Sea straits. Late in 1953 Malenkov evinced an interest in settling certain outstanding financial and border questions with Iran, and the Soviet government began to negotiate a series of trade treaties with other countries without trying to use the bait of Soviet trade to obtain renunciation of the controls over shipment of strategic goods to the Soviet bloc. And again, the bait of a peace treaty and cancellation of all war-born claims was held out to West Germany in order to prevent it from moving further in the direction of European economic and military integration.

To Winston Churchill, once more Prime Minister of England after the Conservative electoral victory in October of 1951, the new fluid elements in the Soviet position seemed to offer a field for diplomatic activity. On May 11, 1953 he called for a Summit Conference similar to those great conferences that had helped shape the world scene in war time, suggesting as he did so that it might be possible to reconcile Russian security interests with European unity. But he ran head-on into President Eisenhower's view that the Soviets should first show good faith by preparing "to allow other nations, including those of Eastern Europe, the free choice of their own forms of government," and "to act in concert with others upon serious disarmament proposals to be made firmly effective by stringent UN control and inspection." The Soviets retorted that to expect them to accept a series of conditions while the United States accepted none was asking too much. This argument struck a responsive chord in many Western Europeans. But the effort to explore further the possibility of a more explicit détente was thwarted not only by the American position, but also by the failure, in the middle of the year, to reach any agreement on the long-delayed Austrian peace treaty.

The Far East and Southeast Asia

The years after Stalin's death brought other Far Eastern developments, and the appearance of a general Russian relaxation after the end of the Korean War. The picture was complicated by the American determination to strengthen its position in the Far East and continued Chinese Communist efforts to press for solutions to conflicts through almost any means, regardless of Russian softness.

In Malaya, despite the steady move toward self-government and intensified efforts to stamp out the Communist rebels in the jungles, the rebellion—outgrowth of the concerted decision in 1948 of Southeast Asian Communist parties to resort to violence—continued. In French Indochina, on the other hand, the war finally came to a conclusion, marking another defeat for France in its attempt to restore its prewar empire. It left extraordinary problems in its wake and eventually brought the substitution of American influence for that of the French.

France's attempt to restore its empire had taken the form of the French Union, a device that would permit various forms of dependency, all leaving France in a position of superiority, and still able to carry out its "civilizing work." * The loss of the long, bitter seven years' war in Indochina, like the much earlier loss of Syria and Lebanon, came as a result of French commitments to an aim that was beyond the strength of postwar France. The commitment was a matter of principle to some conservative groups within France, but was also a

---

* The phrase was used at the Brazzaville Conference of 1944 when basic colonial policy was drafted. According to the Charter, "the purpose of the civilizing work accomplished by France in the colonies excluded any idea of autonomy, any possibility of an evolution outside of the French Empire."

response to pressures from the French colonials within Indochina, who wanted to lose neither their special status nor their investments. In an effort to counter popular support of the Communist-led Vietminh, the French made concession after concession to other nationalist groups whom they tried to set up in opposition to Ho Chi Minh and his Vietminh. There was no purpose in setting up other groups, however, unless they continued to recognize the special status of the French. Yet those who did so, like the chosen French instrument, the Emperor Bao Dai, received no popular support. After years of negotiation, the French and various Indo-Chinese groups reached an agreement, ratified early in 1950, creating the three states of Vietnam, Laos, and Cambodia, within the French Union; in a few days most Western states recognized them. (The Communist states countered by recognizing the Vietminh.) But Emperor Bao Dai had difficulty forming a cabinet and setting up a national army. Any French concessions to him were popularly viewed as having been extracted as a result of pressures of the Communist Vietminh. These increased greatly after the victory of the Chinese Communists established a common border through which supplies could flow, and across which the Vietminh could seek sanctuary, rest, and training. The efforts put forward by the French were enormous yet insufficient to accomplish the job. The war cost France a billion dollars a year, drained her of resources that could have been used for internal investments or for reconstruction in North Africa, and, in a circular process, contributed to the weakening of French governments which in turn could therefore do little to increase the vigor of their efforts. The weakness also aided the nationalist movements in other parts of the French Union, particularly in North Africa.

American aid, supplied after Chinese intervention in Korea, and the use of new and different tactics, proved insufficient. Not until 1953 and early 1954 did France take the final, drastic political step of negotiating and accepting full independence—first of Laos and Cambodia and then Vietnam. The French could argue quite cogently that such a step had been impossible while the fighting continued, and that the fight in Indochina was part of the worldwide policy of containment in which they were doing their unrecognized and unappreciated share. But it was also true that the delay had persisted because French *colons* had not wanted to give Bao Dai what they had refused to hand over to Ho Chi Minh. In Asian eyes, therefore, it was a war of nationalists against colonialists, in which Bao Dai was only a puppet.

In the meantime the battle for Indochina reached a psychological climax in the Communist siege of a French-established strong point, the isolated fortress of Dien Bien Phu. For weeks the bitter attack continued against heroic resistance, while the French airlifted supplies and men. The Communists were determined to capture it: a victory at Dien Bien Phu would immensely bolster their position at the forthcoming Geneva conference, which was to consider the entire Far East situation and which both representatives of the United States and Communist China would attend.

American officials recognized the psychological importance of Dien Bien Phu and nearly committed the United States to the Indochinese war. Already, though the French supplied the manpower, America was paying two-thirds to three-quarters of the cost of the war; the administration had accepted the French contention that a build-up of Vietnamese troops would lead to defeat of the Vietminh within a year if modern arms were available. (Contrary to widely held views, the Vietminh forces were in many cases larger and better-armed than the French.) But since the beginning of 1954 the French position had greatly deteriorated, and all attention was turned to Dien Bien Phu; in April the French government asked for an American air strike against the besieging forces.

Although the administration had previously denied any intent to be involved in the war in Indochina, President Eisenhower now talked of the "domino" theory of Southeast Asia; like a row of dominoes, if one of the weak states went down, the others would certainly go too. Vice-President Nixon launched an off-the-record trial balloon when he mentioned the possibility of using American troops in the area. But Congress registered dismay at the idea, and more sober counsel prevailed, both within the administration and without. After a somewhat belated consultation of European and Asian allies, it withdrew from its extended position. When Prime Minister Churchill told the House of Commons on April 27 that he had made no new military or political commitments and that Britain was not prepared to give any undertakings about military action in Indochina before the Geneva Conference, he was cheered. (One by-product of the consultations was considerable bad feeling between British Foreign Secretary Anthony Eden and Secretary Dulles. Eden thought that Dulles, in an effort to pressure him into supporting intervention, had returned to the United States and publicized as Eden's views the idea that Britain would accept an intervention which in fact Eden opposed.)

Geneva, 1954: The Far Eastern Settlement

The Geneva Conference of 1954 grew out of the sequence of events described in the foregoing narrative. As a result of diplomatic exchanges about the future of Germany and Austria during 1953, and as a result of Churchill's estimate that the changed world situation of 1953 was one in which a "Summit Conference" might produce useful results, the three Western powers had agreed to a four-power meeting of Foreign Ministers with the Soviet Union at Berlin in January 1954. A preliminary conference, at Bermuda early in December 1953, of Eisenhower, Churchill and the French Premier, who happened at the the moment to be Joseph Laniel, did little more than ratify the decision to hold such a meeting.

The chief interest of the United States in the meeting was to demonstrate to its allies and to the growing number of neutrals led by India that the United States was always ready and willing to negotiate, especially when this would reveal the bad faith of the adversary. The European allies hoped for something more, while the Soviet Union used the conference to pursue its aim of securing a broader conference that would consider the Far East and would introduce Communist China to international society. In this the Soviets were aided by the failure, since mid-1953, of all attempts to hold a Korean peace conference. The matter had gone to the United Nations General Assembly in the fall of 1953, where a majority supported the Communist position that the conference should be in the form of a round table rather than a face-to-face confrontation, but had been unable to muster the necessary two-thirds vote in the Assembly.

Three weeks of meetings in Berlin produced continued deadlock over Germany and Austria, as well as a Soviet suggestion for a European security treaty open to all European—not Atlantic—states, and superseding all military pacts. When Dulles returned to the United States his report on the meeting was to the effect that it again indicated that the Russians were completely intransigent and that they still desired to extend their gains while relinquishing none. But to Europeans the absence of propaganda at the meeting led them to hold out hopes that a new conference might, in fact, reach some accommodation. And there would be a new meeting at Geneva in April. Communist China and other Asian states would participate, and the Far East as well as European security would come under discussion. How was it that Secretary Dulles agreed to meet with the Chinese Communists?

The answer lay not only in the necessity to explore further the question of a Korean peace settlement before abandoning all hopes for one, but also the pressures emanating from European states, especially France. Dulles hoped that France would now, after Berlin, proceed to ratify the treaty establishing the European Defense Community, especially if he made some concession to rising sentiment within France for a general negotiated settlement in the Far East. As for Britain, Churchill wanted continued negotiation with the Communists, and the British had begun to be sensitive to the opinion and suggestions of new Commonwealth members—India, Ceylon, and Pakistan—as well as other neutrals like Burma and Indonesia. So Dulles, reassuring Congress that meeting and talking to Chinese Communist leaders did not imply American recognition, prepared to go to Geneva. On February 22 Prime Minister Nehru had appealed for an immediate cease-fire in Indochina, and had subsequently denounced the possibility of American intervention and American plans for a new security organization for Southeast Asia. The Geneva Conference was planned for April 26; on April 28 a number of Asian leaders met in Colombo, Ceylon, where they supported the Indian position on Indochina.

With the military situation deteriorating rapidly in Indochina, the possibility of American military intervention dim, pressures for some settlement growing, and the West in disarray on numerous other issues, the Geneva Conference opened with every prospect that it would lead to deadlock on Korea and either formal ratification of division of Indochina or a breakup over the issue. This, in turn, might lead to more open American intervention or further French disengagement, with possible domestic upheaval in France and disruption of NATO.

The conference lasted, in several phases, from April 26 until July 21, and the problem of Korea brought the expected negative results. Communist proposals for the elimination of American influence clashed with Western proposals that would have eliminated Communist influence and despite strenuous and lengthy efforts no common ground could be found. On June 15 the fifteen United Nations participants and South Korea "reluctantly and regretfully" broke off the negotiations. But in the meantime two events precipitated a new, temporary, and shaky resolution of the situation in Indochina.

The first was the fall of Dien Bien Phu on May 7, with the capture of its beleaguered garrison. The second, following the fall of the Laniel government over policy in Indochina, was the accession to power of Pierre Mendès-France.

Instability of previous French governments and the unresolved problems of the European Defense Community and the Saar brought the new Premier to prominence. Mendès-France was a new and untainted political figure, ironically a leader of the moribund Radical Socialist Party. He used the very weakness of the French executive as a source of power: give him, he asked the French National Assembly, a certain period of time within which to reach solutions to the outstanding problems. They would be painful solutions, but there was no other way to end any of the problems that needed resolution. On June 17 he asked for four weeks to achieve a truce in Vietnam. If the Assembly refused to let him do this, unhindered, and did not accept the unpleasant solution he would devise, chaos and revolution would certainly result. In each case the Gordian knot must be cut, and as far as Indochina was concerned too much good money had already been thrown after bad.

At Geneva, nine nations had taken part in the Indochina discussions: the Big Four, Communist China, the three Associated States of Indochina, and representatives of the Vietminh (or the "Democratic Republic of Vietnam"). The French opened with proposals for a truce and a regrouping of forces—a plan unacceptable to the Communists, who wanted to be able to operate freely throughout Indochina. As a consequence of the French proposals, the Indochinese and especially the Vietnamese representatives began to move away from the French. They wanted no partition, while the Laotian and Cambodian representatives maintained that Communists within *their* borders must be considered invaders from Vietnam, and therefore the conference should see to their being expelled. The stiffer Vietnamese line matched that of the United States; both called for a cease-fire, United Nations supervised elections throughout the area, separate treatment for Laos and Cambodia, and some form of international guarantee for the area. On the last point the Vietnamese looked to the United Nations, while the American representatives were busy lining up support for a new organization for Southeast Asia, more or less modeled on NATO.

A sign of increased flexibility in the Communist position coincided with the coming to power of Mendès-France. The conference took a long breathing spell by creating a commission to study the details of how to stop hostilities. Dulles—old proponent of liberation—now decided not to return to a conference whose inevitable outcome appeared to be partition of Vietnam, with the northern half going to the Communists. Chou En-lai, Communist China's Foreign Minister, spent his time mending fences in conferences with Nehru of India and Burma's Prime Minister U Nu, in which all agreed to noninterference in one another's affairs. In the meantime, the British and Americans, long at odds over the crisis, came to a general agreement on the creation of a new security organization for the area regardless of the nature of the settlement in Indochina. Mendès-France, facing further military pressures by the Vietminh, told his Assembly that if an "honorable" cease-fire could not be secured—one that would allow the evacuation from

Communist areas of those who wanted to go—he would seek authorization to send French conscript troops to Indochina, a move every government had so far avoided. Finally, under the impact of all these developments, the armistice agreements were signed on July 21. Vietnam, which had a new regime under the leadership of the devoutly Catholic political unknown, Ngo Dinh Diem, registered a solemn protest.

Neutralization and demilitarization were arranged for Laos and Cambodia, though within Laos a French military training mission would remain and the dissident Pathet Lao Communist forces of a few thousand would be regrouped but allowed some special relationship. Vietnam was divided along the 17th parallel, and the extensive French positions in the north surrendered in return for Vietminh withdrawal in the south. The agreements forbade the introduction of any new troops or equipment or the building of new bases, provided for free transfer of that part of the population that chose one part of the country over the other, and provided for free, general, secret elections throughout the area within two years. International Commissions composed of Canada, India and Poland would supervise the agreements and elections.

There was little doubt that the Communists accepted the arrangements partly because they were confident that within the two-year period the shaky government in the south would fall, thus allowing them to take over the entire area. But they were also influenced by the threat of stiffened resistance on the part of the West to any further direct military attack, by the tardy French grant of complete independence to the Indochinese states, and by the desire to gain the good will of the new grouping of Asian states.

In subsequent months the agreements were implemented by withdrawal of large numbers of Vietminh units from the south and the southward flow of both military and civilian personnel. Ho Chi Minh's regime in the north behaved in a friendly manner toward French civilians and businessmen; invitations to remain and guarantees of good treatment were extended. In the south, matters changed rapidly. Ngo Dinh Diem's regime began to receive the unqualified American support that made it able to disarm varied opposition sects, some of which controlled police forces and could field substantial armies of their own. American support also enabled Diem to operate more and more independently of the French, who found themselves replaced by American influence, to the dismay of French colonial elements. The United States budgeted $500 million for aid to the Republic in 1955, a year that also saw the end of the French-backed Emperor Bao Dai's attempt to continue to retain influence from his comfortable quarters on the French Riviera. Some 850,000 refugees from the north had to be resettled and with American aid, the Diem regime proved equal to this enormous task. In mid-1955 Ho Chi Minh traveled to Moscow and Peking and signed trade and aid agreements that effectively coordinated the north half of Vietnam with the other Communist states. July also saw the breakdown of attempts to prepare for the forthcoming elections: Diem declared that he could see no conditions under which the Communists in the north would allow them to be truly free. But the 98 per cent of the vote cast for him in the referendum between him and Bao Dai cast some doubt on the freedom of his own electoral processes. By the end of the year Diem was President, Premier, and Defense Minister of the Republic of South Vietnam.

Taiwan and SEATO: The United States Extends Its Alliances

Settlement of the war in Korea and of the struggle in Indochina— however precarious and unstable the agreements might be—nevertheless stopped people from shooting at one another. Soon after the Geneva conference, however, Chou En-lai reaffirmed a basic Chinese Communist aim:

In order that international tension may be further eased, in order that the peace secured through the armistice in Indochina may be consolidated and extended, and that the five principles of peaceful coexistence may be carried through, it is imperative that the People's Republic of China liberate Taiwan and liquidate the traitorous Chiang Kai-shek group.

Nevertheless, during the next year the stalemate in the area continued, as did the arrangements made by the United States and Chiang designed to stabilize the situation and produce a *de facto* and tacit agreement. There were abortive attempts by Britain and other states to promote a two-China policy that would lead to the creation *de facto* and *de jure* of two successor states, both, presumably, to be seated in the United Nations. The two states concerned were unswervingly opposed. Each claimed to be the *only* China (tiny Nationalist China, with a population of ten million, continued to pay the United Nations dues assessed upon it when it was a country of four hundred million, in order to buttress its claim). The Eisenhower administration therefore did two things. Having signed a mutual security treaty with Chiang, it secured, in January 1955 a resolution from Congress authorizing it to act in the event of an attack on Formosa or the nearby Pescadore islands. Although the

President could presumably go to Chiang's defense anyway, this would serve notice to the Communists of American determination, as well as forestall the kind of criticism that Truman met for executive action in meeting the Korean attack without support of Congress. On the other hand the resolution limited American commitment; to all intents and purposes it "released" Chiang since it was accompanied by publication of correspondence about the mutual security treaty that indicated the United States would not aid him if he attempted to attack the mainland. At the same time the administration forced him to withdraw from the Tachen islands, a small group far to the north of Formosa and close to the mainland.

The administration left one thing ambiguous: what it would do if the Communists attacked the Nationalist-held islands of Quemoy (a hundred miles from Formosa and blocking the mouth of the Chinese port of Amoy) and of Matsu (equally far and commanding the approaches to the port of Foochow). Spokesmen declared that if the President felt an attack upon them was a part of and prelude to an attack upon Formosa, the United States would help defend them.

Despite the ambiguity of the last move—one opposed by the British, who would have liked a withdrawal to Formosa proper and the Pescadores—the clear American determination coupled with the retrenching moves eased matters in the area temporarily. Another Asian "settlement" appeared to have been reached.

The American project designed to buttress the new situation in Southeast Asia—the Southeast Asia Treaty Organization—was brought into being at Manila in September 1954. Ceylon, Burma, Indonesia, and India believed that the pact would do more harm than good; the Indochinese states were excluded by the terms of the Geneva settlement. As a result only Pakistan, Thailand, and the Philippines joined with Great Britain, France, Australia, New Zealand, and the United States in the pact. It was not an organization in any way similar to NATO. Although it foresaw some coordination of military strategies for the area, it did not provide for the stationing of the troops of one member state in the territory of the others, and it did not provide for the almost automatic reaction to threat which NATO did.

The United States was in fact the member that stood out against either the creation of a unified command or a unified force or the transformation of SEATO into a large-scale organization for economic development—all of which were proposed by other members. Against the argument that it could not deal with subversion—the kind of threat to security most likely to develop in the area—its proponents contended that once the overt military threat could be removed, action against subversion was easier. The treaty also provided for consultation in case of threats of serious subversion, and was accompanied by a declaration that its guarantees extended to the territories of the Indo-chinese states, even though they could not be parties to it.

More Stirrings in the Non-Western World: Iran, Egypt, Africa

Developments in Asia between 1950 and 1955 showed the importance of China on the world scene and the attention Western states had begun to pay to the views of leaders of such states as India, Indonesia and Burma. In the same period other areas of the world began—sometimes violently—to mark the change in their status *vis-à-vis* Europe and the United States. In most cases these changes demonstrated a lessening of European influence; in some they represented replacement of European by American influence. In no case did the Soviets actually bring about the developments, nor did they profit directly from them. But in the latter years of the period they began to work to use them for their own purposes.

For Iran the period was dominated by Premier Mohammed Mossadegh and his attempt to nationalize the British-owned oil industry. Economic crises, internal instability and corruption, the conservatism of the landed oligarchy, Soviet intrigue—all contributed to a chaotic situation. The Shah of Iran, devoted to the idea of reform, attempted to get economic and military aid from the United States in 1949, but on the basis of reports from the scene, the Truman administration was reluctant to do much for fear that it be pouring out money for nothing, as it had done in Nationalist China. Since large sums were being spent in Europe, where things *were* being done, the administration transmitted its view to the Shah: if he could put his governmental house in order so that the aid might be of some effect, he could expect a warmer reception for his requests. All through 1950, with the aid of the energetic Premier Razmara, the Shah proceeded with reform measures. But the expected aid did not materialize and within the Majlis—the Iranian Parliament—there was agitation to find alternative development funds, by speeding negotiations with the giant Anglo-Iranian Oil Company to increase Iran's share of its profits. Anglo-Iranian had long been the sole concessionaire in Iran, and negotiations for a change in the division of profits had dragged on for a lengthy period. Early in 1951 Mossadegh's parliamentary group began to clamor for nationalization of the oil property and on March 20, following the assassination of Razmara by a Moslem fanatic, a nationalization law passed the Majlis and Senate. Mossadegh became Premier, riots and disturbances erupted all over Iran, and the oil operations shut down.

The Mossadegh regime lasted until the end of August 1953. During that time it rested on an unstable coalition of religious fanatics who resisted the modernization of society, on nationalists of every stripe, student groups, and the large left-wing Tudeh party, which was Communist-led. All were united in only one matter: continued national ownership of the oil properties and defiance of Britain.

Mossadegh counted on Europe's need for the oil and on his ability to sell it on the world market. The British counted on Iran's needs for the oil revenues. Both were mistaken: Europe found its oil in the rapidly expanding facilities in Saudi Arabia and especially the tiny Sheikdom of Kuwait. The Anglo-Iranian Oil Company announced that it would take to court any other purchaser of oil from Iran on the basis that the property had been stolen from the company. Since the major oil fleets of the world were owned by sympathetic companies who were also interested in seeing that nationalization fail, Iran was able to sell very little oil. But lack of foreign revenues was not as quickly disastrous as the British had calculated it would be, even though Iran was unable to get foreign aid from anywhere. Past revenues had largely gone to an upper class that was hurt when it no longer had the income to import the luxuries it was accustomed to—but the government no longer rested on this class.

All attempts failed at negotiation, arbitration, action through the United Nations Security Council, and proceedings at the International Court of Justice. The Iranians steadfastly maintained that nationalization was a purely domestic matter, and they would tolerate no modification of the principle.

Eventually, as economic woes grew and policy had to be devised, the shaky unity of the disparate groups supporting Mossadegh collapsed. He began to rule by decree, resisted deposition by the Shah (who was forced to flee the country), and was finally overthrown on August 19 by units of the army who had remained loyal to the Shah. The Shah returned, and a new regime, receiving emergency American economic aid, negotiated a new oil agreement enabling the Iranian oil industry to resume output. The settlement reflected the fact that no regime could simply have brought back the British: a consortium of eight companies—five American, one French, one Dutch plus Anglo-Iranian—took over the operation of the National Iranian Oil Company.

Although the Iranian episode had future reverberations—it had raised the spectre of nationalization, one never to be allayed—the July 1952 revolt in Egypt had far wider repercussions.

The revolt was the culmination of years of frustration and chaos. The postwar period in Egyptian politics had been devoted to substitution of one political clique by another, while popular dissatisfaction mounted and revealed itself in riots and disorder. The sybaritic King, far removed from popular feeling, had actually tried to rule through the cliques that represented themselves as democratic parties.

Three major issues dominated Egyptian foreign policy: removal of British troops and evacuation of their great Suez base; the future of the condominium with Britain over the Sudan; and relations with Israel. On the first count the political parties had vied with one another in calling for withdrawal. But though the British began negotiations in 1946, they stiffened their stand as Russian pressures mounted. It would be foolish, they felt, to abandon the bases just when they were again needed: World War II had once more proved their strategic importance. No other spot in the Middle East lay athwart such a vital lifeline or possessed such facilities. And as the British stand stiffened, anti-British feeling mounted in Egypt. It culminated in a fight between British and Egyptian troops in Ismaila in January, 1952, and was followed by a great day of rioting in Cairo on January 26, during which numerous landmarks symbolizing British influence were burned and sacked.

Contributing to anti-British feeling was the British attitude on the future of the Sudan. The British argued that the Sudanese should be allowed to choose their own future. Against this, the Egyptians argued for the unity of the Nile Valley: a hostile country athwart the upper Nile could strangle Egypt's livelihood.

Finally, the defeat of the poorly led and miserably equipped Egyptian armies in the Palestine war turned hostile public attention against the regime itself. It was all very well for the politicians to proclaim their nationalism, but if this was the best they could do in defending Egyptian honor, it was far too little. Moreover, the creation of Israel engendered a permanent conflict of interest between Egypt and those Western powers that Egyptian leaders thought had set up and now helped maintain Israel. All through the Korean War Egypt and the other Arab countries abstained from giving any aid to the United Nations effort on the basis that conflict between the United States and the Soviet Union was none of their business and that Russia was no threat to them. The real threat was Zionism, the outpost of Western imperialism.

The Revolutionary Command Council took power with little fuss on July 23, 1952. It represented a "Committee of Free Officers" created back in 1947, and it moved swiftly, first to force King Farouk's abdication, then to destroy the corrupt political parties as well as the powerful Moslem Brotherhood that wanted a return to a theocratic state. A struggle for power within the RCC developed between the man first chosen as a figurehead for the new government, Colonel Naguib, and Colonel Gamal Abdul Nasser, who was the victor. The RCC launched a program of internal reform, concentrating on land reform, labor laws, new irrigation and industrial projects, and studies for even more extensive industrialization. Moving cautiously in the realm of political forms, Nasser eventually established a new authoritarian pattern for Egypt.

In the realm of foreign policy, the Nasser regime liquidated two persistent problems, the Sudan and Suez. Nasser agreed with the British that the Sudanese would be given a transitional period of three years to develop institutions of self-government, after which they would have a free choice of union or independence. Although the Egyptians at first thought the Sudanese would choose union, the possibility became remote and relations deteriorated as the Egyptians redoubled their efforts to create pro-union sentiment in the Sudan. On December 19, 1955 the Sudanese Chamber announced Sudanese independence, and Egypt accepted it.

In 1954, after lengthy negotiations, a new treaty replaced the old 1936 treaty between Egypt and Britain on the Suez Canal. The new one provided for the withdrawal of British troops within twenty months, maintenance of the base by civilian technicians, the right of British re-entry in case of an attack on Egypt, an Arab League state or Turkey, and reaffirmed the Treaty of 1888 that guaranteed freedom of navigation on the Suez Canal. It also recognized that the Canal was "an integral part of Egypt."

In the Middle East people hailed Nasser's diplomatic triumph, and in the West, governments hoped for better relations with the new regime as a consequence of the removal of an old irritant. But because of the Baghdad Pact and Israel—which faced continued Arab blockade and border raids, and retaliated in heavy force—good relations were impossible, and in 1955 the Middle East situation became further complicated and inflamed. International efforts to mediate between Arab and Jew failed one after the other. Arab leaders consistently expressed their determination to destroy Israel, and Israel continued the firm policy of allowing unlimited immigration. On these shoals foundered the effort to work out the "Johnston Plan," for a technical agreement on water-sharing and hydroelectric and irrigation development between Israel and neighboring states. It was an attempt to attack political conflict at the technical level of economic cooperation; its effects would, it was hoped, eventually mitigate the political conflict. Functional cooperation was impossible, however, given the extent and intensity of the political differences. And in Arab eyes the West became further identified with Israel, simply because Western diplomacy, however much it sided with the Arabs on particular matters, nevertheless presupposed the continued existence of Israel within the boundaries set by the Palestine war.

Developments in Iran and Egypt, the role played by India and other Asian states in the Korean and Indochinese affairs and in limiting SEATO, all represent the swiftly changing relationships between Western powers and non-Western areas in the years 1950–55. In North Africa and areas south of the Sahara such changes also began to be evident.

Already in 1949 General Assembly adoption of a resolution on the former Italian colonies had foreshadowed what was to come. It had made Libya independent, federated Eritrea with Ethiopia—restored to independence after the war—and although it had made Somaliland a trust territory, a ten-year timetable had been set for independence. In Kenya in East Africa, the Mau-Mau revolt erupted in 1952, a complicated response to land tenure problems, tribal politics and racism, but which also represented national discontent. The movement was finally crushed by native cooperation with the British authorities; in substance and form it was too backward-looking. But during its course, in 1954, British authorities in Kenya took the step of introducing a new constitution with a large measure of African representation. It was not and could not be completely satisfactory, striving as it did to balance white and nonwhite representation; but it indicated that changes were in the wind.

In the Gold Coast, in Nigeria, in French Africa, Rhodesia, South Africa, as well as in Kenya, African political parties had formed, their nationalism fanned by native wartime service in European armed forces, by the attention paid to them by the United Nations, by the European weakness revealed by the war, and by the facts of new urbanization, education, and industrialization and trade. In the Gold Coast in West Africa, rioting and demonstrations in early 1948 sparked a vast upheaval. They marked the rise of a new African political leader, Kwame Nkrumah (he had been educated in the United States and

England) and the end of any attempt to carry out the 1946 Constitution, which had left non-African appointive members in a clear majority in the Executive Council. An All-African Commission presided over by an African judge drew up a new constitution which took effect in 1951. It came close to providing independence, and promised what was virtually Dominion status in the near future. Nkrumah's nationalist Convention People's Party won a surprisingly large electoral victory, and Nkrumah, jailed for organizing a large-scale illegal strike, was released to become the first Prime Minister.

Change in the direction of self-government and independence came easily in direct relationship to the lack of numbers of white settlers. In the Gold Coast there were few; Kenya was exceeded in its proportion of white settlers only by South Africa, the Portuguese colonies, Algeria, and the Rhodesias. In an effort in 1953 to reconcile the demands of the Rhodesian whites with those of the blacks, Britain formed a new political unit, the Central African Federation. Landlocked, it was bordered on the south by South Africa, whose dominant white minority had begun to take its own peculiar pathway of segregation, known as apartheid, and on either side by the Portuguese colonies, where rigid suppression of black nationalism would continue to be the rule. On the north were the more African states of Tanganyika and the Belgian Congo. The two Rhodesias and Nyasaland, brought together into the Federation by an uneasy British Parliament, represented an attempt to find a compromise between the dominant white minorities who wanted to maintain their special status, and the new African leaders who unequivocally demanded one man–one vote. For the Africans the Federation was an unacceptable compromise because, although it increased native political participation, it still provided for a special political status for the whites. The whole matter was complicated by the presence of Asian minorities, tribal feuds, splits among white workers, white businessmen, and white missionaries, and by the varying degree of white domination in the three component units. Black opposition made its beginning inauspicious, even though it appeared to be a realistic compromise. The Federation was meant to be a bulwark against the harshness of apartheid to the south as well as a bulwark against the advance of radical black nationalism to the north that would inevitably come into open conflict with apartheid and perhaps shatter the continent. In addition, the Federation made economic sense, but the opposition of black leadership dimmed its promise.

Far to the north, along the Mediterranean coast, events took a different turn. The area was affected by its geographical proximity to

European and Middle Eastern political developments and, in Algeria, by the presence of the greatest ratio of white settlers to natives anywhere outside South Africa. Morocco, ostensibly a protectorate, was in fact ruled almost directly through a French-created administrative apparatus and through local tribal chieftains. Moroccan nationalist agitation in this period centered around the person of Sultan Mohammed V whom the French had installed in 1927. The urban groups that formed the core of the movement found in the Sultan an ally with a strong card to play. So long as the French pretended Morocco was merely a protectorate, they had to abide by the rule that the Sultan had to countersign all decrees. He had begun to reject French decrees as early as 1944, and in the early 1950s virtually went on strike, while refusing to disavow nationalist organizations proscribed by the French. The French responded in 1953 by organizing a rural revolt against the Sultan, then deposed and exiled him on the pretext that he had lost the support of his subjects. As the 'fifties advanced, nationalist agitation using the symbol of the deposed king increased in scope and in aims. In 1955 the new government of Premier Guy Mollet returned the Sultan to his throne, and the next year Morocco was granted full independence.

In Tunisia—another French protectorate since the nineteenth century—nationalist agitation centered in the person of Habib Bourguiba, who had been a leader of the Neo-Destour, or Constitution party, since the 1930s. For the first five years after World War II he had toured the world seeking support for Tunisian independence. He was allowed to reenter Tunisia in 1949, with the prospect of internal autonomy held out by the French. But Bourguiba demanded more and was subsequently arrested and deported. As in Morocco, the result was an increase in nationalist agitation, supported now by the new revolutionary regime in Cairo, ready to give aid to any North African nationalist movement. In July 1954, Mendès-France, as part of his effort to cut French losses, flew to Tunis and recognized the right of Tunisia to complete autonomy subject to conventions that were to be negotiated. Bourguiba was released and allowed to return to Tunisia, and within two years Tunisia, too, achieved independence.

In Algeria, flanked by Morocco and Tunisia, the years 1950–55 saw far more ominous developments. Algeria was different; one tenth of the population was of European descent, and the French government had incorporated Algeria into France, creating out of it three departments that were represented in the French Parliament and subject to French law. Native residents, however, were second-class citizens.

As in the cases of Morocco, Tunisia, and other areas of Africa, the impact of modernization and education began to make itself felt quite early in the twentieth century. And again, World War II gave nationalism impetus, as France went down to defeat, other foreign troops entered, the Atlantic Charter and Declaration of the United Nations began to be taken at face value, and native inhabitants found that European states would compete for their allegiance. An outbreak of nationalist violence in 1945 was quickly quelled and followed by French reforms that gave to the mixed Moslem population a greater degree of political participation. The reforms were not far-reaching, nor were they fully implemented. But the French, fully cognizant of the extent to which the Algerian economy was tied to France, were quite confident about the situation in Algeria; it remained relatively stable after the growth of nationalist dissidence in neighboring Tunisia and Morocco. It was immensely disquieting, therefore, when on the night of November 1, 1954—soon after disengagement in Indochina—the French were confronted with a wave of concerted terrorist violence. The first attempts to quell it, based on accurate estimates that a small band were the perpetrators, failed as young Algerians flocked to the movement. By 1955—although the French had not yet realized it—the beginning of the end had come for the French Empire in Africa.

Latin America Enters the World Stage

In the postwar decade the twenty-one American states established the formal inter-American system (see pp. 101–103). In some ways the system gave the impression that all was well with the Americas, that things would take care of themselves under a multilateralized Monroe Doctrine, that Peron of Argentina with his uniforms, his rallies, and his oversized armies was just a fly in the ointment. In fact, clearly visible beneath this facade were some of the same stirrings beginning to animate parts of the non-Western world. Although the similarities were great, there were differences, too, arising from a different historical experience, culture, geography, and economic situation.

During World War II the countries of Central and South America had amassed large dollar credits through shipments of raw materials to feed the enormous American war machine. The second half of the 1940s had seen those balances dissipated, as well as inflation, balance of payment difficulties, and radical shifts in the prices of the single crops or raw materials that many of the countries exported. The result, as usual, had been political upheaval, and constitutional regimes were threatened. The American response had been unsatisfactory: at Bogota, in 1948, when the formal institutions of the OAS were created, there had been Latin demands for an Inter-American Marshall Plan, even on a smaller scale. The United States, with its heavy commitments in the rest of the world, and the State Department worries about the inadequacy of the American military establishment, was prepared only to ease the terms on which the Export-Import Bank would make loans, and to launch a modest program of technical aid. Americans could point to the many programs financed by foundations and missions, and to continued American private investment. But this did not allay a growing feeling that the United States was neglecting its "Good Neighbors" to the south. The Korean War brought another favorable rise in the price of raw materials. But with the end of the war the boom slackened, bringing another drop in the price of many Latin American exports.

Although production increased in most Latin American countries in the years after World War II, it became evident in the early 1950s that Latin American economies were radically unbalanced, and that population increases were swallowing up production increases. The imbalance could be seen in the contrast between the lavish new apartment buildings, hotels, and offices, and their surrounding slums, impoverished countryside, and somnolent villages. Considering these contrasts, radical politics, using the new techniques of mass communication, were bound to flourish.

Moreover, the United States had enjoyed good relations with the ruling classes in the urban areas, creating a situation in which radicals and reformers could charge successfully that the wealth produced by trade with the United States buttressed the political power of the ruling groups. American investments might raise the general level of the economies of the countries in which they were made; but the gains, many charged, went only to the wealthy few. American efforts in the early 1950s to conclude mutual security agreements with Latin American countries and provide military aid and training were viewed with disfavor by many political leaders: armies in Latin America were too potent a political force, and a policy presumably designed to counter the Soviet threat would have primarily domestic political effects. Also, under the Congressional mandate, the mutual security agreements committed recipient countries to facilitate United States access to strategic materials, to cooperate in limiting trade with the Communist bloc, and to help build up the defensive strength of the "free world." In the more democratically governed countries—Mexico, Brazil, Chile and Uruguay—the debates were bitter and vociferous, and anti-American utterances became general.

The gathering of all these threads into widespread anti-Americanism, based partly on certain deep-rooted antipathies, enabled Dictator Peron of Argentina to aspire to a considerable role on the world scene. Peron had successfully resisted American pressures early in his career. He held power in the one country that had long been officially in conflict with American foreign policy and had excluded itself from the American-sponsored inter-American system during World War II. Now he could fish in these troubled waters. In Argentina itself, he attacked the older oligarchies in the name of social justice and based his political power on the new urban masses, whose status he improved. In so doing, and by encouraging a "hothouse" industrialization, he cut into Argentina's export trade and created a need for new imported raw materials and parts as well as creating a new privileged class of workers. The foundations of a difficult future situation were laid: Argentina began to live beyond its means, yet any effort to cut back the unrealistic standard of living would run afoul of the newly strengthened labor organizations; they would resist any cutbacks and would demand that other groups pay for it. Nevertheless, Peron's brand of social justice, partly because it gave to the new masses a measure of political participation (whether manipulated or not), was immensely attractive to groups all over the Americas, whose new nationalism and anti-Americanism incorporated a strong demand for precisely this kind of social change. In the decade after the war Peronism flourished hand in hand with other nationalist and social-reform movements, and it became hard to distinguish and label political movements as democratic, reform, revolutionary, communist, socialist, or fascist. Complex social and economic situations fostered a demand for change. The demand was articulated by intellectuals, college students, professional agitators, labor leaders—sometimes joined by progressive-minded business leaders, churchmen and officers, and sometimes opposed by them. The only constant became the desire for change. Sometimes, as in the Dominican Republic, it was brutally suppressed, sometimes it found, as in Mexico, some measure of peaceful expression after years of revolution.

At the United Nations the Latin American countries voted frequently as a bloc. Their leaders found common policies in an atmosphere in which the Western nations used the General Assembly to pile up massive majorities against the Soviet Union. But the explosive situation in the Americas was certain to break up Latin American unity. The incident that did it took place in Guatemala.

Overthrow of one regime by another was a common occurrence in American states, but this one had special features. Since the war, the regime in Guatemala had moved steadily to the left. Communists had infiltrated several departments of the government, so that they could claim its radical reforms as their own. Agrarian reform—long viewed as necessary in Guatemala—was carried out mainly by expropriating lands owned by the American United Fruit Company, and compensation proposed by the regime was ridiculously small. Then the regime moved against the company-controlled railway and electric power company. To many leaders in Latin America the moves were merely welcome steps in the direction of progress, and that they involved reducing the influence of a Yankee company was not disturbing: only in this direction lay true independence and sovereignty.

But within the United States, where the Eisenhower regime—having promised to rectify Truman's error of ignoring the Americas—confined itself to diplomatic protests, some people called for stronger action. Former Assistant Secretary of State Spruille Braden called Guatemala a "beachhead of international Communism," and censured the administration for its inaction.

Matters came to a head in 1954. A meeting of the Inter-American Conference of the Organization of American States was scheduled for March. Against the resistance of many Latin states, whose representatives wanted to discuss economic affairs, the United States used the meeting to obtain a resolution that "domination or control of the political institutions of any American State by the international Communist movement would constitute a threat to the sovereignty and political independence of the American States, endangering the peace of America." The resolution had been weakened in passage and it did not specify what action would be taken. Countries with military dictatorships of various kinds were less opposed than the more democratic ones, although Argentina joined Mexico in abstaining. A Uruguayan delegate was quoted as saying, "We contributed our approval without enthusiasm, without optimism, without joy and without the feeling that we were contributing to the adoption of a constructive measure." Opposition centered on the notion that this was an unwelcome move toward collective intervention, to which the United States answered that collective intervention was needed to counter *Communist* intervention. Opponents of the American policy also felt there was little reason to single out the Guatemalan dictatorship as against other Latin American ones, particularly since it favored the kind of progressive measures needed in the area.

To protect itself, the regime headed by Arbenz in Guatemala began to step up repressive measures against its internal opponents, and looked for aid from the Soviet bloc. Opponents in neighboring states claimed that the Guatemalan regime was fostering subversion and sabotage within their borders. Then came the revelation on May 18 that Guatemala had received a shipment of arms from Czechoslovakia by way of Poland, and the United States increased its efforts against the government. It called for measures to halt such shipments, it called a meeting of the foreign ministers of the American States, and it authorized increased arms shipments to Guatemala's neighbors, Honduras and Nicaragua, on grounds that these countries were now threatened by the Communist arms. On June 18 a small force crossed the border from Honduras under the command of Colonel Carlos Castillo-Armas, and the Arbenz regime, facing the opposition of the armed forces within Guatemala, quickly fell. Arbenz was later allowed to go to Mexico, and from there he went to Czechoslovakia.

When the revolt—or invasion—took place, Guatemala immediately asked for action in both the Security Council and the OAS, against what it termed "open aggression" by neighboring governments urged on by foreign monopolies. The United States strove to keep the matter out of the United Nations on the basis that it was strictly a regional, and even more, a domestic matter. Thus the importance of the whole matter in the pattern of world politics was revealed: the United States, in trying to block United Nations Security Council action, was concerned with keeping the Soviet Union from becoming openly involved in American affairs. Communist parties had long operated, sometimes effectively, in Latin America. But for the first time since the turn of the century, when the United States had chosen unilaterally to "strengthen" the Monroe Doctrine, a European power—one hostile to the United States—presumed to participate in matters within the Americas. Moreover, the United Nations had been called upon by a Latin American government which, though it could be criticized for undemocratic practices, was still more legitimate and democratic than many other countries on the continent. When, after Nazi Germany's defeat, Peron's Argentina had tried to make itself a counter pole of attraction to the influence of the United States, Peron had grown weaker; he had even begun to court the Eisenhower administration. Now, for the first time, a Latin American country could and did call on a strong and willing alternative source for support, in the context of the United Nations.

Within the Security Council, a Soviet veto prevented the Council from removing the item from consideration, but the United States was able to defer the issue until the Inter-American Peace Committee of the OAS could investigate the matter and report. It never had to complete its work. With mediation by the American Ambassador, John Peurifoy, matters were quickly settled in Guatemala, a new regime established, and in subsequent months the United States rushed it various forms of emergency economic aid.

Although most Americans at the time were not aware of it, the United States had had a direct part in overthrowing the Arbenz government. The Central Intelligence Agency had financed, supplied, and helped train the Castillo-Armas forces, and the American ambassador had informed the contending parties what kind of regime would be acceptable to the United States. The new regime was hardly satisfactory to Guatemalans; but it was non-Communist.

The action was followed by a wave of more overt anti-Americanism throughout Latin-American urban centers, where the whole issue was seen in a different light, and where Communist propaganda stressed how Yankee intervention had again overthrown a regime whose only failing was a lack of subservience to American investors.

While in the north the realities of the unstable Latin-American situation had broken through to the surface, at the southern tip of South America another effort to ride and guide the new waves of discontent came to an end; in Argentina the Peron regime was toppled in a four-day revolution in September 1955. Since the end of 1954, Peron's regime was doomed. His economic policies had disrupted the Argentine economy, inflation had taken on disastrous proportions, members of the armed services were disaffected, and Peron, in an effort to capitalize on anticlerical sentiment, had mistakenly attacked the Church. In the summer of 1955 the Vatican excommunicated him. The end came soon after with a revolt by elements of the army and navy, and a new junta took over. Few could look forward to much stability in Argentina.

Europe, 1950–55

Several issues dominated the five-year period in Europe: German rearmament, political and economic integration of West Europe, the return of West Germany and Italy to the ranks of world powers, accession of a Conservative government in Britain and of Mendès-France in France, continued liquidation of European empires, a new Korean War-born round of inflation followed by the beginning of an economic boom, continued growth of neutralist sentiment, settlement of the difficult Saar and Trieste issues, and—hovering over all in the latter part of the period—a new hope of an accommodation with Russia's new masters. The account of the impact of Korea, the Indochinese settlement and events in North Africa has already treated some of these events, but some parts of the narrative must now be filled in.

The resolution of the question of German rearmament rested in part on events in Britain and France. The Korean War had hastened consideration of the matter and led, in late 1950, to the desperate French expedient of the Pleven Plan, which subsequent French governments were reluctant to endorse. Korea also hastened general rearmament plans in Europe, and these produced a new round of inflation starting in late 1951, for which Europeans tended in large part to blame the United States. By reckless buying of raw materials, they argued, the United States had bid up their prices and produced a scarcity in Europe, whose full share in carrying the burden in Malaya and Indochina Americans did not appreciate. In Britain the long experience of austerity after victory in World War II, coupled with a growing view that nationalization of industry solved little, and with Conservative acceptance of the welfare state, led to a Conservative election victory in 1951. Winston Churchill again took up the reins of government. Since he was a leader in the European movement and had frequently spoken in its support, continental Europeans hoped for greater British participation. They were disappointed. Churchill and his government preferred to continue the close relationship with the United States (cemented during the war years) and the ties of the Commonwealth—sentimental as well as financial. There was, therefore, no question of their joining the proposed European army, although as the situation became thornier, Churchill did pledge (in May 1952) that British armies would not be withdrawn from Germany. This was intended to allay French fears that once Germany was rearmed the British and Americans might withdraw their troops. The United States also joined in this declaration.

But within France opposition to the proposed European Defense Community continued to grow. The Communists were unalterably opposed, and at the other end of the political spectrum de Gaulle also denounced it, declaring that France must regain its independence from both the United States and the Soviet Union and mediate between the two. All other parties (except the Christian Democrats, who had originated the concept and had controlled the Foreign Ministry since 1945) were split on the issue. Distinguished military men pronounced the European army unworkable; others condemned it as a final, fatal surrender of precious French sovereignty. And even many Frenchmen who had worked for some surrender of sovereignty in the form of European integration nevertheless balked at this particular aspect of it.

The Germans had ratified the agreement; everyone waited for the French, and the Anglo-Americans tried both the carrot and the stick. In April 1954 the British signed a far-reaching, binding agreement with the six European Defense Community governments defining various forms of close cooperation with them and the European army within the framework of NATO. The United States, although not going as far, also pledged close cooperation far beyond the expiration date of NATO (1970) if the Europeans wanted it, promising to share weapons and techniques and to coordinate planning, training, and logistics.

On the other hand Secretary Dulles had spoken at one point of the necessity for the United States to indulge in an "agonizing reappraisal" of its policy toward Europe if the European Defense Community were not established. And in mid-1954 he renewed the warning: if Western Europe were to remain divided there might have to be a "basic shift in United States policy." Talk began of rearming Germany with or without the European Defense Community.

Matters came to a head with the Geneva Conference, the coming to power of Mendès-France, and the Indochinese settlement. Mendès-France had pledged himself to dispose of several matters. One was the German settlement, which was complicated by the insistence of previous governments that the dispute with Germany over the future of the coal-rich Saar must be settled prior to ratification of the European Defense Community. In the meantime Russian diplomacy and propaganda increased in variety and scope. The Russians offered to continue the abortive 1954 Berlin conversations to discuss the future of Germany, the Austrian peace treaties, and a proposed European security treaty. Their offer was an appeal to the many elements within France who believed that German rearmament was provocative and who argued that a great part of Russian foreign policy was in fact motivated by fear of a resurgent Germany.

Mendès-France made an effort to change the treaty so it would be more acceptable to his own Assembly, yet still make it palatable to the other countries who had already signed and had been waiting so long for the French. The changes he proposed, however, proved completely unacceptable, and he returned to Paris in August from Brussels, where the negotiations had been futile. Then, on August 30, in the Assembly, he stood by during a debate, not on the merits of the European Defense Community, but on removing the item from the agenda and passing to other business. Emotionalism dominated, although the European Defense Community had been intellectually taken apart in a series of negative committee reports. The motion to move to other business passed; the European Defense Community was dead. Four years of planning a means of German rearmament within the framework of European integration had come to nothing. Dead, too, was the projected European Political Union which was to have given political guidance to the subordinate European army and would have capped the structure of European economic integration.

What next?

Dulles, despite his prior warnings and the pinning of his hopes to the European Defense Community, displayed caution. It fell to Anthony Eden, the British Foreign Minister, to devise a way out of the wreckage. All agreed with Chancellor Adenauer that in some way West Germany must be included in the defense of Western Europe, and on a basis of equality, not subordination. Mendès-France, however, still wanted controls over German rearmament, as did a substantial segment of opinion in other European countries. Eden's solution was to reactivate the Western European Union set up by the Brussels Treaty Organization of 1948 (predecessor of NATO), giving its Council the power to set maximum force levels for *all* members; they could go beyond these only by unanimous consent of the Council members. In addition, when the powers met in London, September 28 to October 3, and then at Paris, October 19–23, they agreed to restore full sovereignty to Germany, while Germany, for its part, renounced the right to build atomic, chemical, or biological weapons and such strategic weapons as missiles and long-range bombers. Britain wrote into the treaty its commitment to keep certain forces on the Continent, and an accompanying protocol admitted Germany to NATO. Mendès-France still made acceptance conditional on prior agreement on the Saar issue, and after hectic negotiations he and Chancellor Adenauer agreed to a form of internationalization: the Saar would become the seat of the European Coal and Steel Community, but France would still retain special economic privileges in the area. But there would be a popular referendum among Saarlanders to approve—or disapprove—the arrangement.

Under a barrage of Soviet suggestions for all-European security conferences and free elections in Germany, the countries proceeded to
ratification of the new agreements. Western leaders argued that once
the arrangements were made it might be the right moment to test the
sincerity of Russian demands for negotiations. The Russians, however,
warned that ratification would unduly complicate the picture and make
a reduction of tensions far more difficult.

Again France was the center of attention. And again, although
willing to admit Germany to NATO and ratify the Saar settlement,
the Assembly voted down the whole Brussels Treaty revision. This
time Mendès-France told the Assembly that German rearmament without controls would be certain, and made the matter a vote of confidence. On December 30, by a vote of 287 to 260, the Assembly accepted the treaty. The change came primarily because Popular Republican supporters of European Defense Community, who had previously voted against Mendès-France because he had allowed their
earlier project to fail, now switched their votes. German rearmament
was finally assured.

It took until May 1955 to complete ratification of the agreements.
In the meantime the Soviet Union threatened retaliation: it announced
that it would create an equivalent organization in Eastern Europe and
that it would denounce the treaties of friendship and alliance it had
signed with Britain in 1942 and France in 1944. In Britain, France,
and Germany, prominent voices were asking that ratification be delayed until the long-called-for summit conference be held. But Churchill, though a proponent of such a meeting, dissented. On May 5 the
fifteen member nations of NATO completed the processes involved
in ratification of the several documents; the occupation of Germany
ended, occupation troops became security troops, Allied High Com-
missioners were transformed into ambassadors, and the German Federal
Republic came into existence. On May 14, in Poland, the eight states
of Eastern Europe signed the Warsaw Treaty, similar to the North
Atlantic Treaty, establishing a joint command for their armed forces
with headquarters in Moscow. Communist spokesmen stressed its defensive purposes, and claimed it was necessitated because "West Germany is being turned into a bridgehead for deployment of large
aggressive forces."

The urgency of the whole matter of German rearmament contrasted
strangely with a prevalent feeling of international relaxation and with
the growing realization that it might take five years to provide the
politically screened and reliable German NATO contribution of

500,000 men or twelve divisions. Even Secretary Dulles shared in the feeling of relaxation. "There is less fear than there was, I am glad to say, of open military activities," he reported on December 7.

German rearmament was only one aspect of the NATO situation in the 1950–55 period. The Korean War had led to creation of an elaborate alliance structure (p. 148), and General Eisenhower had become Supreme Allied Commander in Europe. When he withdrew to enter the presidential race in 1952, the American General, Matthew Ridgway, replaced him. Peace in Korea and the advent of the Eisenhower administration, although it did not forestall German rearmament, brought a new emphasis to NATO strategy and a concomitant renewal of neutralist agitation.

The new strategy was prompted mainly by a reluctance to incur heavy expenditures necessary for the integrated force suggested at Lisbon in 1952. In the United States, this reluctance led to the emphasis on "massive retaliation," in Europe, to a shift back to the idea that the land forces facing the Russians should constitute a "trip-wire" or "plate-glass," designed to trigger retaliation, rather than a really defensive holding force. But it was necessary to assure at least some Europeans that *defense* was possible in case *deterrence* failed to keep the Russians from attacking, and NATO resorted, in 1954, to arming itself with what were called "tactical" nuclear weapons—small weapons that could be used by troops in the field against attacking units, their bases and supply lines. Presumably these would compensate for Atlantic manpower deficiencies *vis-à-vis* the Soviet bloc.

The North Atlantic Council meeting of foreign and defense ministers in December 1954 approved the policy; the finger on the atomic trigger would be American; European troop units would receive training in handling the weapons that could deliver atomic warheads; the atomic weapons would be used even in case of a Russian conventional attack on Western Europe.

The "solution" to the manpower problem—NATO's own "new look"—left many questions unanswered and sparked a long-lasting debate on basic strategy. Some argued that tactical atomic weapons shared the disadvantages of both conventional defense strategy and of the strategy of atomic deterrence. A build-up of tactical atomic strength—like an increase in conventional defense strength—might lessen Russian certainty that the United States would really use its massive retaliatory capacity, and thereby weaken the deterrent effect of the latter. But the tactical atomic weapons shared with the strategic weapons of massive retaliation the unimaginable disadvantage that if used, they would subject Europe to atomic devastation. Could "tactical" atomic weapons be used without leading into a general conflagration? Was not the very term "tactical" a misnomer? Would not the Russians answer by giving their own troops tactical atomic capability, thereby eliminating the advantage the weapons would supposedly give the West? And if the Russians were to "nibble" at some area like Greece or Turkey, or renew their blockade of Berlin, would the West really be prepared to turn to atomic war?

Finally, more and more voices criticized the whole idea of NATO: why equip it with atomic weapons just when a change in Russian leadership appeared to offer a real chance to diminish world tension? The new leaders were different from the suspicious, paranoid, power-mad Stalin. In order to consolidate their power they had begun to offer concessions to Soviet citizens and to relax the police-state methods of Stalin's time. This, some people argued, showed that the ideological erosion of Communism had begun: face to face with new developments—the persistence and spread of nationalism, the development of new and devastating weapons, the strength of Western economic and political institutions—Communist leaders had to revise their dogma and abandon any ideas they might have actually had of conquering the world. (Many people in Western Europe continued to argue that the Soviet leaders had never had such ideas, and others maintained that while the Soviets might really want to spread Communism, this did not necessarily involve an intent to use Russian military power.)

Finally, and perhaps most important, revelations about the awesome power of the new hydrogen weapons affected the discussions. Hydrogen bombs were fundamental to the strategy of massive retaliation. But the general public was shocked by the results of a March 1954 test of one of the new American weapons. Its explosive power, two hundred and fifty times greater than the atomic bomb that had devastated Hiroshima—had apparently not been predicted by scientists, nor had they expected the enormous amount of lethal "fallout" that followed the explosion. Fallout, the radioactive debris that remains long after detonation, can cause painful death, horrible disfigurement to those exposed to it, and threatens subsequent generations with dreadful mutations and malignant diseases like leukemia. Some of this data had come to light because of the exposure to radioactive fallout of the crew of a Japanese fishing vessel, the "Lucky Dragon," which had strayed into a zone from which vessels had been warned away. This zone was in what was traditionally thought of as the high seas, always open to navigation. To the horror of the unknown was added the question of the United States' right to conduct tests in the area.

The Soviet Union had tested its own hydrogen weapons in the fall of 1953, adding to the atmosphere considerable amounts of fallout, the long-term effects of which were equally uncertain. Churchill, in reviewing the available data on hydrogen bombs in the House of Commons on March 1, 1955, said, "The atomic bomb, with all its terror, did not carry us outside the scope of human control and manageable events in thought or action, peace or war . . ." but added that with the hydrogen bomb, "The entire foundation of human affairs was revolutionized and mankind placed in a situation both measureless and laden with doom." He then went on to say, "It may well be that we shall, by a process of sublime irony, have reached a stage in history where safety will be the sturdy child of terror, and survival the twin brother of annihilation." But unlike Churchill, who then justified Britain's decision to build its own nuclear striking force while cutting back on conventional forces, many other people used the information about hydrogen weapons to oppose *all* military strategies, and to argue for renewed efforts at disarmament or neutralism on the part of European countries.

Despite the questioning and argument, NATO governments accepted the new strategy based on tactical atomic weapons in conjunction with massive retaliation.

The debate on Western military strategy attracted considerable public attention. Less dramatic but equally important were developments in the economy of Western Europe. A perilous balance had been regained by the time of the Korean War. The war had upset it again, partly because of the cost of the rearmament effort, partly because of a sharp upward movement in raw material and commodity prices. Nevertheless, with the end of the Korean War, a period of economic growth began in Europe that seemed to mark a fundamental change. In the late 1940s, the Marshall Plan boosted morale, the German "economic miracle" was under way, and the Monnet Plan had started France on reequipment of its industry. Yet Europe was pervaded by a lingering pessimism based on the bitter experience of two generations who had lived through the 1920s and 1930s, when capitalism seemed dying. It had fed on the destruction of the war years. Almost unaccountably, however, the indices of production and employment began to climb in the middle 1950s, and indications were that these were no longer a result of American economic and military aid. A slight recession in the United States in 1954 failed to damp the upward spurt in Europe, although before this it had been assumed that such a recession would cause a sharp drop in European exports to the United States, with serious domestic repercussions. Each year authorities warned that the year ahead might not be so rosy, but 1953, 1954, and 1955 set records far above prewar levels for output, productivity, and employment. Despite the setback to European unity of the defeat of the European Defense Community, Europe appeared to have taken a new lease on life, and even laggard countries like Italy began to show the results of the boom. The index of industrial production for Western Europe published by the United Nations increased from its 1948 base of 100 to 179 by mid-1955. There were soft spots and anachronistic economic practices. Yet governments were tackling them with vigor. In France, Premier Mendès-France set structural readjustments in the French economy as one of the major goals of his government, along with liquidation of the Indochinese war and settlement of the issue of German rearmament; in part readjustments had already begun under the Monnet Plan and the developing Coal and Steel Community. The British, too, began to see some light. Their economic situation had remained precarious. In order to meet their far-flung commitments abroad—including the maintenance of an army in Germany, repayment of World War II debts, and aid to develop overseas territories—the British had to export more than they imported. Yet given the nature of the British economy, many exports contained a large proportion of imported raw materials. A favorable balance of trade came in the first year of the Korean War but gave way, the next year, to an enormous deficit as raw material prices increased and, although World War II rationing was slowly abandoned, a new round of "belt-tightening" took place. All through the 1950s the dilemma apparently inherent in the notion of "belt-tightening" plagued the Conservative government that had come to power because of dissatisfaction with Labour's economic policies: such policies, whose high interest rates and restrictions on consumption were designed to reduce inflationary pressures and decrease imports, also seemed to reduce incentives to increase production and to replace older, worn capital equipment. Moreover, as the 1950s progressed, the British faced increased competition from resurgent Japanese and German production. The two countries, the British noted, were not hampered by the heavy defense expenditures which in Britain took 10 per cent of the gross national product. In 1952 and 1953 the Conservative government tried to persuade the United States to further ease its import restrictions, so that British goods could more easily be sold on the American

market. In this they were somewhat more successful than in another
policy designed to ease their situation—the opening of trade with Communist bloc countries. Conversations with Soviet and Communist
Chinese officials led primarily to irritation in the United States instead
of more exports. Congressional leaders threatened to cut off aid if
Britain succeeded, whereas the conversations themselves brought no
substantial results.

Despite all the problems and the impact of the Anglo-Iranian oil
crisis, the years 1953 and 1954 were the best years for the British
economy since World War II, and both showed a substantial favorable trade balance. Rationing and many other direct controls were
abandoned, inflation was apparently contained, and full employment
and prosperity were achieved. Like the other countries of Europe,
Britain began to share in the mid-century boom. The "post-war"
years were apparently over; the coronation of Elizabeth in June 1953
seemed really to have inaugurated a new Elizabethan age.

In the Far East, Japan—the only Asian country sufficiently industrialized to be compared to Europe—also shared in the boom. Although
exports and imports were still substantially below prewar levels,
although Japanese traders complained about unfair restrictions against
them (the British, in return, accusing the Japanese of unfair trading
practices, tried unsuccessfully to bar them from membership in the
General Agreement on Tariffs and Trade) and although Japan, like
Britain, sought unsuccessfully to penetrate the tempting yet evasive
and ambiguous Chinese market, by 1954 Japan's level of manufacturing stood at 74 per cent over the 1934–36 level, and real income
per capita had risen 5 per cent. The figure was not high, especially
since the comparison is made to depression years. Yet considering the
restriction of the Japanese Empire to the home islands, the ingathering
of people to those islands, and the enormous destruction by American bombardment in the last years of the war, the achievement was
enormous. It had been greatly helped by American aid—to the extent
of $5 billion—and by American purchases and use of Japanese services
during the Korean War. Yet it proved to be a solid achievement: the
base had been laid for a growth that continued at an increasing rate
in subsequent years. No small part of this lay in Japan's successful
tackling of the frightening population problem. Still only dimly seen
in other parts of the world, it was clearly perceived within the confines of the Japanese islands, and governmental action had been forthcoming: in 1949 the Japanese legalized abortion for economic as well
as medical reasons. Now that it was cheaply available through regular

doctors, widespread abortion and increased use of contraceptive practices cut the inflated postwar birth rate almost in half by the mid-1950s.

Developments in the United Nations

The years 1950–55 were bleak for the United Nations. The organization moved into its handsome new quarters in New York. But the Korean War moved out of its control and as efforts to invigorate the concept of collective security failed, regional alliances such as NATO became far more important to many states. Although United Nations agencies continued and even expanded their varied and useful services to the international community in the economic and social fields, on political matters the organization frequently found itself stymied. Final settlements of such matters as the Arab-Israeli dispute, lingering Indonesian-Dutch problems, the status of Southwest Africa (formerly held by South Africa as a League Mandate, now simply held) all proved impossible. The Soviet Union used its veto not only on questions of membership but also on political recommendations, and refused to recognize Secretary General Trygve Lie upon extension of his term of office. To everyone's relief, it agreed to the appointment of Hammarskjold in 1953. But the dismal charade of disarmament talks continued. In 1952 the separate atomic and conventional weapons discussions were combined and a single Disarmament Commission established. But against the background of rearmament efforts occasioned by the Korean War, the American efforts to expand its alliance and foreign base system, the development of the hydrogen bomb, and extensive Russian peace propaganda, the discussions were fruitless. There was some hope that development of the new and more horrible weapons and changes within the Soviet Union might lead to more serious efforts to find a way out of the impasse, particularly since a number of political settlements had taken place. Attention shifted from comprehensive schemes which had many pitfalls, to less ambitious proposals that might lessen the chances of war; both sides acknowledged that existing supplies of nuclear warheads could not be discovered by inspection, and the discussions began to take on a more realistic tone. President Eisenhower's "Atoms for Peace" proposal delivered to the General Assembly in December, 1953 reflected some of the new thinking: transfer of nuclear material—denatured to prevent its use for military purposes—to an international agency for use for development purposes under international control, would convince both sides of the other's willingness to diminish its stockpile, while circumventing the inspection problem. Perhaps such measures might reduce tension without decreasing military security. Yet few could miss the irony of raising new hopes about disarmament at the very moment the West had successfully found a way of rearming Germany. And the deadlock of the issue of admission of new members to the United Nations continued through the 1954–55 General Assembly.

Conclusion

In 1950 people the world over feared the worst—that Korea would be the spark to explode the Cold War into World War III. Yet as the major powers continued to display caution, people began to breathe more easily. Nevertheless, the Korean War and the continued fighting in Indochina had shaped a Western attitude that would prove to be of great significance. The United States led in interpreting the new situation as one in which a well-coordinated Communist bloc, dominated by Russia, had begun to take the offensive. This attitude inspired a major shift in American aid from economic to military categories. It led to a new emphasis on force-in-being for European defense and to wholesale rearming of the West, to a desperate effort to incorporate Germany into the defense system without worrying its neighbors, and to the extension of NATO to the eastern Mediterranean. It allowed the resurrection of Western Germany and Japan, those recently defeated countries whose conquerors had been determined never to let them rise again. They had now become the recipients of extensive American aid and the objects of American blandishment. Whether the thinking behind these shifts was sound remains open to question. There is still disagreement about the relative roles of the Russians and the Chinese in the Korean attack and the long, drawn-out war that followed. But in the United States at the time assumptions about the aims of Soviet foreign policy never came into question; rather, it was the validity of the response to Soviet policy, and the period was marked by an acrimonious and fruitless debate about containment and liberation that did not help in formulating a coherent foreign policy. It did, however, inspire greater distrust of American leadership among America's allies.

The uneasiness was even more intense because, with the threat of general war hanging over the world, both sides now possessed nuclear weapons. Europeans were always ready to argue that Americans did not know what war was really like, since their country had not been a battleground in recent times. Yet as the threat of war receded and a series of precarious settlements were reached in Asia, some people asked whether it was not, indeed, the threat of use of the weapons that had produced the settlements, since no one could benefit from enlargement or continuation of expensive wars.

In any event, the settlements in Asia, the development of thermonuclear weapons, and the changes in Russian leadership occurred just when the enormous reconstruction efforts in Europe were proving to be successful. And as European nations started to enjoy unforeseen economic prosperity, they began to examine their relationship with the United States. Europe had desperately needed America at the end of the war and in the late forties, America had responded. But was America still needed in the same way if more reasonable men were Russia's leaders? The uneasiness about America's posture toward the Soviet Union and about America's apparent inability to understand different interpretations of the world situation, when combined with a desire to be independent, helped to speed the move toward European unity. The Americans themselves had prodded Europe to unite, but the process had faltered with the fiasco of the European Defense Community—itself a product of the Korean War. Still, with the process of recovery virtually completed, Europeans found unity attractive not only in terms of strength *vis-à-vis* the Soviet Union, but also in relation to the friendly but dominating United States.

Thermonuclear weapons sparked a new debate during these years: What did they mean for strategy and international politics? Did they, as Churchill suggested, bring a new and perhaps more stable balance of terror? Or should they call forth a new effort at disarmament? Given their existence, was massive retaliation the correct military doctrine? Past experience hardly provided answers, and the debate was certain to continue.

Weapons, economic developments, internal political changes, and mass attitudes underlay the day-to-day details of international politics, shaping them and giving them patterns, though the patterns were frequently hard to discern at the time. Changes in leadership played a part, too. When Churchill had come back to power in 1951, European leaders hoped that the Labour-imposed isolation from European unity would be reversed. It was not. Churchill put ties to the Commonwealth and trans-Atlantic unity ahead of ties to the Continent. When Eisenhower assumed power many people in Eastern Europe expected to be liberated. They were not. Eisenhower preferred containment. With the death of Stalin, no one knew what to expect. Would his heirs seek to decrease tension in order to consolidate their position at home, or would they increase it to prove that they were the legitimate heirs of Marxism-Leninism-Stalinism? Stalin himself seemed to have sought limited settlements; in the early years, his successors did the same, all the while promising the people of Russia an easier time than before. The latter policy gave promise, too, of a softening of Russian foreign policy. Yet Stalin's heirs had the hydrogen bomb and, as of 1954, the means to deliver it.

Developments in the West, in Russia, in Korea, and in Indochina overshadowed those in the rest of the world. No one yet saw a pattern in the revolt in Egypt, the nationalization crisis in Iran, the new wave of terrorism in Algeria, the revolt and its suppression in Guatemala. Yet these foreshadowed vast changes to come, in which the move for political independence was to be coupled with the idea of social revolution and a desire for some sort of economic independence. They indicated that rejection of Western political domination was likely to include rejection of Western political and economic institutions. Yet if the people in new countries were going to modernize their economic and social structures in order to improve their miserably low standards of living, they could not return to old forms. What alternatives would be open to them?

Conditions in all of the vast belt of "underdeveloped" countries that extended from Southeast Asia across to Africa and South America were such that economic development would be enormously difficult: climate, resources, social structure, population pressure, all would make development a politically difficult task. Those who had begun to call for narrowing the income gap between the poor countries and the wealthier countries of Europe, North America, and Australia-New Zealand hardly realized what they were asking for, and what upheaveal was involved; as yet, they ignored the portents of Egypt, Iran, Algeria, and Guatemala. So far the question of *how* to deal with demands of the new states was discussed primarily on the level that unless they received economic aid they might "go Communist," with the tacit assumption that this meant joining the Soviet bloc as a Russian satellite. Most people thought in terms of a successful Communist revolt or a *coup d'état*. Few saw the alternative suggested by the Guatemalan affair: Russia might reverse its position on the question of cooperation with non-Communist governments whose desire for social and economic change brought them into conflict with the Western powers. If this were to happen, Western leaders might have to search for more new policies. Already some observers had begun to speculate whether the major powers' inability to really threaten the use of thermonuclear weapons might not open opportunities for venturesome new policies that could not be countered by force. The fluid situation in the new states, with their promise of new conflicts with the West, might invite such Communist initiatives. There was one hope—that the major powers would discern a common interest in avoiding mutual annihilation by thermonuclear weapons and find ways to reduce tension. As yet, no one really knew what changes the thermonuclear age would bring.

Part Three

THE HYDROGEN AGE

CHAPTER SIX 1955 and 1956

Coexistence and Conflict—

a New World Balance

Stalin's successors employed more flexible tactics than the old dictator had in his last days. But the elements of continuity in Soviet foreign policy were striking. After the Communist parties' failure in their use of violence in Europe and Asia in 1947–48, after the failure of the Berlin blockade and the split with Tito, Stalin himself seemed to become more cautious. The invasion of Korea was the last new Communist probe; with the stalemate reached there in 1951, much of the dynamism went out of Russian foreign policy, and there are those who believe that Stalin was genuinely in search of a wide-ranging detente, that the West failed to understand, and that American insistence on a military build-up in the Eurasian rimlands combined with talk of "liberation" of captive nations forestalled such an understanding or settlement. Whether or not this is true, the last year of Stalin's life saw the beginning of a new Soviet approach to foreign affairs in which—as his successors took over—vituperation lessened, settlements were agreed to in several areas, and people began to hope. Some argued that this change was the consequence of internal developments in the Soviet Union, that as new men came to power they sought to gain the approval of the masses by increasing consumer goods production, by diminishing the arbitrary use of terror and police methods, and that to do this, they had to reduce the international tension which had been the excuse for those methods. Others argued that the change was due mainly to the resolute effort made by the West to rearm and to put its own house in order, combined with the awareness on each side of the deadly nature of the new weapons each wielded.

Whichever was true—and the problem for policy-makers was that each explanation implied a different policy for the future—the trend culminated in 1955–56. In 1955—despite the Western agreement on

German rearmament and the Soviet response of the Warsaw Alliance—the Russians finally signed a peace treaty ending the occupation of Austria, and Malenkov's successors, Khrushchev and Bulganin, agreed to meet with President Eisenhower, Prime Minister Eden, and Premier Faure at Geneva. The meeting produced the term "the spirit of Geneva"—presumably one of more willingness to discuss and to compromise—and was followed by a meeting of the foreign ministers. At Geneva each assured the other that he wanted no nuclear war, and the conclusion seems to have been reached that indeed neither of the two superpowers could afford to use thermonuclear weapons.

In contrast, however, to the sunny smiles and the handshakes of Geneva and the Austrian peace treaty, there were also the beginnings of what some believed to be a huge new Soviet offensive conceived in nonmilitary terms and conducted under the umbrella of mutual nuclear deterrence. In 1955 the Soviet Union completely abandoned the old Stalinist line that nationalist leaders of new nations were merely bourgeois tools of the imperialists, and replaced it with the view that these same leaders represented a new and progressive force. With this matter safely settled, it became possible to approach them on new terms. The result was a whole set of aid programs, propaganda appeals, wholesale admissions to the United Nations, and visits by Khrushchev and Bulganin to countries all over the world in an efforts to win new friends. A rapprochement with Tito followed, and the gains for the Soviet Union seemed startling. Meanwhile, in 1955, the new states of Asia and Africa made known their own views of their importance on the world scene at a conference at Bandung, Indonesia.

But the period of easing of relations and of peaceful competition ended in 1956 when the Soviet Union's rapprochement with Tito and the attempt to relax Stalinist controls brought an unforeseen response—revolt within the Soviet bloc. At the same time the West was in disarray; serious differences of opinion over how to respond to the new Soviet flexibility led to the Suez war and an American-Soviet alignment against France, Britain, and Israel. What had seemed clear in 1955 became increasingly blurred in the following years, and the Cold War assumed new dimensions.

"Deeds Not Words"

For years, whenever non-Soviet people of any political persuasion suggested that talks with Russian leaders would be a worthwhile effort that might lessen international tension, the standard reply of many Western political leaders was that such talks would be meaningless unless the Russians first proved their willingness to compromise by deeds, not words. But the Soviets could point to many "deeds" since 1952 and in May 1955, came the most striking one of all: Russian signing of the Austrian peace treaty and the subsequent withdrawal of Soviet forces from Austria. Negotiations over Austria had dragged on ever since the end of the war, but conclusion of a treaty had always been prevented by Russian insistence on using it as a bargain counter for other matters—successful resolution of the Trieste crisis, prevention of German rearmament, or some other matter. Moreover, the Soviet government had always insisted on clauses that would have subjected the Austrian economy to Soviet domination.

Suddenly, in the midst of a speech to the Supreme Soviet in February, Foreign Minister Molotov (not yet demoted as a scapegoat for Stalinism) suggested that these conditions might be modified, and the Austrian treaty negotiated on its own terms. Exploratory talks followed and the Russians gave up all their economic demands in return for certain cash payments and a guarantee of delivery of Austrian oil for ten years. The proposed treaty stipulated that Austria would never unite with Germany, and was accompanied by an Austrian declaration that it would remain permanently neutral and never join any military alliance. In short order the wartime allies signed the treaty restoring Austria to sovereign independence; by September 15 all Soviet and other foreign troops were withdrawn from Austrian soil.

The payments to Russia were onerous, and the status of permanent neutrality—although modeled on Switzerland's successful neutrality—might prove difficult to interpret. But the Austrians were jubilant, the West had proof of Soviet willingness to cooperate in "deed," and when the four foreign ministers met to sign the treaty, they agreed to begin preparations for a summit meeting.

Geneva in July

Numerous changes on the diplomatic scene preceded the meeting at Geneva. In the Soviet Union, Malenkov had demoted himself and although Field Marshal Bulganin replaced him as Premier, it became obvious that Party Secretary Nikita Khrushchev was now the leading member in the "collective leadership" that presumably had replaced Stalin's one-man rule. In England, the man who had originally called for a summit meeting in 1953, Winston Churchill, had had to retire, to be replaced by his long-time heir-apparent, Anthony Eden. The new Soviet leaders had begun to effect a rapprochement with Yugoslavia (see p. 208) and had indicated their desire to initiate diplomatic relations with Adenauer's newly sovereign West German Republic.

Technical arrangements for the summit conference were made under United Nations auspices, and the sessions took place at the old League of Nations building now used as European headquarters for the United Nations. The conference proved to be far different from the intimate top-level conversations Churchill had originally envisioned: it took place in a blaze of publicity. In effect, the leaders of the four powers did little more than stake out positions and reassure each other of their peaceful intensions. Not much more could be expected; the agenda covered such topics as German unification, European security, disarmament, and development of contacts between East and West—all highly technical and complicated matters. But more important, the leaders' statements—though laced with expressions of good will—indicated fundamental disagreement on all the agenda topics: the Soviets would not agree to free all-German elections; their idea of a general European security treaty, which would include the two Germanies and lead to an abandonment of all military alliances, was clearly foredoomed since the Western powers were far from ready to abandon NATO. Approaches to the issue of increased contacts between East and West also differed: the Russians were interested in more exchanges of official delegations (presumably because these could be more adequately controlled for national and propaganda purposes) and in a relaxation of Western controls of strategic materials shipments to the Soviet bloc; Western leaders were interested in freer movement of individuals and publications.

In the field of disarmament, President Eisenhower made a dramatic move that immediately caught world attention. Old approaches to disarmament had already been rehearsed. But in a speech in which he turned to the Soviet leaders and, in front of all the apparatus of the world's mass media, vowed that the "United States will never take part in an aggressive war," Eisenhower also advanced a startling proposal: each major power should supply the other with complete blueprints of its military establishment and permit it to make aerial photo-reconnaissance missions over its national territory.

The suggestion was electrifying, even though political leaders—including Americans—soon began to ask exactly what it meant. Like the earlier Atoms-for-Peace plan, presented to the United Nations in 1953, the Open Skies proposal was presented with too little thought about its implementation and perhaps too much thought about the propaganda advantage to be gained. Once sober second thoughts took over, the first propaganda advantage enjoyed by the United States was soon dissipated; people felt they had been taken advantage of. Nevertheless, President Eisenhower impressed many world leaders with his sincerity, and there was evident desire to explore the proposal. Among other things, it reflected a hope that the old pattern of sterile disarmament negotiations might be broken now that the thermonuclear age had arrived. Perhaps one way to avoid the difficulties inherent in any proposal for the actual reduction of weapons might be in schemes to reduce the possibility of surprise attack. Such measures might restore mutual trust and lead to further measures of actual *dis*armament. In subsequent months, however, Soviet leaders entered many objections to the Open Skies idea, and American congressmen questioned the wisdom of allowing Soviet planes to fly over the United States taking photographs while we supplied the Soviet Union with "blueprints"—whatever these might be—of the American military establishment. Nevertheless, the United States worked on the details of implementation, and negotiated on the plan. Various suggestions and countersuggestions for opening different zones for pilot-project aerial inspection were presented. In the end, the proposal came to nothing.

The Geneva conference led to no hard and fast agreements, except to hold further conversations among the foreign ministers in the fall which, in turn, were inconclusive. But it appeared to have two effects. It created an atmosphere of relaxation, an atmosphere the Russians exploited unsparingly in their propaganda during succeeding years: as the Western powers continued moves to maintain their chosen security posture, the Soviets charged them with violating the "Spirit of Geneva," a public charge designed to be heard especially in the newer countries of the world, whose leaders had been so eager to see in the Geneva Conference the beginnings of a real détente. The second effect appeared to be the mutual recognition that nuclear war would be disastrous for all parties.

Behind this apparent tacit agreement lay some complex factors. Within the Soviet Union, it had been forbidden for many years to suggest that nuclear weapons could be decisive in war. The argument had been that since the inevitable course of history would result in the triumph of "socialism," success in war was therefore determined by permanent underlying social and economic factors. Since a capitalist country—the United States—had first developed atomic weapons, unless the laws of Marxist history were wrong, the weapons could not be considered decisive. And under Stalin, the latter became dogma. It did not prevent the Russians from starting a crash program to develop nuclear weapons of their own, however, or from conducting a worldwide propaganda campaign to mark the weapons as significantly different from other weapons, and therefore to inhibit the United States from using them under any circumstances.

But once Stalin was dead and the Soviet stockpile of weapons began to grow and once thermonuclear weapons became a reality, a new debate arose in the Soviet Union. Now it became possible to revise the Stalinist formulations and to discuss the weapons as something new in history that might, indeed, *change* the laws of history. It became possible to argue—as Malenkov did at one point—that both capitalist *and* socialist states might lose disastrously in a thermonuclear war, regardless of the fact that the laws of history *ought* to leave the socialist state triumphant. Malenkov retracted and, after his fall, Khrushchev and Bulganin were more circumspect in their rejection of the old Stalinist line. Khrushchev proceeded to take measures to enable the Soviet Union to fight and, hopefully, survive and even win a thermonuclear war. The whole matter of the importance of surprise attack became open to discussion in the Soviet armed forces press. Previously, for the same reasons of Stalinist dogma, surprise attack could not be viewed as decisive, since this would theoretically give an advantage to a capitalist power that used it. Now the reasoning could be more realistic. Despite Khrushchev's more "circumspect" position— that war might still be possible and therefore that the Soviet Union would have to continue to prepare for it—it became the generally accepted line that for the first time in history the capitalist powers were put into a position that made it suicidal for them to initiate war; for the first time it seemed possible that history might move forward without that last dying convulsion of bitter war so long expected by most good Marxist Communists. Not only had a new period in history dawned with the advent of thermonuclear weapons and their possession by the Soviet Union, but Eisenhower had shown at Geneva that he, too, realized this. While leaders throughout the world believed that Geneva signified tacit agreement by the major powers that nuclear war had become impossible, that a nuclear stalemate existed, to the Soviet leaders, within their framework of thought, it meant something more: the opportunity to pursue foreign policy by other means and to push forward with little or no danger that the capitalist powers would retaliate with nuclear war. Thus, all through 1955 and 1956, they proceeded to take advantage of the stalemate.

New Soviet Initiatives

To the north Soviet leaders demonstrated their good will and removed an irritant by returning Porkkala Naval Base to Finland. Troops began to leave in 1955 and the formal surrender of the base—whose lease, extracted as part of the World War II peace settlement, was to last until 1997—took place on January 26, 1956. Soviet leaders made much of the fact that this, along with the return of Port Arthur to Communist China, liquidated all Soviet bases abroad apart from those required for communications to Germany and those held under the Warsaw Pact; they invited the Western powers to do likewise, since it was well known that foreign bases were a chief cause of international tension. Their moves, they pointed out, gave evidence of their own sincere desire to reduce tension, and the moment the West abandoned NATO and its bases, the Soviet Union would abandon the Warsaw Pact.

Since the Porkkala Naval Base had been held in order to protect the avenue of approach to Leningrad from the kind of attack and the city from a siege such as the one the Germans had carried out in World War II, and since the Soviet leaders now assumed diminished likelihood of any major war (and certainly of any that repeated the pattern of World War II), some observers felt that the move had cost the Soviet Union little.

At the same time, the Soviet leaders initiated a dramatic new peripatetic diplomacy; Bulganin and Khrushchev formed a traveling team that became almost affectionately known in the British press as "Bulge and Krusch." Their first and perhaps most important visit was to the old enemy, Tito of Yugoslavia. It represented part of an overall effort to win Tito back into the Communist fold.

Tito had himself been busy making friends with the leaders of new states—exchanging visits with Premier U Nu of Burma, and receiving Prime Minister Nehru of India. All were receptive to the new Soviet point of view that peaceful coexistence was now not only possible—it was also imperative. All were receptive to the idea that continued American military expenditures and bases abroad threatened coexistence. They reacted more unfavorably to American Secretary of Defense Wilson's statement that nothing at Geneva justified reducing defense expenditures, than to Khrushchev's statement on September 17, 1955.

We are in favor of a détente, but if anybody thinks that for this reason we shall forget about Marx, Engels, and Lenin, he is mistaken. This will happen when shrimps learn to whistle . . . we shall always adhere to the building of socialism. . . . We don't believe that war is necessary to that end. Peaceful competition will be sufficient.

Marshal Tito now received aid from the West; at the same time he appeared to be building some sort of third, neutral force consisting of countries not bound by any military alliances, and in May 1955, he entertained Bulganin and Khrushchev. The earlier attempt to tie Tito more closely to the West through the Balkan Pact had ended quietly. Negotiated in 1952 and signed in March 1953 when Stalin's hostility was still evident, the pact constituted an alliance between Yugoslavia, Greece and Turkey. Since the last two were also in NATO, the pact was, in effect, an indirect way of bringing Yugoslavia into NATO, without exposing Tito to the charge that he had completely abandoned Communism by aligning himself with the most capitalist of nations. But the softer Soviet line led to a quiet death for the pact. How much would Tito now respond to Khrushchev's blandishments? How far could the Kremlin leaders go to repudiate the whole Soviet bloc campaign against Tito?

The answer was that they would go far. The method was simple but rather crude: when Khrushchev arrived at the airport in Yugoslavia, he made the late Lavrenti Beria (executed head of the Soviet secret police) the scapegoat for the whole program of vilification, subversion, and economic and diplomatic pressures against Yugoslavia, for all of which he apologized abjectly. The accusations against Tito "were fabricated by the enemies of the people, detestable agents of imperialism who by deceptive methods pushed their way into the ranks of our party."

The meeting ended with a communique in which Tito supported many Soviet positions on international affairs, and endorsed peace, brotherhood, sovereignty, independence, noninterference, coexistence, and so on. Although much of this was meaningless rhetoric, some at least was an explicit repudiation of Stalin's attempt to dictate to Yugoslavia. Certain more concrete items followed: agreements for expanded trade, cancellation of debts, and provisions for improved communications. In a further move to conciliate Tito, Khrushchev abolished the Cominform. It had originally been created to coordinate Communist regimes, but one of its main tasks had been to organize the campaign against the Yugoslav leader. Yet Tito also moved to reassure the West: he told the United States that he would abide by restrictions on strategic trade with the rest of the Communist bloc (this was necessary for the continuation of American aid) and he received Secretary Dulles cordially when he visited Belgrade in November 1955.

A rapprochement, nevertheless, had been effected. Tito had been restored to a respectable place in the eyes of the Soviet hierarchy, while the West continued to woo him. But if Tito was now respectable, and the whole campaign against him had been a plot of "imperialist" spies, what about all the leaders in other satellite countries who had been purged, sometimes executed, for Titoism? And what about the current leaders who had done the purging? If Tito, who had chosen his own path to socialism, were readmitted to the Communist camp, would other countries be allowed to choose their own paths? No choice had been possible during Stalin's life when the Stalinist model for society *had* to be accepted. Khrushchev's initiative toward Tito had opened a Pandora's box for the Communist bloc: already these questions were being asked in various quarters. The concept of peaceful coexistence had been designed, many thought, to lull the West and bring to the fore the differences among the Western powers that had been eliminated as a result of Stalin's hard policy. But now the policy posed some dangerous dilemmas for the Soviet bloc.

Khrushchev and Bulganin found other fields for the new diplomacy in those new states with which Tito, too, had been seeking solidarity. India's Prime Minister Nehru visited Moscow in June, and later in the year, during November and December, the two Soviet leaders made an unprecedented return visit to India with side trips to Burma and Afghanistan.

There they made full use of existing conflicts with the West. Both India and Afghanistan had quarrels with Pakistan. India's, growing out of partition, concerned mainly the status of Kashmir. Afghanistan's dispute was over its sponsorship of self-determination for the Pathan tribesmen living in the north of Pakistan. The Indian quarrel with Pakistan had been intensified by Pakistan's military aid agreements with the United States signed in 1954, Pakistani accession to the Southeast Asia Treaty Organization, and its signature of the new Baghdad Pact late in 1955. By these moves, Pakistan had aligned itself solidly with the West; so far as India was concerned, this meant an extension of the Cold War to Asia. But, more important, India felt that the increment in Pakistani military power was directed primarily against India: Pakistan was directly involved in conflicts with India, not with Soviet Russia. Only India would feel the weight of the new power, and Indian leaders made their severe displeasure known to the United States.

When Khrushchev and Bulganin arrived, they proceeded to condemn all pacts, and to support the Indian position on Kashmir as well as the Afghanistani position on an independent state for the Pushtu-speaking Pathan tribesmen. Then, with a fanfare of publicity, the Soviet leaders unveiled their own new foreign policy weapon—economic and technical aid. Such aid had long been used by Western powers; the Soviet Union, after abandoning the rigid Stalinist position toward newly independent states, would now also proceed to influence them by helping them. At first the Western press ridiculed the offers of aid as purely rhetorical but aid, trade, and credit agreements were soon forthcoming, and economic ties of the countries to the Soviet bloc began to become a small but important reality. The new Soviet line was not adopted without some strain: domestic Communist parties had long opposed the regimes in these new countries as reactionary, bourgeois, handmaidens of the imperialists. Now that the Soviet line changed, and many of the regimes were welcomed as progressive forces on the world scene, the native Communists also had to change their line. The process was painful and led to serious divisions within several of the parties.

In India, where the Party now announced its support for Nehru, Nehru promptly repudiated it: good relations with the Soviet Union did not necessitate coming to terms with antidemocratic parties *within* India.

The Arab world offered another field for new Soviet initiatives, and again, Soviet leaders were able to capitalize on divisions between countries in the area and on their conflicts with Western powers. In this case, the Arab-Israeli conflict and attempts to extend the Western alliance system to the area gave Russia its opportunity. Although the British had agreed in 1954 to withdrawal of the great base at Suez, they maintained continued influence in Jordan and Iraq (where they trained local armies and maintained base rights), in the smaller sheikdoms of the Persian Gulf (whose oil had proved so important during the Iranian crisis), and in Aden, at the southern tip of the Arabian peninsula. In 1955 they buttressed this remaining influence by the Baghdad Pact—an alliance of the states composing what had been called the "Northern Tier" in the Middle East—Turkey, Iraq, Iran, and Pakistan. Attempts to enlist other Middle Eastern states—Lebanon, Syria, Jordan and Egypt—failed: all saw the pact as a means of continuing imperialist influence in the area just when it should be ending. Egypt's President Nasser was particularly incensed. The alliance potentially strengthened Iraq, and Iraq—though it had less than half the population of Egypt—was Egypt's rival for Arab leadership in an area where Arab nationalism conflicted more and more with the local nationalism in states that had been created only thirty years before. The United States did not join the Baghdad Pact, although presumably giving it full support. In thus trying to have the best of both worlds, the United States only got the worst; the leaders of the Baghdad Pact states who felt the prime purpose of the Pact was to commit the United States to the area were annoyed at it for abstaining, while leaders of the other states that the United States had tried to appease by staying out of the Pact were hostile because they felt that the Pact would not have existed without the United States. Their view focused on American support rather than on American non-membership.

In addition, the Israeli-Arab issue continued to exacerbate relations with the West. In 1950, England, France, and the United States had issued the "Tripartite Declaration" guaranteeing boundaries in the area and imposing something of an arms blockade for the region in an effort to stabilize it. So far as Arab leaders were concerned—especially in the face of massive aid to Israel from private Jewish sources in the United States—this meant that the West backed the existence of Israel. Western powers were also reluctant to force Israel to take back the growing numbers of Arab refugees, or force it to return to the 1947 partition plan boundaries. Therefore they seemed to support Israel in all important matters. It meant little that, in the hope of averting even more Arab hostility, Western powers did nothing to implement Security Council resolutions calling on Egypt to open the Suez Canal to Israeli shipping or Israeli-bound cargoes. And the Eisenhower administration's efforts to improve relations had little effect, even though Dulles visited Naguib in 1953 (leaving him the rather inappropriate gift of a pair of handsome pistols). When Israel adopted a policy of inflicting heavy retaliatory raids on neighboring Arab posts in response to continued Arab sniping and infiltration, the Western powers strongly condemned Israel in the Security Council. Dulles tried to assuage Arab fears that the United States would back Israeli aggression or expansion, and, at the same time, Israel was told by an American Assistant Secretary of State to recognize that it was a Middle Eastern state rather than the "headquarters, or nucleus so to speak, of worldwide groupings of peoples of a particular religious faith who must have special rights within and obligations to the Israeli state." Although Dulles belonged to an administration that had adopted the policy of "massive retaliation," he called on Israel to renounce "the conviction that force and a policy of retaliatory killings is the only policy that your neighbors will understand." He also asked Israel to adopt a policy of restricted immigration; the policy of unlimited immigration fed Arab fears of Israeli expansion in order to accommodate a growing population. (Israel protested strongly that this advice was an interference in Israeli internal affairs.)

At the same time, however, the United States tried to work for some measure of accommodation by promoting the Jordan River Valley development scheme (through which Arab states and Israel would share power and irrigation benefits) and asked the Arab states to "accept the state of Israel as an accomplished fact." In 1955, Dulles offered financial assistance to resettle the Arab refugees, and a guarantee of Israel's borders after "adjustments . . . needed to convert them to boundary lines of safety." In November, Prime Minister Eden went further and suggested—to Israeli horror—a "compromise" territorial settlement.

But, as one Arab spokesman put it, all American offers and all Dulles' initiatives contained "one fundamental flaw." Dulles, he said, "assumes the continued existence of Israel. We don't."

Under these circumstances, Khrushchev could not ignore the opportunities that were present. The Soviet Union had at first supported the Partition Plan and recognized Israel. But gradually, in the 1950s, it veered to stronger and stronger condemnation of Israel, and in late 1955 Khrushchev took a position that strongly backed the Arabs:

. . . from the first day of its existence, the State of Israel has been taking a hostile, threatening position toward its neighbors. Imperialists are behind Israel, trying to exploit it against the Arabs for their own benefit.

More important, the Soviet Union—for the first time since the British began their nineteenth century policy of blocking Russian influence in the Middle East—burst into the area by a simple and spectacular move. The Soviet leaders agreed, in late 1955, to trade Egypt a large quantity of modern arms in return for a heavy proportion of the Egyptian export cotton crop. By this stroke, the Russians leap-frogged the northern tier to establish an undeniable influence in the area, backed the strongest state in the Middle East, took advantage of the Arab-Israeli dispute, and, by upsetting the balance Western powers had tried to maintain, made themselves a force that would have to be reckoned with in all future policy toward the Arab states. Moreover, the move symbolized the manner in which their new initiatives had changed the whole world scene: new states, aggressively nationalist and bent on developing a policy of nonalignment, could now—if they failed to find satisfaction from Western powers—seek support from the Soviet Union. Guatemala, in 1954, had been both a little too early and too close to the United States. But other countries would now certainly follow the example set by Egypt in the military area, and by India, Burma, and Afghanistan in the economic sphere. In short order, Syria and Lebanon began to expand their economic and cultural relations with the Soviet bloc.

The Egyptian move was in fact one of a whole series: Egyptian pilots began to train in Communist-bloc countries and Nasser increased trade contacts with both East Europe and Communist China (to which he extended diplomatic recognition). Meanwhile Nasser spelled out the concept of a "neutralist" foreign policy: the new balance of power allowed a smaller state like Egypt to exist in relative safety without algining itself militarily with either of the two superpowers. An alliance involved subordination to and domination by the larger state, and alliance was not even necessary, since if either of the large states did, in fact, threaten to attack a country like Egypt, the other would probably come to its aid. But even excessive economic and diplomatic links with one bloc might well be the equivalent of domination. For Egypt, Nasser felt, ties of trade and investment in the past had meant exploitation and domination by the West. The new contacts with friendly Communist countries did not bring the dangers that Westerners warned him they would. They were, rather, a way of overcoming excessive reliance on the West, and of establishing real independence.

And, as Nasser proceeded with his program, there were rumors that the Soviet Union had offered to help Egypt with its cherished Aswan Dam.

The projected High Dam at Aswan, on the Nile River was the sort of grandiose project bound to appeal to a government seeking a dramatic move to appeal to its people. One of several different projects for increasing power and irrigation from the Nile River, its cost was estimated at over $1.3 billion and the time required to build it about fifteen years. Nasser's deals with the Soviet bloc prompted the Western powers to attempt to recoup by proffering aid for the dam. In December 1955 Britain, the United States, Egypt, and the International Bank reached a tentative agreement: Egypt would supply $900 million, the International Bank would lend $200 million, and Britain and the United States would supply the rest. The International Bank loan, like all its loans, necessitated an Egyptian commitment to some measure of economic self-discipline. Nevertheless, for Egypt the first fruits of the deal with the Soviet Union had begun to ripen.

The most spectacular of Khrushchev's initiatives involved the new non-Western countries, but the energetic and jovial Russian leader also found time to try his luck with lesser countries in the West. Chancellor Adenauer traveled to Moscow to receive assurance that some of the still-detained German prisoners of war—from more than a decade ago—would be returned. In exchange, Moscow and Bonn traded ambassadors; Adenauer had previously refused an exchange because of Soviet support for the East German government. Neither accepted the others' position about German boundaries in the east nor could they agree on whether West Germany represented all of Germany. But the exchange represented another understanding arising out of Geneva: only Russia could produce German reunification. It would, therefore, have to be on terms acceptable to Russia—a bitter pill for the West German Government to swallow. Adenauer had built his policy on close economic and military ties with the West *partly* as a means toward reunification, and it now became clear that only abandonment of those ties could lead to reunification, and even then only on Russian terms. Domestically, the German Social Democratic opposition made much of this and of the need to test further Russian intentions and the new Communist diplomatic flexibility. Adenauer tried to put the best light on the exchange by countering that Russia had finally been forced to recognize that there was a viable West Germany—one the Soviet leaders would have to do business with.

Although the Soviet leaders held out the bait of reunification within a European security system that would supersede NATO, they also assured the East German Communist leaders that they would not abandon them: by a unilateral Soviet act on September 20, 1955, all Allied (this meant Soviet) controls over the area were ended. East Germany became the German Democratic Republic; it was given complete control over its internal and external affairs, and became a full-fledged member of the Warsaw Pact. The Soviets announced that any questions concerning relations between East and West Germany could now be taken up directly between them. West Germany responded by announcing it would break diplomatic relations with any country recognizing East Germany. Nevertheless, in many areas of the world, countries are forced by circumstances to accept *de facto* situations that they feel are unjust or illegal, and West Germany accepted the fact that many of the newer countries would be involved in trade and cultural negotiations with East Germany. As long as they avoided the formal step of exchanging permanent diplomatic representatives with East Germany, West Germany would not break off relations with them.

Khrushchev and Bulganin made a further effort to test the strength of Western ties. They accepted Eden's invitation to visit Britain in early 1956. Here their appeal was twofold: they stressed Britain's military vulnerability to the Soviet Union's growing strength of new, long-range missiles tipped with thermonuclear weapons, and they played on the enticing possibilities of increased trade. In so doing, they touched a fundamental point of difference between many Europeans and Americans. Most Americans were still suspicious of increased contacts and cooperation with Russia, and judged them solely in terms of whether or how they would help the Soviet Union in the overall strategic balance. Most European leaders, however—while usually not denying the strategic problem—viewed increased contacts as ways of bridging the gap between East and West, ways of reducing tension, and perhaps, in the long run, a means of reducing the strategic problem. The British visit had few concrete results. But it exposed some of the differences among Western powers.

The Bandung Conference

Khrushchev's initiatives arose out of a combination of circumstances: the new and growing economic strength of the Soviet Union, the nuclear balance that appeared to lessen the possibility of war, and the independence of a host of new states, all of which had previously been under the subjection of Western powers in some measure.

Nothing better symbolized the emergence of the new states and the role they aspired to play on the world scene than the conference held at Bandung, Indonesia, April 18–24, 1955. Sponsored by the Colombo Powers—Burma, Ceylon, India, Indonesia, and Pakistan—it assembled representatives of twenty-four other countries from Asia and Africa,* with a population totaling 1.5 billion. Although the main consideration in issuing invitations had been the desire that "all countries in Asia and Africa which have independent Governments should be invited," there were "minor variations and modifications": since all invitations had to be unanimously issued by the sponsoring powers, Israel was not included, nor were North and South Korea, Nationalist China (all of the five sponsoring states recognized Communist China), South Africa, Australia, and New Zealand.

All the countries participating sent high-level representatives—prime

---

* Afghanistan, Cambodia, People's Republic of China, Egypt, Ethiopia, Gold Coast, Iran, Iraq, Japan, Jordan, Laos, Lebanon, Liberia, Libya, Nepal, the Philippines, Saudi Arabia, Sudan, Syria, Thailand, Turkey, Democratic Republic of (North) Vietnam, State of Vietnam, and Yemen.

ministers, foreign ministers, or both. Perhaps most significant was the simple fact that those who attended came with little idea of what the substantive matters before the conference would be. It was not intended to settle any outstanding political or economic problems, and it did not. Their willingness to attend revealed, instead, the importance they themselves attached to a meeting that symbolized their emergence to independence. Moreover, it gave them an opportunity to meet one another. (In the past most of the countries represented had relations primarily with the particular controlling colonial power.) Most of them felt that the heritage of colonial domination and the problem of state-building gave them common interests: Bandung let them establish ties through which in the future they would be able to work out these interests cooperatively. Finally, the conference gave them an opportunity to define a set of general attitudes toward the current international political scene. On this count, despite the expressions of cordiality and common feeling, the conference also revealed that contact might mean not only cooperation and common viewpoints, but also conflict.

Thus the closing communique consisted of promises of cooperation in economic development, technical aid, and cultural exchange, expressions of concern over the status of Dutch New Guinea (which the Indonesians claimed as West Irian) and events in North Africa, and a plea for world disarmament, nonintervention in the domestic affairs of states, and increased membership in the United Nations. It also expressed concern over colonialism, "an evil which should speedily be brought to an end." This phrase represented a compromise reached to a dispute during which the representatives of many states insisted that this must also mean Communist colonialism. The phrase calling for "abstention from alliances serving only the interests of big powers" indicated the split between neutralists and others. Indian's Nehru had wanted a condemnation of all military pacts, but half the members of the conference belonged to military alliances of one sort or another, and the resulting description of the kind of alliance to be avoided was thoroughly innocuous.

Bandung served a useful purpose for Communist China. Foreign Minister Chou En-lai proved himself a thoroughly skilled diplomat. He exuded a spirit of conciliation and friendliness and declared himself willing to negotiate any question with anyone, including the United States, whose representatives he invited to sit down with him in an effort to resolve the Formosa dispute. Secretary Dulles was not in Washington when word came of the Chinese offer, and Under-Secretary Herbert Hoover, Jr.—appointed to administer the department efficiently, and not expected to be well versed in policy matters—answered instead, rejecting the suggestion out of hand. The dismay expressed in other countries was echoed in the United States: again, in a day when the Soviets and the Chinese demonstrated flexibility in the face of new circumstances, the United States appeared to adopt a rigid posture. It was the supposedly inflexible Dulles who hastened to correct the position, and to declare that direct talks might indeed be acceptable and useful. This led, in following years, to a series of protracted but unrewarding conversations at Geneva.

Chou En-lai came away from Bandung with an aura of respectability that served Communist China well. So far as most of the Afro-Asian states were concerned, China was and ought to be accepted as a full-fledged member of the international community. Here and in other places Chou flourished the *Panche Shila,* or statement of five principles which he declared ought to govern the relations between states. Originally stated in a 1954 treaty between China and India in which India acknowledged Chinese sovereignty over Tibet, they were: (1) Mutual respect for each other's territorial integrity and sovereignty; (2) mutual nonaggression; (3) mutual noninterference in each other's internal affairs; (4) equality and mutual benefit; (5) peaceful coexistence. Many states proceeded to pledge adherence to the statement.

Bandung did not represent a complete victory for the neutralists, and Chou En-lai, who had started in a strident manner, tailored his approach accordingly. But it was significant that Sir John Kotelewala of Ceylon, the most strenuous Asian anti-Communist at the Conference, was roundly defeated in an April 1956 election. Although the campaign was fought largely on local issues, it put into power Bandanaraike, head of the heterogeneous but Marxist-oriented United Freedom Party. A thorough neutralist, he quickly established relations with Moscow and Peking, began a program of nationalization, and negotiated withdrawal of the British from the important base they had held at Trincomalee.

Bandung was not the cause, but its spirit was certainly represented in changes that subsequently took place in French-controlled territories. In September 1955, Cambodia, a participant at Bandung as a more-or-less neutralist country, elected a government headed by Prince Norodom Sihanouk, whose first act was to withdraw Cambodia completely from the French Union in which it had remained after the Indochinese settlement of 1954. In early 1956, both Morocco and Tunisia attained full independence from the government of Socialist Guy Mollet. Although Tunisia's Prime Minister Habib Bourguiba rejected neutralism and Communism, he nevertheless proceeded to argue that Algeria, which the French still considered an integral part of France, would also have to attain independence. Finally, in May 1956, France turned over to India a series of small enclaves which it had held for two centuries.

In the same years, Indonesia—seat of the Bandung Conference—acted to increase its own independence through abrogation of the Netherlands-Indonesian Union of 1949 and its accompanying financial agreements. And President Sukarno symbolized his international position by visiting first the United States, then China, and the Soviet Union (which extended technical aid and long-term low interest loans to Indonesia).

December 1955 marked a development in another aspect of the whole decolonization process: end of the membership stalemate in the United Nations with admission of sixteen new members. The Soviet Union had previously vetoed membership for Western-sponsored states because the West had found majorities to block entrance of Soviet-sponsored countries. In this case the veto seems ultimately to have served its purpose: to persuade the great powers to come to a negotiated agreement rather than simply vote against one another. But it could occur only in the spirit of rapproachement that United Nations members seemed determined to salvage from Geneva: Western countries agreed to admit Albania, Hungary, Rumania, and Bulgaria, and the Soviets agreed to the other twelve.* There was the possibility of a last minute breakdown of the package deal when Nationalist China added the Republics of (South) Korea and Vietnam and expressed its determination to block the Mongolian People's Republic, originally included. Pressure on China resulted in abandonment of the proposal of membership for the divided countries, and in return for the exclusion of Outer Mongolia, the Western powers agreed to drop Japan. Informally, all agreed that membership for Japan would be considered at the next Assembly. It was now certain that as new countries became independent, none of the permanent members would take the onus of vetoing their admission. The question of whether United Nations membership should be universal, or whether it should be restricted in

* Jordan, Ireland, Portugal, Italy, Austria, Finland, Ceylon, Nepal, Libya, Cambodia, Laos, Spain.

terms of vaguely stated qualifications in the Charter, had been resolved for all but the divided countries. The march to independence and full international status symbolized by Bandung continued.

But not without pain. The French denied that Algeria had any desire to be or right to be independent. In the face of continued terrorism, France had removed three of its five NATO divisions to Algeria (thus enabling the Soviets and neutralists to claim that NATO aided French colonial suppression). According to the French, Algerian terrorism was supported by only a minority; the majority of Muslims were terrified into passivity. The matter, they said, was strictly domestic, and called merely for pacification; the only thing that made it a matter of international concern was direct interference by Egypt and other countries; they were the ones that should be censured by the United Nations. When in late 1955 the United Nations General Assembly voted to consider the matter of Algeria, the French underlined their point of view by walking out, to return only when the item was removed from the Agenda.

In another spot, Cyprus, the British echoed the French argument. Terrorism had broken out in the tiny island, on which was one of Britain's remaining eastern Mediterranean bases, close to the Suez Canal and the oil fields of the Middle East. The terrorist National Organization for Cyprus Struggle (EOKA) claimed to embody the widespread desire of the Greek Cypriot community for unity with Greece. The British maintained that so long as terrorism existed, there was no way to measure popular feeling, since the people were cowed by the terrorists. To justify continued control, they involved the Turks in the situation. Since almost one-fifth of the population of Cyprus was Turkish and the island lay close to the Turkish coast, the British insisted that Turkey should be consulted. The result was a deterioration in Greco-Turkish relations and bad feeling between the two communities in Cyprus. Britain again imitated the technique used by the French when they had deported the Sultan of Morocco: the British exiled Archbishop Makarios, leader of the Greek Cypriots, charging him with having aided and abetted the terrorists. Attempts to draw up a new constitutional document for internal self-government failed, and Greek agitation for Cypriot self-determination began to undermine Greek relations with NATO. Given the problems of the Turkish minority and British determination to hold Cyprus as a base, the whole issue seemed destined to remain a festering, insoluble matter on which Communist and nationalist could make common cause.

The Soviet Twentieth Party Congress

The year 1955 had seemed an auspicious one in many ways: Bandung had marked the coming to maturity of a group of new countries, and Geneva had demonstrated that, in the face of new weapons, both super powers saw the need to reassure one another that they would try to avoid war, thereby reducing tension. Although Geneva produced no tangible political accords, it was preceded by a series of settlements of outstanding issues on the world scene, and seemed to presage a new era in world politics. Many leaders of new states were especially optimistic, finding as they did on their doorsteps a smiling pair of Soviet leaders who praised their cultures and their efforts at state-building, and who were willing to help them with long-term credits and barter agreements that would avoid the fluctuations of world market prices, plus gifts of new factories or paved roads and technical aid. To Western leaders, the Soviet salesmen seemed much more ominous—precursors, perhaps, of Soviet economic penetration for purposes of political control, and purveyors of the weapons that had upset and disturbed the balance in the Middle East. Nevertheless, the optimists reproached the alarmists. When Secretary Dulles called neutralism "immoral," neutralist leaders like Nehru attacked him bitterly. Dulles' attitude, Nehru said, "left no room for any country to sit on the fence . . . [it divides the world] into two hostile camps, each of which is ready to spring at the throat of the other." Many people felt that Russian internal changes since the death of Stalin involved a genuine liberalization and even democratization. They were even willing to overlook the harshness of the Stalinist period, for Russia, like many of their own countries, had had to industrialize far faster than Western countries, and tough measures had been necessary. Insofar as foreign policy was concerned, Western powers, they thought, had not only been imperialist in the past, but had been reluctant to relinquish their empires, and had done so only under pressure and as a result of weakness. There were things about the new Soviet Union and its surrounding states that one would not wish to emulate, but conditions had vastly improved.

However, the situation within the Soviet Union and the relations between it and its satellite states had been greatly strained by events since Stalin's death and by the very fact of relaxation of international tension. In the first years the main change had been Malenkov's New Course; this involved diminishing the power of the secret police, and increasing light industry and the production of consumer goods at the expense of continued emphasis on heavy industry. The New Course was welcomed in most of the satellites. In some of them it relieved almost intolerable strains imposed by the Stalinist pattern. Although its initiation had been followed by the riots of 1953 in Germany, these had been quelled, and there was no repetition there. Moreover, though Malenkov's foreign policy followed closely upon the course Stalin had begun, involving a search for settlements in various areas, the ties of the Soviet Union to the satellite countries also began to change. Stalin had dictated to them as much as he had to his associates at home. The New Course let them adapt somewhat to local conditions, and to work out problems more on their own. The trend intensified after Khrushchev replaced Malenkov, primarily because the "reduction in tension" symbolized by Geneva appeared to eliminate the whole issue of "liberation" of Eastern Europe from the international scene. This meant to Communist leaders of East Europe that their existence and the stability of their regimes now depended less on the Soviet Union's protection, and they could concentrate on policies that would build domestic support. Finally, the Soviet rapprochement with Yugoslavia appeared to indicate that a country that followed its own policy in both domestic and foreign affairs could be welcome in the Soviet bloc, despite Khrushchev's domestic reversal of Malenkov's emphasis on light industry and consumer goods and his renewed emphasis on heavy industry in the Stalinist pattern.

On the other hand, Yugoslav respectability posed some immediate difficulties for leaders in the other satellite states. Normalization of relations with Tito after years of bloody purges of "Titoists" was ideologically difficult: How could they continue to justify leadership when their particular claim to legitimacy was that they had unmasked Titoists? Poland was in the throes of an intellectual ferment as a result of the de-Stalinization process (as it was already called), and "right-wing deviationists" who had been purged in the past for Titoism—notably Poland's Wladyslaw Gomulka—stood to benefit from Tito's rehabilitation, and endanger the position of existing leaders. Tito pressed home the point, making barbed remarks about Communist heads of state who had followed Stalin's lead which Soviet leaders now condemned. He charged them with having spilled blood of innocent Communists and with lacking "the Communist courage to admit their errors." Satellite leaders responded to the whole development hesitantly. They established correct but not cordial relations with Tito, found scapegoats for past excesses, and praised Stalin's accomplishments while admitting that he had committed errors.

The Twentieth Party Congress in February 1956, however, made their course far more difficult. Khrushchev had been busy consolidating his domestic position by popular reforms. He granted amnesty to some political offenders, laid a greater stress on legal procedures through the courts instead of arbitrary executive action by the police and other administrative branches, allowed greater freedom in the arts, and attacked unpopular bureaucrats. He also proceeded to fill local party positions with his own men. Then, at the Congress—which endorsed Khrushchev's views that parliaments might also serve as organs of "genuine democracy for the working people" and that there were acceptable "separate paths to socialism"—Khrushchev attacked Stalin in the most violent terms, outdoing Western critics in Stalin's time. He spoke of Stalin's dictatorship by terror, of injustice on an unbelievable scale involving the executions of thousands of innocent people. He described how Stalin's closest associates lived in fear of him and his whims: this was what had kept them from protesting or stopping the dictator. Of necessity, Khrushchev did not suggest that the system that permitted such a thing to happen was wrong. The fault, he said, lay in the "cult of the individual," which was now replaced by "collective leadership."

Khrushchev had gone out dangerously on a limb and, in fact, there were many repercussions. Khrushchev had tried to make Stalin the scapegoat for all that had been bad in former years and to identify the new leadership with opposition to the repressive features of the previous regime and absolve them of complicity. But the attempt at absolution was bound to raise further questions about degrees of guilt, as well as about the many leaders who had been deposed for anti-Stalinist activities by Stalinists still in power. (Khrushchev spoke of the many within the Soviet Union who had been rehabilitated since 1953.) Together with the rapprochement with Tito, relaxation of tension with the West and the wooing of bourgeois nationalist leaders, the Twentieth Party Congress speech further jeopardized the position of satellite political bosses and party leaders outside the Soviet bloc.

The Stalemate Shaken: Hungary and Suez

The events of 1955 and early 1956—the détente, de-Stalinization, the new Soviet initiatives in foreign policy, and the rise of new states to a position where they were wooed by both sides—culminated late in the year in two events that shook the world and challenged the whole concept of a nuclear stalemate. They were the revolt in the Soviet bloc and the abortive Suez war.

Within the bloc, Stalin-style industrialization had created an extremely unstable situation in two countries, Poland and Hungary. Czechoslovakia and East Germany were already industrialized to some degree, and in the latter, memories of the failure of the 1953 uprising lingered. Rumania, Bulgaria, and Albania had not suffered such difficult experiences; Bulgaria had a much longer tradition of Russian friendship and was, like Albania, still essentially an agricultural country with a peasant society.

In Hungary and Poland, however, the postwar period of rapid, forced industrialization had created great strain, and Malenkov's New Course was strongly welcomed. In Hungary it brought to power Imre Nagy in 1953, who adopted its tenets. The fall of Malenkov in 1955 had its parallel in Hungary, where Nagy not only had to give up the premiership but was expelled from the party. The Stalinist Rakosi replaced him, but found a dangerous situation: Nagy's reforms had unloosed all the intellectuals' and workers' objections to Stalinism, and had again called forth Hungarian nationalism. Some Hungarian party leaders began to talk of an alternative to Stalinist emulation of Soviet Communism: *national* Communism with national variations determined by local conditions. Moreover, Rakosi assumed power when the Soviet rapprochement with Tito was well under way and when the anti-Stalin campaign was launched in earnest by Khrushchev's Twentieth Party Congress speech. Faced with mounting popular pressure within the country, Rakosi was forced to resign. His replacement by Erno Gero, a leader less tainted with the Stalinist hue, failed to satisfy popular demands for reforms, and agitation grew in Budapest for the recall to power of Nagy and even of non-Communist leaders.

In the meantime, events in Poland had their effect on Hungary. The tension in Poland led in June to workers' riots in the industrial center of Poznan. Although the riots were condemned by the Soviets as engineered by foreign agents, the Polish Communist Party's Central Committee admitted that they were the result of clumsy handling of justifiable complaints about working conditions. Then, on August 4, Wladyslaw Gomulka, ousted in 1949 and imprisoned for Titoism, was readmitted to the party, and by October 16 the situation had so changed that he attended a Politbureau meeting where he was restored to the Central Committee. Since he appeared to stand for radical reform in Poland, he seemed a threat to the delicate new balance Khrushchev had been trying to establish between Soviet leadership and recognition of national differences within the Soviet bloc—a balance made even more precarious by Yugoslav insistence upon its pound of flesh. Alarmed, Khrushchev and three other Politbureau members flew to Warsaw to restrain the course being taken by Polish nationalism. The attempt to intervene, accompanied by undisguised intimidation in the form of troop movements, failed; Gomulka was elected First Secretary of the Polish Communist party on October 21.

These events, including Poland's successful defiance of the Soviet leaders, were watched in Hungary. On October 23, a demonstration began in Budapest demanding Nagy's appointment as Premier, punishment of Rakosi, and the withdrawal of Soviet troops from Hungary. When Hungarian security police fired on the crowd, demonstration turned into outright rebellion. The army, instead of siding with the government, either stood by or, in many cases, sided with the demonstrators. Nagy came to power and made concessions to popular demands, but Soviet troops entered the fighting. The next week was one of extraordinary confusion; church dignitaries and others were freed, a general strike spread through the country while young Hungarians, who fought against the Soviet forces, called for aid from the West. The Communist apparatus in Hungary completely collapsed as Nagy took non-Communists into the government, and it became quite clear that under mass pressures Hungary would actually move out of the Communist camp. Soviet troops became inactive, and on October 30 Khrushchev issued a declaration to the effect that the status of Soviet troops stationed in East Europe was always subject to re-examination; their withdrawal could be negotiated, but only with the concurrence of all signatories. Relations between members of the bloc were governed by the principle of equality and non-interference in one another's affairs. Mikoyan and Suslov, the Praesidium members most concerned with Hungarian affairs, flew to Hungary to discuss the situation. Here they learned of the demand for complete evacuation of all Soviet forces, and found that the Communist party would have a minimal future role if events continued on their course.

Poland and Yugoslavia extended messages of friendship to the new Nagy regime, and the Soviet press declared that a counterrevolutionary *putsch* had been suppressed by joint action of the new Nagy government and Soviet forces. Mikoyan apparently promised the withdrawal of Soviet forces, and in New York, a meeting of the United Nations Security Council, called to consider the situation, adjourned with no action, hoping for the best.

But the situation deteriorated. Under continued internal pressure and on receipt of reports that Soviet armored units had begun to roll across the Soviet-Hungarian border, Nagy and his cabinet withdrew from the Warsaw Pact, announced Hungarian neutrality, and sent a message to the United Nations to this effect, declaring their hope that the United Nations would undertake to guarantee and protect it. During the next two days Soviet units moved to seal off Hungary's border with Austria and to encircle Budapest. In the meantime, the Soviets, having decided on the move, had recruited two members of Nagy's government who would assume power once he was overthrown. On November 2, the Soviets formally agreed to open negotiations for withdrawal of their troops. But the agreement was a ruse. The discussions began in Budapest on November 3, and in the evening shifted to Soviet military headquarters twenty miles away. Here the Hungarian negotiators were arrested and the orders issued for the Soviet forces to crush the Hungarian regime.

They met with extraordinary but futile resistance. Nagy took refuge in the Yugoslav embassy, which he later left on issuance of a safe conduct by the Soviet leaders, who immediately arrested him and subsequently tried and executed him. Desperate Hungarians appealed to the West for help that never came, and eventually two hundred thousand fled the country. Janos Kadar took over the job of making the best of a bad situation as Premier.

The Soviet decision to intervene had tremendous significance. Soviet leaders knew that intervention would cost them heavily among supporters abroad and would greatly damage the image they had been creating during the last few years.* But overwhelming factors seemed to favor intervention: the Hungarian revolution might spread to other satellites, not only to Poland where Gomulka was displaying far more caution and might be swept aside, but perhaps also to Rumania, and even to Germany or Czechoslovakia. Moreover, Khrushchev had faced severe internal opposition to his new foreign policy; it was tremendously important for him personally to keep it from ending in disaster.

Then, too, there was the question of what the West might do, and luckily for Khrushchev the answer came quickly. Eisenhower and Dulles, despite earlier talk of liberation, were not prepared to take

---

* To minimize the extent of the damage, Khrushchev claimed that Kadar, on November 1, had constituted a new and legitimate Hungarian government that had asked Soviet aid against a foreign and fascist-inspired revolution headed by Nagy.

any action in Eastern Europe that might lead to open and armed conflict with the Soviet Union. On October 27, Dulles welcomed the developments taking place within the Soviet bloc and advised the satellites that they could draw American aid even if they did not abandon Communism completely (that is, if they assumed a Titoist or even a Gomulka-like position). He tried to forestall Soviet intervention by assuring the Soviets that the United States did not seek military allies in the area. But earlier he had also declared that the United States could not intervene directly to aid the Polish people because this could precipitate a world war. And Eisenhower declared that America would "do all within [its] peaceful power. . . . We ourselves," he said, "have abstained from the use of force—knowing it to be contrary both to the interests of these peoples and the spirit and methods of the United Nations."

If American reluctance to take direct action was one factor Khrushchev could weigh in favor of intervention, a second aspect of the Western position must have been equally important in his decision. The Western powers were deeply embroiled in the disastrous Suez War, a result of an earlier Soviet venture into the area.

At the very time that the Soviets moved into Hungary, Israeli, French, and British troops were attacking Egypt. World attention, divided, could more easily be diverted to focus on Western imperialism, where, because the United States disapproved of its allies' attack, the Soviet Union could line up *with* the United States and actually secure effective United Nations action impossible to achieve in Hungary.

The attack on Egypt arose out of a series of developments in the Middle East centering on the Aswan Dam project, control over the Suez Canal, and Arab-Israeli hostility. Nasser's prestige in the Arab world had soared since consummation of the Egyptian-Soviet bloc arms-for-cotton deal. Egypt became a center for pan-Arab propaganda and agitation that reached throughout the Middle East and across North Africa. But then the Aswan Dam project (see p. 213), the American counter to Soviet arms, ran into trouble—first with the American Congress, then with the administration. Secretary Dulles, furious with Egyptian attempts to play off the Soviets against the West by spreading rumors that the USSR would perhaps give Egypt a better bargain, decided to administer a public and stinging rebuff to Nasser by withdrawing the offer to help build the dam. In addition to curbing Nasser, the move would serve notice to other new countries that they could not play the same game. A note delivered to Nasser on July 19, 1956, gave several reasons why the United States had to withdraw from the tentative agreement of the year before: Egypt had not reached agreement with other states on the Nile River about the question of dividing of its waters, and Egypt, in the light of its commitment of future foreign exchange resources for purchase of arms, would not be able to contribute its share to build the dam. The United States would, however, continue to help Egypt in other, more feasible development plans. Withdrawal by the United States automatically made void the British and International Bank aid offers.

The timing was not calculated to ease the blow. When the note was delivered, Nasser was conferring in Yugoslavia with the other chief exponents of neutralism, Nehru and Tito. The Egyptian President remained quiet for a week, and then, in an impassioned speech delivered at Alexandria told the roaring crowd that he was nationalizing the Suez Canal. The Canal, he said, had been built by unpaid Egyptian labor (a hundred thousand had died in the process) and Egyptian shares and Egyptian profits had been stolen by the Canal Company. He was retaking stolen property. What did he care about American aid? The company returned profits of a $100 million a year, and he could dispense with the American $70 million a year spread over a five-year period. Americans might complain about the nationalization, but,

. . . whenever I hear talk from Washington, I shall say, "Choke to death on your own fury." . . . I never saw any American aid directed towards industrialization as this would cause us to compete with them. American aid is everywhere directed towards exploitation. . . . Today, when we build the edifice of our dignity, freedom and pride, we feel that it will not be completely sound until we eradicate domination, humiliation and submission. The Suez Canal constituted an edifice of humiliation.

Nasser also linked the seizure directly with the Aswan Dam and declared that Egypt, now able to collect the annual income of the Canal—the $100 million—would "build the High Dam as we want it."

The action and seizure set off a frenzied wave of diplomatic and military activity, of argument and recrimination. In fact, the dam could not be built with the profits of the company—the figure cited by President Nasser was gross profit, from which operating expenses had to be deducted. The United States formally protested the allegations in the speech which, it said, were entirely inconsistent with the friendly relations that existed between Egypt and the United States.

After Nasser's initial outburst Egypt played the diplomatic game skillfully. Egyptian studies had already been prepared on nationalization of the Canal, the concession for which would expire in 1968. Only the occasion was needed. When the American action over the High Dam provided it, the Egyptian Government was therefore ready. It claimed the sovereign right to nationalize a property lying within its borders even if the shareholders were foreign, since it would compensate the shareholders according to fair market value of the shares and would respect the various international treaties that guaranteed freedom of passage to all countries. To those who asked how anyone could expect Egypt to fulfill these commitments, Egyptians had a simple answer: a single country, England, had undertaken them before. Was England more trustworthy than Egypt?

To this, political leaders in France and England retorted that Egypt was certainly not trustworthy. In 1951 the Security Council had declared that Arab armistice agreements with Israel—although not constituting a final peace settlement—gave Egypt no legal right of belligerency, no right of self-defense to block Israeli ships and cargoes from passage through the Canal. Yet Egypt had continued to do so.

Nasser knew that the Western case was weak. Since 1951, although the British had guarded the Canal, Western powers had done nothing beyond the Security Council resolution to ensure Israeli freedom of passage. Therefore it ill-became them to accuse Egypt on this score. Moreover, any further attempt to repeat the Security Council declaration would now be blocked by a Soviet veto.

In his *Philosophy of the Revolution*, Nasser had told the world that he proposed to use Egypt's vital geographical position to build up Egypt. The vital element in that geographical position was Egypt's control of the Canal, through which was shipped almost two-thirds of the oil that had become essential to Europe's economy. Every maritime nation in the world depended upon smooth working of the Canal.

Because of this, as well as Nasser's aid to Algerian rebels, French and British reactions were particularly sharp; Prime Minister Eden took a position from which it would be hard to retreat:

No arrangements for the future of this great international waterway could be acceptable to Her Majesty's Government which would leave it in the unfettered control of a single power, which could, as recent events have shown, exploit it purely for purposes of national policy.

Both he and Premier Mollet of France referred to Nasser as a new Hitler: appeasement would only whet his appetite, and the Canal seizure must not result in another Munich. Both countries immediately considered a military expedition against Egypt.

But both tried diplomacy first, spiked with the threat of economic or military pressures. Here, however, they met confusion sown by the United States; American leaders admitted that a nation might ultimately have to use military pressures to assure its vital interests, but then backed away from the implications of the point. The Administration did support one form of economic pressure: like Britain, it froze Egyptian assets. Then Dulles persuaded the British and French to call a conference of Canal users to prepare a project of international control for the Canal. Nasser, denouncing the idea, refused to attend. Support for his nationalization move was widespread—it was applauded not only in Moscow, but in most of the new countries. Among Arab peoples his prestige had soared; Dulles' move had seriously backfired.

The conference that met in London during August produced a majority and a minority plan. The minority plan—supported by India, Indonesia, Ceylon, and the Soviet Union—would have left the Canal in Egyptian hands and associated some kind of representative body of Canal users with Egyptian management. The majority plan would have taken the Canal from Egypt and given it to an internationally responsible Suez Canal Board. Presentation of the plan to Nasser by a delegation headed by Prime Minister Menzies of Australia produced no result. The United States—now standing by its position that it would not allow the use of force—came up with the idea of a "Suez Canal User's Association" that would employ its own pilots, collect tolls, and coordinate traffic. It would pay Egypt for use of the Canal.

The British and French immediately asked whether, if Egypt refused to cooperate, "SCUA" would run ships through the Canal under threat of force. What did Dulles intend? Statements emanating from Washington gave rise to further confusion; both British and French appeared to think the plan had been meant to exert serious pressure on Nasser. But Dulles explicitly disclaimed any attempt at either boycott or "shooting our way through the Canal." In the months of September and October, as plans for setting up SCUA went forward, the organization looked less and less attractive and such users as Japan and Pakistan refused to join. Some who joined made known their views that it could only be used to negotiate terms acceptable to Nasser.

In the meantime an attempt to show that the Egyptians could not run the Canal by themselves failed. Foreign pilots walked off the job, but hastily trained Egyptian, Russian, and Yugoslav pilots successfully replaced them. The Anglo-French effort to bring Nasser to task therefore shifted to the United Nations Security Council.

Here all the differences between the powers were revealed. Dulles had on one occasion in September said, "I don't think you can go on forever asking nations not to resort to force." Later came his insistence that force must not be used. Then, in a press conference, he had called American differences with the British and French a matter of "colonialism" and of a difference of attitudes on "colonial" issues. Nothing could more infuriate the British and French than this terminology, borrowed from Nasser. Would Dulles consider that opposition to nationalization of American property abroad constituted "colonialism"? Finally, at the United Nations, Dulles seemed to say that if only Egypt accepted the principle that operation of the Canal should be insulated from politics of any one nation everything else would be all right—without any mention of international control. The British and French now felt that Dulles had merely been playing for time to keep them from acting. At the United Nations they came to a broad agreement about principles that should govern operation of the Canal, but there was little satisfaction in this, and they now engaged in private conversations that excluded the United States. By the end of October, as the situation in Hungary worsened, the Anglo-French military buildup in the eastern Mediterranean proceeded rapidly.

While public attention focused on the drama being played out in the Soviet bloc and on the Suez issue, deteriorating relations between Israel and its Arab neighbors came to play a part in the spectacle. The previous two years had seen an increase in pin prick attacks on isolated Israeli border settlements and the development of the Israeli technique of large-scale retaliatory raids. The latter caused far more casualties and earned Israel frequent condemnation by the Mixed Armistice Commissions. In October 1956, Israel was censured by members of the Security Council. Secretary General Dag Hammarskjold had visited the area in an attempt to bring some measure of calm. But Israel's fears for its security—already heightened by growing shipments of Communist arms to Egypt—were increased by October elections in Jordan that returned a large pro-Nasser faction to the Parliament, and by reports that Egypt, Jordan, and Syria were establishing a joint army command for time of war. The Jordanian Chief of Staff was quoted as having announced: "The time has come for the Arabs to choose the appropriate time to launch the assault for Israel's destruction."

The only factor in Israel's favor at the moment seemed to be France's growing enmity for Nasser, whose Canal seizure threatened her economy and who also openly gave arms and supplies to the Algerian rebels.

The French (with approval of the United States, which would not accept the onus of taking the action) had sold modern weapons, including Mystère fighter planes and tanks, to Israel. French technicians were in Israel, and Franco-Israeli diplomatic contacts increased. With one eye on the immediate situation and the other on Soviet embroilment in Eastern Europe, the Israelis mobilized on October 29 and struck rapidly —not at Jordan, as expected, but across Egypt's Sinai peninsula.

Events of the next few days were completely unexpected. As Israeli forces occupied the Gaza strip and cut across and down the Sinai peninsula, Britain and France, instead of acting with the United States on the basis of the Tripartite Declaration of 1950, vetoed an American Security Council resolution calling for a cease-fire, withdrawal of Israeli forces, and denial of aid to Israel. Instead, Britain and France delivered a twenty-four hour ultimatum: Egyptians and Israelis should withdraw ten miles on either side of the Canal which is deep within Egyptian territory. Upon expiration of the twenty-four hour period they proceeded with their plans to intervene to secure compliance: their armed forces moved to occupy the Canal zone.

On October 31 they began aerial bombardment of Egyptian targets and five days later paratroopers and other contingents landed and began to move toward the Canal, occasionally meeting heavy resistance. In the meantime, Egypt had fully blocked the vital waterway with scuttled ships.

The Anglo-French move—one of various alternatives earlier discussed but decided on only at the last moment—proved a monument of miscalculation. Aimed at securing the Canal and toppling Nasser, it did neither. Instead, the two countries found the United States ranged with the Soviet Union and much of the world against them. Under extreme pressure they were forced to withdraw with no objectives achieved, but leaving the Canal blocked. In addition, oil pipelines running from Iraq across Syria to Mediterranean ports (bypassing the Canal) were destroyed by Egyptian sympathizers in Syria. Britain and France thus faced financial difficulties and a potentially large-scale fuel crisis with winter coming, and other European countries that also depended on Canal shipments felt little sympathy for them.

Had it not been for a marvelous piece of improvisation at the United Nations, the threat of Soviet intervention might have become real; Khrushchev first suggested joint military action with the United States, then threatened to send volunteers as well as to attack Britain and France directly by missile. A hasty invention of Lester Pearson of Canada—worked out in detail by Secretary-General Dag Hammarskjold

—provided a face-saving formula for the British-French-Israeli with-drawal: the United Nations Emergency Force.

UNEF was far from the original concept of an international armed force to be set up under the collective security provisions of the United Nations Charter. Its precise makeup, characteristics, tasks, and limitations arose out of an immediate situation: it was a force of some 6000 men, designed only to be interposed between the hostile parties, to fight only in self-defense, to go only where permitted. Moreover, it was composed of men from many nations but from none of the great powers nor the belligerents. Its function was essentially to ease withdrawal of the invaders. As time went on it came to constitute a permanent border patrol along the Israeli-Egyptian border and at Sharm-el-Sheikh, which controls the Gulf of Aqaba and the Straits of Tiran, entrances to Israel's southern port of Elat, hitherto blockaded by Egypt.

England and France tried to delay their withdrawal from Egypt until they had salvaged something from the operation. But President Eisenhower insisted that there must be no rewards for aggression (the collective security argument in purity) and that issues and problems in the area must be negotiated *after* their withdrawal. The two faced many pressures: a run on British currency, Russian threats, and sus-pension of action by an American government-supervised committee of oil companies previously organized to rechannel oil shipments in case of any emergency. In creating the committee no one had envis-aged an emergency caused by Western powers instead of by Nasser or others of his kind. Even oil men had difficulty calculating how bad a European oil shortage might become since the answer depended on many political as well as technical variables. (Not the least of the political problems revolved around state regulation of production within the United States. If state boards, charged with equating supply to demand refused to increase supply, the effect on Europe might be serious. And the Federal government in the United States was loath to appeal to the state boards.)

Under the circumstances, Britain and France played for time, agree-ing to withdrawal if UNEF could keep peace. Hammarskjold obtained Egyptian consent to UNEF entrance, granted because Egypt could then be sure of Anglo-French withdrawal. All excuse for remaining gone, British and French troops began to pull out in early December. They had gained nothing by their actions but blockage of the Canal, further distrust by the new nations, internal political difficulties, and an oil shortage. Israel, however, held out for more and gained something:

from the Egyptian army it had seized large quantities of Russian-delivered supplies; by proving the Israeli army's effectiveness in action, it had enhanced its value as a deterrent; Israel also obtained guarantees before withdrawing from Gaza and Sharm el-Sheikh that both would remain under United Nations control. In fact, Egypt later did re-occupy Gaza, but the border, patrolled by UNEF, remained quiet. The important port of Elat remained open.

On one important matter, Israel was unable to obtain satisfaction: transit through the Suez Canal. When the Canal was reopened to navigation, Israeli shipping was still excluded.

Nasser emerged greatly strengthened. His propaganda pictured the Egyptian army as having roundly defeated the invader (though the fact that UNEF presence hastened the Anglo-French-Israeli withdrawal made this possible). Most countries of the world had supported him, including those that had originally looked with disfavor on his propaganda activities and seizure of the Canal. He also had unquestioned control of the Canal, now being cleared of wreckage under United Nations auspices.

The Soviet Union gained. It successfully posed as the champion of the Arabs, ready to come to their help whenever they beckoned. Moreover, the whole Suez affair helped to deflect attention from what was going on in Hungary. Some observers reproached the United Nations and its member governments with doing too much in the Suez case and too little in Hungary. But the political alignment in each case made effective action in one possible that was impossible in the other. Nations responded with alacrity to the situation in which something could be done. In the Hungarian case, however, they had to content themselves with helping the thousands of refugees.

A curious aftermath to the Suez War typified American attitudes toward the Cold War and the role of the new states in it, and the quite different views maintained by most leaders of these states. The Eisenhower administration believed that British influence in the Middle East was decisively ended. This was the culmination of a process that began in 1947 when Britain informed the United States it could no longer support Greece and Turkey. The new successor states were independent but weak—there was much talk of a Middle Eastern "power vacuum." Moreover, under Khrushchev's new diplomacy the Soviet Union had gained considerable influence and in the process had vaulted over the Baghdad Pact, now even weaker because its members had broken with England over the Suez affair. The administration, therefore, decided that it must step into the breach, just as it had done in Europe in 1947–48 and, more recently, in the Far East and Southeast Asia.

President Eisenhower had just been reelected by a sweeping majority. In January 1957 he went before Congress to ask for passage of a joint resolution that would do several things. It would authorize the President to use the armed forces of the United States to protect any nation or group of nations in the general region of the Middle East requesting such protection against overt armed aggression from any nation controlled by international Communism. In addition, the resolution would authorize military and economic assistance to countries of the area.

It seems doubtful that the Eisenhower Doctrine, as it came to be called, had any of the desired effect. Rather, it revealed the profound gulf between the American administration's world view and that of most Arab leaders, who saw no threat arising from Russia or Communist bloc countries. They had, in fact, just seen one Arab country come under military attack from non-Communists: Israel, England and France. There was little doubt that the Eisenhower administration's position in the Suez War had won it much goodwill throughout the Middle East; Nasser himself emphasized the differences between the United States on the one hand and Britain and France on the other. But the Eisenhower Doctrine was immediately interpreted as an attempt to replace faded French and British domination with American domination, on the basis of a fraudulent issue, and it dissipated all good feeling. A few states whose leaders had already aligned them with the West welcomed it—Iraq (the only truly Arab state) and Iran, Turkey and Pakistan. Nasser spearheaded opposition to it, however; there was no "vacuum" in the area and the Arabs would never again allow their countries to become a sphere of influence for any foreign power. "Arab nationalism was the sole basis on which Arab policy could be formulated." * The threat was not communism but "imperialism, Zionism, and colonialism." The Soviet Union immediately capitalized on these views by expressing its willingness to prevent aggression and interference in the internal affairs of Middle East states. It suggested the withdrawal of all foreign bases and troops and an embargo on shipment of arms into the region, while stepping up its arms shipments and technical aid. By these maneuvers it underlined the contention that its own moves in the Middle East had been a response to the Baghdad Pact and concomitant shipments of Western arms.

* Declaration issued January 19, 1957, by leaders of Egypt, Syria, Saudi Arabia, and Jordan, in Cairo.

In Jordan, a country whose imminent disappearance had been predicted periodically by experts ever since its original formation at the end of World War I, young King Hussein barely escaped deposition. His unstable country had long depended on British subsidy, and the famed Arab Legion—the best-trained force in the Middle East —had been led by British officers. In March 1956, after months of Egyptian agitation, Hussein had courted popularity among his own people by removing long-time British commander John Bagot Glubb, along with lesser British officers. The October elections that returned a pro-Nasser majority to the Parliament were a contributing cause to the Israeli attack on Egypt, although the first indications were that Israel, fearing that Hussein was about to invite Iraqi troops in, might attack Jordan.

Hussein disagreed with the course set by his new pro-Nasser Parliament, particularly when the government of Premier Nabulsi, under the impact of the Eisenhower Doctrine, announced its intention of establishing diplomatic relations with the Soviet Union, of accepting Soviet aid, and of rejecting not only the Eisenhower Doctrine but *any* American aid. When army leaders sided with the government against the King, the very existence of Jordan seemed in doubt. The King, however, was able to rally to his side the Bedouins that composed the mass of the Arab Legion, and an announcement of United States support for the "independence and integrity of Jordan" along with dispatch of the Sixth Fleet to the eastern Mediterranean, enabled him to weather the storm and consolidate his position. Egypt and Syria had earlier promised to substitute their own financial support for British subsidy, but deterioration of relations with Hussein put an end to this possibility. Through the aid of King Saud of Saudi Arabia —ruler of the most anachronistic and backward of the Arab states, assiduously courted by the United States—American financial aid was dispatched to Hussein. In future years his independence was to depend on the United States rather than on Britain.

Conclusion

Although many people failed to see it, 1955 and 1956 marked the emergence of a new, more complicated and complex world balance, one that no longer could be characterized as "bipolar." Churchill had declared in 1953 that hydrogen weapons ushered in a new age, one in which, ironically, the balance of terror might offer more security than had ever been known before; the 1955 Geneva summit conference seemed to prove to many people that he had been right. And if leaders of the two superpowers now felt less fear that the one might attack the other with hydrogen weapons, the leaders of smaller countries found in the situation new opportunities to exercise independence. With less necessity to rely on protection by major powers, they felt freer to act without their approval. Yet the years also showed there were limits to the possibilities open to them: within the Soviet bloc Poland and Hungary tried to go their way, while in the Western bloc Britain and France tried to use force to defend their interests in full knowledge that the United States would disapprove. Within the Soviet bloc the Russians crushed Hungary, while the United States acted to force British and French withdrawal from Egypt. Greater possibilities for action had led men to go too far, and the limits of independence were learned.

Outside the blocs, the years seemed to show that the opportunities for independent action were greater, and neutralism gained more and more adherents. Neutralism explicitly rejected the view that the world was bipolar. It was a view that security would be greater *outside* military alliances with the great powers: alliances brought the greater danger of being in the line of fire if war did come, they provoked counter action by the other side and restricted the freedom of action the neutralists desired. For neutralism also involved the view that economic, diplomatic and cultural links with both sides reduced dependence on either and brought concrete benefits through bids for favor. At the same time, the new neutralism tended to equate both sides in the Cold War and thus gave a moral sanction to the neutralist proposition that the Cold War was not to be viewed as the American response to a Russian Communist threat, but rather as a quarrel between the two superpowers in which neither was better than the other.

The events of these two years marked the breakup of the bipolar world under the impact of the new weapons, of relaxation in the Soviet bloc, of the independence of many countries, and of emerging economic strength in Europe. But the years also marked its limits: the Soviet Union would not allow a real breakup of the Communist world, and the United States would not allow its allies to take strong action toward the newly independent countries that might jeopardize American relations with them. The new situation, then, produced its own new crisis, and it also produced a new series of dilemmas. For the United States, the first one was summed up in the ill-fated Eisenhower Doctrine. In traditional balance-of-power style, the American administration had decided that where weakness existed—as a result of the inevitable withdrawal of British power—it must step in to protect the area against encroachments by the only other power strong enough to step in. The United States would act not only for the sake of the inhabitants of the area, but also to prevent the Soviet Union from the inevitable increase in power that would follow Russian domination of the area. In that case, according to this point of view, the "balance of power" would be upset. But the fate of the Eisenhower Doctrine showed that balance-of-power politics could be successful only where the people in the area concerned saw the Soviet Union as a dangerous opponent. In the era of mass politics and thermonuclear weapons, mass views could no longer be ignored, and in the Middle East, few people shared the American view of the danger.

The second dilemma engendered by the breakup of the bipolar world was intimately linked to the first: the United States found itself, in the Suez case, lined up with the Soviet Union against its own most important allies. This was simply the extreme case of a situation building up since World War II in which the United States consistently advocated independence for the possessions of its allies and argued that the repression of nationalist demands would only create worse situations. Its allies had countered that too rapid independence would lead to chaos, that nationalist demands increased precisely because nationalist leaders found support from the United States, that in many cases so-called nationalist leaders had little real popular base and would merely become local tyrants, and finally, that the United States was indulging in competition with the Soviet Union in supporting nationalist demands —an unfair competition, since the Soviet Union, which stood to benefit from chaos, did not care if chaos followed independence. Moreover, as the Suez case and the Eisenhower Doctrine indicated, once the United States had helped push its allies out of an area, it suddenly saw the necessity for a Western presence in the area and moved clumsily to replace them. Although there might be poetic justice in American difficulties in assuming the role it had helped force its allies to abdicate, this hardly solved the strategic problem that all faced jointly. All through the postwar years the United States struggled with the problem. Its policy-makers were genuinely convinced of the ultimate need to meet new nationalistic demands, both on the grounds of justice and of political necessity, yet their stand often brought them into conflict with their allies and, at times, with what appeared to be strategic necessity.

Finally, the new balance and the Hungarian case raised another issue for the Western powers: Hungary had shown that the Soviet Union would, despite the high political cost, be quite willing to use force to hold its satellites within its bloc, while the United States would not be able to use force to help those within the Soviet bloc who might want to escape. But Khrushchev seemed to believe that the new hydrogen weapons made possible and even required peaceful coexistence—a stage in history in which the socialist camp could now be expected to extend itself by peaceful means. Some Westerners therefore concluded that peaceful coexistence and the various new Russian trade and aid programs meant that the Communist bloc would do everything short of force to draw in new members, but would never relinquish any. In short, as one writer put it, the Russian stand was "what's mine is mine and what's yours is negotiable." But the issue was not so simple; this kind of analysis rested on a bipolar view of the world that what was outside the Soviet bloc was a part of the "free world." A more realistic view had to take into account that there was a Communist bloc, a Western bloc, and a growing number of states uncommitted to either bloc. Despite adherence to dogma that declared that ultimately all states must become Communist, it was primarily toward the latter group that Khrushchev was directing his efforts, which were in the form, as he put it, of peaceful competition. There was little guarantee that the new Soviet activities would, in fact, bring new adherents to the Communist bloc. Although Westerners were quick to warn the new recipients of Communist aid, the recipients were equally quick to respond that they had no fear of Russian domination.

In these two years that revealed the difficulties and problems of the new balance, one development gave hope to many people: the new role assumed by the United Nations and its Secretary-General, whose prestige rose immensely. It seemed quite possible that, given the nuclear stalemate and the possibility for focusing publicity on dangerous spots, intervention by the Secretary-General and the use of such devices as UNEF might keep major powers from the temptation to intervene in them. Many of the twenty-one new states admitted since the 1955 bargain pressed this view strongly: it gave promise of a way to stop the old balance-of-power vicious circle where one major power intervened in the affairs of weak states simply to keep other major powers from so doing, and therefore only provoked the other major powers to try to get there first. It might, in other words, provide a solution to some of the dilemmas the years had revealed. At the same time, however, the new states gave indication of their view that, under modern conditions, collective security was dead and ought to be buried. In expressing hope that Soviet forces would withdraw from Hungary, they expressed the view that under *no* circumstances should force be used. The United Nations, they argued, should concentrate on peaceful settlement of disputes; one of its prime functions should be to hasten and help the process of liquidating nineteenth-century empires and "neo-colonialism," and particular care should be taken not to widen and spread conflicts but rather to localize them. Their admission to the United Nations tended, therefore, to give it a new orientation; but it was one that involved an active role in international politics.

CHAPTER SEVEN   1957–1964 (I)

The New States

and Competitive Coexistence

Several trends mark the years that followed the Hungarian and Suez crises.

A thermonuclear balance continued between the two superpowers, yet technological changes made it unstable and shifting. Both major powers developed intermediate range ballistic missiles and then became able to strike directly at each other with intercontinental ballistic missiles. As a result they began to divest themselves of manned bombers. Despite the events of 1956 the tendency toward a loosening of the blocs was considerably reinforced by missile developments, the growing economic strength of Western Europe, and the appearance of new leaders. Westerners became concerned with the lack of solidity of the North Atlantic Treaty Organization, but disarray among Western powers scarcely matched the splits that developed between Communist China and Russia, and extended to other members of the bloc as well as to Communist parties throughout the world.

For many states, however, the most important trend of these years was the attainment of political independence by more and more former colonial territories. The last great surge took place in Africa, where in some cases the transition was relatively easy. In the Belgian Congo, however, the change produced an international crisis of tremendous significance and embittered relations between the leaders of new African states and Western countries. The years also revealed that political independence was less than a halfway house to the promised land. It brought to the fore a host of new international problems— of relations between the newly independent states and of the boundaries that separated them, of the nature of their relations with economically developed countries, and of what bearing the Cold War might have on them. In Africa, as in other underdeveloped areas, the presence of indigenous Communist parties and the fact of particular kinds of

240

trade relations with the West, widely interpreted as a form of "neo-colonialism," meant that a form of balance-of-power politics between the major powers was inevitably extended to the new countries. But their leaders insisted that the basic problem of world politics was not the division between Communist bloc and the West, but between the rich and the poor.

Neutralism gained wider and wider acceptance; but neutralist senti-ments alone could not make a foreign policy. Neutralists received a shock when Communist China attacked neutralist India and then, two years later, exploded its first atomic weapon. Moreover, relations were not always smooth among new nations. In the Middle East, where most countries had already achieved independence, the clash of local na-tionalism with Arab nationalism helped to perpetuate insecurity. In several places local military action grew more bitter over the years, and in areas like Laos and Vietnam, guerrilla warfare became embroiled in the Cold War.

Finally, developments in Cuba provided a startling and dramatic example of the ties between political independence, "economic in-dependence," and social revolution, all three of which came to be demanded more insistently in one underdeveloped country after an-other. Fidel Castro's desire for all three at once and his particular inter-pretation of the action needed to bring them about put him onto a collision course with the United States and made him turn—successfully —to the Soviet Union for the kind of aid which, earlier, it had not been able to give to Guatemala. The result was an extension of the Cold War to within the Western sphere, and a spectacular confrontation between the Soviet Union and the United States which showed that despite all the loosening of the blocs and the increase in influence of the new states, only the United States and the Soviet Union still had the power to reshape the whole world.

These are the themes of the next three chapters, which will take up in turn the rise of the new states and their role in the international political system, developments in the West and in the Communist bloc, and, finally, the Cuban crisis of 1962.

The New States and Their Search for an International Role

Independence—with all its problems—had already come to much of the Middle East and Asia. In both areas, new states were already quarreling over division of waters, frontiers, and attempts to subvert groups within each other's territory. There, newly independent coun-tries already faced the questions of how to build a unified state, how to promote economic development, and how to react to the Cold War and Soviet offers of foreign aid. Malaya was still to become independent; it achieved that status in 1957 after a gradual process of developing internal self-government and in 1963 joined other territories to form the Federation of Malaysia. There were also numerous enclaves and smaller colonies: British-protected sheikdoms in the Middle East; Portuguese Goa in India; Timor, close to Indonesia, and Macao, in China; sultanates and protectorates such as Sarawak, Brunei, and North Borneo, on the island of Borneo; Pacific islands ranging in size and population from Pitcairn—two square miles and 146 descendants of mutineers from H.M.S. *Bounty*—to the Australian trust territory of New Guinea, with an area of 93 thousand square miles and a population of over one million.

All of these various non-self-governing territories, and self-governing ones that remained colonies, like Singapore, provoked nationalist agitation and provided evidence for those who wanted it that Western colonialism and imperialism had not ended. (When Sarawak, Brunei, Singapore and North Borneo joined Malaya to form a new Federation in 1963, Sukarno of Indonesia argued that the new unit was an even worse form of neo-colonialism, and vowed to mobilize all his efforts to destroy it.) But the major moves to independence in Asia and the Middle East had already taken place. Now came Africa's turn.

In 1956 Tunisia, Morocco, and the Sudan, all former protectorates, joined the ranks of independent Libya, Liberia, Ethiopia, and Egypt. Throughout the African continent that earlier had seemed so settled nationalist pressures grew. Ghana's turn came in 1957. A year later Guinea chose independence over membership in the new French Community created by de Gaulle. In 1960 Somalia, formerly Italian and then a trust territory, reached the ten-year deadline set for its independence by the United Nations in 1950. Within two months the large state of Nigeria, with a population of 35 million, became free. In the same year, the former French territories that had joined the French Community chose independence. These countries spread all across the great western bulge of Africa, down into the central African jungles, and included the Malagasy Republic off the east coast (formerly known as Madagascar). Some chose to retain a status within the French Community, some opted to leave it. Togo and Cameroun achieved independence, and in the Mediterranean the long, bitter struggle over Cyprus finally concluded with the end of British rule and the establishment of a precarious equilibrium between the Greek Cypriot majority and Turkish Cypriot minority—an equilibrium destined to explode into violence. The same year saw the end of Belgian rule in the Congo, the next year the end of British rule over tiny Sierra Leone and Tanganyika; 1962 brought independence to Uganda, to Rwanda and Burundi—formerly held as trust territories by Belgium—and outside of Africa, to Western Samoa, in the Pacific, to Jamaica and Trinidad-Tobago (both of which seceded from the Federation of the British West Indies), to Kuwait in the Middle East, and finally, to Algeria. In 1963 and 1964, Zanzibar, Kenya, and Northern Rhodesia joined the ranks of free African states, with others due to follow.

As each new state achieved new status, it also sought and obtained admission to the United Nations.* The changes in the United Nations, as it grew from its original forty-five members to 114, varied from new pressures on translating facilities, office and living space, and clerical services, to such important matters as shifts in the whole direction and purpose of the organization: the General Assembly sessions were soon dominated by the concerns of the new nations, which the Soviet Union tried in many ways to play upon. Some of the older countries—Britain, France, and Portugal—deplored what they considered to be a tendency to concentrate on internal matters rather than issues of world peace, and to impose what they felt to be a double standard. The United Nations, for example, stood by when India "liberated" the tiny Portuguese territory of Goa in 1961; examined Portuguese conduct in its African territories of Angola and Mozambique; insisted on investigating matters in the Central African Federation; arranged in 1962 for the transfer of "West Irian" from the Netherlands to Indonesian rule under the threat of use of force by Sukarno (if for no other reason). In the case of West Irian, the United Nations was used in a face-saving formula that involved United Nations rule for a six-month period, then Indonesian sovereignty pending a referendum in 1969 on self determination, already described by Sukarno as "internal," not "external" self-determination.

The new African nations thus joined with Asian and other non-Western states to make their views heard on world affairs: the United Nations General Assembly provided them with an excellent forum. Substantively, they tended to keep the attention of the United Na-

---

* In the case of Mauretania, Cold War considerations came to play a rather unusual part: Morocco claimed Mauretania, and the Soviet Union therefore found it easier to resort to its pre-1955 tactic of vetoing a non-Communist state if a Communist state were rejected—in this case, Outer Mongolia. The next year saw the desired trade consummated and admission to the United Nations of both states.

tions on what they considered colonial issues. The Soviet Union, like many other countries, found that their presence in the United Nations required a change in its tactics. In the earlier days of the United Nations it had consistently found itself in a small minority. But its long-time anticolonial stand now brought it new popularity, and it worked hard to see that the United Nations should devote much time to colonial issues. Western powers, however, frequently found themselves embarrassed, and their past use of the United Nations to obtain anti-Russian majorities could no longer be easily repeated.

In fact, the new states had little use for what they considered Cold War issues. Their view of the world was primarily the neutralist one already described, and they tried to avoid entangling themselves in what they saw as American-Russian quarrels. They completely rejected the idea that there was a vast, worldwide Communist conspiracy led by Russia or that Russia was an aggressive power to be feared. When they looked at the situation in Laos and Vietnam, where the United States supported governments against Communist-led rebels, and the situation in Cuba, where Fidel Castro, by leading the country into the Communist group brought bitter American hostility on himself, most nations rejected the view that the United States had to act to keep these countries out of the Communist orbit and to maintain the balance of power. Instead, they saw the United States as intervening in domestic matters against domestic revolutionaries and bolstering unpopular regimes. Their views of relations with the major blocs were shaped in part by their past experience of colonialism, and in part by the American inability to resolve its own racial problem. (America's attempt to pose as a champion of freedom against Communist tyranny appeared hypocritical to black Africans.) But the new nations were particularly influenced by major-power support or lack of support on specific issues such as relations with neighbors, pan-Arab or pan-African movements, increased trade, and economic development. Thus, for a country like Egypt, the desire for arms to buttress its position and back its aims in the Middle East, for long-term sales contracts for its cotton export crop, the need to obtain financing for the High Dam at Aswan (secured from the Soviet Union during 1958)—all dictated the attempt at a policy of maintaining good relations with the Soviet Union which, after all, had backed Egypt at the time of the Suez war. Such relations, however, did not prevent Nasser from suppressing domestic Communists who, he felt, threatened his rule. He would take his chances that increased trade with the Soviet Union might later give the Russians a leverage against him: it would always be possible to turn again to other sources, and for some years after 1959 he found it useful to do so. The same was true of many other new states, with variations. For Middle Eastern countries that relied on petroleum exports for foreign revenue, growing exports of Soviet oil threatened their markets and created ill feeling; yet few of them shared the view of Dulles that a great, sinister Soviet-backed conspiracy threatened them all.

And yet, the Cold War did touch them. To Americans and to many of their allies, the fear of "Balkanization" was very real: large numbers of relatively weak successor states to the old empires might fall into chaos and invite intervention and domination by the Communist bloc, or might align themselves with it. The Russian and Chinese could use subversion, military intervention, and economic penetration. The United States did, indeed, view events in such places as Laos, Vietnam, Cuba, Guinea, the Congo, and Zanzibar in balance-of-power terms as evidence of Communist-inspired Russian and Chinese determination to take advantage of a breakup of empires to extend their sphere of control.

In Laos, for example, a precarious balance of forces had been established after the 1954 Geneva Conference: roughly pro-Western, pro-Communist, and neutralist. In the late 1950s the balance was upset, with the Russians aiding one group, the United States another, while other states tried to find a solution through a coalition of the three. In Vietnam the previously obscure Catholic, Ngo Dinh Diem, secured his position as president over a period of several years and obtained greater American support. But after 1958 Communist guerrilla opposition increased, and in the early 1960s—without ever having made any major decisions—the United States found itself more and more committed to direct military intervention in favor of an authoritarian and seemingly unpopular regime to which there appeared to be no alternative. In the Congo, unforeseen and unprepared independence in 1960 led to riots and Belgian intervention to protect its nationals. The United Nations provided a welcome way to restore order, obtain Belgian withdrawal, and keep the great powers out. But the warring factions that developed within the Congo called for outside intervention in their favor. The Soviet Union was ready to respond in the early period of the affair; it withdrew only when faced with opposition from African and other neutral states it was trying to woo. In 1958, when de Gaulle gave French African states the alternatives of joining his new community or independence, only Guinea, under the leadership of Sekou Touré chose the latter. The French responded swiftly and harshly. They withdrew all their colonial administrators, ended financial aid, and took with them all administrative records. Touré responded by forming a loose union with Ghana and accepting a large loan from it, and also by receiving large-scale aid proffered by Russia. Alarmists in the West began to call Guinea the first Soviet satellite in Africa, and argued that Britain and the United States had missed their chance to forestall the Russians by failing to offer the needed aid. But Touré remained guarded, and when he found the Russian mission being used as a center for subversion, compelled Russia to recall its ambassador.

In the years following 1958 the Russians greatly expanded their efforts throughout Africa. They established a new Department of African Affairs in the Foreign Ministry and proceeded to raise the number of their missions in Africa from three to over eighty, and to send cultural delegations and trade missions. This led to a great increase in trade; by 1960 half of Guinea's imports came from the Soviet bloc. The Soviet Union began to broadcast in African languages, transmissions multiplied rapidly, and magazines were widely disseminated. Thousands of young Africans received technical training and indoctrination in the Soviet sphere. In Moscow the People's Friendship University, established in 1960 with a planned capacity of four thousand students from underdeveloped countries, had its name changed to Patrice Lumumba University, after the slain Congolese national leader whose death was attributed to lack of Western intervention on his behalf.

Most observers felt that Communism would have a hard time making inroads in Africa. Africans might turn to the Soviet bloc for aid, trade, and political inspiration, but would probably not allow ties to the bloc to determine their political future. However, events in one small island, Zanzibar, whose independence was achieved from Britain in December 1963, raised new alarms.

In January 1964, a coup deposed the government of the new state. Confusion at first surrounded the events, but two aspects of the affair emerged clearly: the coup represented African action against the previously dominant Arab minority, which had been long favored by the British, and the new government seemed ready to align itself quickly with the Soviet bloc. It acted to expel Western influence and to break Western ties; many of its leaders had been trained in Moscow, Castro's Cuba, and China; and on January 18, 1964, it proclaimed itself to be the People's Republic of Zanzibar, a one-party state. It received Soviet equipment for its army, Chinese credits and technical aid, replaced British civil servants with Communist bloc personnel, and established diplomatic relations with bloc members, including East Germany and Communist China.

Western newspaper reports began to refer to the first "Soviet outpost in Africa" and commented that Zanzibar might serve as a center for subversion of the rest of the continent. But leadership in Zanzibar was by no means as unified as these views indicated. On April 23 a new and surprising agreement between Tanganyika and Zanzibar created a close union of the two countries, and was ratified within a week. President Karume of Zanzibar, who became the first Vice President, and President Nyerere of Tanganyika sought in the union a way of dealing with extremist pressures in both of their countries. Their chances were good.

The Congo

No other act in the drama of independence so strikingly took the center of the world stage, or involved so many actors, as did the crisis in the Congo. It hardened divisions among African states, engaged the interest of non-African powers, and had incalculable effects on the United Nations. It also showed that, despite a fervently-voiced desire to keep non-African powers out of African affairs, African groups nevertheless frequently did ask them for aid and thus provoked the interest of other states, in a repetition of the old balance-of-power pattern.

The situation in the Congo in 1958 reflected how much Belgian colonial policy had differed from that of its neighbors. Belgium had followed a policy of paternalism, which, in principle, meant the creation of a sound economic base before any political activities would be allowed or civil rights granted. New jobs, education by stages, and the gradual spread of notions of law and government would mean that at some period in the future—perhaps in thirty years—a base would be created for self-government. In this way the painful transition in territories unprepared for self-government would be avoided. In the meantime, however, few Congolese received higher education or held jobs higher than clerical posts in government and business.

But events outside of the Congo interfered with the Belgian program, notably the independence of Ghana, developments in the French Community, and the 1958 conferences that gave Congolese leaders the chance to know one another and to see what was going on in the rest of the continent. They helped stimulate Congolese nationalism and hastened demands for self-government. The economic distress which followed a fall in the world price of Congolese exports made the situation even more difficult, and before long the Belgians, who were still talking of self-government in thirty years, completely lost control. The

Congolese simply refused to obey orders, and native policemen and clerks refused to enforce them. Riots and subsequent Belgian reforms aimed at eliminating the color line occurred in 1959. They were not enough, and in January, 1960, the Belgians held a round-table conference of Congolese leaders in Brussels which, in the space of a week, decided that the Congo would become independent within six months. Nobody, a few months earlier, could have anticipated the pace of change.

Preparations for independence went forward feverishly; under the circumstances they could hardly have been expected to go smoothly. There was suspicion on all sides, particularly on the part of African leaders who thought that the Belgians were trying to retain the substance of control which they exercised through a virtual monopoly of business.

Three Congolese leaders came to personify the forces that would lead to chaos in the months after the independence celebrations of June 30 to July 3. Patrice Lumumba, the first prime minister, emerged as the one political leader of national stature, devoted to the idea of a unitary state with a strong central government. Joseph Kasavubu, head of the Bakongo tribe in the lower Congo region around Leopoldville, became the first President and commander-in-chief of the unruly Force Publique—an ill-trained and undisciplined native force created by the Belgians. Kasavubu had first worked for an independent Bakongo, but when prospects for Congolese independence improved, he accepted the idea of a relatively autonomous region within a federal Congo. Finally, there was Moise Tshombe of Katanga province in the southern tip of the Congo. Katanga's importance to the Congo lay in its fabulous mineral wealth. Contributing sixty per cent of Congolese revenue, it produced—among other things—seventy-three per cent of the world's cobalt and eighty per cent of the world's industrial diamonds. Most of the industry in Katanga at the time of independence was controlled by the Union Minière and Forminière, a giant enterprise whose shares were owned by Belgians, British, and also—after independence—by the Congolese government. Tshombe had never opposed the idea of a unitary state until quite late. Then, with Belgian support, he moved to break up the unity of the Congo.

Independence was preceded by a flight of capital. Soon after this inauspicious start, the Force Publique revolted, asking for higher pay and dismissal of Belgian officers and defense officials. Members of the Force attacked their own officers and white civilians. Belgian officials reacted by flying in paratroopers to take over key points and protect Belgian nationals. At the same time Tshombe announced that he was withdrawing Katanga from the Congo and making it independent. Tribe began to fight tribe, and the whole rickety structure set up for independence came crashing down.

Lumumba appealed to the United States for military aid but Eisenhower and Nkrumah—the latter acting for the independent African states—told him to appeal to the United Nations. From their point of view, it was bad enough to have had the Belgian intervention, against which the Congolese had already lodged an appeal. If the Americans now intervened, they would not only be acting against an ally (as they had done in the Suez crisis) but they would also get embroiled in a situation where African reaction to another white intervention—even though Africans had requested it—was impossible to predict. For the Africans the main issue was to keep the great powers out of the continent. They pointed to the precedent of the United Nations Emergency Force in the Suez crisis. Perhaps the same kind of solution could be reached in the Congo.

Secretary-General Dag Hammarskjold took the initiative in calling a Security Council meeting, and against the reluctance of France, Britain, and the Soviet Union, the Council passed a resolution calling on the Belgians to withdraw their troops and authorizing Hammarskjold to provide the Congo with military assistance until such time as its own troops could secure public order. The Russians tried to include in the resolution condemnation of Belgian aggression and colonialism; they were voted down, and the Belgian representative, though answering charges of aggression by arguing that Belgium had only been protecting its own nationals, agreed that Belgian troops would be withdrawn as soon as United Nations forces could take over. Unfortunately, at the same time Belgium came to the support of Tshombe.

The United Nations had a tremendously difficult job not only logistically and administratively, but also politically. The United Nations troops were primarily African, with some Swedish and Irish contingents. Interpreting the nature of their assignment proved to be the great difficulty: Hammarskjold viewed it as preserving order without interfering in whatever political quarrels existed among Congolese. Order would permit Belgian withdrawal, prevent great power interference or interference by other African states, and create conditions in which, with United Nations technical aid, the Congolese could settle their own affairs. Moreover, the United Nations troops were instructed to use force only in self-defense.

The trouble was that in practice the maintenance of order involved siding with one group or another within the Congo. If the United Nations forces moved into Katanga so that the central government could then follow, one basic question would be settled in favor of the central government. Since in other parts of the Congo other tribal leaders were beginning to follow Tshombe's separatist lead, resolution of the question of central authority appeared absolutely necessary to Lumumba. But Tshombe was now fighting hard for recognition by other states of Katanga's right to self-determination and the authority of his government; he would not let in the United Nations troops. Were they to use force? At whose authorization? Moreover, Lumumba insisted that the United Nations help the central government reimpose unity by transporting Congolese troops and providing them with supplies. But would this not be an expansion of the United Nations force's mandate? Lumumba also registered his impatience with what he felt was the delay in Belgian withdrawal. He announced that unless it took place immediately he might call on the Soviet Union for support in obtaining it.

Again the African states piloted a resolution successfully through the Security Council to intensify pressures on the Belgians to withdraw and to keep other states from intervening. But the Katanga situation grew worse as Hammarskjold moved cautiously, trying to avoid, as he put it, "actions in which Africans kill Africans or Congolese kill Congolese." He flew into Katanga himself, at the head of a body of United Nations troops, to establish the right of United Nations presence in the area. But Tshombe was adamant in refusing to allow government troops to follow, and the debacle quickly followed.

The Soviet Union accused Hammarskjold of dilatory tactics and aiding the colonialists, and found a willing listener in Lumumba who now asked for direct Soviet aid. He quickly began to receive trucks, technicians and transport planes, although other African states had until this time opposed the new move. Then President Kasavubu dismissed Lumumba as Prime Minister and the latter retaliated by dismissing Kasavubu. Chaos was complete.

During one short interval in late 1960, Colonel Mobutu, an army leader, took over the reins of government, ruling without recourse to the Parliament. During this time he forced withdrawal of Soviet representatives and the United Nations worked with him as the one man who held any power. But the United Nations effort to remain neutral between Kasavubu and Lumumba was unsuccessful. Kasavubu imprisoned Lumumba, then turned him over to Katanga, where he was brutally murdered in February 1961. Communists fanned the outraged feelings in new nations throughout the world, and demonstrations against the United Nations and Western powers indicated the depth of feeling that the nationalist leader had not been given sufficient protection. African nationalism had a new martyr. In the meantime Mobutu had forced withdrawal of the Ghanaian and Guinean missions in Leopoldville, accusing them of intervention in Congolese affairs, and a Lumumbist Vice Premier Antoine Gizenga (who earlier had set himself up as interim head of a "legal central government" in the town of Stanleyville) now proclaimed himself the government's head.

These developments split the African countries that had previously backed the United Nations mission. The Brazzaville powers tended to support the general course taken by Hammarskjold. Ghana and Guinea, however, met at Casablanca in January 1961 with Mali, Morocco, Egypt, and delegations from Libya and Algeria, where they voiced strong support for Lumumba, criticism of the United Nations' effort, and also took a completely different position on the issue of Algeria than had the Brazzaville powers. Thus the Congo situation gave impetus to a further cleavage among African states. The Brazzaville powers seemed to be more cautious and conservative in the foreign policy approach; the Casablanca powers more radical.

At this point, too, the Russians used the opportunity provided by African opposition to Hammarskjold's course to attack the Secretary-General personally and the office itself. Khrushchev, arguing that no one could ever be "neutral," declared that the Secretary-General should be replaced by a three-man headship—the so-called "troika" plan, named after a Russian wagon pulled by three horses. One man would represent the West, another the Soviet bloc, and a third the neutral countries (at this point drastically under-represented in the United Nations). In this way, he appealed to the view widely held by representatives of the new states that, in fact, the United Nations had been essentially a Western creation constructed when European empires still existed, and that the United Nations had not been adapted enough to the changed world situation. But the Soviets miscalculated; they found no real support for the plan, even though they threatened to withdraw cooperation from the United Nations if it were not accepted. Various states tried to come up with some compromise plan, keeping in mind that Russian intransigence could destroy the United Nations. Enough countries stood firm, however, and the Soviets dropped the project. Yet the Soviet campaign appeared to have one effect: for the first time—after the death of Hammarskjold—the United

Nations received a non-Western Secretary-General, U Thant of Burma.

In the Congo, vacillation and frustration marked the next two years: each time an improvement appeared to have taken place, disappointment succeeded it. Throughout 1961 and 1962 Katanga remained unintegrated. Tshombe found support in the Portuguese province of Angola, through which he could ship his goods, and in the Central African Federation, which would allow no economic sanctions against Tshombe that involved its borders. These two white-dominated and racist areas, with South Africa, feared that with integration of Katanga the tide of black nationalism would sweep southward. Although Tshombe faced, and ruthlessly suppressed, bitter opposition of tribesmen in the north of Katanga, he maintained order in the mining regions, and with the resulting income (a large part of which ought to have been paid to the central government) he built an army of well-rewarded mercenaries. Britain and France were still reluctant to support strong United Nations measures in the Congo, and the Soviet Union, thwarted in its attempt to capitalize on the chaos, now declared that all United Nations measures taken under authority of the General Assembly were illegal, and therefore refused to pay any assessments for Congo action. France joined in this, and the United Nations found itself not only restrained in the Congo but also faced with a financial crisis at home. If opponents of the Congo action could not stop it directly, they might be able to cripple it indirectly. In 1961, Hammarskjold, patiently avoiding complete commitment to either Congolese faction—the Kasavubu-Mobutu one, supported by the United States, or the Gizenga one supported by the Casablanca powers and the Soviet Union—worked for their reconciliation. In July he obtained a meeting of the Parliament. In August it named a new premier, Cyrille Adoula. Adoula took a reluctant Gizenga into his cabinet as Vice Premier and, after further delay, the Stanleyville regime collapsed. Now India came to the rescue of the Congo operation by providing 5000 troops, and the problem of Katanga and eviction of its mercenary army came to the fore as fighting broke out between United Nations troops and Tshombe's army. Hammarskjold was killed in an airplane crash on his way to persuade Tshombe to relent. The slippery Katanga President willingly signed agreements that would bring Katanga back into the fold, but in practice proved as evasive as ever. He had attacked United Nations troops in late 1961 and found willing backers and propagandists in Britain and the United States who depicted the military incidents as military aggression by a United Nations force that was supposed to be keeping the peace. In these accounts which tried to discredit the whole United Nations operation, Tshombe emerged as the only staunch friend of the West in the Congo, ruler of the only area in which order was maintained, the victim of a Communist plot, and a man legitimately trying to achieve for his country the kind of self-determination that the Congo had achieved from Belgium.

All through 1962, he maintained his position, in spite of a Security Council resolution authorizing stronger action against Katanga. The end, however, came swiftly in January 1963 when a United Nations troop movement brought the collapse of Tshombe's army. To the last he resisted by threatening to destroy the Union Minière installations. But an amnesty and promise by Adoula's government that he would remain provincial president of Katanaga led to surrender of his last stronghold.

The outside world breathed more freely. It seemed that United Nations intervention had preserved the Congo and kept the Cold War out of Africa. Belgium and the United States rallied to help the central government restore its administration and retrain its unruly and unreliable army. Yet, in fact, the Congo's difficulties were far from over, and trouble that had been brewing broke into open warfare in mid-1964 after withdrawal of the last of United Nations forces. Following dissolution of the Congolese Parliament by President Kasavubu, Lumumbists who faced arrest and persecution and who had taken refuge in Brazzaville, capital of what had been the French Congo, began to receive widespread support throughout the Congo. The Kasavubu-Adoula regime was not popular in the country, and the Armée Nationale Congolaise led by General Mobutu commanded little respect. Adoula faced a crisis he could not control as rebel forces seized one provincial center after another, and in perhaps the biggest surprise of the entire Congo affair, Kasavubu replaced Adoula with Moise Tshombe, who now reappeared as the savior of Congolese unity, and patched together a government of national reconciliation which would run the country until elections for a new Constitutional Assembly could be arranged.

But the attempt to bring Congolese factions together failed. Rebel advances continued, and the fact that the government was supplied with American arms and equipment became a point of great emphasis for the rebels, whose portrait of Tshombe as Lumumba's murderer and a puppet of colonial powers, found a receptive audience in other Africans. Tshombe received no response to an appeal he made for

armed forces from other African states to help reestablish order in
the Congo, and he proceeded to recruit some of the old mercenaries
who had previously served him in Katanga. These, in turn, began to
score successes against the rebel armies, and Tshombe himself tried
to paint the rebels as recipients of aid not only from the Congo
(Brazzaville) and from Burundi, but also, through these, from Communist China. He had, perhaps, the gratification that no country recognized the rebels in Stanleyville, who had proclaimed their committee
as the People's Republic of the Congo. Furthermore, it was Tshombe
who represented the Congo at a meeting of the new Organization of
African Unity in Addis Ababa in September. Here, however, under
the influence of the many countries that distrusted him and supported
the rebels, the Organization asked for the end of recruitment of foreign
mercenaries and, refusing to condemn the rebels, created a commission
of conciliation to try to bring all parties together. Tshombe pronounced
himself satisfied, since the Organization had recognized his government
as the only legal one, and the rebels themselves rejected the resolution,
saying that they would never negotiate while Kasavubu and Tshombe
were in power. Within a month, Tshombe was discomfited when he
was excluded from a meeting of the nonaligned states held in Cairo: an
embarrassed Egyptian government found technical reasons for refusing
to allow his plane to land and then, when he came by commercial
craft, held him incommunicado in a villa. Many African leaders were
distressed, fearing the establishment of a general principle of intervention against existing governments. But they were even more alarmed by
events at the year's end.

As the government's mercenary-led troops advanced on the rebel
capital of Stanleyville, the rebels announced that they had seized two
thousand whites in the area and were holding them as hostages. The
International Red Cross tried unsuccessfully to obtain their release, and
the Organization of African Unity immediately began negotiations with
the rebels for the same purpose. Then, suddenly, American planes
flew in several thousand Belgian paratroopers who secured the majority
of the hostages, although a substantial number were killed or wounded.
While the United States and Belgium announced that they had conducted a purely humanitarian operation to prevent a savage massacre,
Africans and Asians reacted strongly: the operation came just at the
time the OAU was negotiating for the release of the whites, and was
therefore a gratuitous insult. But worse, it helped the puppet Tshombe:
it was therefore an imperialist operation designed to help cement
Belgian-American control of the Congo. In reporting the operation,

the Western press had stressed the savagery of the black rebels; Africans condemned the operation because the press made no mention of massacres of blacks by Tshombe's white mercenaries and his Congolese army, and argued that it had brought further massacres: many more blacks were being killed than whites, yet Western powers had acted only to save whites. As for the stress on savagery of the rebels, what white could speak of savagery after World War II, Korea, or Vietnam? African nations arraigned the Belgians and Americans before the Security Council, and the Casablanca powers began to organize help for the rebels, who were not yet defeated after the fall of Stanleyville.

Since the end of the United Nations operation in the Congo, Russia and China had done little about the resumption of strife. But certainly by the end of 1964, with the United States intervening directly to help Tshombe, the Communist powers would find much support if they discreetly helped the rebels. The United Nations operation—a calculated risk—had almost bankrupted the organization, and made it far more difficult to maintain or assume any new peace-keeping functions like the one in Cyprus. And it could hardly be said that the United Nations operation had brought stability to the Congo. Originally designed to ensure Belgian withdrawal, it had then had to face an entirely new situation when Katanga and other provinces tried to break away. A balance sheet would be hard to draw up, but by the end of 1964 the Congo crisis had caused relations between African countries and the United States to be more strained than ever before. It was also significant that when Tshombe stopped to see President de Gaulle, de Gaulle gave him little support. The French leader had little desire to jeopardize the important role he envisaged for France in relations with what the French called the "tiers monde."

White Africa

Two other areas in Africa—Portuguese Angola and Mozambique, and South Africa—raised international problems by trying to resist the tide of African nationalism. But Portugal and South Africa insisted that the only international problem was caused by other African countries, who were interfering in their domestic affairs and lining up support in the United Nations. Portugal (which maintained a system of forced labor within its African territories) transformed its colonies, by a constitutional device, into provinces of Portugal. For years it also followed a practice of raising some detribalized natives to a status equivalent to that of the whites. Although the number was pitifully small, the Portuguese could claim that they were following a cautious but gradual policy of modernization so that the overseas provinces would eventually catch up with the ones at home. Nevertheless, other African states claimed that these were non-self-governing regions and that under the Charter, Portugal was required to report to the United Nations about them. And when in March 1961 full-scale guerrilla warfare started in Angola (requiring a heavy Portuguese repressive effort), African states succeeded in bringing in a Committee Report to the General Assembly that the situation in Angola was a threat to the peace, if only because people in other countries would not let their governments stand by and do nothing. As a result, the Assembly condemned Portuguese practices in Angola and called on Portugal to cease repressive measures. But, although Portugal made reforms, it maintained a view diametrically opposed to the one expressed within the Assembly: the Assembly demanded that Portugal allow self-determination on the basis of freely conducted elections. The Portuguese dictator, Salazar, declared that "unity does not allow transfers, cession or abandonment. . . . Plebiscite, the referendum, auto-determination do not fit into this structure either." Angolan nationalist political parties emerged—but as bitter rivals—and a number of states put diplomatic pressure on Portugal, refusing to sell it arms or closing ports to Portuguese shipping. Throughout 1962 and 1963 the military effort continued to be costly, and the ultimate outcome uncertain.

In another country, South Africa, the outcome of the race relation question was even harder to foresee. Three million whites dominated thirteen million blacks. Again a government claimed external meddling in an internal affair, the policy of apartheid—settling blacks in selected areas apart from the rest of the country, and eliminating them from the normal political processes of the country. Again, African and other countries argued that the matter was of international concern: beginning in 1950 the General Assembly called on South Africa to modify its racial policies and bring them into coordination with its obligations under the Charter. But increased membership of African states after 1955, the increased harshness of apartheid, and the shooting of blacks in Sharpeville in March 1960 during black demonstrations against apartheid, all led to stronger UN measures. The Security Council for the first time considered South African racial practices, repeated the Assembly's call, and asked the Secretary-General to intervene. He visited South Africa and consulted with government leaders but could report no agreement. The various pan-African and neutralist meetings passed resolutions calling for sanctions against South Africa, and when in 1960 South Africa voted to become a republic (the vote split sharply between Afrikaners, the descendants of Dutch settlers, and English-speaking peoples), and asked to remain in the British Commonwealth as a republic, the Commonwealth states demanded concessions on the racial issue. In response, South Africa withdrew from the Commonwealth.

From 1960 to 1963 the Special Political Committee of the United Nations General Assembly, under pressure from new states, went much further and called for the breaking of both diplomatic and economic ties to force South Africa to change its policy. In the General Assembly, such resolutions failed, primarily because various states were afraid to set a precedent on the matter of domestic jurisdiction. It was debatable if the matter was a threat to the peace, and if sanctions would force South Africa to change or might not, rather, hurt South African blacks. But as the years passed, the Assembly left the way open for sanctions by declaring that the situation *did* in fact threaten the peace. In the International Labor Organization, South Africa was barred from all meetings, and African states (though with little effect) carried out their own recommendations on sanctions and made evident their bitterness at the refusal of South Africa's major trading partners to act similarly.

On one other matter, the status of Southwest Africa, international legal complications existed: a German territory before World War I, it became a mandate under the League, administered by South Africa. But South Africa refused to transform it into a trust territory after World War II; in so doing it escaped supervision by the Trusteeship Council of the United Nations, though every year after 1946 the General Assembly has asked South Africa to enter into a trusteeship agreement for the territory. But what had become of its mandatory responsibilities? Mandate powers had been required to report to the League, now defunct, and to undertake certain obligations to the native inhabitants.

The United Nations had recourse to advisory opinions of the International Court of Justice. The latter declared that South Africa had no legal obligation to submit a Trusteeship Agreement, but that it must submit to General Assembly supervision, an equivalent to the supervision exercised by the old Mandates Commission. South Africa, however, argued that these were merely advisory opinions and not legally binding, and therefore refused to carry them out, meanwhile extending apartheid to the region. By 1962 the situation was more tense: nationalist movements had arisen and other African states had asked for stronger United Nations action by revocation of the mandate, evacuation of South African troops, supervision of the move by a United Nations force, and sanctions against South Africa if it refused to accept these actions. In 1962, South Africa for the first time allowed two United Nations representatives to tour the area. They issued a statement to the effect that there was no evidence that affairs within the area threatened international peace and security.

Algeria

In Algeria, at the beginning of the period the situation was similar to the one in South Africa: a small proportion of whites dominated the natives. Like the South African whites, many Algerian whites had lived there for several generations, developed the land, created industries, and considered it their home. Unlike South African whites, however, they had no independent economic base, for they were highly dependent on economic ties to France. Moreover, the insurrectionists who began the 1954 uprising could develop bases of operation in friendly neighboring countries, Tunisia and Morocco. Algeria's geographic situation made it possible to receive outside help.

Vacillating French governments were caught between irreconcilable demands and proved unable to control the situation. Signs of "softness" brought the military insurrection that installed General de Gaulle as Prime Minister. He liquidated the Fourth Republic and installed a new Fifth Republic with a far stronger executive. Brought to power by those who aspired to assimilate Algeria to France, he moved instead toward negotiation for self-determination and independence. But not without fits and starts: his early plans for a vast development program for the area seemed to indicate that he would, indeed, try to make Frenchmen of Algerians. However, he cast off his early supporters, and a series of conferences under his auspices brought a cease-fire, negotiated March 18, 1963, with a promise of self-determination and genuine independence if wanted.

In pursuing this course, de Gaulle withstood attacks on his life and attempts at a military coup by his former supporters. His opponents, in a last ghastly spasm, created the *Organization de l'Armée Secrète*, a terrorist group that attacked de Gaulle supporters everywhere and, in Algeria, killed Muslims indiscriminately while carrying out a scorched earth policy. Algerian restraint and French government firmness prevailed. De Gaulle held a referendum in France on his policy, and the ninety per cent support he received shocked French Algerians still resisting it. On July 1 a referendum in Algeria led to an overwhelming majority for independence, and on October 8, 1962, the new state became the 109th United Nations member.

Independence made little economic sense; a close association with France would help if de Gaulle's generosity were continued. And independence did not mean peace and democracy to Algeria; rather it led to factional struggle by former members of the Algerian Nationalist movement. Ahmed Ben Bella emerged victorious and, like the leaders of most new states, adopted a single-party system and a neutralist foreign policy. But Ben Bella aimed at more: he became a leader among the Casablanca powers in promoting revolution in Africa against Western influence and continued white domination.

Southeast Asia: Neutralism and Guerrilla Conflict

The turbulent emergence of Africa on the world scene did not completely obscure events in other parts of the world. In the early 1960s developments in Asia, the Caribbean, and Europe vied with those in Africa for the attention of harassed foreign office officials.

In Southeast Asia, Thailand, the only Southeast Asian member of the South East Asia Treaty Organization, showed some doubts about its continued alignment with Western powers. For years the wily Field Marshal Pibul Songgram had guided Thai foreign policy in a way that brought largesse from the United States, most of which found its way into deserving pockets. A collaborator with the Japanese who survived a brief detention after the war, he made his way back to power three years later, sending his rival into exile for complicity in the death of the King (which a jury declared was "either accident, suicide, or murder"). But finally, in September 1957, he was ousted by one of his two rivals, Field Marshal Sarit Thanarat, who sent him into exile, and proceeded to hedge somewhat on the question of alignment. Sarit, sensing a growing American tolerance for neutralism and also noting growing Chinese power, made it clear that Thailand's position as a member of the Western bloc could no longer be taken for granted.

In the meantime two other countries long associated with neutralism became more critical of the West. Burma, whose early experiences with Soviet foreign aid had not been too happy, faced internal difficulties that made operation of its democratic system almost impossible. In the circumstances Prime Minister U Nu turned the government over to his Commander-in-Chief, General Ne Win in September 1958. During a period of military rule the various political parties were to purge themselves of corruption and attempt reorganization, while General Ne Win carried forward the fight against Communist guerrillas in the north. The General reviewed relations with the United States, and accepted offers of aid previously rejected as incompatible with Burma's sovereignty. But he had also observed the border difficulties that embittered Indian relations with Communist China, and he managed successfully to conclude a border agreement with the Chinese, thus resolving a potential dispute of long standing.

Return to civilian rule in 1960 under U Nu proved to be brief: in March 1961 General Ne Win seized power, claiming that the political parties had again demonstrated their incapacity to rule and that they had opened the door to Communist subversion. This time the military junta took more severe steps, even blowing up the student center at Rangoon University, which it claimed was a center of Communist subversive activity. But at the same time the junta also ended the aid and research activities of all foreign private groups like the Ford and Rockefeller Foundations. A general curtailment of Western influence followed.

The connection may be slight, but General Ne Win had been Chief of Staff during the entire period since 1950 when the presence of a Nationalist Chinese Army remnant of 12,000 men in the north added to Burma's woes. Named the Yunnan Anti-Communist and National Salvation Army, it was supplied—with the assistance of the American Central Intelligence Agency—by Chiang Kai-shek on Formosa. Besides being a threat to internal order, the army (supposed to remain a pin-prick threat to Communist China's southern flank) was a constant challenge to Burma's security: if it caused trouble, it might bring down Chinese Communist power on Burma. Despite pleas to the United States to bring pressure on the Nationalist government to stop supporting it and to force withdrawal, the task was not accomplished until 1962. Many Burmese leaders held the United States responsible.

Indonesian President Sukarno performed the political miracle of keeping himself in power, consolidating his position, and emerging as a strong man of Southeast Asia, despite the fact that the economic situation in Indonesia had deteriorated steadily since the early 1950s. The feat involved using the army to suppress insurrections on the outer islands which were directed at the growing authoritarian centralization that President Sukarno called "guided democracy." * The loyalty of the army was procured by making it the largest and best-equipped

---

* Although the United States denied all charges, there was some evidence that the United States Central Intelligence Agency provided support for the rebellions.

force in Southeast Asia: enormous supplies of military equipment came from the Soviet Union, which also was able to support whole-heartedly Indonesia's aim of liberating "West Irian" or Western New Guinea. On the other hand, Sukarno, having banned the political activities of most parties other than the Communists—but having also kept Communist leaders from active participation in the government—came to rely more and more on them. The Indonesian Communist party, despite its disastrous effort at insurrection against the Republic in 1948, became the largest and best-trained party outside the Soviet Union. The fact that Sukarno was willing to work with it rather than oppose it, as Nehru did in India, meant that it profited from Soviet and Communist Chinese support in a way the Indian party could not.

After the liberation of West Irian, there was some question about what Sukarno's course would be. Would he now turn his attention to the pressing domestic problems which had been subordinated to the great national task? Emergence of the Malaysia issue in 1963 (see below) showed that he might continue to use foreign issues to help him maintain the balance between the army and the Communist party.

In 1954 Prince Norodom Sihanouk of Cambodia won independence for his country from France. At the Geneva Conference of the same year he managed to avoid having Communist forces in Cambodia regrouped within the country. But with withdrawal of French influence from the area, Sihanouk, who abdicated as king to become head of state and a virtual one-man government of the kingdom, faced increasing pressures from traditional enemies on either side—Thailand and South Vietnam. Thailand had been forced after World War II to relinquish territories seized from Cambodia during the war. South Vietnam, particularly in the years after 1958, claimed that Cambodia afforded a refuge for Vietcong (Communist) guerrillas, and engaged in border crossings and bombings. Since both countries were aided militarily by the United States, Sihanouk blamed American support for continued Thai and South Vietnamese hostility to him. As time passed, and despite large-scale American military aid for his army and economic aid for his country, Sihanouk decided that the American effort to support the regime of Ngo Dinh Diem in South Vietnam was doomed, and that the Communist Vietcong guerrillas would probably win. He decided to find refuge in neutralism and supported the idea of some form of neutralization for the whole region. This, he believed, provided more safety than the American policy of military alliances and support.

After 1957 Sihanouk also turned to the Soviet Union and Communist China for economic aid, and to socialist policies within the country. When the United States, in 1958, refused to mediate a border dispute between Cambodia and Vietnam, he proceeded to recognize Communist China. In 1960 and 1961 he severed ties with Vietnam and Thailand, and became increasingly critical of their American protector. He claimed that internal political opposition to his regime was financed by the American Central Intelligence Agency, and that it was behind plots to overthrow him. In fact, American arms supplied to Vietnam found their way into the hands of Cambodian rebels, and the Prince sought in vain to have the United States make Vietnam find and destroy rebel radio transmitters situated outside his borders. In late 1963, declaring that Communist China was his best source of protection, he asked for termination of all United States aid programs in Cambodia. When he found that neither France, whose President had made rather grand statements about reestablishing France's role in Asia, nor Russia nor Communist China could replace the much needed American aid, he began negotiations to extend the deadline for withdrawal of American personnel. But negotiations bogged down and the projects were terminated. In the meantime, though Sihanouk declared three days of national mourning following the assassination of President Kennedy and temporarily stopped anti-American propaganda and demonstrations, the Cambodian radio, rejoicing in the deaths of Vietnamese President Ngo Dinh Diem and Thai Premier Sarit, also expressed joy over the passing of "the great boss of these aggressors," and Sihanouk declared that "the three enemies of Cambodia are now in Hell to pursue their SEATO meetings." The United States demanded an apology, which was not forthcoming, and though diplomatic relations were never formally broken, the ambassadors and most of their staffs withdrew. Only Sihanouk knew what his next moves would be, and how influential his new Communist Chinese technicians and advisers might be—or his Peking-educated son, whom he named his successor in case of his death.

Finally, in South Vietnam and Laos, growing warfare between Communist and government troops led to an increased American involvement whose outcome was difficult to foresee.

In South Vietnam, guerrilla warfare by the Communist Vietcong began to increase in intensity in 1958. At first foreign observers failed to see the seriousness of the situation, and the government of Ngo Dinh Diem—increasingly autocratic and isolated from the people of South Vietnam—concealed Vietcong successes. But American training missions to the Vietnamese army quickly became aware of the developing threat, and sought increased aid from Washington. It was forthcoming, for the Kennedy administration saw no alternative to aiding Diem, and American personnel in Vietnam rose from 700 in 1961 to 16,500 by the end of 1963. By this time Vietcong forces were estimated at 20,000 to 30,000 regulars and from 100,000 to 300,000 irregulars. They were South Vietnamese, armed primarily with American or French weapons, but the government made much of the fact that some of the Communist cadres had been trained in the north and that they received supplies along what came to be called the Ho Chi Minh trail—a jungle supply route running through Laos and Cambodia. In 1960 the Vietcong announced formation of the National Liberation Front, declaring that unity with Communist North Vietnam was not presently at issue, but might eventually become important—in fifteen to twenty years.

To combat the guerrillas, President Diem increased the size of his army, sought increased American arms aid and regrouped peasants into strategic hamlets, which presumably could be more easily defended. The strategic hamlet program failed, however, and aroused new hostility against the government. Government troops were extortionist; the Diem regime resorted to increasingly rigid security measures; puritanical laws of behavior (inspired by the President's beautiful and ruthless sister, Mme. Ngo Dinh Nhu) were imposed, and the power of her husband and his secret police grew. All of these together weakened the government. Diem, against the opposition of the Catholic Church, tried to impose his Catholicism upon the country and to hinder the functioning of other religions. In 1963 outright warfare developed between the government and Buddhist monks; several monks publicly burned themselves to death to demonstrate opposition to Diem's policy. Mme. Nhu declared that Buddhist demonstrations were Communist-inspired, that American pressures on Diem to reach a compromise with the Buddhists were also Communist-inspired, and exclaimed, "I would clap my hands at seeing another monk barbecue show. . . ."—a remark that hardly eased the situation. Diem in the meantime had alienated army leaders after a coup against him in 1960 failed. To guard against another coup, he constantly transferred them from one post to another (regardless of considerations of efficiency), instituted a system of political commissars for the army, and created a widespread spy network within the armed forces.

Concurrent with the worsening crisis, the Vietcong stepped up its offensives, and for the first time leaders in other countries realized that, in fact, the Diem regime no longer controlled most of the countryside. On November 1 Diem's end came. He and his brother were assassinated, and an army junta took over. But one coup succeeded another, while the Vietcong took advantage of the political instability and of increasing Vietnamese war-weariness. Outside of Vietnam, a debate raged as to what could or should be done.

The Kennedy administration had chosen the alternative of large-scale but specifically limited support for the Vietnamese regime. Americans were not in combat in large numbers, and the fight was carried on against the Vietcong rather than their supporters in the North. Americans were at first surprised to find how deeply involved their government had become in the fight. Then, in 1963, some Americans began to raise specific questions about the whole operation.

There were those who argued that the war should be prosecuted more vigorously and carried to North Vietnam if possible. Others argued for disengagement, declaring that America would simply get deeper and deeper into the morass, with little prospect of victory. George Kennan, author of the policy of containment, asked whether anyone had really considered how strategically valuable Vietnam was to the United States. Hans Morgenthau, prophet of power politics, suggested that American policy was still based on the outmoded view that the Communist countries constituted a single bloc, that it failed to take into account the divergent trends within the bloc. American involvement against the Vietcong coupled with threats of attack against the North forced North Vietnam to rely upon China, which might come to its aid. Yet North Vietnam, though Communist, probably feared Chinese power and, argued Morgenthau, might act as independently as Eastern European countries were doing if American policy would let it.

Morgenthau's argument led him to support the idea of neutralization for the whole area that had previously composed French Indochina and now was occupied by the two Vietnams, Cambodia, and Laos—where the Communist Pathet Lao had also stepped up its attack against government and neutralist troops in late 1963. Outside the United States, the idea of neutralization was put forward publicly by de Gaulle on January 31, 1964.

De Gaulle's independent foreign policy took many forms, including repudiation of French NATO commitments and construction of an independent French atomic striking force. Now, in Asia, de Gaulle proceeded to break with the United States not only by suggesting neutralization and refusing to back the American effort in Vietnam, but also by finally recognizing the government of Communist China and forcing a break with Chiang Kai-shek on Formosa. De Gaulle's attempt to reassert French influence in Southeast Asia in this manner was extraordinarily irritating to the Americans. They feared that such suggestions would undermine whatever Vietnamese will to fight still existed as well as encourage the neutralist tendencies of Sihanouk of Cambodia who, like others, had come to believe that the best course was to come to terms with China.

Despite the questions raised about Vietnam and whether, as a political question it was any longer a Cold War issue (as the United States persisted in treating it), the Johnson administration in the United States at first followed the lines laid down by Kennedy. It continued to aid the new regimes against the Vietcong and appealed to other countries for support. Then, in 1965, it made its decision. It ordered bombing of military targets in North Vietnam and committed to action an increasing number of American troops in the south. (In late 1963 there were 15,500 American advisers in Vietnam. By early 1965 there were still only 27,000. But the spring decisions would probably bring in hundreds of thousands of combat personnel.)

Once more the United States was using direct military force in what its administration interpreted as a continuation of the policy of containment. It did so, however, in an area where for twenty years Vietnamese nationalism had been Communist-dominated, and where local opposition to the Communist-nationalist movement had always had little support—even though most of the population of the south *probably* opposed the Communists. Moreover, containment had originally been directed against a seemingly solid, Russian-dominated Communist bloc. In 1965 the Johnson administration had decided to take the risk that its actions would lead Communist countries to patch over the cracks in what was no longer a single bloc. The alternative seemed to be that a Vietcong victory would lead China and a quiescent Russia to compete once more in aiding "wars of national liberation." But in early 1965, it was anybody's guess how North Vietnam, Russia and China would respond to American escalation of the war.

Difficulties among the New States

No one could have expected that the many new states, whose frontiers were often not of their choosing, and who had a host of different interests, would all live in peace and harmony. Their common background of colonial domination by the West and the long-standing desire of their leaders to throw it off gave them certain common attitudes. The common factor of a low standard of living, of a rhythm of life inexorably tied to the seasons, of similar problems of changing this way of life—all seemed to create a bond of common need. Yet even this proved to be true only to a certain extent: they found themselves competing with the same exports, competing for scarce foreign exchange, or discovering that differences within these broad problems were of great significance.

Within Africa, divisions arose out of ties to the British Commonwealth, to the Common Market, out of Arabism. There were also differing views on how to cope with tribal divisions. Some countries followed Ghana, which had chosen to override them ruthlessly in the interest of creating a strong, central administration; others followed the ideas of Nigeria, which decided to acknowledge them and try to work through a broader and looser federal structure. Such basic divisions of opinion also underlay quarrels over the form that an African political union ought to take. Nkrumah of Ghana tended to support African leaders who agreed with his overall conception of politics, on the basis that these would more readily agree to his ideas for a tight-knit African political union. There were specific conflicts, too. Morocco refused for a time to recognize the sovereignty of Mauretania, to which it laid claim. Somalia argued that parts of Ethiopia and Kenya should be joined into a Greater Somalia. To Somalia's demand for self-determination for tribesmen in Ogaden province in Ethiopia, the government of Ethiopia retorted that what the tribesmen might or might not want was strictly a matter of domestic concern. Sporadic border warfare erupted, and Somalia turned to the Communist bloc for arms and training for its army. In 1963 a bitter border quarrel with ideological overtones led to desert warfare between Algeria, whose leader espoused Arab socialism, and Morocco, a monarchy. Morocco broke off diplomatic relations with Cuba and withdrew its ambassador from Egypt, charging the two states with helping Algeria. The newly created Organization of African Unity (see p. 281) established an arbitration commission in November 1963 which secured an agreement on February 20, 1964 for a withdrawal of troops from a demilitarized zone.

The OAU had a hand, also, in arranging matters in Tanganyika when an army revolt there (and in Kenya and Uganda) in January 1964 forced the governments of these new states to request British military help. It was humiliating to have to make the request and President Nyerere of Tanganyika was helped by an OAU arrangement that brought troops from Nigeria and other countries to replace the British contingents.

Although Africa held the center of the stage after 1957 (mainly because of the rapid change in the status of African territories), there were conflicts and unsettled issues among other new nations. In the Far East and Southeast Asia, South Korea and Japan quarreled over repatriation and fishing rights. The Cambodian dispute with its neighbors increased in bitterness. But it appeared no more menacing than the one that arose from the formation of Malaysia, a state composed of Malaya, Singapore, and the British colonies of Sarawak and North Borneo.

The first suggestion for the Federation of Malaysia came from Malay Prime Minister Tunku Abdul Rahman early in 1961, and it included not only the territories that eventually formed Malaysia, but also the British-protected Sultanate of Brunei. Conversations among the four proceeded so well that the British Government approved formation of Malaysia in November, and formed a commission to make recommendations for implementation. At this point the Foreign Minister of Indonesia welcomed the proposal. In June 1962, after consultations with groups and individuals throughout the area, the Commission made its report, based on findings of widespread support for the Federation and general agreement on most of the problems involved. Only one problem, division of the oil revenues of oil-rich Brunei, was insoluble, and failure to agree kept the Sultanate out of the Federation. The other territories and Great Britain set August 31, 1963 as the day for formation of Malaysia.

But in December 1962, Indonesia began a campaign against the new state and found an ally in the Philippines, whose President Macapagal had earlier laid claim to North Borneo. At a meeting in Japan between the Tunku (the title of the Malay Prime Minister) and President Sukarno, the two agreed to "take every possible measure to refrain from making acrimonious attacks on and disparaging references to each other," and in June, in Manila, representatives of the three countries agreed to set up machinery for regular consultation and to examine a Philippine proposal for a loose confederation of the three. But in July Sukarno claimed that the Tunku had broken his pledge that he would allow a plebiscite in Sarawak and North Borneo. The Malayan retorted that he had never given any such pledge, and Sukarno responded in turn by threatening to "crush Malaysia . . . a British project . . . aimed at destroying the Indonesian revolution."

In an effort to satisfy all parties, the Tunku agreed to allow a United Nations investigation of sentiment in the disputed areas, and to postpone the formation of Malaysia until September 16, 1963. Britain also accepted, while making it clear that it nevertheless retained sovereignty in the areas and could therefore dispose of them as it wished. Secretary General U Thant of the United Nations provided a team to conduct the investigation, with observers from all the interested parties, and the Philippine and Indonesian governments stated they would "welcome the formation of Malaysia provided the support of the Borneo territories is ascertained by an independent and impartial authority, the Secretary General of the United Nations or his representatives."

On September 14 the mission reported that all elections in the area appeared to have been free, and that having reached a wide cross-section of the population, it was convinced that a majority showed a desire to join Malaysia. On September 16, as scheduled, the new state came into being, and Indonesia promptly broke off relations, while encouraging mobs to sack the British and Malay embassies and British homes. All British business properties were taken into protective custody, while Britain tried in vain to find out if this meant confiscation. Indonesia then seized all Malaysian properties, set out on an economic boycott of Malaysia (one that cost its own economy heavily and produced a new round of inflation in Indonesia), and sponsored guerrilla movements within the new Federation.

Sukarno based his "confrontation" on the view that Malaysia represented British neo-colonialism: Britain retained its great base at Singapore and was pledged to give both economic and military aid to Malaysia. He also argued that Malaysian weakness would lure the Chinese Communists into the area. Finally, he claimed that Malaysia, with a population of 10 million, threatened Indonesia, whose population is 100 million. Few foreign observers found the arguments convincing, but in Indonesia Sukarno was unchallenged. Attempts at negotiation failed, and in 1964 the confrontation continued.

The Tragi-Comedy of the Middle East

Nowhere among any group of newly independent states have there been more problems of relations within the group than in the Middle East. Some semblance of unity developed during the Suez war, when leaders vied with one another to proclaim their brotherhood with Egypt and to condemn imperialist aggression. Thus Syrian sympathizers destroyed the pipelines that ran across Syria from Iraq to the Mediterranean; Iraq denounced Britain (with which it was allied in the Baghdad Pact); and Jordan moved to purge itself of further British influence.

Yet there were Iraqi who were unhappy about the loss of oil revenue that resulted from the show of Syrian solidarity. In 1957 came

King Hussein's frantic and successful effort to defend his throne against Nasserite elements within Jordan (see pp. 234–235), and intermittent warfare continued between Yemen and the British protectorate of Aden, and between rebels and the Sultan of Muscat and Oman. Then in late 1957 a curious crisis arose involving Syria, the Soviet Union, and the West.

In Syria a series of revolutions brought to power elements more radical than the country had ever known. In August 1957 they signed a new and extensive economic and military aid agreement with the Soviet Union, discovered an American "plot" against the government, and expelled a group of officials in the American Embassy. Washington's reaction to what Dulles called "the apparently growing Soviet Communist domination of Syria" was to expedite delivery of arms to Syria's neighbors—Jordan, Iraq, Lebanon, and Saudi Arabia. There was talk of invoking the Eisenhower Doctrine. In early October, Premier Khrushchev charged that the United States was inciting Turkey to make war on Syria, warned the United States against its game, and told Turkey that aggression would bring retaliation by rocket. Egypt sent troops to Syria, and they moved immediately to the Turkish border.

Then, almost as quickly as it had begun, the crisis eased when Syria submitted it to the United Nations General Assembly. Although no resolution was passed, the tension was decreased. Khrushchev told the Arab states that the Soviet Union had again, by its intervention, preserved peace in the Middle East, and initiated another economic aid agreement with Egypt.

In 1958, there occurred what appeared to be the most momentous series of events yet in the Middle East. Egypt and Syria joined to form the United Arab Republic, and in Iraq the more-or-less pro-Western monarchy was overthrown. It looked as though Nasser-led Pan Arabism had finally prevailed. The sequence of events began in February 1958, when Nasser and President Shukri al-Kuwaitly of Syria made a joint announcement of union of their countries. The move had broader objectives: the leaders hoped it would provide a base for a greater Arab union. But certainly one of its first effects was to curb the more pro-Russian elements in Syria; Nasser moved rapidly to remove them from office. A second effect was more surprising. In answer to Nasser's initiative, King Feisal of Iraq and King Hussein of Jordan announced a merger of their own two Kingdoms, forming what would be an obvious rival to the United Arab Republic. A strong motive for the second merger was the fear shared by both young kings that Nasserites in their realms would unseat them. Presumably their union would be stronger, although it did not take on the proportions of the UAR, which had already decided to have only one diplomatic service and therefore one seat at the United Nations. Nasser, piqued, predicted that it would be "scattered like dry leaves before the wind." And in short order the UAR took the first step in its expansion—in March Yemen was associated with it.

Then events moved rapidly. In May internal revolt broke out in Lebanon, whose government was always delicately balanced among Christian, Muslim, and Dhruze. The government charged that the rebels were being supported by Nasser's northern province of Syria while Nasser's radio incited the populace to overthrow the government. After an appeal to the United Nations with a formal charge against the UAR and after an attempt to work through the Arab League, Lebanon obtained the services of another hastily improvised United Nations body, the United Nations Observer Group in Lebanon (UNOGIL), that would try to survey the frontiers. In its first report the small group suggested that, in fact, most of the armed groups it observed were Lebanese, although it was possible that some arms had been transferred across the border from Syria. It also could not help noticing that the Lebanese armed forces were not enthusiastic about acting against the rebellion. Then, on July 14, the situation became far more tense: in a bloody coup the young King of Iraq, his uncle the Crown Prince, and the long-time pro-Western strong-man of Iraqi politics, Nuri es-Said, were assassinated. An army clique took over, led by Abdel Karim Kassim.

The results were startling. In the West the coup was viewed as part of the Nasserite wave surging over the Middle East, though the plot itself appeared to be completely internal. Government leaders reacted similarly in strife-torn Lebanon and unstable Jordan: Lebanon immediately cabled the United States for armed help to maintain its sovereignty and King Hussein of Jordan, seeing the breakup of his Jordanian-Iraqi Union, asked for British aid. Both countries responded immediately. Within a day there were 5000 American Marines in Lebanon (the total number eventually reached about 13,000) and within a few days British airborne forces landed in Jordan (as well as in Libya, to which they hadn't been invited).

Once the British and Americans were there, no one knew quite what to do with them. The Iraqi revolution did not spread. Though welcomed by Nasser and cheered by Pan-Arabists all over the Middle East, and though it became obvious that Iraq would eventually leave the Western-sponsored Baghdad Pact, Premier Karim Kassim was not prepared to submit to Nasser's leadership. The revolution had been against the corrupt, oligarchic Iraqi regime. But it was hardly for export. The presence of British troops, however, did ensure continuation of Hussein's government in Jordan, and during the American stay in Lebanon a regime was patched together under the presidency of the Army Commander, General Shihab, who had been reluctant to take sides between the previous government and the rebels.

The armed American intervention in the area provoked cries of "I told you so" from French and British alike. The United States, which had acted against them two years earlier in the Suez crisis when *they* had intervened, now found it necessary to do so itself. But there were other, more important reactions: the violent objections of Nasser's United Arab Republic, the milder but still strong disapproval voiced by other neutral states, especially India, and the threatening attitude of the Soviet Union. Nasser flew to discuss the matter with Khrushchev and to assure himself of Soviet backing if the Western intervention were to go any further. Khrushchev talked of the necessity of a summit meeting to end "the present military conflict," but Eisenhower denied that there was any war. At the United Nations, the Soviets vetoed several Security Council resolutions that would have put a new and expanded United Nations presence in the area to permit a graceful Western withdrawal. In the meantime, Western powers received some reassurances about the nature of the Kassim regime in Iraq, the Soviets called for a meeting of the General Assembly, and the UAR decided not to press the issue further. In the General Assembly it acquiesced to the continuation of the United Nations Observer Group in Lebanon, as well as to the presence of a special representative of the Secretary General in Jordan. The Arab-devised formula hardly dealt with what the United States now had come to consider a new problem: "indirect aggression." But it allowed for withdrawal of troops and permitted some hopes of stability in both Lebanon and Jordan. The new government in Lebanon assumed a somewhat more neutralist pose, explicitly rejecting the Eisenhower Doctrine, to which the previous government had adhered; King Hussein, whose flight abroad for a brief vacation was turned back over Syria, told crowds of excited supporters that UAR fighter planes had tried to shoot him down. But things were relatively calm.

During the next three years this calm prevailed, and the pattern of events was fairly regular. In Iraq, Kassim, having formally withdrawn from the Baghdad Pact in 1959, balanced Communist against other support, taking large-scale aid from the Soviet bloc and putting numerous Communist or pro-Communist sympathizers into office. But he managed to keep them under control. He survived numerous plots against him, usually blamed on Nasser and/or Western imperialist, and until 1963 he was able to play successfully his lone game in the Middle East. When he laid claim to the sheikdom of Kuwait at the time that Britain made it independent in 1961, he found no backers among other members of the Arab League. But the Soviet Union supported him by vetoing Kuwait's application for admission to the United Nations.

Nasser, on the other hand, had to content himself with gains already made in the Middle East, while playing the larger role on the world scene that took him to African conferences and meetings with other neutralist leaders. He dealt harshly with domestic Communists in the United Arab Republic and began, to the dismay of the Syrian business community, a series of reforms under the rubric of "Arab socialism." These involved some degree of nationalization of private enterprise. Khrushchev reproached him for his attacks on domestic Communists, and told the Egyptian President not to aspire to too great a role. Nasser covered his position by gradual moves to improve his relations with Western powers. But at the end of 1958 and in early 1959, the Arab leader signed agreements by which the Soviet Union extended credit and technical aid to build the Aswan High Dam. Despite subsequent ups and downs of relations, the work began and proceeded at a steady pace. Egypt continued to lead the undeclared war against Israel, and tightened its restrictions on shipments to Israel through the Suez Canal while relying on imported German technicians to help it develop modern arms, including rockets that could reach Israeli cities.

King Saud of Saudi Arabia, facing internal opposition, curbed his attempts to be the grand mediator in the Middle East, a role which the United States had helped foster. He had numerous fences to mend, considering the continued popularity of Nasser; under the rising tide of modernism, this friend of the United States even felt it necessary to outlaw slavery in 1962.

And in the meantime, Britain and the United States tried to repair their position by reconstituting the Baghdad Pact as the Central Treaty Organization, to which the United States now gave more support. Turkey and Iran were under continual pressure from the Soviet Union as a result of their membership. Both survived, but the republican regime of Menderes in Turkey was ousted by a military coup in 1961 and, like so many other countries, Turkey (presumably the most modernized of Muslim countries) abandoned democracy. Late in 1961 the army leaders, having purged many members of the previous administration, restored democratic forms, but the new coalition regime remained shaky. The Shah's government in Iran also struggled to keep alive, and tried to impose a revolution from above in favor of the masses and against the strongest political elements. Many doubted the Shah's ability to succeed with the sweeping reforms that seemed necessary. Moreover, the Western alignment was as unpopular with progressive elements in Iran as it had come to be with many elements in Pakistan, the easternmost member of CENTO. There, the government of General Ayub Khan continued to support Western ties amidst growing criticism. When, in 1962, the United States rushed aid to neutral India when it faced a border attack from China, criticism was echoed by Pakistan's leaders. By its alliance Pakistan had put itself in the Soviet line of fire and brought Soviet support to Afghanistan's claims against Pakistan. But it seemed that neutral India, which had maintained good relations with the Soviet Union, could receive United States help too. Was there any point in alliance? Was not a country that helped India thereby aiding Pakistan's enemy? Ayub Khan's answer was to repair relations with his Communist neighbors. Chinese technicians arrived in Pakistan and the two countries arranged border agreements and cultural and barter exchanges. Pakistani Foreign Minister Bhutto warned in mid-1963 that China would come to Pakistan's defense in the event of an Indian attack. Chinese Prime Minister Chou En-lai received an enthusiastic welcome during a visit in early 1964. But Ayub Khan did not cut his treaty ties with the United States.

The years 1961 and 1962 saw another of the kaleidoscopic changes in the Middle East lineup, again involving the clash between Arab nationalism and local nationalisms. In September 1961, the United Arab Republic suddenly dissolved. What was to have been the nucleus for true Arab unity instead foundered on Syrian resistance to Nasser's brand of Arab Socialism, as more conservative elements seized power. Nasser at first tried to prevent the breakup by threatening to use force. The attempt failed, and Syria resumed an independent international role—but an unsteady one, as faction vied with faction for power. Then, in early 1963, there seemed to be another reversal: in Iraq, Kassim's luck ran out on February 8. On February 9, a new regime executed the dictator and installed his former lieutenant and co-conspirator of 1958, Colonel Abdel Salam Arif, who quickly pledged to establish close links with other "liberated" Arab states, that is, countries like Egypt, which had overthrown the kind of royal system still existing in Jordan and Saudi Arabia. But failure of these ties to develop quickly meant that the rulers of those two nations, the last of the "unliberated" states, could breathe more easily. Local differences continued to prevail over sentiments for unity, but among the masses those sentiments remained strong, and Nasser was still the symbol of unity.

War in Yemen

Among the successor states to the old Ottoman Turkish Empire one, Yemen, became the focus of inter-Arab conflict in late 1962. A September coup overthrew the traditional ruler, Imam Mohammed, and established a republic. The change appeared to be another step in the replacement of traditional forms of rule by the newer, Nasserite type. The new republican government announced the death of the Imam and put forward plans for modernization of the semifeudal country, and Communist bloc countries, most Asian states, and the "liberated" Arab countries soon recognized the regime. Saudi Arabia and Jordan withheld recognition, the Imam reappeared in Saudi Arabia, and a royalist government-in-exile was created, supported by tribes in the north.

Clearly, the Saudi and Jordanian monarchies felt threatened by the new Nasserite-style government on their southern border.* To the southeast of Yemen was the South Arabian Federation, a British-sponsored and protected assemblage of small sheikdoms and emirates. The new Yemeni government soon made clear that its neighbors were threatened; Yemen intended to unite the entire Arabian peninsula and liberate it from the "Saudi shame."

Fighting increased on all borders. Saudi Arabia broke off relations with the UAR and signed a defense pact with Jordan, while Yemen signed a similar accord with the UAR, from which it received technical and financial aid. Nasser announced that he had no designs on Saudi Arabia and Jordan; he would withdraw the Egyptian forces now entering Yemen in large numbers if the two countries ended their support of the royalists. The United States and several European countries now announced recognition of the Yemeni republican regime, but Britain, wary of the effect recognition might have on the sheiks and emirs in the South Arabian Federation, refused, declaring that the

---

* It was soon after the new Yemeni regime announced abolition of slavery that the Saudi government felt compelled to do the same.

republican government was not yet in effective control of the territory of Yemen. Despite a United Nations-sponsored disengagement agreement and the presence of a small United Nations observation mission in Yemen, both sides continued to receive outside aid throughout 1964.

The strategic importance of Yemen could hardly be minimized. Nasserite Arabs saw developments there as a flanking move against Saudi Arabia, Jordan, and all the sheikdoms of the Middle East—control of Yemen was a step toward Arab unity. Since—to Egypt—control of Yemen meant control of the Red Sea's southern outlet, Britain viewed developments in Yemen as a threat to its base in Aden (in the South-Arabian Federation), to British influence in all of East Africa, and to vital British oil interests in the Persian Gulf.

Both sides encountered unexpected resistance and costs, and these were responsible for the disengagement agreement as well as an improvement in relations in early 1964. The occasion was a meeting of Arab heads of state called by Nasser to deal with Israeli diversion of waters from the Jordan river for irrigation purposes.

Arab governments had long refused to cooperate with Israel on the use of Jordan River waters, even though in the early 1950s technical talks had reached limited agreement on a formula for division of the flow. They had warned Israel that its diversion of water, even though not exceeding what Arab technicians had earlier agreed to, would be a *casus belli*. In December 1963, Arab chiefs of staff met to consider action, and January 13–16, 1964, the Arab heads of state conferred in Cairo.

The conference communique called on all states to support action against the new Israeli aggression and announced a planned diversion of the northern tributaries of the Jordan that would thwart Israeli actions. Talk followed about establishing a Palestine government-in-exile. But more important, the conference appeared to create an atmosphere of considerable cordiality among the usually hostile Arab leaders: the UAR, Jordan, and Saudi Arabia reestablished diplomatic relations, and Algeria and Iraq announced a willingness to mediate the Yemen dispute. It appeared that Saudi Arabia and Jordan might accept a *fait accompli* in Yemen in return for a measure of Nasserite moderation toward their regimes and, for a time at least, the Arab leaders evinced an unusual warmth toward one another. Yet the Yemen dispute proved to be more intractable than foreseen, for despite heavy Egyptian expenditures 1964 ended without a victory for the republican forces. Jordan and Saudi Arabia had been reprieved more by Egyptian and republican failure than by good will.

Regionalism in Africa

No account of the rise of new states to prominence in international politics would be complete without reference to attempts to bring them together into new groupings, to bridge the old frontiers so often created by balance-of-power considerations. To the story of independence in mid-century, of the search for a role in the international system, of cooperation and conflict with old states, and of conflicts with one another must therefore be added a brief account of movements for creating broader unities and cooperative links.

From the beginnings of nationalist agitation in Africa many leaders dreamed of substituting larger regional groupings or some form of a United States of Africa. Against them were ranged the fact that as states became independent their new ruling elites quickly developed a vested interest in the existence of their particular state, and the fact that despite the unifying bond of a colonial past and of color, many of the states had highly divergent interests. Until 1958 most African leaders had little contact with one another; most of the areas that became independent had little trade with each other; East Africa had been subject to far more Arab influence than had West Africa; the different colonial administrations left different legacies of law, education and African political parties.

But 1958 was the great year of African assertion—and the year that both Soviet and American diplomatic activities increased notably. In January came the Cairo Afro-Asian People's Solidarity Conference, attended by both the Soviet Union and China (though no Western powers were invited). It established a permanent secretariat, and marked what was perhaps the high tide of Egypt's effort to lead Africa. The Bandung Conference of 1955 had had few representatives from Africa, and the Cairo conference stressed the continued effort of other "liberated" states to help their black brothers attain independence. Events moved too quickly, however, and during the year Africans themselves took over the leadership. In Accra, Ghana, the first Conference of Independent African States took place. There were still only three from south of the Sahara—Ghana, and the two anachronistic and archaic states of Liberia and Ethiopia. The others were predominantly Arab states from the north. But the setting of the conference symbolized the leadership Ghana had begun to exert in the movement for African independence, and the extent to which Kwame Nkrumah was known throughout Africa. Until this time, Pan-Africanism as a movement had come mainly from a variety of sources outside Africa. A number of Pan-African congresses had been held. The most notable of these met in Manchester, England, in 1945, bringing together a number of the future leaders of Africa. But Pan-Africanism had concerned itself primarily with achieving independence for African states. Now, under the spell of Nkrumah, the focus shifted to African unity, and the leaders meeting at Accra set up a permanent coordinating group for their United Nations delegations.

In ensuing months many other congresses were held, marking the emergence of pressure groups and parties cutting across state boundaries: the first Conference of North African Political Parties in Tangier in April; the first Pan-African Students Conference in Uganda in July; the first Conference of the Confederation of North African Students in Tunis in August; the first meeting of the Pan-African Freedom Movement for East and Central Africa in Tanganyika in September; and most important of all, the first all-African People's Conference in Accra in December. Here 500 delegates of parties and other nonofficial bodies met to plan, as President Nkrumah put it, "a final assault upon imperialism and colonialism." For Tom Mboya, delegate from Kenya, the theme—in deliberate contrast to the "Scramble for Africa" set off by the Berlin Conference of 1888—was "Scram out of Africa."

While these activities marked the emergence of Pan-Africanism, the new United Nations Economic Commission for Africa—modeled on other existing United Nations regional economic commissions—began operations in Addis Ababa, and in New York, Charles Malik of Lebanon, President of the Thirteenth General Assembly, called it the "African Session," because of the prominence of African issues on the agenda.

Yet the very emergence of African independent states complicated the idea of African unity, and the next years saw a proliferation of groupings, with overlapping and conflicting membership. The union of Guinea and Ghana took place soon after Guinea's independence in 1958, but Guinea's separate membership in the United Nations typified the loose nature of union. Talk began at this time, too, of a union of the Maghreb—Morocco, Algeria, and Tunisia, and indeed, Tunisia's President Bourguiba became embroiled with France over Tunisian aid to the Algerian rebels. Once Algeria achieved its independence, however, the Maghreb union failed to materialize. Instead, in 1963, Morocco and Algeria engaged in warfare over Moroccan claims to Algerian territory. In April 1959 Senegal and the Sudan formed the Mali Federation. It broke up in August 1960, and Senegal's President Leopold

Senghor wrote that Senegal's new role would be to exemplify not a Pan-African but an inter-African policy: the notion of cooperation between independent units began to compete with the idea of an organic unity. The Sudan, which retained the title of Mali, proceeded on the other hand to join the loose Ghana-Guinea union.

In the meantime there were moves to unite the four states that had emerged from French Equatorial Africa—Gabon, the Central African Republic, Chad and the Congo Republic—resulting in a customs union of the four plus the new state of the Cameroons, while the former states of French West Africa, with the exception of Guinea, took a similar step. Then twelve of these—again excepting Guinea, Mali and Togo—met to form an Afro-Malagasy Union to develop cooperation in defense and diplomacy, at the same time creating an Afro-Malagasy Economic Cooperation Organization that would eventually lead to a full-scale common market.

These so-called "Brazzaville Powers" had one other common interest that tended to set them apart from other African states. In Europe, in 1957, the six members of the European Coal and Steel Community signed and ratified agreements to set up the European Economic Community or Common Market. In a momentous decision, Britain, which had kept apart from the European movement, decided not to join. One price that France extracted from the other powers in return for French ratification was a provision that members of the French Union could become "associated states," along with a provision setting up a common development fund. The form of association gave the African states formerly belonging to France access to the new European Common Market without the common tariff barrier that other states would face, including other nonassociated African states. Ghana took the lead in charging that this constituted a form of "neo-colonialism" in that it would subordinate to the Common Market the economies and therefore the politics of the African countries involved.

Association of the former French territories to the Common Market was the only concrete result of the grandiose idea of "Eurafrica." For years, especially in France, men had talked of a Eurafrica that would draw upon the raw materials and manpower on both sides of the Mediterranean—a region in which the Mediterranean would be only a central lake, as it had been under the Roman Empire. Military men pointed to the strategic importance of North Africa, and cited its role in World War II to buttress their arguments. The dream lacked one essential: equality of status between the people who would presumably participate, and a real desire to take part. Nevertheless, the concrete benefits of the Common Market were not to be cast aside.

From the point of view of international relations, however, association of the former French colonies with the Common Market meant another overlapping regional grouping in Africa, competing with others, and working potential hardship on them: behind Ghana's complaint of neo-colonialism lay the fact that it would be harder for African nonmembers to export to the European market. (Latin American countries feared the same thing, and they, along with a few other raw material exporters, tried to pressure the Common Market to keep its outside tariff low.)

While these various groupings formed and re-formed as Africans searched for national identity, one earlier one—the Central African Federation—broke up, and a new one, composed partly out of fragments of the old, seemed imminent. The Central African Federation, composed of Northern and Southern Rhodesia and Nyasaland and created in 1953, had always been unstable. The economic benefits it gave to impoverished Nyasaland and to Southern Rhodesia were apparently at the expense of Northern Rhodesia, even though the latter did share in the general prosperity that followed federation. People in the north felt that the boom would have come anyway, and resented having to share the wealth. The race question was even more important. The federal government worked for some form of racial "partnership" and a multiracial society, but white supremacy was strongly entrenched in Southern Rhodesia, and black Africans in the other parts felt that Federation only perpetuated white supremacy throughout the Federation.

Britain's attempts to deal with the mutually incompatible demands of all parties led to nothing but bitterness. In mid-1963, under pressure from Northern Rhodesia and Nyasaland—whose leaders insisted upon the right to secede from the Federation—the British held a conference on dissolution and the problems that would result: apportionment of the debt, new currencies, the fate of common government services. The conference set December 31, 1963 as the date of dissolution, and the bill providing for it went through the British Parliament unopposed. Planning for independence for Nyasaland and Northern Rhodesia sometime in 1964 raised relatively few problems, but the British government was in an anomalous position about Southern Rhodesia. There a dominant white minority wanted independence in a form that would guarantee its continued supremacy. Britain was unwilling to grant independence until electoral reform took place, leading, within five years, to universal suffrage and majority rule. It insisted on Commonwealth approval for independence; the Commonwealth prime ministers would certainly only approve British terms. African states were therefore in a position of approving the British position, which involved a *refusal* of independence, and disapproving of Rhodesian leaders' demand for independence. But Britain was also prodded in the United Nations to do more to change the situation within Southern Rhodesia.

The Rhodesias, like so many other African countries, were vitally interested in the outcome of the Congo crisis but were also now affected by the Pan-African Freedom Movement for East and Central Africa, led by Julius Nyerere of Tanganyika. Originally envisaging a federation of Tanganyika, Uganda, and Kenya, it came to encompass Zanzibar, Ruanda-Urundi, plus Nyasaland and the Rhodesias. Then members were included from Ethiopia, Somalia, South Africa, South West Africa, and the three British High Commission territories that exist as uneasy enclaves within South Africa: Basutoland, Bechuanaland, and Swaziland. Another grouping was born. How long it might last and with what results, no one could tell.

The Congo crisis further crystallized the two emerging Brazzaville and Casablanca groupings. The former, primarily successor states to the French Empire, had a somewhat less suspicious attitude toward Western countries, tended to see less benefit in immediate African unity, and often accepted a more pluralistic domestic political approach. The Casablanca powers were more radical in their orientation toward colonialism and "neo-colonialism," African unity, and monolithic domestic political systems, and they tended to side with the Soviet bloc on international issues, while nevertheless adhering to the idea of positive neutralism as Nasser had earlier outlined it. The Brazzaville grouping had less objection to Hammarskjold's attempt to remain neutral in internal Congolese affairs, whereas the Casablanca group gave full support to Lumumba, then to Gizenga and his Stanleyville government, and finally in 1964, to the rebels against the central government. (By this time the groupings had re-formed, and the Congo Republic of Brazzaville had become a member of the more radical group.)

In 1961 President Tubman of Liberia attempted to bridge the gap with a proposal for an all-inclusive organization of African states in which each would retain its own identity. But when a meeting of African states took place at his capital city, Monrovia, in May 1961, to discuss the plan, the Casablanca powers stayed away. They also boycotted a second meeting at Lagos, Nigeria, in mid-1962, along with Libya, Tunisia, and Sudan, whose leaders objected to the lack of inclusion of Algeria. In 1963, however, an African summit conference held at Addis Ababa finally brought thirty foreign ministers and heads of state together. Here they succeeded in laying the groundwork of the new Organization of African Unity, a similar but simplified version of the Organization of American States, with a Secretariat in Addis Ababa.

Yet at Addis Ababa it became evident that Kwame Nkrumah of Ghana, with his idea of rapidly developing a United States of Africa—a single political unit—was an isolated figure. Not only was there little response to his plea, but the criticism often voiced in the past of his ambitions came to the fore: many African leaders felt that his Bureau of African Affairs was a center for subversion against other African leaders who failed to share his ideas (like the recently murdered Sylvanus Olympio of Togoland) and some warned openly against "black imperialism" and "African colonialism." Others raised the question of whether Egypt—busy trying to reconstitute the United Arab Republic out of Egypt, Syria, and Iraq—was really African: two-thirds of it seemed Middle-Eastern.

While questions were raised about Egypt, Ahmed Ben Bella of Algeria gained in status: he seemed to be one of the few African leaders actually ready to use his slender resources to promote revolution in the Portuguese possessions, and to fight "neo-colonialism." Nevertheless, the question of whether the Sahara joined or divided Africa was bound to recur.

The new Organization of African Unity soon found use for its slender organizational resources. In the disputes between Morocco and Algeria, between Ethiopia and Somalia, and in the latter stages of the Congo affair, the OAU began to play an important role.

Conclusion

By 1964 the old European empires—product of waves of exploration and conquest between the fifteenth and twentieth centuries—had almost disappeared. Portugal clung to her last remnants, and here and there other isolated segments remained. But by and large they had been replaced by a number of politically independent successor states, most of which faced enormous problems in trying to achieve rapid economic development and social revolution.

The empires had served the function in the old European balance-of-power system of areas in which territorial compensation could take place. They had also been the source of disputes between the major powers. The successor states wanted to avoid being used in the same way by the two superpowers, the United States and the Soviet Union; they also did not want to be fought over. But impelled by balance-of-power considerations, the two inevitably looked at the new states in much the same way, though they could no longer act toward them in the old imperialist manner.

Relations between the new states, the Soviet Union, and the United States, with all their balance-of-power implications, were colored by the legacy of empire. There was much dispute over that legacy: Western states stressed the law and order they had brought, and the investment, schooling, economic development, public health, and modern administration. The new states tended to emphasize the poverty that had been left behind, the centuries of what they considered to be exploitation, the disrupted societies, the lopsided economies, the boundaries founded on neither economic nor ethnic considerations, and the years of degrading racism. They blamed the colonialists for most of their ills, with perhaps too little consideration of the other reasons for them. With the enormous task of nation-building in the face of appalling obstacles, they tended to blame the Western powers for every problem. Like other countries before them, they were not immune from self-seeking new leaders.

For the new, multilevel and dimensional balance-of-power system that superseded bipolarism, all this had a major result: the successor states distrusted capitalism, which they associated with Western domination; they distrusted all Western efforts to protect them as merely new efforts at domination; and they saw little merit in Western political systems. The corollary was that they showed less distrust of the Communist states and were continually influenced by homegrown Communists or Marxist socialists who found Marxism a sound explanation of the phenomena of Western capitalist domination and the meaninglessness of Western democratic forms. Because of past history the Communist states had a built-in advantage in dealing with the new countries. The new states desperately needed economic development; they needed capital. Yet capital from the West was suspect. Moreover in many cases it did create conflict, as in the Middle East, where some countries had the oil that attracted capital and others did not. Nasserism had higher ideals, but hoped all Arabs could share in the oil wealth that only a few now had. In some areas trade with and investment from the West benefited only a small upper class, and created envy and hatred among the poorer classes, who often blamed the West for the existence of a corrupt and wealthy or despotic upper class.

The Soviet Union and China could not provide vast amounts of aid. (Russia tended to concentrate it for quite specific advantages.) But both underlined the non-Westerners' general distrust of Western aid and investment, and posed as examples of how development in the face of great difficulties could take place without foreign capital. In this China, despite its economic difficulties in the early 1960s, was more persuasive than Russia, which had started with a more favorable situation.

The new states had their own foreign policy problems, their widespread neutralism, and their new organizations to try to cope with their own conflicts and to promote cooperation. The result was a rich complexity for international politics: single states had relations with one another, small subsidiary balance-of-power systems developed in various parts of the world, sometimes appealing to the regional organizations, sometimes to the larger members of the world balance of power, who acted on and were influenced by the new weaker states. Sometimes the universal organizations such as the United Nations shared jurisdiction with all of these. The years since the mid-1950s showed that all the states were inextricably intertwined in this new multiple balance; they were not simply in one camp or the other, as in bipolar days. As the next chapter indicates, the two camps themselves had broken into numerous subgroups and balance-of-power systems. In this new situation, neutralism did not mean isolationism.

CHAPTER EIGHT   1957–1964 (II)

The Old Blocs

and Competitive Coexistence

The large number of new states, with the General Assembly as their forum, occupied the center of the world stage for much of the time after 1956. It is possible, however, to exaggerate their importance in the scheme of world politics. The years also witnessed resurgence of a Europe that seemed almost liberated from the burden of empire, and found the United States and the Soviet Union—the two states that had so long dominated world politics—in the midst of troubles that demonstrated their awesome military power but also their increasing inability to use it. They ended, finally, with changes in world leadership: in 1963, President Kennedy was assassinated, and Vice-President Lyndon B. Johnson succeeded him; in 1964, Prime Minister Khrushchev, the man who had initiated de-Stalinization and decisively changed the Soviet Union, was removed from his office in a peaceful coup by other party leaders. Finally, in late 1964, China alarmed the world with its first atomic explosion. The rimlands of Asia were the first to consider its meaning, but it had long-run implications for the rest of the world.

Europe, European Union, and the Atlantic Alliance

The Bandung Conference of 1955 and the Accra conferences of 1958 may serve as convenient symbols of a main trend in international affairs since World War II—the emergence of new states. The Hungarian uprising of 1956 may be used to symbolize another—the growing centrifugal tendencies within the supposedly monolithic Communist bloc and the ever-continuing disposition of Marxists in action to develop factions and to try to move in different directions.

But there is no convenient event to symbolize another, equally dramatic development: the resurgence of a Europe as prosperous as it had been before World War I, but with the prosperity much more

284

widely shared (in a process which nostalgic Europeans called "Americanization"). It was a Europe that had divested itself of Empire and whose geographical boundary was far to the west of where Europe had once extended. Notwithstanding the open questions of divided Germany, or of the nuclear threat, it was a Europe that had regained the confidence and optimism that seemed to have died in the years following 1914.

Some would take Rome, March 25, 1957, as the place and time to symbolize the change: here the treaties were signed establishing the European Economic Community and the European Atomic Community (the Common Market and Euratom). Yet these represented the little Europe of the Six—France, Italy, West Germany, the Benelux countries—and prosperity had begun long before the effects of the Common Market were felt and had also spread to other European countries. Perhaps the most convenient symbol is the growing balance-of-payments difficulties that began to face the United States in 1959; for this, in one way, summed up the change in relationship between the "super-power" United States and Europe. In 1947 the United States had initiated a hasty rescue operation. It had poured aid into Europe and had assumed European commitments abroad. There had been for years a "dollar gap"—result of the need and desire of Europeans (and others) to buy more from the United States than they could sell to it. The gap had been filled by various forms of American aid. Now, though at first only those who read technical financial statistics noticed it, the whole situation had changed. Europeans no longer scrambled for the scarce American dollars needed to purchase from America. Instead they began to hold on to American dollars which they had little immediate need to spend. In the past they might have held them as security, since their own currencies were not trustworthy and there were strict controls over what they could do with them. But in December 1958, European currencies were made freely convertible (thus doing away with the European Payments Union, that necessary organization of the late 1940s). The American dollar might itself come under pressure if the situation that developed in 1959 continued; if people *believed* it would come under pressure, they would hurry to divest themselves of their holdings thereby causing the pressure, through a set of circumstances similar to the one that forced British devaluation of the pound in 1948. The United States was, in fact, still selling more abroad than it bought. The new reverse gap developed, however, because the United States continued foreign aid expenditures, American tourists were buying European services in such quantities, American expenditures for troop maintenance abroad continued at a high level, and American investors, so long encouraged to fill the old dollar gap by increasing their investments in other countries were, in fact, doing just that. Unfortunately, from some foreign policy viewpoints, they were not investing in the new undeveloped countries that needed it most but that offered little inducement to private investors. Instead, they invested in the booming Western European economies and bought European securities that yielded current high interest rates. Thus, in 1959, the world was treated to the spectacle of the American Secretary of the Treasury pleading with Europe to eliminate some of its postwar restrictions on imports of American goods while the United States government considered cutting some of its military commitments abroad in order to reduce its payments gap. Finally, the Kennedy administration took even more stringent measures.

Moreover, the payments problem represented not only the new economic balance between Europe and the United States, but the shifting strategic situation as well. For years the United States had provided the NATO sword through its Strategic Air Command—the retaliatory deterrent on which basic NATO strategy rested. Neutralist currents were always strong in Europe, but governments accepted the strategy for Europe, though they questioned its validity for other areas. After the Korean War there was dispute over the size of the necessary "Shield," to balance Soviet atomic power. But there was little question about SAC. Now, in the years after the Suez War, with a stronger Europe and a Russia armed with thermonuclear weapons, the whole relationship was again called into question.

Central to both these shifts was the posture assumed by the man brought into power through the Algerian crisis, de Gaulle. Some saw him as embodying outworn conceptions of a nationalist past, but others saw him as a political genius who grasped the fundamental meaning of these two shifts and faced up to their consequences.

The story of the economic and political aspect of European resurgence begins with the failure of the European Defense Community and the proposed European Political Community in 1954. These were to have been added to the functioning European Coal and Steel Community, and would have permitted German rearmament. Instead, German rearmament was secured through German membership in NATO and reactivation of the Western European Union.

The setback to "Europe" provided by the collapse of EDC did not deter those groups working for tighter unity who realized that

Western European Union was merely a means to rearm Germany. Within a few months they began planning a broad customs union—an association of states in which trade barriers among them would be eliminated and a common tariff to the outside world established around them. Negotiations continued among the six—the members of the Coal and Steel Community—throughout 1956 and into 1957. The British, observing the discussions, took the same position as toward the ECSC and EDC: commitments to the Commonwealth and a special relationship to the United States in the Atlantic community precluded British membership. The French, in early 1957—still attempting to reintegrate Algeria into France and trying to forge a new set of relationships with their other African territories not yet independent—almost halted the negotiations with their demand that some kind of associated status be arranged for overseas territories. In the end the other countries paid the price to get the Common Market: overseas territories would have access to the Common Market without having to pay the common tariff. They could, however, maintain their own external tariffs against the rest of the world. Moreover, their developing industries could retain some protection against European products that would not be allowed to regular Common Market members. The price also included establishment of a Common Market development fund to be channelled to the associated territories (which also included the Belgian Congo and Ruanda-Urundi). But other states also received concessions, notably Italy. The Common Market included a Bank to channel funds to low-income areas within the Market—which meant, in practice, southern Italy.

In the end, the voluminous treaty signed in Rome showed that its signers understood one thing: establishment of a common customs boundary around a free-trade area meant that the countries involved would eventually have to bring into harmony their social security laws, tax systems and fiscal policies, and policies on investment. Many people who worked for establishment of the Common Market were confident that as time passed and brought each of the stages provided for in the treaty (each of which led to greater and greater economic integration), the countries involved would find that the easiest way to bring all such matters into line would be through common political organs. The Common Market, they hoped, would lead to true political unity.

But people could support the Common Market on the basis of economics alone. They could believe that its aim—the creation of a huge internal market—could be achieved through cooperation rather than unity. The treaty provided, moreover, that the organs of the

Common Market—the Council of Ministers, the Parliamentary Assembly and the Court of Justice—would assume greater powers as the Market evolved through the stages outlined in the treaty. This would take from twelve to fifteen years. Events might well modify some of the later stages, and escape clauses could be invoked. Thus people with different views were able to support the Common Market and ratification proceeded with relatively few difficulties. The treaty and its companion one establishing the European Atomic Energy Community took effect on January 1, 1958. Across the board internal tariff cuts of ten per cent began on January 1, 1959, with additional ones in each succeeding year. Various other internal restrictions—quotas, subsidies, discriminatory transport charges, and so on—also underwent rapid change. In surprisingly short order, and despite political upheaval in France, the Common Market became a thriving concern, with intra-European trade rising sharply.

But as the volume of intra-European trade rose, so did imports and exports for the whole Common Market area, thus belying one of the great fears of countries outside it: that it would operate to restrict external trade as much or more than it freed internal trade. From the beginning the United States—which had long urged measures of unity with little careful thought of their implications—expressed this fear. So did England and other European countries, African countries that did not form a part of the French Community, Latin American countries that were afraid the special privileges of associated states would enable them to supplant Latin America in supplying tropical products to Europe, and even the Communist bloc. All shared the fear, and brought varying diplomatic pressures to bear.

The most important of these was the British-led attempt to form a greater European Free Trade Association. This would eliminate trade barriers betwen its members but, unlike members of the Common Market, each member would keep its own external tariff toward the rest of the world. The European Free Trade Association would, besides, involve far less cooperation in other social and economic fields. Such a free trade area would allow Britain to maintain its special ties to the Commonwealth. But original British thought on the subject was that such a free trade area could include the Common Market as one of its several members, and in 1957 an inter-governmental committee at the ministerial level considered the proposal.

All through 1958 the committee wrestled with the difficult problems involved. In France there was considerable hostility to the whole idea. Many French officials felt that Britain was asking far

too much, that it would get the benefits of Common Market membership while retaining those of its Commonwealth preferential tariffs.
Moreover, as in the Common Market negotiations, the problem of
agriculture was formidable. Each country had protected agriculture
through subsidies in some form or another; it took the Common Market
countries until January 1962 to reach an agreement on how they would
proceed to free agricultural trade of the restrictions earlier imposed.
But from the start, England wanted guarantees that proved unacceptable.

Europeans argued that Britain demanded a one-sided bargain—
benefits without the responsibilities of the Common Market members. At the same time, those who looked to the Common Market as the
basis for a closer political community saw in Britain's bid a formula
that would dilute the supranational aspects of the EEC. The *coup de
grace* to the idea, however, came from one who was opposed to
supranational institutions, de Gaulle.

The collapse of the Fourth Republic was a peculiar one. Never
had France been more prosperous, never had its economy achieved
such a base for a continued dynamism. But persistent governmental
instability overshadowed everything else. France had lost in Indochina and lost out in the Suez war. The government was unable to do
anything about the worsening situation in Algeria. All attempts to steer
a course between Algerian nationalist demands for self-determination
and independence, and French settlers' demands for maintenance of a
French Algeria failed. Four hundred to five hundred thousand troops
in Algeria, mostly withdrawn from the NATO command, could not
decisively defeat the terrorists. The cost mounted and so did opposition within France. But discovery of significant quantities of petroleum
in Algeria—which promised to diminish France's dependence on the
seemingly precarious Middle Eastern supply stiffened French resolution. The government wavered again and again. In May 1958,
de Gaulle's supporters, who for a long time had seen the only solution
to France's instability in elimination of parliamentary supremacy and
the party system, found the army and Algerian settlers ready to act.
The army, in particular, was bitter: it had fought long, hard, and
heroically in Indochina. Government instability, officers felt, had sabo-
taged their effort. The army had gone into Suez; at home a weak government had capitulated and forced it to withdraw. Now it seemed
that the officers' efforts in Algeria were to be undermined. Instead,
they seized power there, and officers in France refused the government's demand to order them to relinquish it. They seized the island

of Corsica, and threatened to land paratroopers on the mainland, demanding that General de Gaulle be invested as Prime Minister.

The Parliament and President bowed, de Gaulle was invested, and given the power to rule for six months without recourse to Parliament and to draw up a new constitution. This document—giving far more powers to the President and drastically curbing those of the Parliament—was completed and submitted to public referendum on September 28. It received a 4 to 1 vote in its favor. The Fourth Republic vanished, and the Fifth—with de Gaulle as its new president—began. Subsequent changes approved by referendum further strengthened the presidency.

How would this affect the French approach to European integration? De Gaulle was known to prefer cooperative ventures among sovereign states and to believe that a resurgent and purified France should have a larger role in the determination of Western policy.

On October 29 de Gaulle's government declared that it *would* proceed with implementation of the Common Market treaty. On November 14 the French cabinet announced that France would *not* agree to link the Common Market with the proposed free trade area. But to cushion the initial shock of the Common Market's moves of January 1, it announced that certain tariff cuts would be extended to other European countries.

Britain and the other European countries now turned to another expedient: in July 1959 the Ministers of Austria, Denmark, Norway, Portugal, Sweden, Switzerland, and Britain agreed to establish the European Free Trade Association. It embodied the original idea of the free trade area, but without the Common Market as a member. Although it promised some economic benefits, most people viewed it as a way of generating greater bargaining strength for purposes of resuming negotiations with the Common Market.

The impetus for bargaining came primarily from the United States. It was concerned with its balance of payments situation—that could be worsened by Common Market discrimination—with the disastrous potentialities of an irrevocable split in Europe between the Six and the Outer Seven, and with the effect on other underdeveloped countries of association of the former French territories. In January 1960, therefore, the United States proposed a series of committees to examine relations between the EEC and EFTA, the question of aid to underdeveloped countries, and suggested reorganizing the old Organization for European Economic Cooperation, originally set up to help carry out the Marshall Plan.

Results were mixed: the OEEC was indeed transformed into a new agency in which the United States and Canada were full members—the Organization for Economic Cooperation and Development (OECD). The new organization would try to see that the various economic communities would operate within an overall framework of Atlantic cooperation, and at the same time coordinate aid and trade policies toward underdeveloped countries. This would serve two purposes. It would help convince a more prosperous Europe to share further the burden of foreign aid with the United States (American foreign aid helped to create the balance of payments problem). At the same time it would bring pressure on the EEC not to discriminate against underdeveloped countries outside the associated states.

But the negotiations between the EEC and EFTA were futile, and as a result Britain made a momentous decision. Despite formation of EFTA, and after years of deliberately staying out of Europe, it applied for membership in the Common Market.

Several factors prompted the decision. Britain's overall trade with the Commonwealth countries had declined as a percentage of her total trade, and Europe had become a more important trading partner (trade with the United States had increased even more). Since de Gaulle had indicated that the new Europe would be a looser-knit political union than previously proposed, it became easier for Britain to conceive of joining it. More than this, however, other economic facts stood out: growth rate within the Common Market was at a far higher level than in the comparatively stagnant British economy (Italy, for example—so long a laggard country—had the highest rate of industrial expansion in the world next to Japan in 1960); Common Market area exports had increased 115 per cent since 1951 while British exports—a matter of life and death to Britain—had increased by only thirty per cent, trade among the Common Market countries was increasing enormously. In the years 1959–60 French imports from the other five members had increased by fifty per cent, exports to them by seventy-nine per cent. The Macmillan government in Britain hoped membership in the Market might provide the stimulus of competition to British industry that it appeared to need so badly.

The British decision involved severe problems: its partners in EFTA might feel they were being left out. But Denmark and Norway joined Britain in making application for membership, and others sought associated status. Commonwealth countries reacted more severely; their trade with Britain might be only a small percentage of overall British trade. (*Total* exports to the Commonwealth constituted forty-two per cent of British exports.) In many cases, however, it was a major percentage of their own trade: ninety per cent of New Zealand's meat and dairy products went to the United Kingdom. At Commonwealth meetings they expressed their concern. The Macmillan government assured them that it would work for an overall low external Common Market tariff, so that they, too, would have access to the growing European market. In this, the English argued, lay the best course.

There was plenty of opposition within Britain too. Old Tories deplored the idea that Britain should join with continental foreigners. Britain was the oldest nation-state; her Parliament, upon which so many others had been modeled, was the oldest functioning one, and Britain had been politically stable for centuries, fortunately isolated from continental conflicts by the Channel and British control of the seas. Labour party leaders argued that Britain's economy suffered because of policies followed by the Conservative government, and that joining the Common Market as a way of dealing with Britain's ills was really a Tory way to evade the problem of internal reform. Nevertheless, Macmillan staked his prestige on the application.

And then, on January 14, 1963, at the same time that he declined to enter into new military arrangements for NATO suggested by the Kennedy Administration, and with superbly contemptuous disregard for the views of other EEC members, de Gaulle vetoed British entry into the Common Market, arguing that it would lead to Anglo-American domination of the area. De Gaulle then moved to strengthen his ties with a somewhat reluctant Germany. Many Germans were suspicious that Britain was too soft on the issues of Berlin and German reunification, and during a recent Anglo-German quarrel over the costs of maintaining British troops in Germany, strong anti-German sentiments were fanned in Britain. German leaders nevertheless preferred having Britain *in* Europe and were reluctant to follow de Gaulle's lead. Nevertheless, aware that de Gaulle could wreck the Common Market, whose overall benefits were becoming apparent, Germany acquiesced, and on January 22 signed a new treaty of friendship and cooperation, subsequently ratified by an uneasy Bundestag.

Britain, left out in the cold, nevertheless indicated that it would probably reapply for membership later. But Macmillan was obviously chagrined.

What lay behind de Gaulle's veto? The answer is complex, but one major factor may be singled out: de Gaulle's long-standing distrust of England and the United States. This stemmed from his reading of history, was reinforced by British and American disregard for French interests as he defined them at the time of the Liberation in 1944, and finally confirmed by recent military developments. Since the latest weapons put the United States directly in the line of attack, he believed the United States would not really use its deterrent power to defend Western Europe unless it were itself attacked. At the time of the Indochina debacle in 1954, the United States had been unwilling to come to the rescue of the French unless the action took on an international character—and Britain was unwilling to lend it such a character. At the time of Suez, the United States had acted forcefully against its own allies. Finally, at the Nassau meeting in December 1962, Britain was virtually forced to abandon its own independent deterrent and accept subordination to the United States (see p. 296). This was not the kind of Britain that de Gaulle wanted in the Europe he envisaged, a Europe independent of the United States, made up of co-operating sovereign states stretching—eventually—from the North Sea to the Urals. While de Gaulle believed that Britain and the United States hindered the achievement of his grand design, he also decided that the developments in the Soviet bloc during this period bore promise of such a future.

The United States had long encouraged European recovery and any form of unity that the Europeans chose. It had been disappointed when the British refused to join the Coal and Steel Community, and disturbed by the exclusive character of the Common Market and the split with the Free Trade Association. The United States found it hard to accept, too, that the resurgent Europe, with which it was now much harder to deal, really represented spectacular success of the earlier American recovery policy. Strengthened Europe required a readjustment of American policies, however, and the new Kennedy administration tried to provide this. The chief move on the economic front was to pass a new Trade Expansion Act which gave the President greater bargaining power than the earlier Reciprocal Trade Acts had done. Equipped with this, the administration hoped that it could persuade the new Europe not to discriminate against American exports, especially agricultural exports. There was much talk of a new "Atlantic Partnership," but it seemed that as long as the distrustful de Gaulle remained in power—and perhaps afterward, too, if he really represented French reaction to the changed relationship of Europe to the United States—that Atlantic Partnership failed to promise much.

The development of the hydrogen bomb and the desire to reduce military expenditures from Korean War levels raised a number of questions concerning military strategy during the first half of the 1950s. The American doctrine of massive retaliation was matched by European acceptance of nuclear arms for NATO. Both of these policies raised more questions than they answered, particularly from 1955 onward, when the Russians and then the United States developed ballistic missiles that could supplant the manned bomber as a means of delivery.

At the time of the Suez crisis Khrushchev's threat to rain rockets on Europe gave Europeans a feeling of enormous vulnerability. Then, during the revolt in Hungary, the West, fearing that direct interference in the Soviet sphere might well result in all-out war, specifically ruled out the use of force to help the rebels. It also became clear at this time, particularly in the light of the fighting in Algeria and radio-stimulated uprising in the Arab lands, that political aggression could take many forms. In referring to the Middle East, Dulles had talked of "indirect aggression," while in Algeria a modern army was pinned down by guerrilla fighters.

Oddly enough, these factors led the British to formulate a new strategy of reliance on massive retaliation and tactical nuclear weapons modelled precisely after the American "New Look," which most commentators felt had been wrong from the outset. A White Paper produced by the Macmillan Government that replaced Eden's after the Suez disaster, proposed an increased reliance on nuclear striking power and a reduction of British conventional forces overseas. The strategy was dictated partly by economic factors and partly by the difficulty of holding overseas bases in the face of nationalist agitation. As a part of the cutback, Britain planned to reduce its forces drastically in Germany, even though it had not consulted with its NATO allies on the matter, and even though Germany had as yet only begun to field its first three divisions.

The strategy was influenced by British advances in thermonuclear weapons (the first British H-bomb was exploded on May 15, 1957), but it was also affected by British reluctance to rely entirely on American deterrence after American opposition during the Suez War. Duncan Sandys, the Defense Minister, put it quite clearly:

We think it is just as well to make certain that an appreciable element of nuclear power shall, in all circumstances, remain on this side of the Atlantic, so that no one shall be tempted to think that a major attack could be made against Western Europe without the risk of nuclear retaliation.

The same questions that had been raised in the United States about the "New Look" were to be raised about the new policy. How would the country now respond to a non-nuclear attack, or an uprising aided by the Soviet bloc? Would the new strategy open the way to a Soviet "nibbling" process? And some people suggested that new weapons developments called for increased efforts at reaching some disarmament agreement with the Soviet Union.

But British military thought expressed in the new policy received something of an endorsement on October 4, 1957, when the Soviets boosted into orbit the first man-made satellite. There had been much fanfare about American preparations, but the Russians not only did it first—in the next few months they lifted larger satellites than the Americans were able to, and they did it when the highly publicized American program produced an ignominious failure before its subsequent successes.

The Soviet success came at a time when the United States, impelled by budgetary considerations, had been cutting back heavily on all research and weapons development programs. At first members of the administration tried to downgrade the importance of the Soviet accomplishment, but the administration soon responded by bringing forth new American crash programs, at considerable more cost and inconvenience than would have been the case had the earlier cutbacks not taken place. More than this, the Soviet "sputnik" revealed Russian superiority in missiles: apparently Khrushchev had not been boasting when he had told the United States that the Soviet Union could strike at it directly with intercontinental missiles.

On this basis the Macmillan Government could argue that now the United States was more directly in the Russian line of fire than before, and therefore that it had been correct to think in terms suggested by the White Paper: Britain needed its own deterrent.

To reassure its allies, the United States offered to station Intermediate Range Ballistic Missiles (named Thor and Jupiter) in Europe, though the warheads would still be under American control. Britain accepted, but other NATO countries showed little enthusiasm, and only Turkey and Italy joined Britain. The argument against the missiles was that there was still no guarantee the United States would actually use them. But more than this, they were liquid-fueled, above-ground missiles, and needed considerable time to fire. In the case of a Soviet attack, they would probably be destroyed before they could be fired. Thus they appeared to add little retaliatory or deterrent capacity; rather they seemed to be missiles that could be used only in a *first* strike, rather than as a response to aggression. They might, therefore, constitute a provocation, a statement to the Soviet Union that the West might—in spite of President Eisenhower's declarations to the contrary—actually *start* a thermonuclear war. And possession of the missiles might bring a country into a line of fire which it might otherwise escape.

Although commentators raised these issues at the time, installation of the weapons was completed and the weapons stayed in place until 1963, when they were finally replaced with weapons that apparently overcame these objections: Polaris missiles fired by submarines while still underwater that would be able to survive a first attack.

The British decision proved to be a mistake. The force of bombers built to carry the weapons became obsolete rapidly. The British in the meanwhile began construction of a missile that would replace the bombers—the Blue Streak—but abandoned it (as too expensive) and came to rely on an American-supplied missile—the "Skybolt"—to be fired from their bombers in flight. Planes that fired the Skybolt while still a thousand miles away from target could presumably escape the modern antiaircraft defenses that had made them obsolete: their useful life would be lengthened. But in 1962 the United States government decided to abandon development of the Skybolt. It was too expensive to make reliable, given the alternatives of the new "family" of intercontinental ballistic missiles and the unforeseen rapidity of development of the submarine-based Polaris. To compensate the British, whose dependence on the United States was thus emphasized, Kennedy suggested to Prime Minister Macmillan (at the December meeting in the Bahamas) establishment of a multinationally manned and controlled seaborne force which the United States would equip with Polaris missiles. It was first thought that the force would be one of nuclear submarines; then it was decided that surface ships equipped with the Polaris would be quicker and cheaper to construct. (The effect of all this upon de Gaulle and Britain's application to the Common Market has already been described.)

The British effort to construct an independent deterrent was thwarted by the speed of change in military technology that had simply outstripped Britain's economic capacity to keep up.

But Britain's example inspired the French. For years they had been constructing reactors for power and experimental purposes. By the late 1950s, these reactors were in a position to produce fissionable products for weapons purposes, and in February 1960 the French tested their first nuclear weapon in the Sahara. Their tests continued despite African and other protests, as de Gaulle determined to build France's own retaliatory force, the "Force de Frappe," based first on high-speed low-level bombers that could escape the radar and anti-aircraft devices devised to cope with the high altitude bombers of the 1950s. In 1963 the French government developed a site in Tahiti, in the South Pacific to test hydrogen bombs.

The French decisions discomfited the United States and others. The French argument that they were only doing what the British had done was met with the retort that times had changed since the early British decisions. But the basic French argument reflected thinking widely held in Europe, and it had also been the basis for the earlier British effort. If the Soviet Union could strike directly at the United States, could Europe really rely on the United States to use its power in defence of Europe—not only now, but in the unforeseeable future? Despite American assurances, Europeans could cite former American Secretary of State Christian Herter's testimony before a Congressional Committee:

> I can't conceive of the President involving us in an all-out nuclear war unless the facts showed clearly that we are in danger of devastation ourselves, or that actual moves have been made toward devastating ourselves.

The Suez war was crucial in reinforcing the NATO allies' view that they might well have interests different from those of the United States, and therefore would need independent means for asserting them. Equally important was a series of accounts written by Dulles and published in *Life* magazine in which he argued that to deter the Communists the United States had had to go to the "brink of war" and threaten the use of its nuclear might. This had been done over the islands of Quemoy and Matsu in the Far East—islands that America presumably defended as essential to the security of Taiwan. The French and others asked whether they were to be devastated by a nuclear war for islands they believed the United States was wrong to defend. If they had their own nuclear deterrent they could threaten retaliation themselves. And if the American deterrent were not based on their soil, where the enemy would have to destroy it, they might escape the disastrous consequences of American folly.

Once de Gaulle was in power he suggested that NATO be revised. He envisaged leadership by a triumvirate of Britain, France, and the United States, all acting as equals. But American authorities balked, fearing that such a move would mean sharing control over atomic weapons. De Gaulle therefore determined that only greater independence would serve his purposes.

This view was reinforced by events in late 1962, when American cancellation of the Skybolt—for budgetary reasons—changed British plans, and when the United States almost came to war with the Soviet Union over Cuba (Ch. 9) without consulting its allies. With the end of the Algerian war in March 1962 and withdrawal of French forces from Algeria, de Gaulle made no move to replace the forces which had been withdrawn from the NATO command, and in 1963 even removed most of his Channel and Atlantic naval units from the NATO lineup.

There had been many attempts to devise NATO formulas that would satisfy European demands. When President Kennedy replaced Eisenhower, he increased America's conventional forces. The move was a response to the criticism that New Look policies of equipping ground troops with nuclear weapons had put the West into a difficult position: it would either have to respond with nuclear war to a non-nuclear situation—and thereby face total annihilation—or would fail to respond at all. With stronger conventional forces, the West could make the Soviets pause while the consequences of pushing war further became clearer, and the mutual desire to avoid annihilation would come into play. There had also been various suggestions to build a multilateral NATO nuclear force—NATO Commander General Norstad had proposed a NATO intermediate range ballistic missile force in 1959, and Secretary of State Herter had endorsed a modified proposal for a Polaris force the next year. Then in 1962 President Kennedy adopted the idea in his discussions with Macmillan and tried to convince European allies of its validity.

The "multilateral force" (MLF) or "mixed-manned fleet" idea never satisfied anyone, and by late 1964 it became the center of a NATO crisis. The idea was an attempt to compensate the British for the Skybolt cancellation, but it was also based on the long-run consideration that the fleet would avoid proliferation of national nuclear forces. Germany, in particular, might eventually want more direct participation in its own defense, and the fleet would be a way to avoid the world crisis that would surely be precipitated by a German demand for nuclear weapons. Yet in all discussions of the concept one thing seemed clear: the United States would still have a veto on the use of the weapons supplied to the fleet. Behind the American agonizing lay a terrible dilemma. So far the Russians had not shared nuclear weapons with anyone, nor did they seem to want to; yet the NATO allies threatened to go their own nuclear way if the United States did not share. The MLF was an attempt to find a way out.

But de Gaulle would not tolerate the idea. In late 1964, after his return from a tour of South America, he mounted an offensive against MLF and produced a crisis in Franco-German relations by virtually forcing a hapless German government to choose between cooperation embodied in the Franco-German treaty of 1963, or cooperation with the United States—in which case a united Europe might come apart.

The result of all this was continued confusion about NATO strategy. By late 1964, MLF was still in effect only a project for discussion. Heavy financial pressures had still not swayed de Gaulle from having his own deterrent force.

Meanwhile the Kennedy administration had rejected the possibility of "limited atomic war"—war that involved small-scale nuclear weapons that would only be used against battlefield targets—and evolved a new policy of limited strategic atomic war. This would use large-scale atomic weapons against strategic targets, but instead of aiming at population centers—as massive retaliation would have done—would only aim at military targets. The strategy rested on the same argument that supported earlier concepts of limited atomic war: in order to avoid mutual annihilation, both sides would have a common interest in keeping any war limited. Kennedy had rejected as unfeasible the idea of massive retaliation only to find that the alternative—a build-up of conventional forces—was enormously expensive. The "counter force" strategy was a new attempt to find a deterrent that would avoid the dilemma. The United States would threaten to destroy only military targets in the Soviet Union if the Soviets initiated large-scale conventional attack; it would thus destroy most of Russia's capacity to strike directly at the United States. Yet by sparing Russian cities, while still retaining the capacity to strike at them if Russia aimed at American cities, the Soviet Union would be deterred from using its remaining atomic power against American cities.

If the Soviet Union hardened its own missile sites sufficiently, however, a United States strike could not destroy them, and the strategy would be put in doubt. By 1964 this seemed probable; moreover the Russians were developing Polaris-type missiles that would also escape destruction in the event of a first American strike. In addition many people rejected the workability of this or any other "limited atomic war" strategy. They felt that if atomic weapons were used, the passions of the moment would ensure an all-out war. In order to guard against the possibility of unwanted escalation of conflict, the United States persuaded the Soviet Union to sign an agreement in early 1963 to set up a direct teletype wire linking Moscow and Washington; if war started by accident—and this would be an increasing possibility if there were proliferation of nuclear weapons and therefore more fingers were on the button—rapid communication could be established between the two capitals to call the whole thing off. The "hot-line" could perhaps also be used if a smaller incident that provoked greater mutual military responses threatened to get out of hand. It was the first success in the long and difficult round of disarmament discussions that seemed to have started afresh in Geneva in 1955, and to which we may now briefly turn.

Disarmament: 1957–1964

From the demise of the Baruch Plan in 1947, disarmament discussions had been wearying sessions, consisting mainly of one propaganda gambit after another. During the Communist charges of germ warfare in Korea, they hardly seemed worthwhile carrying on. Nevertheless, the weapons existed and were getting bigger and better. Once the Soviet Union and the United States had hydrogen weapons and the means of delivery, people began to worry about the spread of nuclear weapons to other countries. England exploded its first atomic bomb in 1952 and planned to build hydrogen bombs. France had an atomic program under way that could lead to atomic bomb production. Other industrialized countries had the capacity to produce the weapons, and although the means of delivery built by the United States and the Soviet Union were immensely costly, sophisticated, and beyond the means of any other single country, there were easier ways of using the weapons, especially against local enemies. In the early 1960s Egypt —with the help of German technicians—began to produce 250-mile range missiles, even though it did not yet have atomic warheads for them. And it was always possible that one of the major powers might give away rockets or atomic warheads. If the United States equipped NATO or its NATO allies with such weapons, why should the Soviet Union restrain itself?

Thus, the thermonuclear age—whose arrival appeared to have been recognized by the participants of the 1955 Geneva Conference—gave a new impetus to disarmament negotiations. The Geneva Open Skies proposal, moreover, indicated that the search for solutions might broaden to include means to prevent surprise attack or keep a small war from "escalating" into a larger one. In the following years there was much discussion about what came to be called "arms control"—

methods of providing some measure of stability that did not necessarily involve actual reduction of arms.

There were several broad assumptions behind the new initiatives. One was that arms races are symptoms of existing conflict; although they are not in themselves the cause of war, they may make the conflict worse. As each side tries to outstrip the other, it is tempted to strike while it has the advantage; small wars may escalate into big wars; each side may miscalculate the ends or motives of the other power and respond in too harsh a manner, thereby provoking the other side to respond equally. The various strategies adopted by NATO could be seen as attempts to bring a measure of stability to an unstable international situation in which a basic conflict existed. But given the destructiveness of the new weapons and the possibilities of escalation that neither side would want, it seemed that the military strategies adopted were not sufficient. More was required for stability

There were almost as many suggestions as there were people concerned. In Europe especially, many people argued for unilateral disarmament by the West. Some thought that the Soviet Union would be unable to use its great military force under modern circumstances. Others thought that the nature of modern weapons—that they were essentially agents of mass destruction—had strengthened the moral argument for pacifism. Wars in the past were bad enough, but now the distinction—such as it was—between combatant and noncombatant had disappeared and all civilization was threatened. For some, passive resistance was the answer. Others believed the Russians probably acted as much out of fear as we did, and that removal of the Western nuclear threat would in fact eliminate the conflict.

In England the various groups calling for unilateral disarmament moves grew rapidly (some, however, asked for unilateral disarmament not by the West as a whole, but only by England: they hoped that other states might then be impelled to follow the British lead). But no government in the West accepted the unilateral argument. Small states like Sweden and Switzerland continued their traditional neutrality, but maintained it in a state of military preparedness—and both considered adopting nuclear arms.

On the other hand, in the late 1950s there was serious discussion of the idea of "disengagement." Suggested by George F. Kennan, the author of the "containment" doctrine, in a lecture series in England, a concrete proposal was actually put forward by Poland as the "Rapacki Plan" in February, 1958.

The Rapacki Plan and other similar ideas suggested simply that the major powers should withdraw their forces from a certain area where they currently faced each other. Many of them called for withdrawal from East and West Germany, Poland, and Czechoslovakia. The Rapacki Plan itself was more limited, calling for establishment of an atom-free zone embracing these countries.

One feature was very attractive. Many felt that the Hungarian uprising had taught the Soviet leaders that the satellite states were a liability; disengagement might therefore be a way for the Soviet Union to withdraw from them on the basis of compensating moves by the West.

All such proposals met with the usual suspicion. NATO military leaders argued that withdrawal of American forces from the area would leave them no other place to go whereas the Russians would withdraw only a short distance and could easily surge forward. An atom-free zone would disrupt the whole forward strategy designed to actually protect Germany with tactical atomic weapons. Arguments that possession of atomic weapons in reserve would guarantee that neither side would try to reoccupy the evacuated area were met with others that no one would dare use the weapons. In the end, nothing came of the idea of disengagement in central Europe except suggestions for atom-free zones in other parts of the world—the Middle East or Africa.

Discussions of disarmament measures at the government level assumed a more serious tone in 1955, even before President Eisenhower announced his spectacular Open Skies plan. The French and British had advanced a new set of comprehensive proposals. On May 10, 1955, the Soviets issued a new statement that went far toward meeting the French and British views approved by the Americans. Harold Stassen had been appointed as President Eisenhower's Disarmament Assistant —a new post that showed the new emphasis the President had come to place on disarmament. All these events pointed to possible progress, particularly when the Geneva heads of state meeting appeared to have generated good feeling, even though it settled no political issues.

Several aspects of the various plans gave evidence of a new approach. The Soviets no longer demanded immediate prohibition of all nuclear weapons, or percentage cuts in manpower, and they no longer rejected control in the early stages of disarmament—and Stassen's reaction was to reserve all previous American positions. In other words, the United States now admitted that its previous plans—to which the new Soviet proposals closely corresponded—no longer conformed to American strategy or the facts of atomic life. It was now impossible, for example, completely to verify if stockpiles had been destroyed. The United States therefore moved in other directions, towards plans to build confidence. It suggested cutting off arms production, and proposed that all future fissionable material be channeled into an international agency that would use it for peaceful purposes under the Eisenhower Atoms-for-Peace Plan. Stassen also stressed rapid communications in order to prevent surprise attack. The Soviets agreed to ground inspection and control-posts, but insisted on force-levels below the ones that the United States, with its commitments abroad, would accept.

At this stage, in early 1957, after the Hungarian uprising and the Suez war (with the Russian threat of missiles against France and England), people felt negotiations might really result in some agreement: the dangers had been so great, and all sides *seemed* ready for agreement. The disengagement proposals had been made, and it appeared that early warning systems and progressive stages of control and inspection along with production cut-offs and the end of nuclear testing were possible.

But the whole effort blew up in mid-1957. American allies were alarmed. The British and French wanted a ban on testing and nuclear development only if the United States shared its technical knowledge more than current legislation permitted. The President's military advisers, members of the Atomic Energy Committee and Secretary of State Dulles were alarmed; the United States had almost signed an agreement which they felt contained loopholes, and Stassen was virtually replaced by Dulles as the chief negotiator. A stiffer "package plan" was prepared and presented to the Russians, and negotiations broke down. Then, on October 4, the Russians put their first artificial satellite into orbit around the earth, and the whole tone of the discussions degenerated into propaganda. Khrushchev was eager to transform his prestige and propaganda victory—which implied Soviet rocket superiority—into political victories; the United States, which had cut back on many military programs during the summer, wanted to "catch up."

Yet the earlier pressures were still there: fear of where the arms race might lead, of accident, economic pressures, or fear of the spread of weapons. Moreover, the widened interest in arms agreement during the brief period when possible agreement had seemed near (1955–57) stimulated the concern of scientists and others who believed the disarmament problem had never been treated carefully in terms of its implications; rather it had been seized as a wonderful opportunity for propaganda. Nothing was easier than to load an attractive proposal with one or more small features that would make it unacceptable to the other side; meanwhile it was possible to pose as a generous and plausible savior of mankind.

The new interest led to a spate of books and articles concentrating on arms control measures of various sorts. Negotiations, however, came to center on just one kind—a cessation of nuclear tests.

In the 1956 presidential campaign, Democratic candidate Adlai Stevenson proposed that the United States stop testing hydrogen bombs. He was promptly called soft on Communism and eager to weaken the United States. However, the administration had itself been considering such a proposal, particularly since the uncertain effects of radioactive fallout were receiving worldwide publicity, and demands to cease testing were heard from various quarters. Although the Soviets were involved in a large-scale testing program, Communists throughout the world echoed the call for cessation. The Soviets had suggested it in their May 10, 1955 proposal, and they widely publicized the Western tests. Cessation would also work against the British and French efforts to develop their own nuclear arsenals.

In mid-1957 the Soviets proposed a test ban with control posts to verify compliance, and accepted the idea of a two or three year ban rather than complete cessation. But the United States position was that the parts of the American "package plan" could not be treated separately. This meant no discussions could be carried on to see whether agreement was possible on the hard questions of manning the control posts, how many and where they would be, what would constitute inspection, and so on. In 1958, however, when other agreements seemed impossible and pressure for a test ban had mounted, a remarkable meeting of scientists and technicians from both sides reached agreement on criteria for an inspected test ban agreement. President Eisenhower voluntarily suspended all nuclear tests for one year; so did Britain; the Soviet Union, after rushing through a series of tests, then followed suit. When talks began at the end of October 1958, the United States agreed to negotiate a test ban separately from other disarmament measures. It looked as though the long road of disarmament failures might be coming to an end. A test ban would be a partial step. But it would have immediate benefits in the cessation of radioactive fallout and, if it generated more confidence, might lead to further measures.

There were many who questioned its value. But more important, early in 1959 the United States introduced new data that showed that the 1958 criteria would have to be modified. New techniques of testing underground in large holes had been developed which could "muffle" explosions and make them harder to detect. A larger number of control posts and inspections than had been agreed on was now necessary. In the United States, those who argued that any agreement reached with the Russians was a bad agreement, claimed that under the new circumstances hidden testing could "tip the balance of power." (When the testing moratorium was broken two years later, the United States at first carried out underground tests, but soon returned to atmospheric tests because the expensive underground techniques did not yield enough new data. Thus those who believed in 1959 that the strong American position on underground tests was something of a red herring were apparently justified.)

The Russians at first refused to consider the new material; negotiations stretched on and reached the stage where a partial test ban was considered. This would prohibit all but very small explosions, and research on means of detecting them would continue. But in 1960 even this hope faded as political events throughout the world dragged negotiations back to the level of political propaganda. The propaganda effort was initiated by Premier Khrushchev during his spectacular visit to the United States in late 1959. At the United Nations General Assembly he called for complete general disarmament, down to police levels. Western officials were pondering the vague and general proposal when suddenly, in May 1960, the lid blew off.

The United States had finally consented to a summit conference. It met in Paris—Khrushchev, Macmillan, Eisenhower, and de Gaulle attending—a few days after the Russians announced they had shot down an American U-2 spy plane that was flying across Russia from a base in Pakistan to Norway. The United States government proved embarrassingly unable to cope with the revelation. At first it denied the flight, then admitted it. U-2 planes of the type shot down had been carrying out aerial surveillance of the Soviet Union since 1956. The Soviet Premier could have chosen to accept President Eisenhower's statement that such flights would be discontinued. Instead, he arrived in Paris, delivered a blistering attack, demanded a personal apology, and declared that negotiations with the United States were meaningless until the fall elections had replaced its moribund leadership.

The reasons for the failure of the summit meeting and Khrushchev's blow-up are still subject to conjecture. The Soviet Premier chose to claim that the spy flights had put him in a difficult position. In the Geneva Conference and in his trip to the United States he had staked his position on a friendship with Eisenhower; against opposition within the Soviet bloc he had argued for peaceful coexistence and come close to accepting Western disarmament proposals. In 1958 he had raised the issue of changing the status of Berlin (see pp. 309–313), yet he had taken no decisive action. Now, in the arms field, the West had responded to his overtures by placing intermediate range ballistic missiles in Europe and flying across the Soviet Union in an extraordinarily provocative way. In addition to the U-2 incident, Khrushchev made propaganda capital out of Soviet destruction of an American RB-47 bomber shot down over the Barents Sea; he claimed that it had violated Soviet air space. The United States answered that it had been thirty miles out over the ocean and that Soviet fighter planes, having failed to force it over the Soviet Union, had shot it down. Whichever story was true, the worried British warned the United States that they wanted prior notification of such flights. To send this type of plane within even thirty miles of the Soviet Union seemed provocative and a courting of disaster in a period when retaliation times were becoming shorter and shorter. And Khrushchev, who had invited Eisenhower to visit the Soviet Union, coldly told him he had better "postpone" his visit.

On February 13, 1960, de Gaulle's government exploded its first atomic bomb in the Sahara. Other explosions followed later in the year, and de Gaulle pushed his plan to build France's own *Force de Frappe* through a reluctant Parliament. In November the United States launched the first submarine armed with Polaris missiles and negotiated an agreement with Britain to use Holy Loch, in Scotland, as a base for a submarine tender for the new Polaris submarines thus provoking new British disarmament demonstrations.

The world situation looked grim. There was a new crisis in Cuba (see p. 333), Japanese demonstrations forced President Eisenhower to call off a scheduled visit to that supposedly reliable ally in the Far East, revolts broke out against old governments in Turkey and Korea, in Europe there was a break between the Common Market and Outer Seven, and the Congo crisis was straining the United Nations. Under these circumstances, what could be expected of Soviet policy?

The answer came in 1961: Khrushchev told the West he felt it would be wise to abandon test-ban talks that were separate from discussions of complete general disarmament. The Russians pointed to continued French testing, claimed that America was preparing to resume tests too, and announced that the moratorium was over. In the fall they embarked on a series of tests that included the largest yet—explosion on October 30 of a weapon equivalent to 50 to 60 million tons of TNT.

All attempts to reach any kind of disarmament agreement, including a test ban treaty, seemed at a dead end. Yet in mid-1963 the situation changed again. Research on detection of underground tests, initiated when the United States changed its mind about inspection requirements, produced more sensitive detecting instruments as well as new information about the nature of earthquakes. The Kennedy administration also seemed to accept that all the talk about underground explosions was primarily theoretical. In 1958 the Americans had thought that every suspicious tremor ought to be subject to inspection; the American draft treaty of August 1961 asked for twelve to twenty on-site inspections. By mid-1963 the number had been lowered to seven, and at the beginning of 1963 the Russians, for the first time in several years, agreed to the principle of on-site inspections, although they argued that three a year should be sufficient. And under present, improved, knowledge, such a number meant that exploding a very small nuclear weapon underground would be courting exposure.

Suddenly, in mid-July, shortly after the Cuban missile crisis (see pp. 340–344), the deadlock broke. Averell Harriman, former American Ambassador to the Soviet Union, and English Viscount Hailsham flew to Moscow. On July 25 they signed a partial test ban treaty—something the Soviets had earlier opposed—that would eliminate tests in the atmosphere, the oceans, and in outer space. By this means, the parties avoided the whole question of inspection: such tests are detectable. (Prior to ratification, the Kennedy Administration proved its "toughness" by conducting a series of underground tests.) De Gaulle served notice that he would not sign, and Communist China denounced the treaty. Signature by the East German regime caused the West Germans to hesitate, seeing in the maneuver a further effort on the part of the Russians to render respectable the East German puppet government. Nevertheless, the ban brought some hope. Perhaps the endless cycle of more and bigger bombs—apparently far beyond the needs of national security—might be brought to a halt. Although the United States Senate paid attention to the views of scientist Edward Teller—"father of the H-bomb"—who argued that tests in the atmosphere were necessary to perfect an anti-missile missile, they ratified the treaty. With installation of the "hot-line" teletype between the Kremlin and the White House, two halting first steps of open, agreed arms-control measures had finally been taken.

The Eighteenth General Assembly of the United Nations adopted a resolution banning emplacement of nuclear and thermonuclear weapons in outer space. In early 1964 the Johnson Administration in the United States and Khrushchev both announced a mutual cutback in production of fissionable materials, suitable for bomb production.

Communist Foreign Policies After 1956

Communist foreign policies were only partly responsible for the differences among Western countries revealed so violently at the time of the Suez war and never fully bridged thereafter. Significantly, the gaps between Communist countries revealed at the time of the Hungarian uprising also widened, and the story of Communist foreign policies in subsequent years is primarily one of growing differences between members of the bloc, and how these affected policies toward the rest of the world. The original break—between the Soviet Union and Tito's Yugoslavia—developed into a breach between the Soviet Union, on one hand, and Poland and Hungary, on the other. At that time, Communist China helped to bring the bloc members back into line. But the period from 1957 to the present is one in which China and Russia split on numerous issues and competed for the allegiance of other bloc members and Communist parties abroad.

The first part of this period—roughly from the beginning of 1957 to the abortive Paris Summit Conference of May 1960—saw Khrushchev struggling to maintain his hold over the world Communist system when it was badly shaken by events in East Europe. His policy since the fall of Malenkov was to seek some sort of détente with the West while energetically establishing good relations with the national bourgeoisie of new countries. This general approach had also led him to the rapprochement with Tito. Coming at a time when a return to emphasis on heavy industry had encouraged Stalinists in countries like Hungary and Poland, yet at the same time that Khrushchev's attack on Stalin at the Twentieth Party Congress was widely known, the resultant tensions had led to revolt in Poland and Hungary. Khrushchev's policies had led to trouble; he had to justify his position or face the possibility of being overthrown.

At home, Khrushchev's capacity for infighting served him well: in the early months of 1957, by alliances with one faction, he disposed of one set of possible rivals—labeled as the Anti-Party Group—and then, in the same manner as Stalin earlier, disposed of his allies. "Collective leadership"—supposedly correcting the "cult of the individual," that is, excessive adulation of a Stalin who wielded absolute power—now existed in name only. Khrushchev had triumphed. In the meantime, he gained a great propaganda victory by launching the first "sputnik" in October.

With this and the elimination of internal rivals, Khrushchev was well prepared in November for the fortieth anniversary celebration of the

October Revolution, and he used it to reassert the need for unity of the whole Communist movement. The Chinese delegation supported him, urging others—especially Wladyslaw Gomulka, ruler of Poland—to acknowledge Soviet leadership. But no one could persuade Yugoslavia. In the next year, relations between Yugoslavia and the Soviet Union further deteriorated as Khrushchev continued his campaign to secure his position. The new Draft Program of the Yugoslav party declared that the cause of the danger of war was the existence of the two power blocs rather than simply the policies of the capitalist bloc. This particular point and others in the program were evidence of the extent to which the Yugoslavs had set themselves to compete with the Soviet Union for influence among the neutral states. Publication of the program brought denunciation from Russia, China, and satellite states: Bulgaria and Albania renewed their claims over Yugoslav border areas.

But relations with the West with one exception, the issue of Berlin —were conducted on a plane of more cordiality than had ever existed before. Disarmament discussions showed signs of progress; in 1959 Khrushchev visited the United States in a circus-like atmosphere; the program of cultural exchange was expanded. Popular acclaim for a young American pianist, Van Cliburn, in the Soviet Union when he won the international Tchaikovsky competition, was matched only by the ovation given to the spectacular Moiseyev dancers in the United States. Khrushchev continued to make much of the view that nuclear war was something to be avoided at all costs, and something that *could* be avoided now: the new weapons had brought the era of peaceful coexistence.

There were some developments in which Khrushchev could not resist getting actively involved. One was the Syrian crisis of 1957, and another the Lebanon and Jordan adventure of 1958, when he suggested a summit meeting and then retracted his call, meanwhile interfering with matters at the United Nations. And finally, in late 1958, when the East German regime seemed to be in good shape, he initiated the Berlin crisis.

In a speech delivered on November 10, 1958 and in notes delivered two weeks later, Khrushchev suggested that the time had come to end the four-power status of Berlin—a status left over from Allied occupation of Germany. He proposed either that the city be united and absorbed into East Germany or else, since he did not think that the first proposal would be acceptable, that the three western sectors be established as a separate "free city"—neutralized, disarmed and barred from carrying on subversive activities against its neighbors.

From the time of the end of the Berlin Blockade of 1948, West Berlin had been integrated more and more into the economy and polity of West Germany, which gave it special subsidies. It had become a thriving, booming, and colorful city—and a thorn in the side of drab East Germany surrounding it. It provided an escape route for the continued flow of refugees who wanted to leave behind the economic hardships of the East, and its radio and television stations constantly interfered with Communist attempts to isolate their people from the West. All of this would cease under Khrushchev's plan. He gave the West six months to negotiate a solution. At the end of this time he would turn over all Allied rights to East Germany, which would then control the roads, rail lines, canals and airlanes leading to the city. One thing was certain: an airlift of the 1948 variety would not keep the city alive. Its total imports and exports were ten times what they had been in that drab era of post-war impoverishment.

But, though the allies met to discuss the situation and issued statements of unity to cover a typical situation of disagreement, nothing happened. (It was a time when uncertainty about de Gaulle, the Common Market, and the Free Trade Association made agreement about anything difficult.) The allies rejected the Soviet proposal and talked about reinforcing their military strength. Yet President Eisenhower rejected the possibility of using force to fight through to Berlin if the East Germans imposed a blockade. In early 1959 Soviet Deputy-Premier Mikoyan made a goodwill tour of the United States. He denied that the six-months period had been a time limit or ultimatum, and thereby reopened the possibilities of negotiation: the Western powers had said nothing could be done under the shadow of an ultimatum. Instead, the Soviets asked for a summit conference to deal with all major international differences.

Prime Minister Macmillan favored it; de Gaulle and Eisenhower felt it would serve no useful purpose unless a lower-level meeting of ministers indicated the possibility of genuine agreement; and Adenauer feared it at this time, thinking that the British were far too willing to barter away German demands for unity under free elections, and that de Gaulle was too ready to settle for the Oder-Neisse line as the eastern boundary of Germany. As a result, the four agreed with the Soviets to a Foreign Ministers conference to meet during the summer. It met and accomplished nothing, but recessed in a spirit of optimism at the news that Khrushchev was to visit the United States in September.

While in the United States, the Soviet Premier dispelled any notion of a renewed ultimatum on Berlin, and seemed anxious to avoid any difficulty that might prevent the summit conference he wanted. The spirit of goodwill engendered by the tour and the meeting with the President at Camp David, made the Russians appear ready for genuine negotiation on disarmament. Although Khrushchev then went before the General Assembly to call for general complete disarmament within four years (a demand which many people interpreted as a return to propaganda), some observers noted that the Soviet proposal included references to a comprehensive system of control to be achieved by stages, and to aerial observation and photography—a form of control the Soviets had resisted until now.

Then at the beginning of 1960 the peripatetic Soviet leader took a second trip to South and Southeast Asia, where he visited India and Indonesia, making promises of economic aid. While in Indonesia he also announced the opening of Friendship University in Moscow—an institute specially designed for the training of personnel from the underdeveloped countries. (The university was subsequently renamed Patrice Lumumba University.) In part the trip may have been an effort to counter the good impression created by President Eisenhower on his own Asian trip in December 1959, when he drew enormous and enthusiastic crowds. In any event, Khrushchev's visit led to large aid commitments to India and Indonesia: total Soviet credits to help India fulfill its third five year plan amounted to $500 million in rubles.

There were rumblings: during the months preceding the summit conference Khrushchev returned again and again to the theme that Russia must sign a peace treaty with East Germany. This would eliminate all allied rights in Berlin which would have to be renegotiated with East Germany. Yet Westerners who saw a pattern of conciliation in the Soviet Premier's moves could argue that he really *did* believe that if the Berlin issue were resolved on his terms, peaceful relations between the Communist sphere and the Western sphere would be even more likely: a Berlin settlement would signify acceptance on both sides of a common dividing line. But then came the revelation of the American U-2 spy plane, and the angry blowup by Khrushchev at the 1960 Paris conference. This was followed by Soviet threats to launch rockets at countries who permitted such planes to use their bases, a disruption of disarmament negotiations with the statement that the United Nations General Assembly was the place to resume them, the RB-47 incident, and a series of harassing incidents along the approaches to Berlin. In the fall of 1960 Khrushchev spurred attendance of heads of state at the United Nations General Assembly, and here, before representatives of the new states, he launched into a tirade against imperialism and colonialism. Here, too, he produced the plan—designed to appeal to these states—of replacing the Secretary General with a three-man committee, or "troika," and justified Soviet intervention in the Congo as a response to imperialist intervention through the mechanism of the United Nations. Khrushchev also suggested that neutral states now participate along with the major powers in disarmament negotiations, and agreed with neutralist leaders that there should be a summit conference with whatever new American president replaced Eisenhower. Publicly, he embraced and cultivated a young head of state, Fidel Castro of Cuba, who, during the course of the year had defied the United States and turned to the Soviet bloc for help.

In 1961 relations continued to be bad. There was a series of crises; but none were pushed to the point of no return, so that many people found it possible to ascribe continued caution to Khrushchev. Perhaps the most serious was the situation in Laos, where the truce broke down among three factions: the more-or-less pro-Western royalists, neutralists under Souvanna Phouma, and Pathet Lao Communist forces aided by North Vietnam. The tiny land-locked kingdom with its rugged jungle terrain and long, poorly defined borders became the scene of fighting in which the Pathet Lao maintained a consistent upper hand against troops apparently uninterested in the struggle. The Soviet Union intervened directly by airlifting supplies and military equipment to the Pathet Lao troops; once again, people found it possible to interpret this as a reaction to American policy. In 1959 the United States had tried to build up the right-wing forces so that they could decisively defeat and drive out the Pathet Lao, and steer Laos away from the precariously balanced neutralism established at Geneva in 1954. But it had failed miserably. All the aid had not made the right wing popular: its best troops defected and objected to the proposed course. Yet the United States was unwilling to intervene decisively itself. The Kennedy administration tried to salvage something by agreeing once more to a neutralist Laos, and the Soviet Union again assumed what appeared to be a reasonable position. Its representatives met with the Western and neutral states at Geneva during the summer of 1961 to reach a solution to the Laotion situation. Here they agreed on a neutralist coalition government and—during negotiations that dragged on through 1962—persuaded Laotian leaders to form one. Foreign troops were to be withdrawn, except for a few French military instructors.

An uneasy peace was established, after the curious spectacle of the United States cutting off aid to its right wing allies in order to force them into a coalition with neutralists and Communists.

Then, in 1961, with more Soviet rocket successes behind him, Khrushchev finally solved the Berlin question, at least to his temporary satisfaction. When he first raised the issue, East Germany was in good shape, and it appeared to be a question of moving from strength to eradicate what was an annoying anachronism to the East Germans. But in 1961 East Germany's economic situation deteriorated badly. At Vienna, at a meeting with President Kennedy, Khrushchev renewed his demand for a solution to the Berlin question. He became more and more insistent in ensuing weeks. With this threat in the air, the flow of refugees to West Berlin began to swell: among them were many of the technicians, doctors, and other professional men most needed by the East German regime. In July Khrushchev informed Western powers that a proposal he had made the previous year to cut Soviet armed forces by one-third would have to be rescinded in the light of the ominous world situation. President Kennedy responded by asking for increased military appropriations and draft calls; then, on August 13, came the long-awaited Soviet move—but it was not the one expected. The Soviets simply closed the border between East and West Berlin to any traffic by erecting a wall across the city and, as the months went by, greatly strengthened "The Wall."

It was a shocking move, dividing families, people from their place of work, friend from friend. It was, in its way, a confession of failure, too. Yet it left West Berlin intact, as well as the route to it.

Kennedy responded by sending a small, extra combat force to Berlin, and by sending Vice-President Lyndon Johnson and then General Clay—of Berlin airlift fame—as his personal representatives. There were intense protests and solemn resolves that the Wall must come down. But the West was not ready to risk war for freedom of movement between East and West Berlin, and attempts to knock down the Wall could have resulted in death and little else. The Wall stood.

To add to the tension provoked by the Wall, Khrushchev abandoned the nuclear test moratorium that had prevailed for three years. The West tried to gain a propaganda advantage by stressing that it was Khrushchev who had first resumed testing; he responded by pointing out that the French had never adhered to the moratorium and had gone on testing, and argued that the United States was preparing to resume tests. Moreover, the original moratorium had lasted only a year, at the end of which President Eisenhower had declared that since no test ban had been signed, the United States would feel free to renew testing. During the next few weeks the Soviets conducted over forty atmospheric tests, including the largest ever carried out. In response, the United States began with small, underground tests that produced no fallout: it was true that the Atomic Energy Commission, certain military men, and numerous Congressmen had urged resumption. In mid-1962 the United States resumed atmospheric testing.

Although 1962 was marked by continued conversations, harassment, charges and countercharges on Berlin, Soviet propaganda about its continued space triumphs, and expressions of genuine Soviet concern about the emergence of the Common Market, there was nothing new in Soviet foreign policy until late in the year. The event was as explosive as any during the postwar period—the shipment of Soviet rockets to Cuba.

A more or less rational response to Khrushchev's policy moves required some explanation of what he actually wanted and intended to do. But it was difficult to account for the shift from the relatively peaceful period following the Hungarian crisis—marred by the Berlin demand on which, however, Khrushchev temporized—to Russian militancy after the blow-up of the Paris summit conference of early 1960, following upon the U-2 incident. President Kennedy obviously hoped that Paris, the RB-47 incident, the attack on the United Nations, Soviet intervention in the Congo, and aid to Castro might be only isolated instances of Russian troublemaking. When he went to meet Khrushchev in Vienna early in his term of office, he hoped to explore ways of bringing about a genuine détente. But he came away depressed. The incidents could not be explained away as temptations the Soviet Premier could not resist; there seemed to be more fundamental causes. In later months came the Laotian intervention, the Berlin Wall, and resumption of nuclear tests with the much publicized 50-megaton blast.

Many analysts found an explanation in the development of conflict within the Communist bloc between China and the Soviet Union, and in Khrushchev's resultant need to show that he was still the militant leader of the entire bloc.

The Chinese-Russian Break

In 1954 China became a member of the world community at Geneva, and in 1955 received the approbation of large numbers of the leaders of new states at Bandung. It was just before this, in late 1954, when they were relieved of the burden of both aid to North Korea and aid to the Vietminh in Indochina that Chinese Communist leaders turned their attention to consolidating their hold over all of China; they proposed to "liberate" the island of Taiwan, held now by what was generally referred to as "the gangster Chiang Kai-shek clique."

But in bombarding the tiny Nationalist islands lying immediately offshore, they provoked the United States into action. The Eisenhower administration took a dual initiative: it forced Chiang to evacuate the Tachen islands far to the north, and it obtained an overwhelming vote from Congress for a resolution empowering the President to defend Formosa. Although the resolution did not mention the island groups of Quemoy and Matsu, close to the mainland shore, the administration spelled out its position: if it considered that an attack on these was a prelude to an attack on Formosa itself, it would come to their defense. Tension grew in the light of this uncertain commitment and of Chiang's proclaimed aim to liberate the mainland. But at the time that Chou En lai went to charm his new neutral friends at Bandung he offered to negotiate the matter with the United States—and the United States, after some fumbling, agreed to talk. The crisis was temporarily over although the Communist Chinese claim remained. Many states that accepted China's claim to Taiwan felt that the United States had in fact intervened in what was essentially a domestic civil war.

In 1955 Communist strategy still seemed well-coordinated. Yet the kind of problems that led to the Polish and Hungarian uprising were already present beneath the surface of smooth bloc relations. Even Stalin, who dictated to other Communist parties as effectively as he had to the Soviet Union, had not been able to dictate to the Chinese, who followed their own path to power. Khrushchev was even less able to control them. In 1956 and 1957 the Chinese, although they disapproved of Khrushchev's secret anti-Stalin speech at the Twentieth Party Congress, played a leading role in supporting Khrushchev's attempt to bring Eastern European parties back together.

Significantly, the Moscow November 1957 meeting at which the Yugoslavs refused to sign a manifesto of unity was a meeting of parties; it appeared that the Chinese were already concerned that meetings of the Communist Party of the Soviet Union alone should not be the occasion for launching any more new ventures—like Khrushchev's de-Stalinization campaign. Equality among parties ought to be the basis for Communist unity. The Communist Party of the Soviet Union had always claimed primacy in Stalin's time since it was the sole Communist party in power and provided the base of operations for all others. This was no longer true, and leadership, the Chinese felt, must be exerted on the basis of consultation. In 1956, Togliatti of the Italian Communist party had coined the world "polycentrism" to describe the new situation.

In 1958 Russian influence was still evident everywhere in China: there were Russian books, Russian language signs, Russian technicians. Improved communications in the form of frequent jet flights were matched by efforts to link the countries by rail across China's western deserts. Some people had predicted that China would take a separate— perhaps Titoist—course. It had national interests that clashed with Russia's, border areas it disputed with Russia, its leaders had come to power on their own, and the Chinese revolution—of which Chinese Communism was only a part—was directed against humiliation by all of the West, including Russia. Almost ten years of unbroken Communist solidarity appeared to belie the predictions of Sino-Soviet conflict, but in 1958 these factors and others took effect. A break began that came into the open in 1960 with Russian economic sanctions against China, and in the next few years with Russian aid to those whom the Chinese were fighting. There still seemed little chance of what de Gaulle, among others, foresaw: an alignment of Russia with the West against China. Yet the break went much further than others had thought it would. Analysts who tended to explicate the well-springs of Communist foreign policy entirely in terms of Communist ideology and viewed ideology in rigid terms failed to interpret events correctly. Newspaper accounts of international relations after 1957 were in many cases drastically distorted because they viewed Chinese and Russian foreign policy as one in which the moves of each were part of one well-coordinated plan.

The central point of difference that began in 1958 concerned relations with the United States. Khrushchev, from that time on, appeared to have sought a summit conference to deal with a wide range of differences. He asked for one when American troops landed in Lebanon. It would have included India, not China, as a representative of Asian countries. Yet after a hasty conference in Peking, he dropped the project. It seems plausible that the Chinese, who had insisted on formal as well as *de facto* recognition as one of the Big Five, objected to Khrushchev's courting India as if it were to play that role.* Moreover, the United States remained China's chief enemy—it was the country that continued to block Chinese entry to the United Nations, blocked absorption of Taiwan and supported a rival government claiming the

---

* G. F. Hudson argues this point in G. F. Hudson, R. Lowenthal, R. Mac-Farquhar (eds.), *The Sino-Soviet Dispute* (New York: Praeger, 1961).

mainland, it supported South Vietnam and South Korea, and worked actively against Communist parties elsewhere. Was Khrushchev genuinely trying to reach agreements with this country without taking into account China's quarrels? In August 1958, the Chinese, perhaps merely to create tension, intensively bombarded Quemoy and Matsu, thus resuming the crisis over Taiwan where it had stopped three years before. Again American weapons in the hands of Chiang's troops proved sufficient to prevent an attack.

But 1958 marked the beginning of another episode that came to figure in relations between the two Communist giants. China's Communist leaders had maintained and extended their administrative control over China to a degree that no other Chinese regime had ever found possible. Their material accomplishments were enormous yet they had also encountered trouble caused by some of China's basic problems—an enormous population concentrated in small areas that for centuries had been farmed as intensively as possible, and the resistance of a people pushed almost beyond endurance. They had tried the un-Marxist practice of government-encouraged birth control—"un-Marxist" because in the past poverty was viewed as a function of the capitalist maldistribution of wealth—and they had tried, beginning in 1956 (when liberalization affected the entire Communist bloc) a period of intellectual liberalization. "Let a hundred flowers bloom," said Mao Tse-tung. "Let diverse schools of thought contend."

But far more intellectual resistance to the regime was revealed than its leaders had anticipated, and repression followed in 1957. In 1958 the regime set out to solve its economic problems by radical new methods summed up in the phrase, "The Great Leap Forward." Month after month production quotas were raised. People were herded into factories, and small backyard factories and blast furnaces were established everywhere; in the most dramatic move, the collective farms and the villages were consolidated into 26,000 "communes" in which people slept in dormitories and ate in messhalls. Men and women worked side by side in brigades while children were kept in nurseries and schools. Production figures indicating enormous successes, and the labor shortages that developed prompted the regime to drop the birth control program.

The Great Leap Forward meant more than a departure from traditional Communist methods of industrialization, for the Chinese proceeded to make grandiose ideological claims. China, they argued, was approaching true communism faster than other states, including the Soviet Union; the communes were the key factor.

The Soviet Union thus found itself challenged on the issue of ideological leadership by virtue of Chinese internal development policies. The fact that initial reports of success of the Great Leap Forward had to be modified in late 1958 did not lessen the problem.

In 1959 there were further clashes. China came into a conflict with India—a conflict which Khrushchev publicly deplored. The dispute involved the tragic suppression by China of a revolt in Tibet, where it had established its sovereignty in 1951. India, which had long seen Tibet as a buffer area, had at first objected, but then agreed. But in encouraging Chinese immigration into the area and establishing its own Communist form of organization, the Chinese stimulated a resistance that took the form of open revolt. The Indians had softened their objections to growing Chinese influence in the tiny border state of Nepal and had not protested loudly to Chinese maps that included substantial sections of India and Burma within Chinese territory. But when the Chinese brutally crushed the Tibetan revolt, abrogated the 1951 Sino-Tibetan agreement allowing local autonomy, and made incursions into Indian territory, the Indian government changed its position. It opened its borders to thirteen thousand Tibetan refugees, including the Dalai Lama, the spiritual leader of Tibetan Buddhists. Nehru refused to back the Lama's plea to the United Nations, since, he said, Tibet was legally Chinese territory, but he did react bitterly to Chinese charges that India had instigated the revolt, and for the first time he publicized the Chinese border problem. The issue quieted down during the next three years. The Chinese spent their time strengthening their position in the Himalayas, but India failed to do so. Then in September 1962, fighting broke out again in several border areas, and the better equipped Chinese troops moved into the border areas to which China laid claim.

A storm broke in India, where the government had worked hard to establish good relations with the truculent neighbor to the north. The United States rushed military aid and equipment while India hastily passed increased appropriations and encouraged emergency enlistment in the armed forces. Although India's neutral neighbors tried to provide some form of conciliation, Nehru, under internal pressure, dropped his unpopular Secretary of Defense, Krishna Menon, long a bitter critic of the Western powers. India and China exchanged acrimonious notes to no avail, while speculation arose concerning Chinese motives. These ranged from views that the Chinese needed an external incident to divert attention from the miserable failure of the Great Leap Forward—for failure it was, in spite of the grandiose claims for it and in spite of the Chinese attempt to generalize from it in Marxist terms as the true future course for all Communist countries. Others saw the aggression as limited, merely aimed at rounding out frontiers long claimed by the Chinese. Significantly, the Chinese Nationalist government of Chiang Kai-shek supported the Communist Chinese claims to the areas under dispute and condemned Western aid to India in the circumstances. Yet others saw in the attack an attempt to discredit India as a power in Asia. They buttressed this view by noting that China had signed an amicable border agreement with Burma the year before and one in early 1963 with Pakistan. (The latter agreement concerned an area of Kashmir, and India accused Pakistan of taking illegal action concerning territory that should be India's. The new dispute led to a breakdown in conversations between India and Pakistan instigated by the West in an effort to have the two unite against the common enemy, China.)

Would the Soviet Union continue economic and military aid to India while it was under attack by a Communist neighbor? The answer was that it would. Perhaps it believed that the Chinese aims were limited, and that the aid would not prove crucial. But, through Walter Ulbricht of East Germany, it strongly condemned the Chinese attack on India.

If in 1959 the Sino-Indian dispute became an element in the growing friction between China and the Soviet Union, it was also in 1959 that the Chinese expressed dismay at Khrushchev's tour of the United States and his private conversations with President Eisenhower at Camp David. As a conciliatory gesture, Khrushchev made haste to go to Peking soon afterward. But the meetings there were cool, and in 1963, when the Chinese accused Khrushchev of having literally broken hundreds of agreements with China, they dated this from his 1959 meeting with Eisenhower.

Despite the 1960 summit conference failure at Geneva, Sino-Soviet relations continued on a steadily downward trend in the next three years. The Chinese, with a moderate aid program of their own to certain selected countries, attacked the Soviet Union for its large-scale aid to backward nations led by bourgeois nationalists at a time when genuine Socialist countries—that is, China—needed aid. In 1960 Khrushchev boasted that the Soviet Union would outstrip the Western countries in productivity and production within a few years, and even surpass the United States. In this version of peaceful coexistence, competition between the economies of the two leading exponents of Communism and capitalism would be the key factor, and as people saw

Communism winning, they would voluntarily adopt it. "Your grand-children will live under Communism," he told Americans. Yet this came at the very time when the Great Leap Forward first began to falter; the Chinese attacked a program that would subordinate bloc development to Russian development, and their attacks on the con-cept of "peaceful coexistence" and "competitive coexistence" became stronger and more bitter. In late 1960, Soviet technicians and aid per-sonnel began to leave China.

The year 1960 marks the development of the struggle between Khrushchev and the Chinese to win the allegiance of other Communist parties. Two major meetings took place: one at Bucharest in June, and another, with representatives of eighty-one Communist parties at Moscow, in November and December. The Moscow meeting—the more important of the two—appeared to patch over some differences, but the polemics began anew soon afterward.

Khrushchev staked out an ideological position the way the Chinese had done in 1958: the Soviet Party was recognized by other, equal parties as the leader, not because (as in Stalin's time) it was the first to make the revolution, or the only Communist party with a territorial base, but because it was the only one to have entered the stage of Communist development. The claim was reinforced by certain internal reforms that involved administrative decentralization and reinvigoration of "people's courts" outside the regular system of justice; these moves presumably indicated some withering away of the state.

During the 1960 conference the Soviets also launched sweeping attacks against the Chinese for trying to build support among other parties to unseat Khrushchev, for their incorrect denunciations of his travels in the West and efforts to settle matters peacefully, and for their factionalism, which tended to split the world Communist movement.

The Chinese, however, added other items to their bill of particulars: they carried forward their drive against the paucity of Soviet bloc aid and denounced Khrushchev's approval of different paths to socialism, which had allowed a rapprochement between the Soviet Union and Yugoslavia in the early 1960's. In 1956, the Chinese had come to Khrushchev's aid to combat revisionism; now they accused *him* of the sin.

Albania's association with China was partly due to Albanian isola-tion following the Soviet-Yugoslav rapprochement, and partly the work of Albanian Stalinists, who had won out in intraparty strife. After conversations with the Albanian leaders, Khrushchev declared that he could more easily come to an understanding with Macmillan than with them.

On the whole, Western European Communist parties supported Khrushchev. But the Chinese gained support for their more militant stand among parties in Asia and the Middle East, especially where Khrushchev's policy had been one of cooperative friendship with governments engaged in crushing the local Communist parties. In India the party was forced to oppose Chinese incursions, and sections of it rallied to Khrushchev; Khrushchev tried to obtain the backing of the Pathet Lao by aiding it during the Laotian crisis. And in one part of Asia—Outer Mongolia, which Khrushchev ushered into United Nations membership—the Russians succeeded in destroying growing Chinese influence.

There is no doubt that the Soviets and the Chinese shared common views about the new and emerging nations: that they must be liberated from colonialism, that the national bourgeoisie was a vital element in achieving this process (one with which local Communists and the Communist bloc could ally itself), and finally, that ultimately the national bourgeoisie would have to be replaced by the forces of socialism. Russia's acceptance of many paths to socialism, however, made it possible for Russia to find merit in radical movements that were not a part of the international Communist movement. Khrushchev seemed to believe that these movements might be converted peacefully especially as the Soviet Union proved its economic superiority to the West (a strategy which, as pointed out earlier, involved economic sacrifice of the rest of the bloc. In general the Chinese argued that violent struggle was necessary, and that cooperation with the national bourgeoisie must be very limited. After the Soviet rocket triumphs of 1957, the Chinese insisted that the balance in the world power structure had shifted to the side of Communism and that more risks could be taken in wars of national liberation. Khrushchev had to accept that such wars were just, but he appeared to have seen far more danger in their breaking out into general war that would be as dangerous for the Communist bloc as for the capitalists.

In addition to these differences in emphasis, China's experience was clearly more relevant than Russia's to the problems of underdeveloped countries. They, as well as China, wanted to move faster than had the Soviet Union. And finally, the Russians—like the colonial oppressors—were white men. The Chinese were not. And in Africa and Asia, China began to play on the racial theme.

As a result the struggle within the bloc was transferred to relations with the governments of new countries as well as to relations with their Communist parties. The Chinese were more likely to uphold local Communist parties' efforts to overthrow the new nationalist governments where the Russians counselled cooperation. In some countries the Chinese were more influential with radical governments than the Russians, or were able to support a government where the Russians found it difficult: the Chinese developed more influence in Somalia because they upheld its claim to a greater Somalia—something the Soviet Union could not easily do since it enjoyed good relations with Ethiopia, from which a good part of Greater Somalia would come. In the Algerian struggle, the Chinese gave more support than the Russians because Khrushchev wanted to avoid antagonizing de Gaulle, whose general approach to the Atlantic alliance he found attractive. At the time of the Lebanon crisis of 1958 when Khrushchev abandoned his summit conference demand after a conference with the Chinese, it now appears that the Chinese demanded active intervention with volunteers to oust the Americans. All through Africa in the period under review the Chinese made large-scale efforts to get in touch with the more radical elements and to encourage their visits to Peking. At first their success on this level was mainly confined to the Casablanca group; the Nationalist Chinese cultivated relations with other African states in order to have their votes maintain the Nationalist Government's status in the United Nations. But in 1964 the Communists made further progress.

Communist parties have always been subject to factionalism, to disputes between those who interpret the objective political situation as one demanding immediate and rapid action, and those who counsel caution. The dispute between Chinese leaders and Khrushchev took on the same quality, and factions were able to find support among one or the other of the two bloc leaders; in turn, the two sought to strengthen the particular factions supporting them in order to build strength for their positions in the overall world Communist movement. In Indonesia, Korea, Vietnam, Japan, Thailand, and Malaya, the Chinese found more favor than Russia, particularly after Khrushchev's attack on Albania at the Twenty-Second Party Congress. By mid-1964 Khrushchev was ready for a trial of strength with the Chinese: against the advice of other Russian-oriented party leaders, he decided to call a special Congress of Communist parties from throughout the world, where he intended to read the Chinese comrades out of the movement. One thing intervened: on October 13 the world learned the surprising news of Khrushchev's deposition by what was evidently a unanimous vote of the Party Presidium. He was succeeded by two men, Leonid Bhreznev and Aleksei Kosygin. The precise reasons for the dismissal remained in doubt. They combined, however, the Russian military's resentment at his emphasis on consumer goods production, and annoyance at his ten-year failure to solve the farm problem in the Soviet Union (ignominiously, in 1964 the Russian government had had to spend scarce foreign exchange on large-scale purchases of foreign wheat). In addition there was also the clumsy handling of the dispute with the Chinese and his volatile approach to both domestic and foreign affairs.

Yet the man was not all of Russian policy; objective factors provide the guidelines and limits to personal policy decisions. Although the new leaders could postpone the showdown with Communist China, two weeks of talks between Chou En-lai and the Russians revealed one thing: personal invective might disappear, but the basic reasons for the split still existed.

The Soviet Union, Communist China, and the countries of Eastern Europe had been plagued in recent years by economic difficulties which had contributed to their squabbles and altered their foreign policies. In China the collapse of the Great Leap Forward in the early 1960s had led to curtailing the aid programs to such radical neutrals as Guinea, Ghana, and the United Arab Republic. (It should be noted that by 1964 concentration on agriculture appeared to be paying off and recovery from the disasters of the Great Leap Forward to be more or less complete.) There was no doubt that the economic break with Russia had hurt China: factories begun with Russian help stood idle without parts, and Russian machinery was useless. In Russia, on the other hand, little was heard of Khrushchev's boasts that had so alienated the Chinese. No one talked about overtaking the United States in per capita food production, and the need to purchase large quantities of wheat testified to the failure of all Khrushchev's experiments to solve the Russian farm problem. Russian fears of Common Market success were expressed by the propaganda directed against it. The Communist leaders were genuinely concerned that it might discriminate too strongly against essential Soviet foreign trade, and they suggested some kind of special associated status for themselves.

Russia also tried harder to coordinate production in the entire Communist bloc. Here again, years of effort showed little result. National planning in each state made any coordination of their economies difficult (there were also different pricing practices that made it difficult to measure relative efficiency) and nationalist differences also interfered. Rumania, in particular, rejected Russian demands to turn away from its old-line Stalinist emphasis on heavy industry, and rely instead on other Communist countries. The Rumanian leaders wanted to have their own heavy industry. One result was that in 1962 Rumania began to increase greatly its trade with Western countries, including the United States. Czechoslovakia, East Germany, and Poland, too, failed to escape the economic difficulties that had plagued the Soviet Union and helped bring Khrushchev's downfall. The trouble was not serious enough to threaten their regimes; throughout Eastern Europe people had come to accept that they might as well make the best of the system. But the troubles were serious enough to make Communist leaders rethink economic planning. Yugoslavia's boasts about decentralization were listened to, and in other countries schemes of profit-making as a guide to investment were seriously considered.

It meant, also that the use of foreign aid as a technique of foreign policy had to be more selective. Cuba remained a burden, and the Aswan Dam project and help for Egypt could not be abandoned. There was evidence, however, that the Russian leaders did not want to take on the burden of more aid projects. There had been complaints within the Soviet Union that Khrushchev's large-scale foreign aid programs, initiated in 1955, had brought the Soviet Union little return.

This did not mean that other foreign policy techniques were closed to Soviet and Chinese Communist leaders. Disposal of a little surplus military equipment never cost much and could bring all sorts of results, and support of local Communist guerrillas or Communist parties was cheap. Depending on their internal economic conditions and the way the world outside their borders developed, there would always be a fluid situation that required flexibility. The Cuban situation of recent years (Chapter 9) provides a good example of how fortuitous circumstances could produce an unexpected situation to which the Communist leaders had to respond—not by prearranged plan, but on the basis of a combination of previous attitudes and immediate improvisation. There was no Communist master plan.

This account has dealt primarily with the years since Hungary in terms of the growing split within the Communist bloc. Certainly it constitutes one of the developments in international affairs comparable to the resurgence of Europe, the independence of new states, and the development of hydrogen weapons. But this perspective alone may distort. What of China's foreign-policy aims over this period? How successful were Mao Tse-tung and those around him?

The answer must be that Mao was not very successful, but that he still had before him possibilities and prospects of great successes. The Chinese Communists had failed to destroy Chiang and liberate Taiwan. They had failed to win South Korea despite costly efforts. Earlier, Communist guerrilla efforts had been defeated in Burma, Indonesia, Malaya, and the Philippines. Only in Indonesia had the movement recovered fully; there, with Sukarno ailing, the party had a good chance. In Burma, Marxist ideas were strong and the government had made peace with China. In Cambodia, as a consequence of the situation in Thailand and Vietnam, China was a favored nation. In Vietnam, Chinese aid after 1949 had helped secure victory in the North for the Vietminh in 1954. But against all expectation, Diem had consolidated his rule in the south. After 1960, however, guerrilla activity in the south increased rapidly, and 1964 brought the Communist Vietcong to a new peak of strength. In Tibet, the Chinese had successfully reasserted a traditional domination that Tibet had long resisted. Although they had lost something of their international status as a consequence, they had reclaimed border territories which India had long claimed as her own. Finally, in Africa, their 1964 diplomacy had brought them increasing prestige and recognition from African states (as well as from France).

In terms of expansion, therefore, the record was mixed. Moreover, China, aspiring to international status, failed to gain entry into the United Nations. There were many who could not see this as any victory for the Western powers but it appeared to have been a failure on the part of the Soviet Union; and the Soviet Union failed the Chinese signally in the matter of economic and technical aid. Direct economic aid never reached the proportions of Chinese grants to *its* satellite states, North Korea and Vietnam, and technical aid from the Soviets came to a sudden halt in mid-1960. The volume of Russo-Chinese trade dropped enormously, too, after the open quarrel began, although China had depended heavily on imports of Soviet machinery. Between 1960 and 1961 the dollar value of these fell from 500 million to 100 million. The program of economic development failed disastrously in 1960–61 through a combination of mismanagement, natural disasters, overwhelming exhaustion, and continued population growth. A severe retrenchment took place with much more modest goals; the first order of business was recognized as simply to be able to feed the population, and extensive moves were taken both to improve agriculture and to curb population increase.

The Russians provided the Chinese with one success. By returning to China what had been granted to Stalin at Yalta, they withdrew from control of the Manchurian Railway, Port Arthur, and Dairen. Significantly, at no time did Russia help China with the development of strategic weapons—bombers, missiles, or atomic or thermonuclear bombs. In 1963 the Chinese charged that among the many earlier promises broken by the USSR was the pledge to help China develop its own nuclear weapons. But in mid-October 1964, at the time of Khrushchev's deposition, the Chinese exploded their first nuclear device. The event again showed how a totalitarian system facing enormous shortages can nevertheless concentrate its resources on particular projects. More important, however, it raised the specter of a China with plenty of nuclear weapons in the future, and raised the question of what this might mean for Asia and the whole international system. Would China be able to brandish these weapons with any more success than Russia or the United States? What effect would the event have on India, where there were already calls for nuclear arms to match China's but where the government—for the time being at least—rejected the notion? What of Southeast Asia, where the successor states to Indochina were under strong Communist pressures, where Burma had tried to come to terms with China, where, in Indonesia, the largest Communist party outside the Communist bloc operated, and where Malaysia and Thailand counted on American support? What, finally, might it mean for Australia, a country that had, only twenty-two years earlier, barely escaped a Japanese invasion?

Conclusion

"Peaceful coexistence" meant several things for the developed countries. So long as all believed that there was a tacit agreement between the United States and the Soviet Union to accept the other's sphere of influence, the regimes of the lesser states in each bloc no longer feared attack from outside the bloc, and therefore felt less dependent on protection by the Soviet Union or the United States. Paradoxically, the dropping of the goal of "liberation" from the lexicon of American foreign policy had the effect that Communist bloc countries actually had the opportunity to become more independent of Moscow, while lessened fears in Western European countries gave leaders like de Gaulle the opportunity to defy the wishes of the United States.

There were limits: the lesson of 1956 had been learned. The Soviet Union had crushed a Hungarian regime that wanted to drop Communism and withdraw from the Warsaw Pact, and the United States forced the British and French to withdraw from their independent foray into Egypt. But within these broad limits there were many divergencies. The Communist bloc divided into several groups, and only the most doctrinaire anti-Communist could now speak of *the* Communist conspiracy or *the* Communist bloc. China and Albania heaped vituperation on Russian leadership, called for its overthrow, and became the first to applaud the event; Rumania defied the Russian demand for economic unity of the Communist bloc and Yugoslavia continued its long course of Communist neutralism. Among Western countries France exchanged diplomatic representatives with Communist China, withdrew its contingents from NATO, and continued to build its own nuclear *Force de frappe*. And when Turkey and Greece engaged in a bitter quarrel over Cyprus, the United States found it difficult to do anything to reconcile the two NATO members.

Weapons were not the only cause of the change. The economies of Western countries had reached heights previously unimagined, and the threat of Communist subversion had virtually disappeared. Within the Soviet bloc, on the other hand, economic difficulties had forced leaders to seek increased trade with Western countries. Finally, in the face of various alternatives open to him, Khrushchev, despite his long record as a faithful Stalinist, had been a generally conservative actor on the world scene. He had made probes into the Congo and the Middle East, he had threatened and blustered, blown hot and cold. But the Chinese attacks on him give some indication of what some other Communist leaders thought he *should* have done, and of how conservative they felt he had been: he had refused to give China nuclear weapons and to back its attack on India. In Europe he had never pressed the issue of a German peace treaty or the status of Berlin to any conclusion. He had withdrawn from the Congo. Although he had quarrelled with Nasser over Nasser's policies, he had never cut off aid for the Aswan Dam. He had resolved border issues with neighboring states. And the Cuban adventure of late 1962 (see Chapter 9), in which he had boldly—some Communists said too boldly—challenged the United States by placing missiles a hundred miles from the American coast, had ended in Soviet withdrawal. The period of belligerence which had begun in 1960 with the blow-up of the Paris summit conference ended with the resolution of the Cuban crisis, and in the next years Khrushchev concluded the first arms control agreement with the United States—even while increasing his own arms spending to close the missile gap his Cuban move had tried to redress. By the end of the period under review, French spokesmen could argue that de Gaulle's policies were justified because, in effect, the Cold War had been won: the 1947 situation that had brought forth containment had now ended, and new and more flexible policies were required.

In *both* blocs, the desire for independence had become real. Western Europe was preoccupied with what had come to be called economic colonialism—the taking over by giant American firms of European companies that needed capital to expand. In Europe it was hoped that the European Economic Community might give market opportunities to European firms that would enable them to grow to rival American ones, with their enormous resources for research and marketing, and their ability to absorb losses when necessary. But so far it had not done so, and in the meantime, for many politicians, the need to combat American economic hegemony was as great as the need to struggle against political and military hegemony.

On the other side of the world the Chinese atomic explosion, coming at the same time as Khrushchev's downfall, symbolized China's unwillingness to be guided by the Soviet Union and also its awesome potential power. All through underdeveloped Asia annual statistics consistently revealed the failure to keep economic development ahead of population increase. This had seemed true of China in the early 1960s, yet China appeared to be one of the few states with the centralized administrative control that might enable it to win the race. If it did, it could dominate Asia. How it might wield its power in the world, would depend in large part on its relations with the Soviet Union. They might clash directly, or they might find once more the common ground that would enable them to operate together. In either event, even though the United States had no diplomatic relations with China, the nature of the political settlement of the Eurasian rimlands would necessarily have to depend on China.

In the new structure that supplanted rigid bipolarism, the United Nations found a precarious new life that might yet be snuffed out by financial strains. The organization helped to provide a fairly orderly dismantling of past empires; it helped to find ways of settling disputes in many areas; it tried—with limited resources—to help the new countries to find their own pathways to economic development and it served them as a useful and economical channel for communication with other countries. With one embassy in New York, a new nation could meet with representatives of almost all the countries of the world.

On the Cold War front the United Nations' usefulness remained limited, and the major protagonists worked out their conflicts with little reliance upon it. Yet even the major powers found that the organization might provide useful face-saving formulas for withdrawal from extended and embarrassing positions: United Nations action, supported by the United States had, for a while, kept the Congo from becoming a Cold War battleground. But departure of the United Nations —itself weakened by the Congo action—brought back chaos and renewed the possibility of open intervention.

When President Kennedy died from an assassin's bullet (to be replaced by Lyndon B. Johnson), the period brought a tragic change in the personnel that act out the scenario of world politics. It brought the end of thirteen years of Conservative government in England, the end of the Fourth French Republic and the rise of de Gaulle, death to Prime Minister Nehru of India, and the end of the Khrushchev years— years that had witnessed a fundamental liberalizing of the Soviet state that would be difficult for his successors to reverse. Kennedy and Khrushchev were the two leaders to play major roles in one dramatic event of international politics in the period under review that has yet to be touched on. This was the confrontation between the Soviet Union and the United States over Cuba—a confrontation that raised questions about the structure of the international political system that have yet to be answered.

CHAPTER NINE

Cuba, the United States and Latin America, and the Great Confrontation of 1962

In late 1962 Cuba became the scene of a direct confrontation between the Soviet Union and the United States, one that involved nuclear weapons. Never since the Berlin blockade fourteen years earlier had the two staked out such mutually incompatible positions with so much at stake. This time, since the confrontation involved thermonuclear weapons, the threat was infinitely more ominous. In the end both retreated somewhat, the Soviet Union more. But people the world over had been reminded that, regardless of the emergence of China, Europe, and the new countries of Asia and Africa, only the Soviet Union and the United States possessed thermonuclear weapons and the means of delivery in any large quantity. And some people noted that leaders of neither country had bothered to consult with others before taking steps that might have precipitated nuclear war: in some ways, then, it seemed still the bipolar world of two superpowers that people talked about in the late 1940s. Yet the opposite conclusion might be drawn from the fact that both leaders backed down: nuclear stalemate *did* exist, limiting the action each of the two might choose and allowing small states to take advantage of the situation.

Castro and Cuba

Fidel Castro came to power in Cuba in January 1959. The bearded, cigar-smoking revolutionary had had created for him an aura of Robin Hood romanticism; his tiny band of rebels in the mountains vanquished an army and sent an unsavory dictator into exile; he conquered all odds and swaggered into Havana to the delighted shouts of the masses, and with the open support of the educated and professional

330

classes and the more respectable business groups. Millions of Americans had seen him on television; a popular and staunchly Irish-Catholic television personality had gone into the mountains to interview him, and Castro had agreed with one of his observations: since most of Castro's men wore crucifixes, they couldn't be Communist.

From the beginning, however, Castro made it clear that this was not to be a revolution like so many other revolutions in Latin America, a mere change in the ruling clique, from one comfortably corrupt group to another. The revolution, he said, had just begun. What most Americans and most Cubans did not realize (and many could not understand) was that Castro was determined to make a genuinely social revolution, one that involved radically changing the entire social, economic, as well as political, structure of the tiny country. It is quite doubtful that at the time Castro had any definite picture of how he would do it. He was no Communist, although there were some Communists and fellow-travelers around him; he had received no support from the Cuban Communist party as such during the campaign that put him into power. But the radical-nationalist viewpoint he espoused brought him their support and he came to rely upon them more and more.

This radical-nationalism and Cuba's proximity to the United States were what made the Cuban revolution so important on the international scene. Chapters 4 and 5 have already pointed out how underlying social tensions, exacerbated by population increases, contrasted with the facade of inter-American relations. Peronism in Argentina and the abortive Guatemala revolution were reactions to a set of like factors that combined differently in each Latin American country. All of them had extremes of wealth and poverty, a facade of modernization against a background of peasant society, an entrenched landlord class and an Indian peasantry. Everywhere the military was a factor in politics; intellectuals chafed against the form of society while defending their culture against the materialistic barbarism of Yankee culture imported by the moneyed classes, and a Catholic priesthood existed that was too often identified with reaction. In many of these countries American investment in mineral extraction and plantations fostered resentment against absentee ownership: in Cuba people believed widely that American sugar plantation owners conspired with a well-bribed government to avoid paying of taxes and to ensure that land would not be used for other purposes.

In these circumstances, ideas for radical change abounded. Political legitimacy was hard to come by as one revolutionary regime succeeded another and, in fear of the next, tried to crush opposition, thereby forcing it to adopt revolutionary means of expression. The cycle was and is self-perpetuating. And only in a few cases had revolution produced any real social change. Castro set out to do this, and attracted the attention and support of radical elements all through Latin America. He also set out on a direct collision course with the United States. Unlike Arbenz in Guatemala five years earlier, he obtained support for his revolution from the Soviet Union and ended up declaring himself to all intents and purposes a member of the Communist bloc.

Castro did not need anti-Americanism to mobilize popular support. There was some fear of Castro in the United States, but also much goodwill and a desire to rectify the errors of the past. Inside the government and out, many Americans felt that past policy of maintaining good relations with any regime, so long as it kept order and protected American investments, had been wrong. True, a different policy might involve the United States in intervention on the side of those whom it saw as "the good boys"; nonrecognition of governments had hardly produced good results in the much earlier cases of the Soviet Union, Mexico, of Japanese conquests in the Pacific, of Communist China. Yet the Caracas declaration of 1954 made a Communist government incompatible with the inter-American system: didn't this imply a kind of collective intervention to regulate the internal form of government?

In the Cuban situation, at first, the dilemma did not have to be faced. The administration by and large looked upon Castro with cautious favor, and Castro received a ringing welcome when he visited the United States. But Castro saw himself as the leader of a revolution that would spread throughout Latin America, one that was bound ultimately to be blocked by a United States whose foreign policy—so he argued—was dictated by its business interests. On the one hand, he set in motion a program of domestic reform; on the other, he began to replace the non-Communist elements that had brought him to power by more radical elements. Right-wingers who accused *all* reform elements of Communism seemed to be crying "wolf," and only confused an already complicated situation. Castro seized on the emotion of pride in the revolution and encouraged Cubans to believe that American imperialism meant to crush it; it was easy to cry "he who is not with us is against us," and to eliminate as opponents of the revolution those who at first welcomed and supported it. Castro had only to wait until they began to object to growing Communist influence and totalitarian methods.

In the meantime a program of wholesale nationalization and expropriation, mass execution of Batista men, and demands that the United States return Batistianos as criminals rather than political refugees strained the worsened relations between the two countries. The American press and Congressmen criticized the Cuban leader, and he cried out that the United States opposed the revolution. As they talked of growing Communist influence, Castro was enabled to equate anti-Communism with counter-revolution; in a series of moves in late 1959 he dismissed or arrested some of his most important supporters because they objected to Communist infiltration of the most important branches of government.

The United States played into Castro's hands. It was slow in preventing anti-Castro groups from using small airfields in Florida to launch hit-and-run air raids on Cuba; its reaction to land reform was to demand compensation; the outcry about public executions sounded hypocritical coming from a country that had not objected to Batista's brutality and had maintained correct relations with the regime until the end (though many chose to forget the United States embargo on arms to Batista after March 1958). There was in the United States a kind of patronizing and mocking attitude taken toward the young revolutionary that betrayed a terrible failure to understand the appeal of his radical idealism throughout Latin America.

In early 1960, Major Ernesto Guevara, head of the powerful Agrarian Institute, made it clear that more expropriation of American business was in order; the Cubans blamed the United States for explosion of a munitions ship in Havana harbor, and Castro and other Cuban spokesmen began to talk of the necessity to "defeat" the United States. An extensive new trade agreement, accompanied by Soviet credits of $100 million, resulted from the visit of Soviet Deputy Premier Anastas Mikoyan in February. About this time Guevara argued that the American quota for imports of Cuban sugar constituted economic enslavement, but the Cuban government also—paradoxically—cried "economic aggression" at the hint that the United States might reduce the Cuban quota.

The quota was a result of United States protection of its own sugar producers. It allowed only certain unilaterally determined amounts to enter the United States and, under the circumstances, the United States paid a higher price than the world price. Guevara's argument that Cuba thus had to buy United States goods above world prices had little merit; the dollars could have been spent elsewhere. The quota, however, was set by the United States alone, and it was true that low

Cuban tariffs to American goods tended to direct trade with the United States. Once the idea was implanted that the quota might be reduced, however, American critics of Castro began to agitate for it, giving the Castro regime full opportunity for its propaganda. "Cuba Si, Yankee No!" became a popular war-cry, and Cuba a magnet to discontented revolutionaries all over Latin America who applauded defiance of Goliath by David. Cuban broadcasts and shipments of propaganda materials to the rest of Latin America increased; at home Castro moved to establish totalitarian controls as opposition increased. The stream of refugees flowing into Miami swelled, and opposition began to organize inside and outside Cuba. There was validity to Castro's charge that the United States was helping refugees who wanted to overthrow him; subversion on the part of the American Central Intelligence Agency had already begun.

The mood of the summer of 1960 conspired to make the situation worse. The summit conference blow-up in Paris had occurred and the United States was involved in an election campaign in which Cuba was to become a central issue. Kennedy hammered hard at the theme that American prestige had suffered grievous blows during the later years of the Eisenhower Administration, while that of the Soviet Union, particularly with its successful sputniks, had soared. But he wanted to leave open the possibility for pursuing a détente with the Soviet Union. Khrushchev, whose policies before the U-2 affair appeared aimed in that direction, had suggested another summit meeting with whoever succeeded Eisenhower. One result was a deliberate decision not to attack the Soviet Union but rather Communism in Cuba. In this way, Democrats could avoid the "soft-on-Communism" issue that the Republicans were always eager to pin on them, but at the same time avoid attacking the Soviet Union directly. Kennedy quoted rabid right-wingers on how the Eisenhower administration had been misled by pro-Communists about Cuba. Democrats and Republicans in Congress were entangled in the battle, and Eisenhower did his campaign stint for Nixon: he asked Congress for stand-by power to lower the sugar quota. The Democrats disliked giving it to him; each party accused the other of being "soft on Cuba"; but the law passed.

In the meantime Castro had won another victory by importing Soviet crude oil (at a lower price than oil from the United States). The American oil companies operating refineries in Cuba refused to refine it (it was one of their grievances that Castro imported the oil to avoid paying debts due to the oil companies). In retaliation Castro nationalized the refineries, a move popular throughout Latin America, where

American oil companies are always a target for nationalist resentment about American theft of natural resources.

The fall of 1960 brought the heads-of-state meeting of the General Assembly in New York, and Castro emulated other world leaders in seeking the spotlight. He and Khrushchev embraced each other before newsmen, and the Cuban leader took the opportunity to call both the United States presidential candidates "beardless, brainless youths." Khrushchev had warned the United States that an attack on Cuba would bring a rain of rockets in retaliation, though when Castro repeated this to cheering crowds in Cuba, Khrushchev told him that it had been only figuratively speaking, and Castro proceeded to recognize Red China and North Korea. In January, before inauguration of the new American president, Castro ordered all but eleven members of the United States embassy staff to leave Havana within 48 hours. Eisenhower retaliated by breaking off diplomatic relations.

In more serious moments, Cuban delegates to the United Nations complained of American training of would-be guerrillas preparing to invade Cuba, a charge that was palpably absurd and easily turned aside. But it was also true.

Under the Eisenhower administration plans had gone forward to help Cuban refugees on the grounds that Castro's totalitarian methods made it impossible to overthrow him from within. The job was handled primarily by the American Central Intelligence Agency, which appears to have botched it badly. Unable to tell left from right, it relied on unpopular former Batista men, could not patch up quarrels among factions, failed to inform the underground in Cuba of what it was doing, and drastically underestimated Castro's ability to meet the small force that it finally helped land on Cuban soil on April 17, 1961. Ill-concealed training bases sprang up, not only in Florida and Louisiana, but also in Guatemala, and the anti-Castro forces were equipped with American weapons.

When Kennedy became President, this policy and many others came under review. The new President agreed to go on with the training and equipping of the forces. He would allow them to carry out the operation against Cuba *if* his advisers assured him of success even if the United States itself carried out no overt military operations. Both the Central Intelligence Agency and the military gave him this assurance, as well as several of his personal advisers. Pressures in favor of the operation included what had been said during the political campaign, as well as a genuine conviction that Castro's growing alignment with the Communist bloc posed a severe danger to the

Americas in the light of his popularity among left-wing groups. More-over, what was to be done with the trained forces already in existence and the organized Cuban political groups that were supposed to take over after the overthrow of Castro? Finally, it became known that Soviet jet fighters were on their way to Cuba and Cuban pilots were training in Czechoslovakia. It might soon be too late, and the President of Guatemala told American authorities that the camps in his country would have to be closed by summer.

In the circumstances, the President authorized an invasion that turned out to be a perfect failure. Fifteen hundred men landed and were attacked by Castro's air force, which also kept them from being re-supplied. Castro was able to mobilize his army and militia of over 250,000 men, and bring his forces rapidly to bear on the small beach-head at the Bay of Pigs. Within three days it was all over. There were no multiple landings to force him to divert his forces; because the Central Intelligence Agency was unable to establish reliable contact with any of the underground within Cuba, there was no internal uprising. When President Kennedy was asked to authorize an American air strike at a time the invasion attempt was palpably failing, he re-minded those appealing to him that he had authorized the operation only on the basis that no American forces need be directly involved: the United States was not to be charged with its own Hungary. More-over, no one could now assure him that more would not be required. The United States had already jeopardized its good name by backing the invasion; it would not go further.

And it seriously jeopardized its reputation and prestige. There were many previous Castro supporters among the ranks of the invaders, but Castro was also able to parade Batista murderers from among them. The American Ambassador at the United Nations, Adlai Stevenson, had told an emergency meeting that two B-26 bombers that landed in Florida on April 15 were Cuban air force planes flown by defecting pilots. He was wrong. They were American-supplied planes flown from bases in Nicaragua to destroy Castro's air force on the ground—a job at which they failed. (There was to have been a second air strike, but as the press began to unravel the story of the first one, President Kennedy cancelled it.) Stevenson at least had not lied in the United Nations: he had been misled by his own administration, and the United States had put itself—to say the least—in an awkward position. Re-action against the American-sponsored invasion mounted throughout the rest of the world and especially Latin America, where the Cuban revolution had touched wellsprings of emotion never tapped during the Guatemala affair.

The Bay of Pigs invasion came close to wrecking at the outset the new administration's plan to deal with the tensions and frustrations throughout Latin America that had led to Castro in Cuba and would probably lead to more radicals in power in other countries. A suggestion by Castro himself, in mid-1959, that the United States embark on a long-range multilateral aid program amounting to $30 billion, had received scant consideration. A year earlier Vice President Richard Nixon had set out on a goodwill tour of Latin America which had been a total failure. Nixon was pelted with eggs, physically attacked, and his wife endangered by radical hoodlums. President Eisenhower alerted a force of a thousand marines in the Caribbean to protect him. The move was scarcely likely to endear the United States further to Nixon's host countries, but they had hardly provided hospitality. The tour might have served to give the Administration some indication of how badly relations with countries to the south had deteriorated. But for years they had been seen as Latin playgrounds, the source of new dances, the province of Pan American Airways and Grace tour liners, picturesque neighbors who could be counted on to vote the American way in the United Nations, united by a tradition of revolution against foreign domination and devotion to ideals of individual freedom. All of these attitudes were hard to drop. Revolutions, Americans knew, took place; but they generally meant that one military junta replaced another. Only Peron in Argentina and Cardenas in Mexico had tried to do more, and Roosevelt in pursuit of his good neighbor policy in the 1930s had tolerated the nationalist eccentricities of Mexico. Many American citizens found it was nice to work for an American company in Latin America; they could live well very cheaply and find so many servants. And many saw no further than this pleasant life.

Nixon's unpleasant treatment made headlines in the American press and raised some puzzled cries of "Why?" But when a group of Latin American leaders suggested a long-range multilateral aid program, the administration gave them a cold shoulder: traditional policies were sufficient. These included extension of credit by the Import-Export Bank for the purchase of American exports, loans from the International Bank, Point Four technical aid programs, military aid to help increase the strength of Latin American armies so that they might resist Russian invasions, and suggestions to follow conservative fiscal policies that would avoid foreign exchange deficits and consequent import controls.

In 1960, when Democrat and Republican vied with one another to attack Castro verbally, the administration belatedly changed its mind: it suggested a $500 million aid program for the rest of Latin America, for which people throughout Latin America ironically thanked Castro; it agreed that American aid could go to state-controlled enterprises or nationalized industries; and it joined in setting up an Inter-American Development Bank.

The new administration was staffed with thinkers from the universities who, caught up in the academic concern for the problems of emerging countries, had worked out elaborate schemes of the economic, social, and political requisites for economic development. They conceived the Alliance for Progress. The Alliance would be the answer to Fidelismo, to Communism, to the whole tense situation throughout Latin America that produced the need and demand for radical solutions.

Therefore, while Kennedy did battle with Castro over captured Cuban refugees (whose ransom by private groups he later felt impelled to sanction), he also presented a new broad-scale program that would attack the underlying causes. At a conference of finance ministers at Punta del Este, Uruguay, in August 1961, the American states signed a series of multilateral agreements that provided for three aspects of the Alliance: a promise of $20 billion for development aid from the United States over a ten-year period; commitment to fundamental social change on the part of participating governments, in the form of land reform and changes in the frequently regressive and inequitable tax structures; and a plan to make a group of Latin American economists working under the Economic and Social Council of the Organization of American States a clearing house for coordination of long-range development plans presented by participating states. In this way development funds could be equitably apportioned and perhaps some measure of economic integration be achieved. Cuba was specifically excluded from the Alliance.

The Alliance has so far provoked a large measure of pessimism: loans in its first years were condemned either as having strings tied to them (which was true) or as having been extended *without* the necessary strings, on a crisis basis—which was not the intent of the program. One thing became clear as statistics mounted: Latin America, especially around the Caribbean, faced the most drastic population problem outside Asia. Unless methods were devised to cope with this, in the one part of the world where religious objections were particularly important, Alliance programs would not prevent a fall in the standard of living.

While the Kennedy administration expanded Eisenhower's programs to deal with fundamental problems of Latin America, the Organization of American States became the scene of an American attempt to obtain multilateral action against a Cuba more and more closely tied to the Communist bloc. Castro, in December 1961, announced that he was and always had been a Marxist-Leninist (not, as some immediately translated it, a Communist Party member). Khrushchev still hedged his bets on Castro in 1961, seeing him as a too romantic rebel; economic support was still tentative, and Soviet technical aid personnel vied with many from China. But Castro's personal blend of Marxism-Leninism had wide appeal in Latin America, his subversive activities became more intense and, in the United Nations, Cuba became to all intents and purposes a member of the Communist bloc. The process was a strange one. It was not one of Russian and Communist subversion; rather Castro, influenced by Communists and radicals around him, handed Cuba to Khrushchev as a satellite state. There was much evidence to support the view that Khrushchev was unsure what to do with the gift, particularly one as provocative to the United States.

But the United States *was* determined—in a more respectable manner —to do something; there was evidence that as Castro continued his activities even left-wing forces in the Americas were becoming fearful of having their thunder stolen by someone too closely tied to Russia. On the basis of this growing disenchantment with Castro, the United States suggested that the Organization of American States undertake collective sanctions against his regime, now that it had come under extrahemispheric domination.

Under considerable pressure from the United States fourteen of the OAS Foreign Ministers, meeting at Punta del Este in January 1962 voted to exclude Cuba from participation in the inter-American system. Brazil, Argentina, Chile, Ecuador, Bolivia, and Mexico—the most populous and in most cases the most democratic of Latin American states—abstained. There were internal repercussions from the voting, too. In Argentina, the military forced President Frondizi to reverse his position and assume a harder line against Castro. The issue then figured in an election which saw heavy returns for Peronists, and brought a confusing military coup to annul the returns. In April 1962 the Brazilian government, following a more "independent" line in foreign policy, reestablished diplomatic relations with the Soviet Union. (But this government, too, was later overthrown by a military coup.) Collective intervention appeared to achieve few results in Cuba.

The Missile Crisis

Quiet reigned in Cuban-United States relations for a few months; the Caribbean was more concerned with a coup that ended the long and hated Trujillo regime in the Dominican Republic, with the effort to replace it by a more democratic regime and an attempt by the Trujillos to regain power—foiled partly by a show of force on the part of United States naval forces. Then in mid-year, it appeared that the Soviet Union had decided to provide massive support for Cuba. The economic situation in the island appeared grave; Khrushchev apparently decided that he could not allow the first Soviet bloc member in the Americas to collapse. Increased shipments from the Soviet Union, however, included a large number of modern weapons, accompanied by military technicians. In September American Congressmen charged that the Soviet Union was shipping nuclear rockets to Cuba.

Military analysts, with little corroborating evidence, were skeptical. Many had long thought that American liquid-fueled rockets around the Soviet Union were obsolete and ought to be withdrawn: such rockets, which could easily be destroyed in a first strike, had no retaliatory value. This would also be true of Soviet weapons in Cuba and, given the superiority in American nuclear weapons under the increased procurement program of the Kennedy administration, the Russians would know that they could not afford a first strike.

In August, in response to stepped-up Soviet shipments and intelligence information, the administration increased aerial surveillance of Cuba; in September flights were hampered by bad weather and by publicity over Chinese destruction of a U-2 plane sold to the Nationalist Chinese. Then, in early October, and unmistakably by October 14, photographs showed emplacements for Soviet intermediate range ballistic missiles plus assembled Soviet jet bombers. What Khrushchev had never done for China he had now done for Cuba, ninety miles away from the American coast.

The Kennedy administration reacted promptly. Discarding the alternatives of protesting to the Soviet Union, or of bringing the matter up before the United Nations or the OAS, it considered three others: a direct attack upon Cuba, mounted swiftly and preceded by an air strike to destroy missiles and planes before they could be launched; an air strike alone; or a naval blockade of the island until Khrushchev would withdraw the weapons.

The first two might provoke nuclear war, and would certainly cause a tremendous reaction and revulsion against the United States throughout the world. They would cause not only Cuban deaths, but also Russian deaths. If Cubans resisted, banded behind Fidel Castro, there might be a nasty prolonged situation in Cuba after the initial conquest. Although it was unlikely that Khrushchev would immediately retaliate against the United States, given American power to strike back, he might respond in Berlin, in Turkey, in Iran, or in Iraq, and escalation would be a possibility.

The third choice had its own special dangers. If the Russian ships tried to run the blockade (which would extend only to weapons), this would force further, more painful decisions. It was also possible that the weapons build-up had been completed and that the Soviet Union would now only be shipping the kind of conventional supplies to which the blockade did not extend. In this case, the policy would be insufficient, and further steps would have to follow.

Nevertheless, the administration decided on the naval blockade, calling it a "quarantine" in order to conform in some way to traditional international law (whose legal categories, however, hardly appeared to cover the kind of new situation that involved an internal build-up of rapid-fire nuclear weapons). It kept in reserve a contingency invasion plan.

Preparations for the quarantine were carried out in utmost secrecy, using the cover of previously scheduled naval maneuvers in the Caribbean. Florida was heavily reinforced, and the administration took what precautions it could against the outbreak of a large-scale conflagration. On Monday evening, October 22, President Kennedy, having previously informed the Soviet Union of his intention, broadcast to the nation his decision to institute the quarantine on October 24. Having first taken the action, he then called the Security Council and the OAS Council into session. The latter voted 19 to 0 to authorize the use of armed force to prevent further Soviet arms shipments into Cuba. In the Security Council of the UN the Soviet Union found itself caught in a falsehood when it denied the presence of weapons which the United States was able to prove were there. It then argued that there were no *offensive* weapons in Cuba: the Soviet Union had supplied missiles to Cuba so that the Caribbean country could deter the United States from attacking it, and the Bay of Pigs incident and subsequent American actions gave ample evidence to suspect that an invasion was imminent.

Secretary General U Thant of the United Nations asked both sides to suspend action for a two- or three-week period so that the crisis could be resolved by peaceful negotiation. Khrushchev agreed, and

Kennedy agreed to negotiate—on condition that the blockade would continue until negotiations for withdrawal of the bases.

Never before had world tension been so high. Modern communications made the confrontation a public matter everywhere. Throughout the world, people waited anxiously to see what course would be taken by the twenty-five Soviet vessels heading for Cuba. Would they turn back? Would they submit peacefully to American search? Or would the first encounter lead to nuclear war?

A number of the vessels, presumably carrying arms to Cuba, turned back. Others, carrying only petroleum and similar products, were allowed to proceed after search. Khrushchev had drawn back. The orders to the Russian ships were accompanied by an offer to Kennedy for mutual withdrawal of bases from Cuba and bases in Turkey, but Kennedy refused the offer, and Khrushchev agreed to stop work on bases, dismantle the weapons under United Nations supervision and ship them back to Russia. Kennedy, in return, pledged that he would not invade Cuba and that the quarantine would be lifted when the United Nations had taken the necessary measures.

But what of Castro? It appeared that he had been a pawn in a great power play, and that Khrushchev was now abandoning him without consultation. The Cuban Premier, after inviting U Thant to Havana, refused to allow United Nations or Red Cross inspection, and asked for American withdrawal from the Guantanamo naval base, which was on Cuban territory.

At this point, Kennedy made his concession; despite knowledge that domestic criticism would rise, satisfied that the Soviet Union was beginning a withdrawal, he determined to rely on naval and aerial surveillance. The United States did not insist on further inspection. In short order the weapons were withdrawn.

It was an extraordinary episode. Khrushchev, criticized bitterly by the Chinese for his cautious revisionist attitudes, had gambled heavily. Two men made it clear again to the world that in spite of the appearance of new centers of power, they and they alone had the awesome power to destroy much of the world. Khrushchev apparently wanted to bolster his position within the Communist world by one bold stroke, to solidify the shaky position of the Cuban regime in the face of growing American concern and in the same move increase its subversive possibilities. But he was also trying to restore a nuclear balance that his military experts must have told him was shifting numerically to the side of the United States. He withdrew with two gains: an enhanced reputation in the non-Communist world for acting cautiously at a dangerous moment, and a promise that the United States would not invade Cuba to overthrow Castro.* But he still faced the Chinese and their allies, who screamed hysterically that Khrushchev had again displayed his cowardice before the United States, a "paper tiger." Relations between Moscow and Peking became worse in the ensuing months, with the charges and countercharges even more bitter. The Sino-Indian border war seemed almost an attempt to prove that the Chinese, at least, were still willing to act.

Kennedy found much support for his firm stand and the restraint which he, too, displayed. Still, outside of the United States he was criticized for having instituted the dangerous blockade instead of having chosen a less risky alternative, and many thought he should have bargained away the obsolete American bases in Turkey (which, in fact, the administration had already decided to abandon). Some thought that this was the sole motive for Khrushchev's action: it would make the United States realize what it meant to have such bases so close to its borders. Yet while many people drew a comparison between the two sets of bases, others pointed out that in fact the many Soviet bases were on the borders of the Western bloc, and that only a United States move to establish such bases in a country previously friendly to the Soviet Union—Poland, for example—would have been comparable. They also knew that Kennedy, by limiting himself to the action taken, would come under further attack at home for not having liquidated the whole Cuban problem—and he did.

Some expected great negotiations to follow, and, perhaps, a dramatic denouement, but there was none. However, two moves did follow the Cuban crisis. The United States, while denying domestic criticism that a deal was involved, announced withdrawal of its missile bases in Europe. They would be replaced by Polaris submarines. These carried weapons that could be used for retaliation, and hence for deterrence. Then, in early 1963, the Kremlin agreed to a "hot wire" between Moscow and Washington. A direct teletype link had long been under consideration: it would allow rapid communication between the two capitals in case of a nuclear accident, a small outbreak of violence that threatened to escalate, or a confrontation such as had occurred in Cuba. In a time when almost instantaneous response was possible, it might give the two major powers a chance to avert a response neither wanted. Finally, conclusion of the partial test-ban agreement in mid-

---

* The United States Government ultimately withheld any formal pledge, since one condition in the Kennedy-Khrushchev correspondence was never fulfilled: on-site verification of the withdrawal. Castro himself prevented it.

1963 might be viewed as having stemmed from the crisis, as well as Kennedy's avowal that it was time to take another look at the whole Cold War, to avoid recriminations, and—in a spirit of understanding that it was not all black and white—to find new ways of easing tension.

On the other side of the ledger, the crisis apparently strengthened French determination to build an independent deterrent force despite increased evidence in 1963 that its cost would be greater than anticipated and the return small.

Cuba, despite Castro's apparent disenchantment with Khrushchev, remained firmly in the Communist bloc into which Castro had taken it. Like other members of the bloc since 1957, it had its own peculiarities, and its leader frequently suggested that for their own good the Russian and Chinese comrades should get together. In any event, there it stood, ninety miles from the United States, and it also stood for future trouble. Americans, who had become used to the idea that the Communists had taken over one country after another by subversive conspiracy, curiously failed to realize that Cuba was the only one that might fit into the category. All the others in the Communist bloc had either been conquered from Germany or Japan by the Red Army in World War II or—as in the cases of China and North Vietnam—had resulted from success of indigenous Chinese Communists in the vacuum created by Japanese loss. And even Cuba did not exactly fit the picture; its leader had handed it to a previously weak Communist party.

Conclusion

The Cuban confrontation showed that despite the apparent breakup of the bipolar world the leaders of the Soviet Union and the United States still held the future of much of mankind within their hands. The very weapons that made it difficult for them to influence events in so many places still gave them the power virtually to eliminate those places. President Eisenhower had said at one point that war had now become unthinkable. But to many people the Cuban affair appeared to prove that all-out war was still possible, and that academic discussion of the outbreak of major war by escalation, miscalculation, or even rational calculation, had a base in reality. Khrushchev had, in fact, miscalculated, and as a result the world had held its breath.

Yet Khrushchev withdrew, and so did Kennedy, after his firmness had shown the Russian leader his mistake. Both displayed prudence in the face of the awesome possibility of thermonuclear war. Deterrence had worked.

According to their bent, people could stress either the first point (how close war had come) or the second (that war had not broken out). The lesson drawn from the Cuban affair by the first group was that efforts toward arms control and disarmament must be redoubled. And in fact, the first frail successes in obtaining overt rather than tacit agreements in this area came after Cuba: the test ban treaty, the hot-line agreement, the cutback on nuclear materials production. The next two years—despite increased Russian arms expenditures after the failure of the Cuba gamble—led to a decrease in international tension.

But the incident also contributed to the Russian-Chinese quarrel: the Chinese charged Khrushchev with recklessness in putting the missiles into place, with abject cowardice in then withdrawing them, and accused him of making an agreement to divide up the world with the United States. (The charge of recklessness was repeated in the Soviet Union when Khrushchev was deposed in 1964.) While many people praised him for withdrawing the offensive arms from Cuba, others stressed the fact that he had dared to put them there in the first place, and claimed that deterrence worked only because a determined American president had threatened war. In Britain and France the fact that an American president had dared to make the terrifying decision without consulting his allies, strengthened the determination of leaders in both countries to try to maintain an independent deterrent.

The balance sheet of the Cuban experience was hardly a clear one. But the confrontation seemed to lead to greater caution. Though it confirmed the qualitative difference in physical power between the superpowers and the rest of the world, the Cuban incident also demonstrated the centrifugal nature of the international political system.

Conclusion

Twenty years after World War I the world was on the verge of a second and even more devastating war; almost twenty years have passed since the second one. Few people involved in World War II now find it possible to accept the passage of the years. Few foresaw the pattern of international politics that would prevail.

Many who fought in World War II thought that this time it was truly a crusade, a war against an identifiable evil: fascism in all its forms, a philosophy that denied individual dignity and freedom. (General Dwight D. Eisenhower captioned his memoirs *Crusade in Europe*.) Once the evil was crushed, a new and better world would emerge; there were high hopes that, under the auspices of the new United Nations, international relations would take a radically different turn.

When America dropped the atomic bombs upon Hiroshima and Nagasaki, the hope was turned to certainty: in the face of this ultimate horror, something *must* be done to eliminate the old tendencies of balance-of-power politics, now thoroughly out of date. Wendell Willkie, the Republican presidential candidate in 1940, had already written his plea for *One World;* state legislatures in the United States began to pass resolutions in favor of world government; former Secretary of Agriculture and Vice-President of the United States, Henry A. Wallace, began to advocate help from the wealthier nations of the world for the poorer ones.

What emerged in the chaotic, postwar years was very different from "one world." Statesmen like Churchill and professional diplomats were not caught by surprise. National sovereignty could not be abrogated by any single state or group of states: all would have to do it, all would fear that some might not, and therefore none would do it. Individual differences of sovereign states were too deeply rooted for them to adopt any single form of overriding government. Thus all the tendencies of a political system with no central political authority continued to bring states face to face with the security dilemma, despite

346

all the changes in communications, weapons, and ideologies. These made the situation highly unstable, yet the old system survived the predictions of those who argued that advent of the atomic age had made world government imperative.

But it survived with many changes. From chaos emerged first the bipolar world, with consolidation of the two superpowers' spheres after conflict over the extent of each sphere. The Soviet Union appeared to have scored a major triumph with the victory of the Chinese Communists. Yet the forces that began to break up the Western sphere and to fragment the old Western empires were at work in the Soviet sphere, too. In the late 1940s Western military strategists customarily added satellite armies to the Soviet army in order to arrive at the grand total under Communist arms; it was soon clear that the exercise was meaningless.

The United Nations, whose Charter defined an attempt to set up a political authority without destroying national sovereignty, could never work as originally envisaged. In fact, at the outset there was considerable disagreement about what was envisaged. The emergence of new states in the context of bipolarism, and the reluctance of the two "superpowers" to use their major weapons helped make the United Nations into a special field of operation for the new nations, where they could try to redress the injustices caused by the old balance-of-power system that had depended partly on using them as pawns in the game of power.

The combination of new developments and the persistence of the sovereign, independent state ruled out the possibility that any single state could transform the system. But new habits of action and response were required, and they were often hard to acquire. Conservatives in the modern world who try to adhere to Burkean formulas are faced with a dilemma: changes outside their borders occur so rapidly that frequently only radical new policies can cope with them and conserve the values of the old order. But to choose appropriate policies in the face of uncertainty involves terrible risk and potentially horrible consequences in the modern world. Preventive war was possible in the nineteenth century; several people advocated it for the United States in the late 1940s, without realizing its implications. In the light of what was still an American monopoly of atomic weapons, it seemed barely plausible from a purely military viewpoint. But none of its advocates seemed to consider what "victory" might bring in terms of American commitments or responsibilities, and they were apparently untroubled by the moral issue. In later years, when the temporary monopoly was ended and both sides possessed H-bombs and means for delivering them, the whole idea became ridiculous; President Eisenhower could even call war "unthinkable." Yet in Cuba, in 1962, the "unthinkable" almost happened, and civilian strategist Herman Kahn titled a book on military policy, *Thinking About the Unthinkable*. War had not vanished from the world, yet it would be disastrous to undertake war as in the past. Many limited wars dotted the years from 1945 to 1964, and the last years found the United States supporting for a short while limited war in Laos and, apparently for a longer period, a form of limited war in Vietnam. Other states fought small wars in other areas—Tibet and Yemen are only two instances.

Old-fashioned notions concerning "intervention" no longer appeared valid when radio could carry ideology across national boundaries and incite mobs to overthrow their rulers. But the old idea of the "just war" became popular again in terms of intervention. Arabs referred to "liberated" as opposed to "unliberated" states, and intervened to bring "liberation." Africans threatened force to "liberate" Portuguese colonies, Indonesia to "liberate" West Irian, India used force to "liberate" Goa, and the Chinese poised forces on the coast ready to "liberate" Taiwan, having already accomplished the task in Tibet. China ran into the United States in the Pacific, however, and American views that the United States ought to "liberate" Cuba were not appreciated elsewhere: such an intervention would presumably not be "just."

Any attempt to intervene decisively and by force in the major spheres of one or the other of the superpowers was too risky; it took a long time to appreciate that this inhered in the new pattern of bipolarism. In 1951 *Time* Magazine bitterly criticized Secretary of State Acheson for his aim of merely containing the Soviet Union. John Foster Dulles talked loudly of "liberation," and a new American administration swept into office on the idea. It learned the hard way, however, that destruction of Communism or victory over Communism were empty slogans in the modern world. In the next decade the pattern of loosened ties within the two blocs became the dominant one; the previously monolithic Communist bloc, although still successfully preventing overt intervention by outsiders into its conflicts, became even more divided than the western bloc. Yet American frustration with the apparent failure to "win" the Cold War was such that in 1964 one American presidential candidate, Barry Goldwater, seriously returned to the old ideas of the early 1950s. Leaders in the rest of the world watched in dismay and breathed a sigh of relief when he received a crushing defeat, but they still wondered how much Americans had really learned if such a man could receive the presidential nomination.

In the 1950's and early 1960's the Russians had had to learn some of the same lessons as the Americans. Polycentrism in the Soviet bloc had allowed Western nations to establish useful relations with individual members of the bloc; Communist states found that they could make friends among statesmen outside their bloc. But bringing new members *into* the bloc was a far harder task; many failures attested to it. Castro had come in, but on his own, not Russian initiative. Still, competition between the Soviets and Chinese Communists might make both of them try harder, and Communist parties abroad could find support for their aims from one if none was forthcoming from the other. In some areas of the world, notably Southeast Asia, bitter jungle warfare by Communist guerrillas and growth of indigenous Communist parties still promised gains for the Communist bloc; yet no one could now ignore the question this immediately raised: which bloc?

In the American sphere the control of its members by the most powerful member was never as extensive as in the Soviet bloc. Even so, the United States had dominated: it had brought pressure on its allies to give up their empires; it had opposed them completely and forced a humiliating defeat on them at the time of Suez; it had made France accept a complete reversal of its immediate postwar aims toward Germany; it had gone its own way in the Far East and had run the risk of bringing its allies into war over policies they opposed, and since the early 1950s its giant industries had begun to buy controlling interest in more and more European concerns, giving rise to fears of domination by American absentee ownership.

But by 1964 changes had taken place on both the economic and military fronts. European resurgence made it less economically dependent on the United States. The presence of H-bombs and the fact that Russia could strike directly at the United States increased European desire to be able to threaten retaliation without depending on the United States. American withdrawal from Mediterranean and North African bases and reliance instead on Polaris missiles and the intercontinental Atlas, Titan, and Minuteman rockets could be and were interpreted as a return, under pressure of new developments, to a kind of fortress-America isolationist policy. In any event, these developments meant that European states sometimes worked out foreign policies in complete defiance of the United States: polycentrism existed in the West, too, and French recognition of Communist China and refusal to sign the partial test ban treaty were symbols of it, while the European Common Market came to be looked upon as a device to resist American economic domination.

The decline of policies of "contingent necessity" was less clear as a pattern, but equally important. It was less clear because, so long as semi-sovereign states existed side by side, they would be driven by security considerations to try to block other states from gaining ascendancy in an area by establishing themselves there first. Thus in 1957 the United States launched the Eisenhower Doctrine to keep the Soviets out of the Middle East, and in 1964 it was bogged down in the Vietnamese war in an effort to keep the Communist bloc—particularly Communist China—from extending its power throughout Southeast Asia. Yet in the Middle East the small states had by and large rejected the Eisenhower Doctrine, claiming that they could protect themselves. There, and in Africa, the United Nations had provided a "presence" that served to keep major powers from seeing a necessity to assert their power to forestall their rivals. This peace-keeping function rested on two factors: the presence of nuclear weapons, which made infinitely more dangerous the risk of a clash over influence in an area, and the development of mass communications, which threw a spotlight on the maneuvers of states, and made it unpleasant for a major power to risk a clash with the slender force built up from the armies of the very neutral nations it so often wanted to court. In the Congo, the United Nations force had for several years prevented direct great-power intervention; there was some hope that the new-born Organization for African Unity might assume some of the same functions.

Yet the very success of the United Nations device limited its future usefulness. Opposition to it caused such an acute financial crisis in the United Nations that unless circumstances changed radically, any new United Nations force would be impossible. Events in Southeast Asia and Formosa showed that in some areas the major powers would do anything they could to keep the others out, and would not trust to the limited possibilities the United Nations seemed to them to present.

And yet, Balkanization of the world had not brought the desperate scrambles for power that some people had feared. The very factors that had made possible the limited use of United Nations forces also served to curb natural tendencies toward balance-of-power policies.

On the other hand, smaller balance-of-power systems had also developed within the larger world system: in Southeast Asia and the Middle East, medium-sized powers vied with each other for strategic advantage. They had no atomic weapons and were, therefore, still willing to risk the use of force. But if any ambitious African states set off a scramble for power, it was unlikely that fragile, developing African institutions could offer much resistance, and great power politics might prevent any successful United Nations intervention.

The one political world envisaged in the United Nations Charter had turned into a world system of far more states in contact with one another than had ever existed before, and these in turn formed political blocs and groupings of various kinds. In terms of economic relations, the same process had occurred. The North Atlantic area, with the EEC in it, came to comprise a group of countries that trade more and more among themselves and with Japan, Australia, and New Zealand. Highly industrialized, accounting for two-thirds of the world's trade, their policies adhered closely to the original guidelines for the world economy set down in the United Nations system. A second group of states, in the Communist bloc, also came to trade more and more among themselves, although the political cracks in the bloc in later years were represented by increased trade between dissident members and states outside the bloc. The Communist trade bloc was outside the United Nations system, but by 1960 it began to trade more with the countries of two other groupings: the semi-industrialized states and the underdeveloped countries. The semi-industrialized group included Argentina, Brazil, Mexico, Finland, Yugoslavia, India, and South Africa, and although its members belonged to the United Nations system, they made the most use of its escape clauses; with twenty per cent of the world's population they accounted for six per cent of its trade. The final group—the rest of Asia, Africa, the Middle East, and Latin America—with thirty per cent of the world's population, did twenty per cent of its trading. Little of their trade was with one another; most of them exported a few raw materials or commodities in return for manufactured goods.

Within the Atlantic group, there was a substantial division between the smaller European Six and the others that was unlikely to be bridged in the near future. More important political problems lay in the relations between the two poorer groups and first two, more industrialized groups. In this sphere a haphazard political battle was fought between the Atlantic grouping and the Communist bloc in which there were few clear victories.

Channeling aid through the United Nations represented an effort to keep aid out of the political arena, and a number of useful United Nations agencies testified to a modest success. But the capital-rich states still preferred to maintain more control over the flow of their funds than was offered through the United Nations.

One thing seemed certain in terms of world stability: political Balkanization had created many states that, given their population increases, were not economically viable. Some leaders believed that economic regional groupings that offered larger markets for prospective industries and more scope for labor mobility were the solution. A Latin America Free Trade Area and a Central American Free Trade Area were formed in response to this view, and the African and Arab states also responded with new groupings. But aspiration was not so readily transformed into reality. Political upheaval seemed inevitable; action in this sphere might moderate it. In the meantime, the poorer states continued to look to the first two groups to help them accumulate capital. One of the ironies of the postwar situation was that without the stimulus of the Cold War, both sides might have been less generous to the underdeveloped states. Yet many of the leaders of the new states argued that the Cold War was only a foolish exercise between the two major powers, one that they ought to abandon, and that the real problem for world politics, the one most urgently in need of resolution, was the great gap between the rich sets of states in the north and the poor ones in the south. It was this discrepancy, they believed, that would lead to conflict in the future.

*   *   *

For most people, most of the time, what Dr. Johnson wrote two hundred years ago remains true:

> How small, of all that human hearts endure,
> That part which laws or kings can cause or cure.

International politics and foreign policies are still remote from the citizen—difficult to understand and impossible to alter. Yet to a mob in Teheran nationalization of the oil industry becomes an immediately important matter; a South Vietnamese peasant, who may not understand why American soldiers are present, but who is all too conscious of Vietcong guerrillas and government troops, is immediately touched by international politics; an Englishman, forced by increased taxes to cut his consumption in order to rectify a dangerous balance of payments deficit, feels the pinch of international relations.

In some cases remote, in others immediate, the unfolding pattern of international affairs—determined by the search for power or security, for wealth, for status and prestige in a world of semi-sovereign, semi-independent states—creates the framework and limits within which, on a local level, individual human beings are enabled to work out their own lives.

Bibliography

The area covered by this book necessitates a highly selective bibliography. It consists mainly of nontechnical and relatively general works in English which in themselves can lead the reader to other, more specialized sources. No attempt has been made to include books in the more specialized areas of international relations such as international law, economics, or finance, since the focus of the book is political history. With isolated exceptions, textbooks have not been included. Numerous works are included which are dated from the point of view of history or policy recommendation, but which serve as sources for how events and developments were viewed at the time the books were written.

The bibliography should serve, therefore, primarily as a useful source for works that will take the reader more deeply into the events summarized in this book, and to other, more analytical and technical works.

For the reader who wants to keep abreast of the development of world events and go beyond the too often shortsighted reporting in his daily newspaper, numerous periodicals and yearbooks exist that provide useful summaries and articles. A number of them are listed below. All readers should also be familiar with several major bibliographical sources: the volumes published at ten-year intervals of the *Foreign Affairs Bibliography*, New York: Bowker (for the Council on Foreign Relations), and the yearly and quarterly volumes of the *Public Affairs Information Service Bulletin*, which lists periodical articles and pamphlets as well as books. For ready reference on names, places, dates, and excellent summaries of events, *Keesing's Contemporary Archives*, London: Keesing Publications, is indispensable.

PERIODICALS

Carnegie Endowment for International Peace *International Conciliation* pamphlets
Current History
Foreign Affairs
Foreign Policy Association *Headline* Series
International Affairs
World Politics

There are also numerous excellent periodicals on the politics of various regions of the world.

YEARBOOKS

Année Politique. Paris: Presses Universitaires.
Annuaire Européen–European Yearbook. The Hague: Nijhoff.
Annual Register of World Events. New York: Longmans.
Chronologie Internationale. Paris: Documentation Française.
Stebbins, Richard P., et al., *The United States in World Affairs.* New York: Harper (for the Council on Foreign Relations).
Survey of International Affairs. New York: Oxford University Press (for the Royal Institute of International Affairs).

GENERAL

Aron, Raymond, *The Century of Total War.* Garden City: Doubleday, 1954.
Black, Joseph E. and Kenneth W. Thompson (eds.), *Foreign Policies in a World of Change.* New York: Harper and Row, 1963.
Burnham, James, *Containment or Liberation? An Inquiry Into the Aims of United States Foreign Policy.* New York: Day, 1953.
(The) Economics of Competitive Coexistence. Washington: National Planning Association, 1959–1961 (8 vols.).
Fleming, Denna Frank, *The Cold War and Its Origins, 1917–1960.* Garden City: Doubleday, 1961 (2 vols.).
Herz, John, *International Politics in the Atomic Age.* New York: Columbia University Press, 1962.
Kaplan, Morton A. (ed.), *The Revolution in World Politics.* New York: Wiley, 1962.
Kennan, George F., *Russia, the Atom, and the West.* New York: Harper, 1958.
Lukacs, John A., *A History of the Cold War.* Garden City: Doubleday, 1961.
Seton-Watson, Hugh, *From Lenin to Khrushchev: The History of World Communism.* New York: Praeger (2nd edition), 1960.
———, *Neither War Nor Peace: The Struggle For Power in the Post-War World.* New York: Praeger, 1960.
Wolfers, Arnold (ed.), *Alliance Policy in the Cold War.* Baltimore: Johns Hopkins University Press, 1959.

UNITED NATIONS

Annual Review of United Nations Affairs. New York: New York University Press.
Boyd, Andrew, *United Nations: Piety, Myth and Truth.* Baltimore: Penguin, 1962.

Burns, Arthur Lee and Nina Heathcote, *Peace Keeping by United Nations Forces: From Suez to the Congo*. New York: Praeger (for the Center of International Studies, Princeton University), 1963.

Claude, Inis L., Jr., *Swords into Plowshares*. New York: Random House (3rd revised edition), 1964.

Everyman's United Nations. New York: United Nations Sales section.

Holcombe, Arthur N., et al., *Strengthening the United Nations*. New York: Harper, 1957.

Lash, Joseph P., *Dag Hammarskjold: Custodian of the Brushfire Peace*. Garden City: Doubleday, 1961.

Lie, Trygve, *In the Cause of Peace*. New York: Macmillan, 1954.

Miller, Richard, *Dag Hammarskjold and Crisis Diplomacy*. New York: Oceana Publications, 1961.

Rosner, Gabriella, *The United Nations Emergency Force*. New York: Columbia University Press, 1963.

Yearbook of the United Nations. New York: Office of Public Information, United Nations.

WEAPONS, STRATEGY, AND DISARMAMENT

Amrine, Michael, *The Great Decision: The Secret History of The Atomic Bomb*. New York: Putnam, 1959.

Barnet, Richard J., *Who Wants Disarmament?* Boston: Beacon Press, 1960.

Björklund, Elis, *International Atomic Policy During a Decade*. Princeton: Van Nostrand, 1956.

Brennan, Donald G. (ed.), *Arms Control, Disarmament, and National Security*. New York: Braziller, 1961.

Brodie, Bernard (ed.), *The Absolute Weapon*. New York: Harcourt, 1946.

Eckstein, Harry (ed.), *Internal War: Problems and Approaches*. New York: Free Press of Glencoe, 1964.

Fowler, John M. (ed.), *Fallout: A Study of Superbombs, Strontium 90 and Survival*. New York: Basic Books, 1960.

Gavin, James M., *War and Peace in the Space Age*. New York: Harper, 1958.

Kahn, Herman, *On Thermonuclear War*. Princeton: Princeton University Press, 1960.

———, *Thinking About the Unthinkable*. New York: Horizon Press, 1962.

Kecskemeti, Paul, *Strategic Surrender: The Politics of Victory and Defeat*. Stanford: Stanford University Press, 1958.

Levine, Robert A., *The Arms Debate*. Cambridge: Harvard University Press, 1963.

Nutting, Anthony, *Disarmament: An Outline of the Negotiations*. New York: Oxford University Press (for the Royal Institute for International Affairs), 1959.

Paret, Peter and John W. Shy, *Guerrillas in the 1960's*. New York: Praeger (for the Center of International Studies), 1962.

Spanier, John W. and Joseph L. Nogee, *The Politics of Disarmament: A Study in Soviet-American Gamesmanship.* New York: Praeger, 1962.

WORLD WAR II AND AFTERMATH

Churchill, Sir Winston, *The Second World War.* Boston: Houghton, 1948–1953 (6 vols.).

Command Decisions. New York: Harcourt (prepared by the Office of the Chief of Military History, Department of the Army, under the general editorship of Kent Roberts Greenfield), 1959.

de Gaulle, Charles, *War Memoirs,* Vols. II and III. New York: Simon and Schuster, 1959 and 1960.

Feis, Herbert, *Between War and Peace: The Potsdam Conference.* Princeton: Princeton University Press, 1960.

———, *Churchill-Roosevelt-Stalin: The War They Waged and the Peace They Sought.* Princeton: Princeton University Press, 1957.

———, *Japan Subdued: The Atomic Bomb and the End of the War in the Pacific.* Princeton: Princeton University Press, 1961.

Morison, Samuel Eliot, *Strategy and Compromise.* Boston: Atlantic (Little, Brown), 1958.

Snyder, Louis L., *The War: A Concise History, 1939–1945.* New York: Messner, 1960.

UNITED STATES

Adams, Sherman, *Firsthand Report: The Story of the Eisenhower Administration.* New York: Harper, 1961.

Brown, William A., Jr. and Redvers Opie, *American Foreign Assistance.* Washington: Brookings Institute, 1953.

Bundy, McGeorge, *The Pattern of Responsibility.* Boston: Houghton, 1951.

Byrnes, James F., *Speaking Frankly.* New York: Harper, 1947.

Carleton, William G., *The Revolution in American Foreign Policy* (revised edition). New York: Random House, 1963.

Donovan, Robert J., *Eisenhower: The Inside Story.* New York: Harper, 1956.

Eisenhower, Dwight D., *The White House Years: Mandate For Change, 1953–1956.* Garden City: Doubleday, 1963.

Freymond, Jacques, *de Roosevelt à Eisenhower: La Politique Etrangère Américaine, 1945–1952.* Geneva: Droz, 1953.

Gelber, Lionel, *America in Britain's Place: The Leadership of the West and Anglo-American Unity.* New York: Praeger, 1961.

Goldman, Eric F., *The Crucial Decade and After: America, 1945–1960.* New York: Vintage Books (2nd enlarged edition), 1961.

Kennan, George F., *American Diplomacy, 1900–1950.* Chicago: University of Chicago Press, 1951.

Lippmann, Walter, *The Cold War: A Study in United States Foreign Policy*. New York: Harpers, 1947.

Millis, Walter (ed.), *The Forrestal Diaries*. New York: Viking Press, 1951.

Reitzel, William, et al., *United States Foreign Policy, 1945–1955*. Washington: Brookings Institute, 1956.

Ridgeway, Matthew B., with Harold H. Mastin, *Soldier: The Memoirs of Matthew B. Ridgeway*. New York: Harper, 1956.

Ross, Thomas B. and David Wise, *The U-2 Affair*. New York: Random House, 1962.

Rostow, W. W., *The United States in the World Arena: An Essay in Recent History*. New York: Harper, 1960.

Spanier, John W., *American Foreign Policy Since World War II*. New York: Praeger, 1960.

Taylor, Maxwell D., *The Uncertain Trumpet*. New York: Harper, 1960.

Truman, Harry S., *Memoirs*. Garden City: Doubleday, 1955–1956 (2 vols.).

United States Relations With China: With Special Reference to the Period 1944–1949. Based on the files of the Department of State. Washington: Department of State, 1949.

Williams, William A., *The Tragedy of American Diplomacy*. Cleveland: World, 1959.

USSR

Allen, Robert L., *Soviet Economic Warfare*. Washington: Public Affairs Press, 1960.

Berliner, Joseph S., *Soviet Economic Aid: The New Aid and Trade Policy in Underdeveloped Countries*. New York: Praeger (for the Council on Foreign Relations), 1958.

Brumberg, Abraham (ed.), *Russia Under Khrushchev*. New York: Praeger, 1962.

Crankshaw, Edward, *The New Cold War: Moscow and Peking*. Baltimore: Penguin, 1963.

Dallin, Alexander, *The Soviet Union at the United Nations*. New York: Praeger, 1962.

Dallin, David J., *Soviet Espionage*. New Haven: Yale University Press, 1955.

———, *Soviet Foreign Policy After Stalin*. Philadelphia: Lippincott, 1961.

Dinerstein, Herbert S., *War and the Soviet Union*. New York: Praeger (revised edition), 1962.

Garthoff, Raymond L., *Soviet Strategy in the Nuclear Age*. New York: Praeger (revised edition), 1962.

Hudson, G. F., et al., *The Sino-Soviet Dispute*. New York: Praeger, 1961.

Laqueur, Walter Z., *The Soviet Union and the Middle East*. New York: Praeger, 1959.

Moseley, Philip E., *The Kremlin and World Politics*. New York: Vintage, 1960.

Shulman, Marshall, *Stalin's Foreign Policy Reappraised*. Cambridge: Harvard University Press, 1963.

Sokolovskii, Vasilii, *Soviet Military Strategy in the Nuclear Age*. Englewood Cliffs, N.J.: Prentice-Hall, 1963.

Zagoria, Donald S., *The Sino-Soviet Conflict, 1956–1961*. Princeton: Princeton University Press, 1962.

EASTERN EUROPE

Armstrong, Hamilton Fish, *Tito and Goliath*. New York: Macmillan, 1951.

Brzezinski, Zbigniew K., *The Soviet Bloc: Unity and Conflict*. New York: Praeger (revised edition), 1961.

Dedijer, Vladimir, *Tito*. New York: Simon and Schuster, 1953.

Gibney, Frank, *The Frozen Revolution. Poland: A Study in Communist Decay*. New York: Farrar, Straus, 1959.

Hoffman, George W. and Fred Warner Neal, *Yugoslavia and the New Communism*. New York: Twentieth Century Fund, 1962.

Kecskemeti, Paul, *The Unexpected Revolution: Social Forces in the Hungarian Uprising*. Stanford: Stanford University Press, 1961.

Korbel, Josef, *The Communist Subversion of Czechoslovakia, 1938–1948: The Failure of Coexistence*. Princeton: Princeton University Press, 1959.

Laqueur, Walter Z. and Leopold Labedz, *Polycentrism: The New Factor in International Politics*. New York: Praeger, 1962.

Lukacs, John A., *The Great Powers and Eastern Europe*. New York: American Book, 1953.

Seton-Watson, Hugh, *The East European Revolution*. New York: Praeger (3rd edition), 1956.

Ulam, Adam B., *Titoism and the Cominform*. Cambridge: Harvard University Press, 1952.

Vàli, Ferenc, *Rift and Revolt in Hungary: Nationalism Versus Communism*. Cambridge: Harvard University Press, 1961.

Zinner, Paul E., *Revolution in Hungary*. New York: Columbia University Press, 1962.

EUROPE: GENERAL, EUROPEAN UNION, AND ATLANTIC ALLIANCE

Ball, M. Margaret, *NATO and the European Union Movement*. New York: Praeger (for the London Institute of World Affairs), 1959.

Benoit, Emile, *Europe at Sixes and Sevens*. New York: Columbia University Press, 1961.

Boyd, Andrew and Francis, *Western Union*. Washington: Public Affairs Press, 1949.

———, *Britain in Western Europe*. New York: Royal Institute of International Affairs, 1956.

Buchan, Alastair, *NATO in the 1960's: The Implications of Interdependence.* New York: Praeger (for the Institute for Strategic Studies, London) (revised edition), 1963.

Clay, Lucius, *Decision in Germany.* Garden City: Doubleday, 1950.

Defense in the Cold War. New York: Royal Institute of International Affairs, 1950.

Diebold, William, Jr., *Trade and Payments in Western Europe.* New York: Harper (for the Council on Foreign Relations), 1952.

Florinsky, Michael T., *Integrated Europe?* New York: Macmillan, 1955.

Haas, Ernst B., *The Uniting of Europe.* Stanford: Stanford University Press, 1958.

Holborn, Hajo, *The Political Collapse of Europe.* New York: Knopf, 1951.

Kraft, Joseph, *The Grand Design: From Common Market to Atlantic Partnership.* New York: Harper and Row, 1962.

Osgood, Robert E., *NATO: The Entangling Alliance.* Chicago: University of Chicago Press, 1962.

Price, Harry Bayard, *The Marshall Plan and Its Meaning.* Ithaca: Cornell University Press, 1955.

Reynaud, Paul, *Unite or Perish: A Dynamic Program For a United Europe.* New York: Simon and Schuster, 1951.

Robertson, A. H., *The Council of Europe.* New York: Praeger (for the London Institute of World Affairs) (2nd edition), 1961.

———, *European Institutions.* New York: Praeger (for the London Institute of World Affairs), 1959.

Shanks, Michael and John Lambert, *Britain and the New Europe: The Future of the Common Market.* London: Chatto and Windus, 1962.

Ward, Barbara, *The West at Bay.* New York: Norton, 1948.

WESTERN EUROPEAN COUNTRIES

Davison, W. Phillips, *The Berlin Blockade: A Study in Cold War Politics.* Princeton: Princeton University Press, 1958.

Eden, Anthony, *Full Circle: The Memoirs of Anthony Eden.* Boston: Houghton, 1960.

Epstein, Leon, *Britain—Uneasy Ally.* Chicago: University of Chicago Press, 1954.

Fitzsimons, Matthew A., *The Foreign Policy of the British Labour Government, 1945–1951.* Notre Dame: University of Notre Dame Press, 1953.

Freund, Gerald, *Germany Between Two Worlds.* New York: Harcourt, 1961.

Freymond, Jacques, *The Saar Conflict: 1945–1955.* New York: Praeger (for the Carnegie Endowment for International Peace, European Center), 1960.

Furniss, E. S., Jr., *France, Troubled Ally: de Gaulle's Heritage and Prospects.* New York: Harper (for the Council on Foreign Relations), 1960.

Grosser, Alfred, *La IVème République et Sa Politique Extérieure.* Paris: Colin, 1961.

Litchfield, E. H., et al., *Governing Post-War Germany.* Ithaca: Cornell University Press, 1953.

Mander, John, *Berlin: Hostage for the West.* Baltimore: Penguin, 1962.

Montgomery, John D., *Forced to Be Free: The Artificial Revolution in Germany and Japan.* Chicago: University of Chicago Press, 1957.

Vandenbosch, Amry, *Dutch Foreign Policy Since 1815.* The Hague: Nijhoff, 1959.

Walker, Patrick Gordon, *The Commonwealth.* London: Secker and Warbury, 1962.

Werth, Alexander, *France: 1940–1955.* New York: Holt, 1956.

Whitaker, Arthur P., *Spain and the Defense of the West: Ally and Liability.* New York: Harper (for the Council on Foreign Relations), 1961.

Williams, Francis, *Twilight of Empire: Memoirs of Prime Minister Clement Attlee.* New York: Barnes, 1962.

Woodhouse, Christopher, *British Foreign Policy Since the Second World War.* New York: Praeger, 1962.

DECOLONIZATION AND NEW STATES

Buss, Claude A., *The Arc of Crisis.* Garden City: Doubleday, 1961.

Calvocoressi, Peter, *World Order and New States: Problems of Keeping the Peace.* New York: Praeger (for the Institute of Strategic Studies, London), 1962.

Duroselle, Jean-Baptiste and Jean Meyriat (eds.), *Les Nouveaux Etats dans les Rélations Internationales.* Paris: Colin, 1962.

Easton, Stewart, *The Twilight of European Colonialism: A Political Analysis.* New York: Holt, Rinehart and Winston, 1960.

Emerson, Rupert, *From Empire to Nation.* Cambridge: Harvard University Press, 1960.

Kahin, George McT., *The Asian-African Conference.* Ithaca: Cornell University Press, 1956.

—— (ed.), *Major Governments of Asia.* Ithaca: Cornell University Press, 1958.

Martin, Lawrence W. (ed.), *Neutralism and Nonalignment: The New States In World Affairs.* New York: Praeger (for the Washington Center of Foreign Policy Research, School of Advanced International Studies, Johns Hopkins University), 1962.

Zinkin, Maurice, *Development for Free Asia.* New York: Oxford University Press (for the Institute of Pacific Relations) (revised edition), 1963.

MIDDLE EAST

Bromberger, Merry and Serge, *Secrets of Suez.* London: Sidgwick and Jackson, 1957.

Bullard, Sir Reader William (ed.), *The Middle East: A Political and Economic Survey.* New York: Royal Institute for International Affairs (3rd edition), 1958.

Campbell, John C., *Defense of the Middle East: Problems of American Policy.* New York: Harper (for the Council on Foreign Relations) (revised edition), 1960.

Cremeans, Charles D., *The Arabs and the World: Nasser's Arab Nationalist Policy.* New York: Praeger (for the Council on Foreign Relations), 1963.

Ellis, Harry B., *Israel and the Middle East.* New York: Ronald Press, 1957.

Finer, Herman, *Dulles Over Suez.* Chicago: Quadrangle Books, 1964.

Ford, Alan W., *The Anglo-Iranian Oil Dispute of 1951–1952.* Berkeley: University of California Press, 1954.

Hoskins, Halford L., *The Middle East: Problem Area in World Politics.* New York: Macmillan, 1954.

Hurewitz, Jacob C., *The Struggle for Palestine.* New York: Norton, 1950.

Kirk, George E., *Contemporary Arab Politics: A Concise History.* New York: Praeger, 1961.

Lacouture, Jean and Simone, *Egypt in Transition.* New York: Criterion Books, 1958.

Laqueur, Walter Z. (ed.), *The Middle East in Transition: Studies in Contemporary History.* New York: Praeger, 1958.

Lenczowski, George, *The Middle East In World Affairs.* Ithaca: Cornell University Press (3rd edition), 1962.

Nasser, Gamal Abdul, *The Philosophy of the Revolution.* Buffalo: Smith, Keynes, and Marshall, 1959.

Peretz, Donald, *Israel and the Palestine Arabs.* Washington, D.C.: Middle East Institute, 1958.

Polk, William R., David M. Stamler, and Edmund Asfour, *Backdrop to Tragedy: The Struggle for Palestine.* Boston: Beacon Press, 1957.

Shwadran, Benjamin, *Jordan: A State of Tension.* New York: Council for Middle Eastern Affairs Press, 1959.

———, *The Middle East, Oil and the Great Powers.* New York: Council for Middle Eastern Affairs Press (2nd revised edition), 1959.

Wheelock, Keith, *Nasser's New Egypt: A Critical Analysis.* New York: Praeger, 1960.

ASIA

Brecher, Michael, *The New States of Asia: A Political Analysis.* New York: Oxford University Press, 1963.

Clubb, Oliver E., Jr., *The United States and the Sino-Soviet Bloc in Southeast Asia.* Washington: Brookings Institute, 1962.

Fifield, Russell H., *The Diplomacy of Southeast Asia: 1945–1958*. New York: Harper, 1958.
——, *Southeast Asia in United States Policy*. New York: Praeger (for the Council on Foreign Relations), 1963.
Kahin, George McT. (ed.), *Governments and Politics of Southeast Asia*. Ithaca: Cornell University Press, 1959.
Modelski, George (ed.), *SEATO: Six Studies*. Melbourne: Cheshire (for the Australian National University), 1962.
Rosinger, Lawrence K., et al., *The State of Asia: A Contemporary Survey*. New York: Knopf (for the Institute of Pacific Relations), 1951.
Thorp, Willard L. (ed.), *The United States and the Far East*. Englewood Cliffs, N.J.: Prentice-Hall (for the American Assembly) (2nd edition), 1962.
Vinacke, Harold M., *Far Eastern Politics in the Postwar Period*. New York: Appleton, 1956.

ASIAN COUNTRIES

Ball, William McMahon, *Japan: Enemy or Ally?* New York: Day (for the Institute of Pacific Relations), 1949.
Barnett, A. Doak, *Communist China and Asia: Challenge to American Foreign Policy*. New York: Harper (for the Council on Foreign Relations), 1960.
Berkes, Ross N. and Mohinder S. Bedi, *The Diplomacy of India*. Stanford: Stanford University Press, 1958.
Lord Birdwood, Christopher, *India and Pakistan: A Continent Decides*. New York: Praeger, 1954.
Borton, Hugh, et al., *Japan Between East and West*. New York: Harper (for the Council on Foreign Relations), 1957.
——, *Japan's Modern Century*. New York: Ronald, 1955.
Boyd, R. G., *Communist China's Foreign Policy*. New York: Praeger, 1962.
Brecher, Michael, *Nehru: A Political Biography*. New York: Oxford University Press, 1959.
Callard, Keith B., *Pakistan: A Political Study*. New York: Macmillan (in cooperation with the Institute of Pacific Relations), 1957.
Chakravarti, Prithwis Chandra, *India's China Policy*. Bloomington: Indiana University Press, 1962.
Elegant, Robert S., *The Dragon's Seed: Peking and the Overseas Chinese*. New York: St. Martin's Press, 1959.
Fall, Bernard B., *Street Without Joy: Indochina at War, 1946–1954*. Harrisburg: Stackpole, 1961.
Feis, Herbert, *The China Tangle*. Princeton: Princeton University Press, 1953.
Hammer, Ellen J., *The Struggle for Indochina*. Stanford: Stanford University Press (for the Institute of Pacific Relations), 1954.

Higgins, Trumbull, *Korea and the Fall of MacArthur: A Précis in Limited War, 1950–1953.* New York: Putnam, 1962.

Hsieh, Alice Langley, *Communist China's Strategy in the Nuclear Era.* Englewood Cliffs, N.J.: Prentice-Hall, 1962.

Kautsky, John H., *Moscow and the Communist Party of India.* Cambridge: Technology Press; New York: Wiley, 1956.

Korbel, Josef, *Danger in Kashmir.* Princeton: Princeton University Press, 1954.

Leckie, Robert, *Conflict: The History of the Korean War, 1950–1953.* New York: Putnam, 1962.

Lord Lindsay, Michael, *China and the Cold War: A Study in International Politics.* New York: Cambridge University Press, 1955.

Mende, Tibor, *China and Her Shadow.* New York: Coward-McCann, 1962.

Moraes, Frank, *Revolt in Tibet.* New York: Macmillan, 1960.

Mosley, L. O., *The Last Days of the British Raj.* New York: Harcourt, Brace, and World, 1962.

Pye, Lucian, *Guerrilla Communism in Malaya.* Princeton: Princeton University Press, 1956.

Talbot, Phillips and S. L. Poplai, *India and America: A Study of Their Relations.* New York: Harper (for the Council on Foreign Relations), 1958.

Warner, Denis, *The Last Confucian: Vietnam, Southeast Asia, and the West.* New York: Macmillan, 1963.

Whiting, Allen S., *China Crosses the Yalu: the Decision to Enter the Korean War.* New York: Macmillan, 1960.

Wildes, Harry Emerson, *Typhoon in Tokyo: The Occupation and Its Aftermath.* New York: Macmillan, 1964.

AFRICA

Alwan, Mohamed, *Algeria Before the United Nations.* New York: Speller, 1959.

Brace, Richard and Joan, *Ordeal in Algeria.* Princeton: Van Nostrand, 1960.

Clark, Michael K., *Algeria in Turmoil: A History of the Rebellion.* New York: Praeger, 1959.

Gordon, King, *The United Nations in the Congo: A Quest for Peace.* New York: Carnegie Endowment for International Peace, 1962.

Hodgkin, Thomas, *Nationalism in Colonial Africa.* London: Muller, 1956.

Hovet, Thomas, Jr., *Africa in the United Nations.* Evanston: Northwestern University Press, 1963.

Kraft, Joseph, *The Struggle for Algeria.* Garden City: Doubleday, 1961.

Legum, Colin (ed.), *Africa: A Handbook to the Continent.* New York: Praeger, 1962.

——, *Congo Disaster.* Baltimore: Penguin, 1961.

Legum, Colin, *Pan-Africanism: A Short Political Guide.* New York: Praeger, 1962.

McKay, Vernon, *Africa in World Politics.* New York: Harper, 1963.

Merriam, Alan P., *Congo: Background of Conflict.* Evanston: Northwestern University Press, 1961.

Nkrumah, Kwame, *Africa Must Unite.* New York: Praeger, 1963.

Padelford, Norman J. and Rupert Emerson (eds.), *Africa and World Order.* New York: Praeger, 1963.

Rivkin, Arnold, *Africa and the West: Elements of a Free-World Policy.* New York: Praeger, 1962.

Tillion, Germaine, *Algeria: The Realities.* New York: Knopf, 1958.

———, *France and Algeria: Complementary Enemies.* New York: Knopf, 1961.

Wallerstein, Immanuel, *Africa: The Politics of Independence.* New York: Vintage Books, 1961.

THE AMERICAS

Arévalo, Juan José, *The Shark and the Sardines.* New York: Lyle Stuart, 1961.

Berle, Adolf A., Jr., *Latin America: Diplomacy and Reality.* New York: Harper and Row (for the Council on Foreign Relations), 1962.

Dreier, John C. (ed.), *The Alliance for Progress: Problems and Perspectives.* Baltimore: Johns Hopkins Press, 1962.

———, *The Organization of American States and the Hemisphere Crisis.* New York: Harper and Row (for the Council on Foreign Relations), 1962.

Eayrs, James, *Northern Approaches: Canada and the Search for Peace.* New York: St. Martin's Press, 1962.

Lieuwen, Edwin, *Arms and Politics in Latin America.* New York: Praeger (for the Council on Foreign Relations) (revised edition), 1961.

Meyer, Karl and Tad Szulc, *The Cuban Invasion: The Chronicle of a Disaster.* New York: Praeger, 1962.

Pachter, Henry M., *Collision Course: The Cuban Missile Crisis and Coexistence.* New York: Praeger, 1963.

Scheer, Robert and Maurice Zeitlin, *Cuba: Tragedy in Our Hemisphere.* New York: Grove Press, 1963.

Schneider, Ronald M., *Communism in Guatemala: 1944–1954.* New York: Praeger, 1958.

Szulc, Tad, *The Winds of Revolution: Latin America Today, and Tomorrow.* New York: Praeger, 1963.

Tannenbaum, Frank, *Ten Keys to Latin America.* New York: Knopf, 1962.

Whitaker, Arthur P., *The Western Hemisphere Idea: Its Rise and Decline.* Ithaca: Cornell University Press, 1954.

Index

Abdullah, King of Transjordan, annexes Arab Palestine, 119
Acheson, Dean, 58, 139, 143, 153, 348; and Marshall Plan, 90; and Far East policy, 135; and "Uniting for Peace" proposal, 152
Aden, 210; and Yemen war, 269, 275
Adenauer, Konrad, 109, 204; and German inclusion in West European defense, 186; and relations with USSR, 214; and 1960 Summit Conference, 310
Adoula, Cyrille, 252, 253
Afghanistan, 209, 213; and Pathan tribesmen, 210; supported by Soviets against Pakistan, 273
Africa, 351; and decolonization, 240; and Russia, 246; influence of Congo crisis on, 251; states sanction of South Africa, 257; and British Commonwealth, 266; regionalism in, 276–281; association with Common Market, 266, 278; as "atom-free" zone, 302; Chinese Communist efforts in, 325
Afro-Asian Peoples' Solidarity Conference (Cairo, 1964), 276; and Egypt's role in Africa, 276
Afro-Malagasy Union, 278
Albania, 223; communization of, 52, 53; entry into United Nations, 218; and claims on Yugoslav border areas, 309; and relations with China, 320; Khrushchev attack on at 20th Party Conference, 322; attack on Russian "revisionism," 327
Algeria, 176, 177, 218; terrorism in, 177–178, 196; France sends NATO based troops to, 219; independence of, 243; and "Casablanca group," 251; and Tunisia and Morocco, 258; and de Gaulle, 258, 289; and Organisation de l'Armée Secrète (OAS), 258; and war with Morocco, 266, 281; offers to mediate Yemen crisis, 275; and Maghreb Union, 277; and Chinese Communist support of rebels, 322
All-African Peoples' Conference (Accra, 1958), 277
Alliance for Progress, established at Punta del Este, Uruguay, 338
Allied Control Council for Germany, 31, 36
Angola, 243, 252
Anti-Fascist People's Freedom League (Burma), 69, 120
ANZUS Pact, 150
Arab League, 119, 174, 272
Arab Legion (Jordan), in Palestine war, 118
Arab socialism, 272
Arbenz, Jacobo, 182, 332
Argentina, 100, 101, 152, 101, 102, 339, 351; and Peron, 180, 331; end of Peron regime, 183 (see also Peron)
Arif, Col. Abdel Salam, 273
Atlantic Charter, 178
"Atlantic Partnership," 293
Attlee, Clement, becomes Prime Minister, 34; and Palestine Question, 65; and Indian independence, 66; and Korean war, 142
Atomic bomb, 13; first experimental explosion Alamagordo (1945), 35; and "containment," 127, 128; proposed use of in Korea, 142

Atomic Energy Commission, 157
Aung San, 69, 120
Australia, 12, 57, 215, 326; mutual defense treaty with U.S., 150; and SEATO, 170
Austria, 23, 218; independence of, 9; and Moscow Conference (1947), 89; Russian offers for peace treaty with (1954), 185; treaty ending occupation, 202, 203; neutrality of, 203; and EFTA, 290
Austria-Hungary, 5, 15, 65
Axis powers, defeat of in World War II, 12
Azerbaijan province, 72

Badoglio, Marshal Pietro, 21, 25
Baghdad Pact, 174, 209; signing of, 210; becomes CENTO, 272
Balance of Power, 5–7, 12–13, 42, 283; Peace of Westphalia and, 5; imperialism and, 6; impact of political liberalism and nationalism on, 7; and industrialization, 7; and World War I, 8; and World War II, 12; and developments in weapons, 13; and effects of political and social revolutions on, 15; and U.N. Charter, 43, 347; and Communist subversion, 245
Balfour Declaration, 65
Balkan countries, defeat in World War II, 11
Balkan Pact, 208
Ballistic missiles, 13–14, 240
Bandaranaike, Solomon, 217
Bandung Conference (1955), 202, 215–218, 220, 276, 284, 314–315
Bao Dai, 121, 163, 168–169
Baruch, Bernard, 81 (see also Disarmament)
Basutoland, 280
Battle of Britain, 11
Baxter, James Phinney, 80
Bechuanaland, 280
Belgium, 26, 57, 112, 113; and post-war trade, 56; and Schuman Plan, 95; and monetary reform, 115; and independence of Belgian Congo, 243; and paternalism in the Congo, 247;

aids Congo government, 253; intervention in Stanleyville, 254
Belgian Congo, 56, 176, 240; independence of, 243; association with Common Market, 266 (see also Congo, Republic of the)
Ben Bella, Ahmed, 259, 281
Benelux Customs Union, 112, 285
Beneš, Eduard, 55; alliance with Stalin, 22; and communization of Czechoslovakia, 103, 104
Beria, Lavrenti, 160; as scapegoat in rapprochement with Tito, 208
Berlin, 110, 201, 305; blockade of, 96; 1954 Foreign Ministers' meeting, 165; Khrushchev and crisis in, 309–314; and Berlin Wall, 313
Bermuda Conference (1953), 165
Bernadotte, Count Folke, 117, 118
Bessarabia, 21, 50
Bevin, Ernest, 35, 83, 110, 112; and NATO formation, 95
Bhreznev, Leonid, 323
Bhutto, Zulfikar Ali, 273
Bipolarism, 47, 86, 129, 235, 347; and United Nations, 131; break-up of, 236, 347; and nationalism, 237; and neutralism, 244–245
Bogota Charter, 102
Bolivia, 339
Bounty, H.M.S., 242
Bourguiba, Habib, 177, 218, 277
Braden, Spruille, 181
Brazil, 100, 180, 339, 351
"Brazzaville Powers," 251; and Common Market, 278; effect of Congo crisis on, 280
"Bricker Amendment," 154
Brunei, 242; joins Malaysia, 267
Brussels Conference (1960 on the Congo), 248
Brussels Treaty, 112, 186
Bukovina province, 50
Bulganin, Nikolai, 160, 202, 203, 206; and 1955 tour with Khrushchev, 207–209; efforts to win back Tito, 207; trip to Britain with Khrushchev, 215
Bulgaria, 9, 22, 27, 92, 223; independence of, 9; post-war status, 36, 48;

peace settlement with, 50; communization of, 54; membership in U.N., 218; and claims on Yugoslav border areas, 309

Bunche, Ralph, 118

Burma, 12, 125, 171, 209, 213, 215, 325, 326; independence of, 69, 120; leaves Commonwealth, 70; opposition to U.S.-Japan treaties, 150; and SEATO, 170; internal difficulties, 259; cuts off U.S. aid, 260; and Nationalist Chinese army remnants, 260; Chinese Communist territorial claims on, 318; agreement with China over border areas, 260, 319

Burundi, 243

Byrnes, James F., 34; at Potsdam Conference, 35; view on Soviet occupation of East Europe, 49; and demilitarization of Germany, 52, 54; and UNRRA, 58; and McCarthy charges, 139

Cairo Conference (November, 1943), 23

Cairo Conference of Arab leaders (1964), 275

Cambodia, 61, 167, 217, 218, 325; independence of, 163; withdrawal from French Union, 217; relation with France, 262; dispute with Thailand and South Vietnam, 261, 267 (*see also* Sihanouk, Prince Norodom)

Cameroun, 242, 278

Canada, 168; and formation of NATO, 96; and Korean war, 144

Caracas Declaration (1954), 332

"Casablanca Powers," 251; on U.S.-Belgian intervention in Stanleyville, 255; Congo crisis effect on, 280; Chinese Communist support of, 322

Castillo-Armas, Colonel Carlos, 182, 183

Castro, Fidel, 241, 244, 330–335; and Khrushchev, 314, 335; and Communism, 331, 332–333; execution of Batista men, 333; and conflict with United States, 333; at U.N. General Assembly (1960), 335; and Bay of Pigs invasion, 336; and Soviet missiles, 341, 342 (*see also* Cuba)

Central African Federation, 176, 243, 252; break-up of, 279 (see Rhodesia and Nyasaland)

Central African Republic, 278

Central American Free Trade Area, 352

Central Intelligence Agency (U.S.), and Guatemala, 183; in Burma, 260; in Indonesia, 260 (n.); and Sihanouk, 262; and Cuba, 334; and training of Cuban refugees, 335; and Bay of Pigs invasion, 336

Ceylon, 166, 215, 217, 218; independence of, 120; and SEATO, 170; and Trincomalee base, 217; opposes Suez Canal Users Association, 229

Chad Republic, 278

Chapultapec, Act of, 101

Chiang Kai-shek, 19, 74, 75; at Cairo Conference, 23; and Yalta, 30; and struggle with Communists, 75–77; and Marshall mission, 77; and Communist victory, 124; and Eisenhower, 155; and Taiwan status, 169, 325; and Burma, 260; breaks relations with France, 264

Chile, 100, 101, 180, 339

China, 18, 23; military operations and World War II effect on, 19, 42–43; and U.S. view of post-war role, 21; at Yalta, 30; and U.S. policy, 74, 75; Sino-Soviet agreement, 77; and Marshall mission, 77–78; Communist victory in, 86, 123–125 (*see also* Republic of China, Peoples' Republic of China, Chiang Kai-shek *and* Mao Tse-tung)

China, Peoples' Republic of, 316, 332, 347; Sino-Soviet agreement (1949), 125; and Communist bloc, 130; and Korean war, 133, 140–142; recognition of, 125 (n.); effect of Korean war on relations with U.S., 145, 152; and Bandung Conference, 216; treaty with India on Tibet, 217; attacks India, 241, 273; use of subversion, 245; aid to Congo, 254; and border agreement with Burma, 260, 319; aid to Indian Communist party, 261; and

Cambodia, 261; at Cairo Afro-Asian Peoples' Solidarity Conference, 276; and aid to underdeveloped nations, 283; explodes first A-bomb, 284, 326–328; denounces Test-Ban treaty, 307; and relations with Soviet Union, 308, 309; and Taiwan, 315, 325, 348; and destalinization, 315; relations with U.S., 316; and "Great Leap Forward," 317; dispute with India over Tibet, 318, 348; claims to border areas in Burma and India, 318; agreement with Pakistan over border, 319; reaction to Khrushchev visit at Camp David and "peaceful coexistence," 319; reaction to Soviet-Yugoslav rapprochement, 320; and Albania, 320; influence in Somalia, 322; loses influence in Outer Mongolia to Soviets, 321; support to Algerian rebels, 322; and Lebanon crisis, 322; support to "Casablanca group," 322; Collapse of "Great Leap Forward," 323; foreign policy aims of, 324–326; fails to enter U.N., 325; economic relation with USSR, 325; Russians return Yalta acquisitions to, 325; attack on Russian "revisionism," 327; attacks Khrushchev on Cuban missile crisis, 342, 343, 346 (see also Chou En-lai)

China, Republic of (Nationalist) 215; impact of Korean war, 140; membership in U.N., 218; supports Chinese Communist border claims in India and Burma, 319; relations with African states, 322 (see also Formosa and Chiang Kai-shek)

Chinese-Russian break, 314–326; and Communist bloc, 321–322; and emerging nations, 321–322

Chou En-lai, 125, 167, 216, 315; and Korean war, 141; views on Taiwan, 169; at Bandung Conference, 216; visit to Pakistan, 273; talks with Soviets after Khrushchev deposition, 323

Christian Democratic parties, and European unity, 113

Churchill, Sir Winston, 20, 21, 22, 23, 43, 110, 187, 235, 346; and strategy in World War II, 20; at Cairo Conference, 23–24; at Teheran Conference, 24; and Poland, 24–25; and Tito, 26; at Quebec and Hyde Park Conferences, 26; and Moscow Conference (1944), 27; and de Gaulle, 28; Roosevelt distrust of, 29; at Yalta, 30; conversations with Joseph P. Davies, 33; defeat in 1945, 34; speech at Fulton, Missouri, 48; opposition to French policy in Middle East, 62–63; on Indian independence, 67; supports European movement, 112; calls for Summit conference (1953), 161; on Indo-China, 164; on negotiation with Communists, 166; elected (1951), 184; and European defense, 184; and hydrogen weapons, 190, 195; retirement of, 203–204

Clay, General Lucius B., 51; and Berlin blockade, 96; sent to Berlin (1961), 313

Cliburn, Van, 309

Collective security, 44; impact of Korean war on, 151–152; failure of, 193; and U.N., 238

Colombia, 101, 111

Colombo Plan, 120, 166

Cominform, 105

Comintern, 105

Common Market (see European Economic Community)

Commonwealth of Nations, 120, 166; and Africa, 266; and Britain's application to the Common Market, 291

Commonwealth Prime Ministers Conference (London, 1949), 69

Communist Bloc, 103–106; and bipolarism, 130; and Titoism, 130; and China, 130; and Western powers, 133; and relaxation of Stalinist control, 202; and relations with U.S., 215; internal situation and destalinization, 220–221, 222; splits within, 240, 308–309, 315; and Sino-Soviet dispute, 321–322; and economic coordination of 323–324; and polycentrism, 349; as a world economic group, 351

Communist propaganda, 131; and sputnik, 303
Conference of the Confederation of North African Students (Tunis, 1958), 277
Conference of Independent African States (Accra, 1958), 276, 284
Conference of North African Political Parties (Tangiers, 1958), 277
Congo, Federal Republic of the, 327; independence of, 243; revolution in, 245, 247–255; influence of crisis on African groupings, 251; crisis and U.N. financial problems, 252, 306, 328; unpopularity of Kasavubu-Adoula regime, 253; Chinese Communist aid to, 254; rebellion in Stanleyville, 254; effect of crisis on Casablanca and Brazzaville groups, 280; and U.N. presence, 350 (*see also* Belgian Congo)
Congo, Republic of the (Brazzaville), 278
Congress Party (of India), 67
"Containment," 85, 129, 153; and "liberation and rollback," 154, 221; Vietnamese war and U.S. containment of China, 350
Council of Europe, 112–113, 146
Council of Foreign Ministers, and peace settlements, 47–50; and Korea, 79; at Moscow (1947), 86, 89, 90; 1949 Conference in Paris, 110
Council for Mutual Economic Aid (Comecon), 105
Cuba, 241, 244; and Communist subversion, 245; crisis over, 306, 314, 327, 330–337; Soviet aid to, 324; and C.I.A., 334; 1960 elections and Cuba, 334; breaks diplomatic relations with U.S., 335; and Bay of Pigs invasion, 336–337; member of Communist bloc, 339; exclusion from OAS, 339; and Soviet missiles, 340, 342 (*see also* Castro, Fidel)
Curzon Line, 21, 32
Cyprus, 242, 327; and British action in, 219; National Organization for Cyprus Struggle (EOKA), 219

Czechoslovakia, 22, 92, 223, 225; independence of, 9; communization of, 55, 86; and invitation to join Marshall Plan, 103; and Comecon, 105; rioting in, 160; aid to Guatemala, 182; economic problems in, 324; trains Cuban jet pilots, 336

Dairen, 30, 325
Davies, Joseph P., 33
De Gaulle, General Charles, 25, 83, 113, 184, 310, 322; and Churchill, 25, 28; and Admiral Leahy, 25; U.S. *de facto* recognition of, 26; and French world role, 28; and view of Allies, 28; signs 20-year treaty of alliance with Stalin, 29, 110; and Oder-Neisse line, 32 (n.); and Potsdam Conference, 36; French troops in, 62; and French Community, 242; and Tshombe, 255; brought to power with Algerian crisis, 258, 286, 289; and Vietnam, 264; recognizes Chinese Communist government, 264, 325, 327, 349; and British entry into EEC, 289, 292, 293; and collapse of Fourth Republic, 289, 290, 329; and Common Market, 290, 291; and EFTA, 290; treaty of friendship and cooperation with Germany, 292; and revision of NATO, 297, 298; and MLF, 299; and 1960 Summit Conference, 305, 310; and "force de frappe," 306; refuses to sign 1963 Test-Ban treaty, 307, 349; views on Sino-Soviet split, 316, 327; and defiance of U.S., 326, 349
De Tocqueville, Alexis, 129
"Decolonization," 71, 131; and U.N. membership of new states, 218; in Africa, 240; implications of, 282
Denmark, 113, 114; in World War II, 11; and NATO, 97, 148; and EFTA, 290; applies to Common Market, 291
Dewey, Thomas, 154
Diem, Ngo Dinh, 168–169, 325; and support of, 168, 245; and Vietcong, 261, 262; assassination of, 262
Dien Bien Phu, 164, 166
Dirksen, Everett M., 87

Disarmament, 302; played down in U.N. Charter, 44; negotiations (1947–1950), 80–82; Atomic Energy Commission of U.N., 81; Baruch Plan, 81, 126, 300; U.S. and Soviet Union sign "hot line" agreement, 300, 307, 343; negotiations (1957–1964), 300–307; Geneva Open Skies proposal, 300; and "arms control," 300, 301; and Rapacki Plan, 301–302; impact of Suez and Hungarian revolt on, 303; ban on nuclear test, 304, 307; complete general disarmament proposal by Khrushchev, 305, 311

Disengagement (in Europe), proposal by Kennan, 301–302; Rapacki Plan, 301–302

"Dollar Gap," 60, 285

Dominican Republic, 180; and overthrow of Trujillo, 340

Dulles, John Foster, 14, 135, 164, 188, 245, 303; and "massive retaliation," 14, 156–157, 188; supports "liberation," 154, 348; views on foreign policy, 158–159; agrees to meet Chinese Communists, 165–167, 215; and "agonizing reappraisal," 185, 186; and Tito, 208; and Egyptian relations, 211; and Arab refugees, 212; and "neutralism," 220; and Hungarian revolt, 225; withdraws aid to Aswan project, 226; and Suez crisis, 229–230; and 1957 Syrian crisis, 269; and "indirect agression," 294; and "brinksmanship," 297

Dumbarton Oaks Conference (1944), 37

Dutch East Indies, 61, 63 (see also Indonesia)

East Germany, 223, 225, 309, 313; revolt in 1953, 156, 160, 221; establishment of German Democratic Republic, 214; and Warsaw Pact, 214; signs Test-Ban treaty, 307; and Berlin crisis, 310; economic problems in, 324 (see also Germany, Walter Ulbricht)

East Prussia, 35

Eastern Europe, 11, 24, 33, 84, 103; Russian activities in, 35, 48, 86; violation of Yalta agreements, 36; effect of World War II on, 42; communization of, 52–55; and Marshall Plan, 92; "liberation" of, 221 (see also individual countries)

Economic Cooperation Administration, 89 (see also Marshall Plan)

Ecuador, 339

Eden, Anthony, 34, 164, 294; and German rearmament, 186; at Geneva (1955), 202; replaces Churchill as Prime Minister, 203; and Arab-Israeli problems, 212; and Suez Canal control, 228

Egypt, 64, 111, 117 119, 242, 244, 268; and Korean war, 136; Officer's revolt in, 173–174, 196; and British base at Suez, 173–174; effect of Palestine war on, 173; rejects Baghdad Pact, 210; Aswan Dam project, 213, 226, 244, 272, 324, 327; and Suez crisis, 226, 230, 326; attack by Israel, Britain and France, 231; relations with Hussein of Jordan, 235; and "Casablanca group," 251; and Tshombe, 254; and Syrian crisis, 269; and formation of UAR, 269, 281; produces nonnuclear missiles, 300 (see also United Arab Republic)

Eisenhower, General Dwight D., 20, 28, 58, 162, 195, 298, 344; as Supreme Allied Commander, Europe (SACEUR), 148, 188; elected U.S. president, 155; opposition to "Captive Peoples' resolution," 155; "unleashes" Chiang Kai-shek, 155; almost intervenes in Indo-China, 164; secures "Formosa Resolution," 169; and Latin America, 181; and "Atoms for Peace" proposal, 193, 204, 303; at Geneva 1955, 202; and "Open Skies" proposal, 204; on nuclear war, 206; and relations with Egypt, 211; and Hungarian revolt, 225; and Suez crisis, 232; and Eisenhower Doctrine, 233, 234; and Congo crisis, 249; and Lebanon crisis, 271; suspends nuclear testing, 304, 313; and 1960 Summit Conference, 305, 310; cancels visit to

Japan, 306; and Berlin crisis, 310; meets Khrushchev at Camp David, 311; visits Asia (1959), 311; and Formosa crisis, 315; and Cuban crisis, 334; memoirs, *Crusade in Europe*, 346; calls nuclear war "unthinkable," 346, 348

Eisenhower Doctrine, 233, 234, 236, 350; and 1957 Syrian crisis, 269; rejected by Lebanon, 271

Emmanuel, King Victor (of Italy), 25

England (*see* Great Britain)

Eritrea, 111; federated with Ethiopia, 175

Estonia; independence of, 9; reincorporation into USSR, 21

Ethiopia, 50, 242, 276, 280; and Eritrea, 175; and conflict with Somalia, 266, 281

Europe, 47, 82, 183–184; movements for reunification of, 86, 112; and break-up of old Empires, 129; and bipolarism, 130; and rearmament of Germany, 133; effect of Korean war on, 145; resurgence of prosperity in, 284; and disarmament, 301 (*see also* Eastern Europe, Western Europe, *and* individual countries)

European Advisory Council, 23, 27

European Atomic Community (EURATOM), 285, 288

European Coal and Steel Community, 94, 191, 278, 286–287 (*see also* Schuman Plan)

European Defense Community, 147, 165, 185; defeat of, 184–186, 286

European Economic Community, 278 285, 310, 328; and Africa, 266; Britain rejects membership, 287; and French territories' associated status, 287; effect on other areas, 288; and de Gaulle, 290; negotiations with EFTA, 290, 306; Britain applies to, 291; and Russia, 323; as means to resist U.S. economic domination, 350

European Free Trade Association, 310; establishment of, 288, 290; and de Gaulle, 290; and EEC negotiations, 290

European Payments Union, 94, 112, 285

European Political Union, 186, 286

European Recovery Program, 91 (*see also* Marshall Plan)

Export-Import Bank, 101, 107; and Latin America, 179

Far East, 9, 84, 162–170, 349, 351; limited U.S. commitment, 134; (*see also* individual countries)

Farouk, King of Egypt, 32; abdication of, 174

Faure, Edgar, at Geneva (1955), 202

Federation of British West Indies, 243

Feisal, King of Iraq, 269; and merger with Jordan, 269; assassination of, 270

"Fertile Crescent," 119

Finland, 22, 92, 114, 207, 218, 351; independence of, 9; post-war status of, 36; peace settlement with, 50, 104; Russian pressures on, 104; and Marshall Plan, 104, 115

Formosa, 24, 124, 216; and U.S., 134; and U.S. Seventh Fleet, 140; and U.N. seat, 161; crisis over, 317 (*see also* China, Republic of, Chiang Kaishek, *and* Taiwan)

France, 74, 83, 98, 113, 236, 325; in 1930's, 9–11; defeat in World War II, 11; membership on European Advisory Commission, 29; membership in U.N. Security Council, 29; at Yalta, obtains zone and seat on Allied Control Council, 31; effect of World War II on, 42; and implementation of Potsdam agreement, 51; and Lend-Lease, 57; post-war colonial policies, 62; and Democratic Republic of Vietnam, 63; Communist agitations in, 86, 108, 131; 1947 economic crisis, 93; and Schuman Plan, 95; and European unity, 112; and Germany, 113, 349; and monetary reform, 115; rejection of EDC, 147–148, 184–185; defeat in Indo-China, 162, 289; and French Union, 162; and Brazzaville Conference (1944), 162 (n.); and SEATO, 170; and Algeria, 177–178, 219, 289; and German rearmament, 184, 187;

and Suez war, 202, 226, 231, 289, 326; and Tripartite declaration, 211; and Indian enclaves, 218; and new states in U.N., 243; and Guinea, 245; and Congo crisis, 249, 252; refuses to pay U.N. contribution, 252; and "Eurafrica," 278; and "force de frappe," 306, 344; associate status for African colonies in Common Market, 287; and nuclear stategy, 296–297, 300, 301; explodes first A-bomb, 306 (see also de Gaulle and Mendès-France)

Franco, Generalissimo Francisco, 149

French Community, 242, 247

French Union, 62, 162; Cambodia withdraws from, 217

Frondizi, Arturo, 339

Gabon, 278

Gandhi, Mohandas, 66, 67

Gaza Strip, 233

General Agreement on Tariffs and Trade (GATT), 41, 94, 192

Geneva Conference (1954), 164–168, 185; establishes international commissions, 168

Geneva Conference (1955), 202–205, 220, 235; "Spirit of Geneva," 205; and tacit agreement on nuclear war, 205; "Open Skies" proposal, 300

Germany, 23, 65, 74; in 1930's, 9, 10; in World War II, 11; dismemberment of, 21, 24; post-war plans for, 26; and Morgenthau Plan, 27; occupation zones at Yalta, 31; and Potsdam Conference, 35; effect of World War II on, 42; reparations and occupation, 48, 51; creation of "Bizonia," 52; and Moscow Conference of 1947, 89; and European unity, 112–113; Nazi Germany and Latin America, 182 (see also Adenauer, West Germany, and East Germany)

Gero, Erno, 223

Ghana, 242, 247, 266, 276; and "Casablanca group," 251; and Guinea, 277; Chinese Communist aid to, 323 (see also Nkrumah)

Gizenga, Antoine, 251, 280

Glubb, John Bagot, 235

Goa (Portuguese), 242

Gold Coast, 175 (see also Ghana)

Goldwater, Barry, 348

Gomulka, Wladyslaw, 221, 223–224, 309

Gottwald, Clement, 55

Great Britain, 74, 83, 98, 113, 184, 236; in 1930's, 9, 10, 11; and French in Syria, 33; position at Potsdam Conference, 35; and Greece, 36; effect of World War II on, 42; clash with Russia in Near East, 47; post-war trade situation, 56; U.S. post-war loan to, 58; economic situation 1947, 60; post-war colonial policy, 64; and Turkish policy, 74; inability to support Greece and Turkey, 87; and European unity, 112, 114; devaluation of £, 116; promotes two-China policy, 169; and SEATO, 170; and German rearmament, 184; and EDC, 185; economy in 1950's, 191–192; trade with Communist bloc, 192; and Anglo-Iranian oil crisis, 171–172, 192; coronation of Elizabeth II, 192; and Suez war, 202, 210, 226, 228, 268, 326; and Tripartite declaration, 211; and aid for Aswan Dam, 213; and Cyprus crisis, 219; and new states in U.N., 243; in Congo crisis, 249, 252; and "crush Malaysia" program, 268; aid to Jordan, 270; transforms Baghdad Pact to CENTO, 272; and Yemen, 275; and Common Market, 278, 288, 291; and establishment of EFTA, 288, 290; Commonwealth and British application to EEC, 291; and nuclear strategy, 294–296, 300, 301; and "Skybolt," 296; suspends nuclear testing one year, 304; and use of Polaris missiles, 306 (see also Churchill, Bevin, Attlee, Eden, and Macmillan)

Greece, 22, 27, 36, 113, 161; guerrilla war, 48; and Truman Doctrine, 86, 87; and NATO, 97, 148; and Balkan Pact, 208; and Cyprus crisis, 219, 327

Groza, Petru, 53

Guatemala, 196, 212; revolt in, 181, 331;

aid from Soviet bloc, 182; and bases for training Cuban refugees, 335, 336

Guevera, Ernesto, 333

Guinea, 242, 245–246, 278; and Ghana, 246, 277; and "Casablanca group," 251; Chinese Communist aid to, 323

Hague Round-Table Conference (on Indonesia, 1949), 122

Hailsham, Viscount (Quintin Hogg), 307

Hammarskjold, Dag, 161, 193, 280; and Suez crisis, 230, 231; and Congo crisis, 249, 250; death of, 251, 252

Harriman, Averell, 27, 93, 307

Hatta, Mohammed, 64, 123

Herter, Christian, 93, 297; and NATO, 298

Hinnawi, Colonel Sami, 119

Hiroshima, 13, 36, 346

Hiss, Alger, 139

Hitler, Adolf, 11, 19

Ho Chi Minh, 63, 121, 163, 168–169

Hobbes, Thomas, 5

Hoffman, Paul, 93

Honduras, 182

Hoover, Herbert, 145, 154

Hoover, Herbert, Jr., 217

Hudson, G. F., 316 (n.)

Hull, Cordell, 19, 22; attitude on foreign policy, 23; distrust of Churchill, 23; and de Gaulle, 25

Hungary, 27, 59, 92, 223, 226, 236, 237; independence of, 9; post-war status, 36; communization of, 53, 90; and Comecon, 105; revolt in, 156, 224–225, 284, 294, 302, 326; membership in U.N., 218; withdraws from Warsaw Pact, 225; effect of revolt on Communist bloc, 308, 324; relations with Soviet Union, 308

Hurley, General Patrick J., 77

Hussein, King of Jordan, 119, 235, 271; struggle with Nasserites, 269; merger with Iraq, 269, 270; asks British aid, 270

Hyde Park Conference (1944), 26

Hyderabad, 67, 69

Hydrogen bomb, 13, 195; effect on military strategy, 157–158; and "fallout," 189 (see also Nuclear strategy)

Ibn Saud, King of Saudi Arabia, 33, 65

Iceland, NATO membership, 97

Import-Export Bank, 337

Indeterminacy, in foreign policy, 3–4

India, 12, 57, 120, 125, 151, 166, 168, 171, 209, 213, 215, 271, 316, 351; independence of, 66; Muslim League and problem of princely states, 66, 67–69; and partition of Palestine, 117; and Korean war, 136, 142, 144; opposition to U.S.-Japanese peace treaty, 150; and SEATO, 170; treaty with China on Tibet, 217; gains control of French enclaves, 218; opposes Suez Canal Users' Association, 229; attacked by China, 241, 273, 327; and attack on Goa, 243, 348; sends troops to Congo, 252; visit by Khrushchev (1960), 311; dispute with China over Tibet, 318; Chinese Communist claims to border areas in, 318, 325; reaction to Chinese Communist A-bomb test, 326 (see also Nehru)

Indochina, French, 121, 125, 135, 171, 218; defeat of France in, 162–164, 289; and SEATO, 170–171; and European inflation, 184; Chinese aid to, 314 (see also Vietnam, Laos, and Cambodia)

Indonesia, 48, 121, 171, 215, 322, 325, 326; independence under Japan, 62; independence of, 63; and U.N., 122; U.S.S. *Renville* truce, 122; and West Irian, 122–123, 216, 243, 348; and SEATO, 170; abrogates union with Netherlands, 218; opposes Suez Canal Users' Association, 229; and Malaysia, 267; visit by Khrushchev (1960), 311 (see also Sukarno)

Inter-American Development Bank, 338

International Bank for Reconstruction and Development, 40, 41, 44, 99, 107, 337; and Marshall Plan, 92; aid to Aswan project, 213

International Civil Aeronautics Organization, 41

International Court of Justice, 39; and
Iran, 172; and South Africa, 257
International Labor Organization, 41;
bars South Africa from meetings, 257
International Monetary Fund, 40, 41,
44, 94, 107, 115, 126
International Refugee Organization, 88
International Ruhr Authority, 113
International Telecommunications
Union, 41
International Trade Organization, 40,
41, 44, 126
"Intervention," and idea of "just war,"
348
Iran, 23, 24, 84, 273; end of Russian
occupation of, 48; and Nazi Germany, 72; allied invasion of, 72;
separatist agitation in, 72; and partition of Palestine, 117; and Korean
war, 144; settlement of border issues
with USSR, 161; and Anglo-Iranian
oil crisis, 171–172, 192, 196; Shah of,
171, 273; signs Baghdad Pact, 210,
272; and Eisenhower Doctrine, 234
Iraq, 117, 119, 210, 268, 269; signs
Baghdad Pact, 210; and Eisenhower
Doctrine, 234; withdraws from Baghdad Pact, 271; coup in, 273; offers
to mediate Yemen dispute, 275 (see
also Feisal and Kassim)
Ireland, 113, 218
Israel, 161, 174, 215; independence of,
86, 116–118; and "Johnston Plan,"
175; and Suez war, 202, 226, 230; and
conflict with Arab states, 210, 211,
226, 230; and Western support of,
211; censured by Security Council,
230; attacks Egypt, 231; port of Elat
blockaded by Egypt, 232, 233; use of
Jordan River, 275 (see also Palestine)
Italy, 113, 183, 218; in 1930's, 10; in
World War II, 11; occupation controls in, 21, 36; and U.S.-British
clash over, 25; and Moscow Conference (1944), 26; effect of World
War II on, 42; peace settlement with,
50; Communist agitation in, 86, 108,
109; 1947 economic crisis, 93; and
Schuman Plan, 95; and Nato, 97;

148; and former colonies, 111; and
monetary reform, 115; and Common
Market, 285, 287, 291; U.S. stations
IRBMs in, 295

Jamaica, 243
Japan, 35, 74, 78, 125, 291, 322, 332; in
1930's, 10; in World War II, 11, 18,
36; encourages nationalism in Asia,
61; economic competition with Great
Britain, 191; economy in 1950's, 192;
and U.N. membership, 218; refuses to
join Suez Canal Users' Association,
229; conflict with Korea over fishing
rights, 267; and demonstrations
against Eisenhower, 306
Johnson, Lyndon B., 284; follows Kennedy policy in Vietnam, 265; sent
to Berlin, 313
Johnson, Dr. Samuel, 352
"Johnston Plan" (see Jordan River
Valley Development Program)
Jordan, 119, 218, 235, 268, 269, 275, 309;
and British influence, 210; rejects
Baghdad Pact, 210; and Suez crisis,
230; and Yemen, 274 (see also Hussein)
Jordan River Valley Development Program, 175, 212
Junagadh, 67, 68

Kadar, Janos, 225
Kaganovich, Lazar, 160
Kahn, Herman, Thinking About the
Unthinkable, 348
Karume, Abeid Amani, 247
Kasavubu, Joseph, 250, 252
Kashmir, 67, 68, 209; and Lord Mount-
batten, 68
Kassim, Abdel Karim, 270; withdraws
from Baghdad Pact, 271; claims Ku-
wait, 272; executed, 273
Katanga Province, 248, 253; secession
of by Tshombe, 249
Katyn Forest massacre, 25 (n.)
Kennan, George F., and U.S. and Viet-
nam debate, 264; and "disengage-
ment," 301, 302
Kennedy, John F., assassination of,

262, 284, 329; aid to Ngo Dinh Diem, 263; and Trade Expansion Act, 293; and Macmillan in Bahamas, 296; and NATO strategy, 298, 299; and test-ban talks, 207; meeting with Khrushchev at Vienna, 313–314; and Cuba, 314, 334, 335; and Bay of Pigs invasion, 336; and Alliance for Progress, 338; and Cuban missile crisis, 341–343, 344

Kenya, 176, 266, 277, 280; Mau Mau revolt in, 175; independence of, 243; army revolt in, 266; and British military aid, 266

Khan, General Ayub, relations with China, 273

Khrushchev, Nikita, 202, 203, 206, 238, 294; succeeds Stalin, 160; rapprochement with Tito, 202, 207–209; 1955 tour with Bulganin, 207, 209; abolishes Cominform, 208; and Arab world, 210, 212; and Bulganin visit to Britain, 215; and destalinization, 221–222; flies to Warsaw, 224; and peaceful competition, 238; and "troika" proposal, 251; and 1957 Syrian crisis, 269, 309; and Lebanon crisis, 271, 309, 322; and Nasser, 272; removed from office, 284, 322–323, 326, 328–329; and sputnik, 295, 303; visit to U.S., 1959, 305; complete general disarmament proposal at U.N., 305; and 1960 Summit Conference, 305; and U-2 incident, 306; foreign policy of, 308–314, 327; disposes of "anti-Party" group, 308; and "peaceful coexistence," 309; and Berlin crisis, 309; meets Eisenhower at Camp David, 311; at U.N. 1960, 312; and Fidel Castro, 312, 335; and Berlin Wall, 313; abandons nuclear test moratorium, 313; and Chinese Communists, 315, 319; drops 1958 Summit proposal, 316, 322; and aid to Pathet Lao, 321; attack on Albania at 20th Party Congress, 322; and Soviet missiles in Cuba, 340

Koenigsburg, 35

Korea, 23, 24, 78, 201, 215, 325; and Allied occupation policy, 79; and Syngman Rhee, 79; and U.N. Temporary Commission for, 127; withdrawal of U.S. and Soviet forces, 127; Korean war, 133, 135–145; and effect of, 145, 190, 194; Korean war and Western views of USSR foreign policy, 140; reaction to Chinese intervention, 142; armistice negotiation, 144, 161; at Geneva Conference of 1954, 166; Korean war and European inflation, 184; Korean war effect on role of Germany and Japan, 194; membership in U.N., 218; conflict with Japan over fishing rights, 267; coup in, 306 (*see also* Rhee, Syngman)

Korea, People's Republic of, 215, 314, 322; attacks South Korea, 136, 137; Chinese Communist aid to, 325

Kosygin, Aleksei, 323

Kotelewala, Sir John, 217

Kovaks, Bela, 53, 90

Kurile Island, 30

Kuwait, 172, 243; claimed by Iraq, 272

al-Kuwaitly, Shukri, 269

Labour Party (in Britain), rejects participation in Europe, 114

LaGuardia, Mayor Fiorello, 58

Laos, 61, 167, 218, 241, 244, 245; independence of, 163; International Commission for, 168; and Communist guerrillas, 262; crisis in, 312, 348; Geneva Conference on, 1961, 312

Latin America, 100, 351; post-war situation in, 178; and Korean war effect on, 179; anti-Americanism in, 180; and Common Market, 279; and Alliance for Progress, 338; and population problem, 338 (*see also* individual countries)

Latin American Free Trade Area, 352

Latvia, independence of, 9; reincorporation into Soviet Union, 21

League of Nations, 9–10, 38–39

Leahy, Admiral William D., 20(n.), 25

Lebanon, 62, 117, 162, 269; rejects Baghdad Pact, 210; ties to Soviet bloc, 213; crisis in, 270, 309, 322; and UNO-

GIL, 270; asks U.S. aid, 270; rejects Eisenhower Doctrine, 271
Lend-Lease, diverted to Far East, 33; termination and settlements by Truman, 57
"Liberation," 154, 201, 326
Liberia, 242, 276
Libya, 36, 111, 218, 242; independence of, 175; and "Casablanca group," 251, 281; British intervention in, 270
Lie, Trygve, 126, 161, 193
Life magazine, 154, 297
Linggadjati Agreement, 121
Lippmann, Walter, 128
Lithuania, independence of, 9; reincorporation into Soviet Union, 21
Lucky Dragon, 189
Lumumba, Patrice, 248–250, 280
Luxemburg, 112, 113; and Schuman Plan, 95

MacArthur, General Douglas, 19, 153; and occupation of Japan, 48, 78; named Supreme Commander in Korea, 136, 137; and Inchon landing, early success in Korea, 141; relations with Truman, 142–143
McCarthy, Joseph R., 138–139, 153
Macmillan, Sir Harold, 292; and nuclear strategy, 294, 298; and Kennedy at Bahamas, 296; and 1960 Summit Conference, 305, 310
Macao, 242
Macapagal, Diosdado, 267
Machiavelli, Nicolo, 6
Maghreb, Union of, 277
Makarios, Archbishop Myriarthefs, 219
Malagasy Republic, 242
Malaya, 69, 70, 242, 322, 325; and Communist guerillas, 141, 162, 261; and European inflation, 184; and formation of Malaysia, 242, 267 (*see also* Malaysia)
Malaysia, 242, 326; and Indonesia, 267; relations with Philippines, 267; and U.N., 267
Malenkov, Georgi, 157, 160, 161, 202, 203; on thermonuclear weapons, 206; and "New Course," 220–221; fall of, 308

Mali, and "Casablanca group," 251
Mali Federation, 277; and Afro-Malagasy Union, 278
Malik, Charles, 277
Manchuria, 24; railroad, 30, 325; Russians withdraw from, 48
Mandate system (League of Nations), 10, 39
Mao Tse-tung, 77, 124–125; and "Hundred Flowers" campaign, 317; foreign policy aims of, 324–326
Marshall, George C., 95, 139, 143; and mission to China, 77; and Marshall Plan, 86, 91; as Secretary of State, 86; and containment of China, 134
Marshall Plan, 86, 90–95, 134, 190; and Economic Cooperation Administration, 89; and Committee of European Economic Cooperation, 92; effect of, 95; and Czechoslovakia, 103; and Finland, 104; and Communist propaganda, 131
Masaryk, Jan, 104
Matsu, 170, 297, 315
Mauretania, 266; and Morocco, 243 (n.)
Mboya, Tom, 277
Menderes, Adam, 272
Mendès-France, Pierre, 166–167, 184; and settlement in Indo-China, 166–168; and Tunisian independence, 177; and German rearmament, 185–187
Menon, Krishna, 318
Menzies, Robert, 229
Mexico, 180–182, 332, 337, 339, 351; Mexican Revolution, 100
Mexico City Conference (1945), 37, 101
Michael, King of Rumania, 53
Middle East, 47, 48, 86, 241, 245, 327, 351; and Israel, 116–117; and Suez crisis, 219; and Nasserism, 269; as "atom free" zone, 302 (*see also* individual countries)
Midway, battle of, 12
Mikolajczyk, Stanislaw, 55
Mikoyan, Anastas, 224; and U.S. goodwill tour, 310; visit to Cuba, 324
Mobutu, Joseph, 250, 252; and Armée Nationale Congolaise, 253
Moch, Jules, 108

Mohammed V, Sultan of Morocco, 177

Mohammed, Imam, 274

Moiseyev dancers, and U.S.-Soviet cultural relations, 309

Mollet, Guy, 177, 218; and Suez crisis, 228

Molotov, Vyacheslav, 35, 160; demands on Italy and Japan, 48; agrees to peace terms for Axis satellites, 49; and Austrian treaty, 203

Mongolia, Peoples' Republic of, 30, 218

Monnet Plan, 190

Monroe Doctrine, 178, 182

Monrovia Conference (1961), 280–281

Montgomery, Field Marshal Bernard, and battle of El Alamein, 12

Morgenthau, Hans, 264

Morgenthau, Henry, 26–27, 57; and Morgenthau Plan, 31

Morocco, 242, 266; independence of, 177, 218; and Mauretania, 243 (n.); and "Casablanca group," 251; and Algeria, 258, 266, 281; and Union of Maghreb, 277

Mossadegh, Mohammed, 171

Moscow, Conference of (1943), 23

Moscow, Conference of (1944), 26, 27

Moscow Meeting of Communist Parties (1960), 320

Moslem brotherhood, 174

Mountbatten, Lord Louis, 21, 67

Mozambique, 243

Muscat and Oman, Sultan of, 269

Muslim League, 66

Mussolini, Benito, 111; deposed by Badoglio, 21

Mutual Defense Assistance Program, 146

Nabulsi, Suleiman, 235

Nagasaki, 36, 346

Naguib, Mohammed, 211

Nagy, Ferenc, 53, 55

Nagy, Imre, 223; in Hungarian revolt, 224

Nasser, Gamel Abdul, 174; reaction to Baghdad Pact, 210; and "neutralist" foreign policy, 213, 280; prestige from Suez crisis, 226, 233; nationalization of Suez Canal, 227–228, 229; opposes

Eisenhower Doctrine, 234; suppression of Communists, 244; and Pan-Arabism, 269; and revolt in Lebanon, 270, 271; and "Arab Socialism," 272; and Yemen, 274; and Khrushchev, 327

National Liberation Front, 263 (*see also* Vietcong)

Ne Win, General, takes over Government in Burma, 259, 260; border agreement with Chinese Communists, 260

Nehru, Jawaharlal, 66, 67, 166–167, 207, 208, 216; visit to Moscow, 209; and Indian Communist party, 210, 261; and Dulles' attitude toward "neutralism," 220; death of, 329

Neo-Destour Party (Tunisia), 177

Nepal, 218; Chinese Communist influence in, 318

Netherlands, 26, 112, 113; in World War II, 11; and Indonesia, 63, 121; and Schuman Plan, 95; hands over West Irian, 243

"Neutralism," 236, 241; growth of in small countries, 128, 133; and hydrogen weapons, 158; and bipolarism, 241, 244–245

New Guinea, 242

New Zealand, 12, 57, 215, 291; mutual defense treaty with U.S., 150; and SEATO, 170

Nhu, Madame Ngo Dinh, 263

Nicaragua, 182; and planes in Bay of Pigs invasion, 336

Nigeria, 242, 266

Nixon, Richard, 139, 164; and 1960 presidential campaign, 335; and Latin American tour (1959), 337

Nkrumah, Kwame, 175–176, 266, 277; in Congo crisis, 249; and Pan-Africanism, 276–277; isolation of, 281

Non-Western countries, and relations with West, 196–197

Norstad, General Lauris, 298

North Africa, 175, 216

North Atlantic Treaty Organization (NATO), 86, 95, 112, 126, 134, 188, 240; Brussels Treaty, 95, 112; Korean War and transformation of, 145–149;

Lisbon meeting (1952), 148, 188; and Spanish participation, 149; and European Defense Community, 185; strategy and nuclear weapons, 188; and U.N., 193; and Balkan Pact, 208; and Cyprus crisis, 219; and Strategic Air Command, 286; and de Gaulle plans for revision, 297, 298; and Multilateral Force, 298

North Borneo, 242; joins Malaysia, 267

Norway, 11, 26, 113, 114, 305; defeat in World War II, 11; and NATO, 97, 148; and EFTA, 290; applies to Common Market, 291

Nuclear strategy, post 1950's, 294–300; and U.S. IRBMs in Europe, 295; and Polaris missiles, 296; France and, 296; and Skybolt, 296 (see also Hydrogen bomb)

Nyasaland, 176, 280 (see also Central African Federation)

Nyerere, Julius, 247, 266; and Pan African Freedom Movement for East and Central Africa, 280

Oder-Neisse boundary, 32, 54, 310; and Stalin, 32; and de Gaulle, 32(n.); discussions of at Potsdam Conference, 35

Olympio, Sylvanus, 281

Open Door Policy, 75

Organisation de l'Armée Secrète, 258

Organization of African Unity (OAU), 350; meeting on Congo crisis (Addis Ababa, 1964), 254; and revolt in Tanganyika, 266; formation of, 281; and Morocco-Algeria dispute, 266

Organization of American States (OAS), 102; creation of, 179; and Inter-American Conference of 1954, 181; and Guatemala, 182; Inter-American Peace Committee, 183; and Economic and Social Council of, 338; and U.S. effort for multilateral action against Cuba, 339; and exclusion of Cuba from, 339

Organization for Economic Cooperation and Development, establishment of, 291

Organization of European Economic Cooperation, 94, 112; transformed into Organization for Economic Cooperation and Development, 291

Outer Mongolia, 243(n.); Russians overcome Chinese Communist influence in, 321 (see also Mongolian Peoples' Republic)

Pakistan, 166, 215, 305; independence of, 67; and SEATO, 170, 209; and Baghdad Pact, 209, 210, 273; and conflict with India, 209; refuses to join Suez Canal Users Association, 229; and Eisenhower Doctrine, 234; and relations with Soviet Union, 273; agreement with China on border areas, 319

Palestine, 64; and American Zionist Organization, 64; Roosevelt and Ibn Saud, 64; Anglo-American Committee of Inquiry, 65; war in, 86, 117; partition plans, 117; Arab refugees, 118, 211, 212; war and effect on Egypt, 173 (see also Israel)

Pan-African Freedom Movement for East and Central Africa, in Tanganyika, 277, 280

Pan-African Students Conference in Uganda, 277

Pan-Africanism, 276–277

Pan-American Union, 102 (see also OAS)

Pan-Arabism, 269

Panama Canal, 99

"Panche Shila," 217

Pathet Lao, 168, 312; and Khrushchev aid to, 321

Patrice Lumumba University, 246, 311

Peace Treaties, World War II, 47–50

"Peaceful coexistence," 326

Pearl Harbor, 11

Pearson, Lester, and U.N. Emergency Force in Suez, 231–232

Peron, Juan, 101, 178, 180, 337; pressured by U.S., 101; overthrow of, 183; and Peronism, 231

Persian Gulf sheikdoms, 210

Pescadore Islands, 24

Peurifoy, John, mediation of Guatemala crisis, 183
Philippines, 111, 325; independence of, 70; Hukbalahaps, 71; mutual defense treaty with U.S., 150; and SEATO, 170; and Malaysia, 267
Pitcairn Island, 242
Pleven Plan, 146, 184
Point Four Program, 86, 98–99, 337
Poland, 11, 27, 59, 92, 182, 221, 223, 236; independence of, 9; territorial settlement after World War II, 21, 32; Russian domination of, 24, 25; and Churchill, 24–25; recognition of Polish Committee of National Liberation, 24, 27; Warsaw uprising (1944), 25; and Curzon Line, 32; communization of, 54; and Comecon, 105; and Warsaw treaty, 187; and Poznan riots, 223; defiance of USSR, 224, 308–309; reaction to Hungarian revolt, 225; and Rapacki Plan, 300; economic problems in, 324 (*see also* Gomulka)
Population, and international politics, 16; and Communist position, 16; and Japan, 192; and Latin America, 338
Port Arthur, 30, 207, 325
Portugal, 218; and NATO, 97; Portuguese colonies, 176, 255, 256, 281, 348; and new states in U.N., 243; and EFTA, 290
Potsdam Conference (1945), 27, 34–36; issue of Germany, 35, 50
"Preventive war," 145
Priestley, J. B., 129
Punta del Este Conference, 339; and exclusion of Cuba from OAS, 339

Quebec, Conference of (1944), 26
Quemoy, 170, 297, 315

Rahman, Tunku Abdul, 267
Rakosi, Matyas, 223, 224
Rapacki Plan, 301, 302
Rayburn, Sam, 59
Razmara, General Ali, 171
Reciprocal Trade Agreements Act, 101
Reparations, allied views at Yalta, 31; Allied Commission on, 35; at Potsdam, 35; Molotov demands for, 48; Clay on suspension of, 51; at Moscow Conference 1947, 89
Rhee, Syngman, 79, 161; signs military assistance agreement with U.S., 135; efforts to disrupt armistice negotiations, 144–145
Rhineland, 90
Rhodesia, Southern, independence of, 279
Rhodesias, 176, 243, 280 (*see also* Central African Federation)
Ridgeway, General Matthew B., replaces MacArthur in Korea, 143; as Supreme Allied Commander Europe, 188
Rio de Janeiro Conference (1947), 102
Roosevelt, Franklin D., 23, 154; at Cairo Conference, 23; at Teheran Conference, 24; at Quebec and Hyde Park conferences, 26–27; and U.S. withdrawal from Europe, 29; and distrust of Churchill, 29; at Yalta, 30; conference with Haile Selassie, 32; and admission of Jews to Palestine, 33; death of, 34; and Iran, 72; and "Good Neighbor" policy, 337
Ruanda-Urundi, 243, 280; association with Common Market, 287
Ruhr area, 35, 90
Rumania, 9, 22, 27, 59, 92; independence of, 9; post-war status, 36, 48; peace settlement with, 50; communization of, 53; membership in U.N., 218; reaction to Hungarian Revolt, 225; rejects economic coordination of Communist bloc, 324, 327
Russia, 9, 15 (*see also* Soviet Union)

Saar, 90, 114, 184, 185, 186
es-Said, Nuri, 270
Sakhalin Island, 30
Salazar, Antonio de Olivera, 256
San Francisco Conference (1945), 37
San Francisco Peace Conference (1951), 150
Sandys, Duncan, on British nuclear strategy, 294
Sarawak, 242; joins Malaysia, 267

Sarit Thanarat, Field Marshal, 259; death of, 262

Saud, King of Saudi Arabia, 119, 235, 272

Saudi Arabia, 172, 269, 275; and Yemen, 274; breaks relations with Yemen and UAR, 274 (see also Ibn Saud and Saud)

Scandinavia, 112, 114 (see also individual countries)

Schuman, Robert, and Schuman Plan, 94–95, 114; and Pleven Plan, 146, 184

Schuman Plan, 94–95, 114, 148 (see also European Coal and Steel Community)

Selassie, Emperor Haile, 32

Senegal, and Mali Federation with Sudan (French), 277

Senghor, Leopold, 278

Sharpeville Massacre, 256

Shihab, General Fuad, 271

Sierra Leone, 243

Sihanouk, Prince Norodom, 217; and Thailand and South Vietnam, 261; and U.S., 261; and Soviet Union and Chinese Communists, 261, 262; and C.I.A., 262; and neutralism, 265

Singapore, 70, 242; joins Malaysia, 267

Sjharir, Sutan, 64

Socialist Parties, and European unity, 112

Somalia, 242, 280; conflict with Ethiopia, 266, 281; Chinese Communist influence in, 322

Somaliland, 111, 175 (see also Somalia)

Songgram, Field Marshal Pibul, 259

South Africa, 176, 215, 252, 280, 351; and settlement on Lend-Lease, 57; and apartheid policy, 256; Sharpeville massacre, 256; withdraws from Commonwealth, 257; barred from I.L.O., 257; sanctions by African states, 257; administration of Southwest Africa, 257; and International Court of Justice, 257

South Arabian Federation, 274

Southeast Asia, 11; effect of World War II on, 43; and Korean truce, 133; and settlement of 1954, 164–171; and

SEATO, 170; neutralism and guerrilla conflicts in, 259–265, 349

Southeast Asia Treaty Organization, 170–171

Southwest Africa, 280; administration of by South Africa, 257

Souvanna Phouma, Prince, 312

Soviet Union, 74, 82–83, 332, 347; in 1930's, 11; in World War II, 18; and Manchuria, 32, 36; position at Potsdam Conference, 35; annexation of East Prussia, 35; and war with Japan, 36; effect of World War II on, 42; post-war position, 47; claims on Libya (Tripolitania), 48; plans for rebuilding Germany, 52; and Middle East affairs, 63, 119, 234; and Azerbaijan, 72; pressure on Turkey, 73; Sino-Soviet agreement, 77; reaction to U.S. policies, 86; and Marshall Plan, 91–92; and Berlin Blockade, 96; and Communist victory in China, 124; and Sino-Soviet agreements (1949), 125; post-war military position and A-bomb, 128, 129; and Communist bloc, 130, 308–309; failure of intervention outside bloc, 130; and Korean war, 136, 137; explodes H-bomb, 157, 190; and Stalin foreign policy mistakes, 159; 19th Party Congress, 159; changes in foreign policy, 159–161; and policy toward U.N., 161; settlement of border issues with Iran, 161; proposals for German and Austrian peace treaties, 185; and German rearmament, 185, 187; and NATO strategy, 189; change in foreign policy of, 201; and nuclear strategy in 1950's, 205; liquidation of Soviet bases, 207; and economic aid program, 210; and arms deal with Egypt, 212; policy on German reunification, 214; on U.N. membership, 218, 243 (n.), 244; 20th Party Congress of C.P.S.U., 222, 322; crushes Hungarian revolt, 225, 236; opposes Suez Canal Users Association, 229; opposes Anglo-French invasion of Egypt, 231, 233; and Cuban crisis, 241, 314; use of subversion, 245; in Laos, 245; and Africa, 246; and Congo crisis, 249, 250; refuses to pay U.N. financial contribution, 252; aid to Indian Communist party, 261; and Cambodia, 261; and 1957 Syrian crisis, 269; and Lebanon crisis, 271; offers credit for Aswan Dam, 272; relations with Pakistan, 273; at Cairo Afro-Asian Peoples' Solidarity Conference, 276; and decolonization, 282; and aid to underdeveloped nations, 283; launches sputnik, 295; and disarmament, 300, 301; suspends nuclear testing one year, 304; and U-2 incident, 305, 306; and test-ban talks, 307; agreement, 327, 344; announces cut-back on production of fissionable materials, 307; aid to India and Indonesia, 311; intervention in Laos, 312, 321; overcomes Chinese Communist influence in Outer Mongolia, 321; and Common Market, 323; economic coordination of Communist bloc, 323–324; burden of aid to Cuba and Egypt, 324; and Chinese Communist admission to U.N., 325; and economic relations with China, 325; and missiles in Cuba, 340–344; establishes "hot wire" to Washington, 300, 307, 343 (see also Malenkov, Molotov, Khrushchev, and Stalin)

Spaak, Paul-Henri, 113

Spain, 149, 218; exclusion from NATO, 97; demands in U.N. for action against, 149; supported by Arab and Latin American states, 149

Stalin, Joseph, 11, 21, 36, 84, 105, 130, 201, 315, 325; at Teheran Conference, 24; and de Gaulle, 29; at Yalta, 30; at Potsdam, 35; demands trusteeship over Libya, 36; and U.N. organization, 37; defines World War II, 48; and break with Yugoslavia, 106–108, 209; and Communist victory in China, 124; death of, 133, 159, 195, 220; and nuclear weapons, 206; attacked by Khrushchev, 308; and Chinese Communists, 315

Stalingrad, battle of, 12

Stanleyville, 251; rebellion in, 254; U.S.-Belgian intervention, 254–255

Stassen, Harold, 302, 303

Stevenson, Adlai, 158; proposes end to H-bomb testing, 304; and Bay of Pigs crisis, 336

Sub-Carpathian Ruthenia, 55

Sudan (French), and Mali Federation, 277

Sudan, 281; independence of, 174, 242

Sudan, Anglo-Egyptian, 64, 173 (see also Sudan)

Suez Canal, 64; Suez crisis, 202, 219, 226–235, 308; and Suez Canal Users Association, 229; and European oil crisis, 231, 232; and France, 289

Sukarno, Achmed, 64, 123, 325; visits U.S., China and USSR, 218; and Malaysia, 242, 267; obtains West Irian, 243, 261; and Indonesian army, 260; on C.I.A., 260 (n.); and Communist party, 261

Summit Conference (Paris, 1960), 305, 308; and U-2 incident, 305, 306, 311

Sun Yat-sen, 75

Supreme Headquarters Allied Powers in Europe, 98

Suslov, Michael, 224

Swaziland, 280

Sweden, 56, 97, 113, 301; neutrality and NATO, 114–115; and EFTA, 290

Switzerland, 56, 97, 203, 301; and EFTA, 290

Syria, 62, 117, 119, 162, 230, 268; rejects Baghdad Pact, 210; ties to Soviet Bloc, 213; relations with Jordan, 235; 1957 crisis in, 269, 309; and UAR, 269

Tachen Islands, 170

Taft, Robert, 87, 97, 154

Tahiti, and French nuclear strategy, 297

Taiwan, and SEATO, 169–170; and Communist China, 315 (see also China, Republic of and Formosa)

Talal, King of Jordan, 119

Tanganyika, 176, 243, 280; union with Zanzibar, 247

Teheran Conference (1943), 24

Teller, Edward, 307

Thailand, 322, 326; and SEATO, 170; and Field Marshal Songgram, 259; and Cambodia, 261

Thorez, Maurice, 108

Tibet, 1954 Sino-Indian treaty, 217; Chinese Communist intervention in, 318, 325, 348

Time magazine, 143; on Acheson, 348

Timor Island, 242

Tito (Josip-Broz), 23, 201; and Russia, 26, 106–108; and Churchill, 26; problems with Italy over Trieste, 33; and Greek Communist guerrillas, 89; and China, 130; Khrushchev rapprochement with, 202; attempts to build third neutral force, 208; and Balkan Pact, 208

"Titoism," 86, 209

Togliatti, Palmiro, and "polycentrism," 316

Togo, 242; and Afro-Malagasy Union with Mali, 278

Touré, Sékou, 245

Transjordan, 64, 117, 119 (see also Jordan)

Transylvania, 50

Trieste, 184, 203; dispute between Italy and Yugoslavia, 33, 50, 111

Trinidad-Tobago, 243

Tripartite Declaration (on Israel-Arab borders), 211

Truman, Harry S., 139, 143, 153; and Churchill's view of USSR in 1945, 33; at Potsdam, 34; and U.N. organization, 38; and Palestine question, 65, 117; and "containment" policy, 85; Truman doctrine, 87, 91; and Point Four program, 98; and Far East policy, 135; and Korean war, 136; relations with MacArthur, 142–143; and Iran, 171

Tshombe, Moise, 248, 255; support from Angola, 252; collapse after U.N. troop pressure, 253; becomes premier, 253; at OAU meeting (1964), 254; and de Gaulle, 255

Tubman, William, 280

Tunisia, 242, 281; independence of, 177, 218; and Algeria, 258; and Maghreb Union, 277

Turkey, 5, 15, 57, 65, 113, 161, 174; in World War II, 73; and Truman doctrine, 86, 87; and NATO, 97, 148; and Balkan Pact, 208; and Baghdad Pact, 210, 272; and Cyprus crisis, 219, 327; and Eisenhower Doctrine, 234; and 1957 Syrian crisis, 269; ouster of Menderes, 272, 306; U.S. stations IRBMs in, 295, 343

U Nu, 120, 167, 207, 208; turns over Government to General Ne Win, 259

U Thant, 252; and Malaysia, 268; and Cuban missiles crisis, 341, 342

Uganda, 243, 280; army revolt in, 266

Ulbricht, Walter, 319

Umberto, Crown Prince, 25

"Unconditional surrender," 19

United Arab Republic, 269, 271, 275; joined by Yemen, 270; dissolution of, 273; Chinese Communist aid to, 323 (see also Egypt, Nasser and Syria)

United Kingdom (see Great Britain)

United Nations, 15, 24, 37–42, 47, 82, 125–127, 153, 204, 242; Security Council functions, 37; veto, 37; General Assembly, 38, 65, 98, 111, 117; and political change, 38; Trusteeship Council, 39, 117, 257; role of Secretary General, 39; Economic and Social Council, 40, 117; and balance of power, 43, 283, 347; Special Committee on Palestine, 65, 116–117; and Kashmir, 68; and Iran, 73; and Greek problem, 88, 126; and technical aid, 99; regional organizations provisions, 101; Security Council and Trieste, 111; Security Council and Palestine, 117, 126, 193, 211; and Indonesian independence, 122, 126, 193; General Assembly and Korea, 127, 141, 144; Temporary Commission on Korea,

127, 136, 137, 151; Security Council and Korea, 136, 151; and bipolarism, 131; Commission for Unification and Rehabilitation of Korea, 141; new posture after Korean war, 145, 151–153, 193; demands for action against Spain, 149; "Uniting for Peace" resolution, 151; Peace Observation Commission, 151; Collective Measures Committee, 151; Security Council and Iran, 172; General Assembly resolution on Italian colonies, 175; and Latin America, 180; Security Council and Guatemala, 182; and NATO, 193; and status of Southwest Africa, 193; and Soviet Union, 193; and disarmament in 1950's, 193–194; membership in, 218; General Assembly and Algeria, 219; Security Council and Hungary, 224–225; action by in Suez, 226, 230–232; Security Council and Suez freedom of navigation, 228; Security Council censure of Israel, 230; U.N. Emergency Force and Anglo-French-Israeli withdrawal, 232, 249; and role of Secretary General, 238; impact of new states on, 243–244; and Congo crisis, 249, 253, 255; and Emergency Force in Congo, 249; and Khrushchev "troika" proposal, 251, 312; withdrawal of troops from Congo, 253; General Assembly report on Angola, 256, and apartheid, 256–257; and Malaysia, 267; General Assembly and Syrian crisis, 269; and Observation Group in Lebanon (UNOGIL), 270; and Jordan and Lebanon crises, 271; General Assembly and "African Session," 277; and Southern Rhodesia, 270; and financial strains, 328; and Khrushchev disarmament proposal, 305; General Assembly resolution on nuclear weapons in outer space, 307; and Chinese Communist admission, 325; and Castro, 335; Security Council and Cuban missile crisis, 341–342; and "contingent necessity" policies, 350–351; and world economic groupings, 351, 352;

and economic aid, 351 (*see also* Hammarskjold *and* Lie)
United Nations Economic Commission for Africa, 277
United Nations Educational, Scientific and Cultural Organization (UNESCO), 41
United Nations Mixed Armistice Commission, 118
United Nations Relief and Rehabilitation Administration (UNRRA), 41–42, 57, 58
United States, 129; in 1930's, 9, 10; in World War II, 18; and Japan's Pacific islands, 21; effect of World War II on, 42–43; post-war position, 47, 56; and demilitarization of Germany, 51; post-war loan to Britain, 58; post-war policy on China, 74–75, 138; and Truman Doctrine, 86; and interim aid and Marshall Plan, 90–94; diplomatic pressure on Peron, 101; U.S. aid to Tito, 107; and Middle East crises, 117–119; and Russian A-bomb, 128; and decolonization, 131, 282; and Korean war, 133; prepares to abandon Formosa, 134; military assistance to Korea, 135, 145; domestic pressures during Korean war, 138–140; Mutual Security pact with Korea, 145; effect of Korean war, 145, 194; and Mutual Defense Assistance program, 146, effort to build alliance system, 149; and Spain in NATO, 149; bilateral agreements with Spain, 150; treaties with Japan, 150; mutual defense treaties with Philippines, Australia, and New Zealand, 150; failure of Middle East Command, 150; and effect of 1952 campaign, 155–156; "New Look" in U.S. military establishments, 157; and SEATO, 170, 209; and Latin America, 179–180, 336–338; and Guatemala, 182; and German defense, 184; and European Defense Community, 185; interpretation of Communist foreign policy in 1950's, 194; and Soviet Union in Suez crisis, 202, 226; and Baghdad Pact,

211; Tripartite Declaration, 211; aid to Aswan project, 213; differences with Europe on contact with Communist bloc, 215; opposes Anglo-French invasion of Egypt, 231, 236–237; supports Hussein, 235; and collective security, 238; and Cuban crisis, 241; opposition to Communist-led revolutions, 244, 348; fear of "Balkanization," 245; aid to Congo, 253; intervention in Stanleyville, 254; and Cambodia, 261; Johnson and massive intervention in Vietnam, 265; and Malaysia, 267; and 1957 Syrian crisis, 269; and aid to Lebanon, 270; transforms Baghdad Pact into CENTO, 272; and Yemen, 274; and balance of payments, 285; and SAC in NATO, 286; and "Atlantic Partnership," 293; and Trade Expansion Act, 293; post-1955 nuclear strategy, 294–300; establishment of IRBMs in Turkey, Italy and Britain, 295; and Skybolt, 296; and disarmament, 300, 304; and U-2 incident, 305, 306, 311; and Polaris missiles in Scotland, 306; and Test-Ban treaty 1963, 307, 327, 344; announces cut-back on production of fissionable materials, 307; intervention in Laos, 312, 348; relations with Communist China, 316; and "economic colonialism" in Western Europe, 328; initially favors Castro, 332; conflict with Castro, 333 (ff.); 1960 election campaign and Cuba, 334; breaks relations with Cuba, 335; aid and training of Cuban refugees, 335; and effort in OAS for multilateral action against Cuba, 339; and Soviet missiles in Cuba, 340; and Guantanamo naval base, 342; and withdrawal of missile bases in Europe, 343; establishes "hot wire" to Moscow, 300, 307, 343; "polycentrism" in U.S. sphere of control, 349; activity in Far East, 349; and Common Market, 350; and Vietnamese war, 350 (see also Eisenhower, Truman, Kennedy, Harriman, Herter, Hoover,

Hull, Hurley, Roosevelt, U.S. Congress, U.S. Senate, and U.S. State Department)
United States Congress, approves aid to Greece and Turkey, 88; Economic Cooperation Act, 93; and NATO, 97; and "Captive Peoples," 155
United States Senate, ratification of U.N. Charter, 41; approves aid to Greece and Turkey, 88
United States State Department, 117; and China White Paper, 134; and charges of Communist infiltration in, 139, 143
Ural Mountains, 293
Uruguay, 100, 101, 180, 181

Vandenburg, Arthur H., 96, 97
Vatican, excommunication of Peron, 183
Vietcong, 261; and Ngo Dinh Diem, 262
Vietminh, 163–164, 325; recognition by Communist states, 163
Vietnam, 61, 167–169, 241, 244; independence of, 163; membership in U.N., 218; and Communist guerrillas, 245, 262–265; and Cambodia, 261; and U.S. intervention in, 263–265; and de Gaulle, 264 (see also France, Indochina, Vietcong, Vietminh, and Vietnam, Democratic Republic of)
Vietnam, Democratic Republic of, 63, 222, 325; and Ho Chi Minh trail, 263; Chinese Communist aid to, 325

Wallace, Henry, 87, 346
Warsaw Pact, 133, 202, 207, 326; signature of, 187
Washington Conference (1943), 21
West Germany, 109, 113, 183; currency reform 1948, 94; and Schuman Plan, 95; Adenauer foreign policy, 109; and Basic Law, 110; monetary reform, 115; and rearmament of, 133, 146–148, 184, 202–203, 286; and Pleven Plan, 146; and European Defense Community, 147; and Soviet Union, 161; ratifies EDC, 185; Russian offers for

peace settlement 1954, 185, 327; renounces building of ABC weapons, 186; admission to NATO, 186; obtains sovereignty, 187; and "economic miracle," 190, 191; Socialist Democratic position on reunification, 214; and diplomatic relations with East Germany, 214; and Common Market, 285; treaty of Friendship and Cooperation with France, 292, 349; and nuclear weapons, 298; and protection of, 302; and East German signature of Test-Ban treaty, 307 (*see also* Adenauer *and* Germany)

Western Europe, 50, 56; post-war trade patterns, 56; Communist parties in, 108; reaction to U.S. foreign policy 1947, 110; integration of, 183; economy of in 1950's, 190–191; relations with U.S. and Soviet Union, 195–197; and U.S. "economic colonialism," 328; as part of industrialized trading group, 351 (*see also* individual countries)

Western European Union, 112, 186; and German rearmament, 286, 287

Western Hemisphere (idea of), 99

Western New Guinea (West Irian), 122–123, 243; "liberation" of by Indonesia, 348

Western Samoa, 243

Willkie, Wendell, 346

Wilson, Charles, 207

World Health Organization, 41

World War I, 42, 346

World War II, 18, 42, 346; military operations, 19; diplomacy during, 21; end of in Europe, 33; effect on Latin America, 178

Yalta Conference, 29–32; German occupation zones, 31; settlement in Far East, 32; Declaration on Liberated Europe, 32

Yemen, war with Aden, 269; joins UAR, 270; revolt and war in, 274–275, 348; strategic importance of, 275; and Britain, 275

Yugoslavia, 9, 22, 27, 92, 129, 161, 351; independence of, 9; and Trieste, 33, 50; communization of, 52–53; break with Soviet Union, 86, 106–108, 130; and Palestine partition, 117; and Korean war, 136; opposition to U.S.-Japanese treaties, 150; and Balkan Pact, 208; rapprochement with Soviet Union, 221, 308; refuses to sign unity manifesto 1957, 315; and economic decentralization of, 324; and "Communist neutralism," 327 (*see also* Tito)

Zaim, Husni, 119

Zanzibar, 243, 280; and Communist subversion, 245, 246; revolt in, 246–247; union with Tanganyika, 247

Zhukov, Georgi, 160

Zionism, 64–65, 173

Zorin, Valerian, 103